ACTION 21

International Development
Research Centre

Ottawa
•
Cairo
•
Dakar
•
Johannesburg
•
Montevideo
•
Nairobi
•
New Delhi
•
Singapore

**ABSTRACTS
REVIEWS
AND COMMENTARIES**

Edited by Theodora Carroll-Foster

Published by IDRC Books, PO Box 8500, Ottawa, ON K1G 3H9

© 1993, International Development Research Centre

All rights reserved. No part of this publication may be reproduced, stored in a retrieval system, or transmitted, in any form or by any means, electronic, mechanical, photocopying, or otherwise, without the prior permission of the publisher.

Canadian Cataloguing in Publication Data

Carroll-Foster, T.

Agenda 21: Abstracts, reviews, and commentaries. Ottawa, ON, IDRC, 1993. 322 p.

/Sustainable development/, /environmental management/, /resources conservation/ — /waste management/, /capacity building/, /children/, /women/, /indigenous population/, /international cooperation/, IDRC/, /abstracts.

UDC: 574   ISBN: 0-88936-688-8

Distributed in Canada by Code International, 323 Chapel St., Ottawa, ON K1N 7Z2

Abstracts have been published in French under the title « Action 21: Résumés »

TABLE OF CONTENTS

INTRODUCTION 6
ACKNOWLEDGMENTS 8

SECTION I
SOCIAL AND ECONOMIC DIMENSIONS 9

CHAPTER 1   PREAMBLE TO AGENDA 21   10

CHAPTER 2   INTERNATIONAL COOPERATION AND RELATED DOMESTIC POLICIES   11

CHAPTER 3   COMBATING POVERTY   17

CHAPTER 4   CHANGING CONSUMPTION PATTERNS   27

CHAPTER 5   DEMOGRAPHIC DYNAMICS AND SUSTAINABILITY   31

CHAPTER 6   PROTECTION AND PROMOTION OF HUMAN HEALTH   39

CHAPTER 7   PROMOTING SUSTAINABLE HUMAN SETTLEMENT DEVELOPMENT   47

CHAPTER 8   INTEGRATING ENVIRONMENT AND DEVELOPMENT IN DECISION-MAKING   53

SECTION II
CONSERVATION AND MANAGEMENT OF RESOURCES FOR DEVELOPMENT 63

CHAPTER 9   PROTECTION OF THE ATMOSPHERE   64

CHAPTER 10   INTEGRATED APPROACH TO THE PLANNING AND MANAGEMENT OF LAND RESOURCES   73

CHAPTER 11	COMBATING DEFORESTATION	79
CHAPTER 12	COMBATING DESERTIFICATION AND DROUGHT	87
CHAPTER 13	SUSTAINABLE MOUNTAIN DEVELOPMENT	95
CHAPTER 14	PROMOTING SUSTAINABLE AGRICULTURE AND RURAL DEVELOPMENT	103
CHAPTER 15	CONSERVATION OF BIOLOGICAL DIVERSITY	110
CHAPTER 16	ENVIRONMENTALLY SOUND MANAGEMENT OF BIOTECHNOLOGY	115
CHAPTER 17	OCEANS AND THEIR LIVING RESOURCES	121
CHAPTER 18	FRESHWATER RESOURCES	128
CHAPTER 19	ENVIRONMENTALLY SOUND MANAGEMENT OF TOXIC CHEMICALS	135
CHAPTER 20	MANAGEMENT OF HAZARDOUS WASTES	142
CHAPTER 21	SUSTAINABLE MANAGEMENT OF SOLID WASTES AND SEWAGE-RELATED ISSUES	148
CHAPTER 22	SAFE AND ENVIRONMENTALLY SOUND MANAGEMENT OF RADIOACTIVE WASTES	153

SECTION III

STRENGTHENING THE ROLE OF MAJOR GROUPS 159

CHAPTER 23	STRENGTHENING ROLE OF MAJOR GROUPS: PREAMBLE	160
CHAPTER 24	GLOBAL ACTION FOR WOMEN TOWARDS SUSTAINABLE AND EQUITABLE DEVELOPMENT	161
CHAPTER 25	CHILDREN AND YOUTH IN SUSTAINABLE DEVELOPMENT	169
CHAPTER 26	RECOGNIZING AND STRENGTHENING THE ROLE OF INDIGENOUS PEOPLE AND THEIR COMMUNITIES	179
CHAPTER 27	NON-GOVERNMENTAL ORGANIZATIONS	188
CHAPTER 28	LOCAL AUTHORITIES' INITIATIVES IN SUPPORT OF AGENDA 21	197

CHAPTER 29	STRENGTHENING THE ROLE OF WORKERS AND THEIR TRADE UNIONS	205
CHAPTER 30	STRENGTHENING THE ROLE OF BUSINESS AND INDUSTRY	210
CHAPTER 31	SCIENTIFIC AND TECHNOLOGICAL COMMUNITY	217
CHAPTER 32	STRENGTHENING THE ROLE OF FARMERS	224

SECTION IV

MEANS OF IMPLEMENTATION 231

CHAPTER 33	FINANCIAL RESOURCES AND MECHANISMS	232
CHAPTER 34	TRANSFER OF ENVIRONMENTALLY SOUND TECHNOLOGY, COOPERATION AND CAPACITY-BUILDING	235
CHAPTER 35	SCIENCE FOR SUSTAINABLE DEVELOPMENT	243
CHAPTER 36	PROMOTING EDUCATION, PUBLIC AWARENESS AND TRAINING	249
CHAPTER 37	NATIONAL MECHANISMS AND INTERNATIONAL COOPERATION FOR CAPACITY-BUILDING	260
CHAPTER 38	INTERNATIONAL INSTITUTIONAL ARRANGEMENTS	265
CHAPTER 39	INTERNATIONAL LEGAL INSTRUMENTS AND MECHANISMS	269
CHAPTER 40	INFORMATION FOR DECISION-MAKING	274

CONVENTIONS AND OTHER DOCUMENTS 287

    CONVENTION ON BIOLOGICAL DIVERSITY 288

    STATEMENT OF PRINCIPLES ON FORESTRY 298

    FRAMEWORK CONVENTION ON CLIMATE CHANGE 306

    RIO DECLARATION 313

ACRONYMS 317

LIST OF REVIEWERS AND COMMENTATORS 319

INTRODUCTION

The International Development Research Centre (IDRC) was created by the Parliament of Canada in 1970 to stimulate and support scientific and technical research by developing countries for their own benefit and purposes.

To date IDRC has financed over 4,500 projects in more than 100 developing countries. At least 45 Canadian academic institutions and 58 other organizations, including non-governmental organizations (NGOs), associations, and private sector companies, have participated in and collaborated on IDRC-funded research.

In Rio de Janeiro, Brazil, in June 1992, at the United Nations Conference on Environment and Development, also known as UNCED or the Earth Summit, the Government of Canada mandated IDRC to be one of the key Canadian agencies for implementing Agenda 21. IDRC's mandate was broadened to emphasize the environment and sustainable development, and to help move forward Agenda 21, the global action plan for sustainable and equitable development. During the last several months IDRC has launched an extensive consultative process to develop and strengthen strategic partnerships dedicated to working together to improve the quality of life, to protect or restore the environment, and to conserve Planet Earth's resources for future generations. As part of this process, one of the tasks IDRC set for itself was an analysis of the 600 page long Agenda 21 document which in four broad sections deals with 40 different topics or sectors.

The reasons for undertaking this analysis of Agenda 21 were threefold. First, because the document is so lengthy, complex, and complicated, there was a need to understand the contents of Agenda 21, the interrelationships between the different themes and sectors, and the types of programs or activities which were advocated and agreed to by the negotiators of Agenda 21. Second, there was a need to identify the strengths and weaknesses of Agenda 21, its gaps and deficiencies, and the various roadblocks or constraints to its effective implementation. Third, from an IDRC perspective, there was a need to ascertain what research had been identified as a basis for the implementation of the programs and activities in a number of different areas, what research had been left out or neglected, and what possible future research challenges or opportunities might exist for IDRC and its partners.

Before embarking upon a chapter-by-chapter analysis of Agenda 21, the two Conventions and the Forest Principles, a common analytical format was devised for the Reviews, or the first cut at the analysis. Another format was devised for the Abstract of the Reviews, or the one-pagers that condense the 10–20 page Reviews. And a third format was set up for the Commentaries, which were the peer reviews of the original Reviews and which demonstrated quite clearly that even among colleagues with approximately the same interests there are differing viewpoints. A list of IDRC specialists from various disciplines, was prepared and each person was assigned one or more chapters to review, analyze and critique. When these Reviews were completed, others were asked to prepare either Abstracts of or Commentaries on the Reviews. In addition, drafts of these documents were circulated to and shared with specialists outside IDRC to obtain their inputs and feedback. As well, because a number of Canadian and developing countries' governmental departments and organizations, were likewise trying to come to grips with the exhaustive contents of Agenda 21, the preliminary drafts were requested for inputs into reviews being conducted by other agencies or organizations. The culmination of all this work is this document.

The reader will find that most chapters commence with the one-page Abstract, proceed to the Review, and finish with a Commentary. In a couple of instances, where the chapters are no more than brief preambles, no review was necessary or undertaken. In a few instances, where the peer reviews coincided with or completely agreed with the original reviewers, no Commentaries have been inserted since they would be otherwise redundant. For readers who are interested in delving further into the arcane of Agenda 21, two other publications will be appearing simultaneously. These are: *A Guide to Agenda 21 — Issues, Debates and Canadian Initiatives;* and *Agenda 21: A Green Path to the Future.* These are available from: IDRC Books, PO Box 8500, Ottawa, Canada K1G 3H9.

Much attention has been focused on the controversy and disagreements surrounding UNCED, and much negativism has been directed at Agenda 21. Neither were without their faults. But each was also a step forward, towards reconciling environmental and developmental imperatives. In reviewing and analyzing Agenda 21, IDRC's reviewers have tried to identify the challenges and the opportunities for moving the global agenda forward yet another step. We hope that you might find elements in *Agenda 21: Abstracts, Reviews and Commentaries* — "ARC" that will also be helpful to you in keeping on the Rio momentum towards a more environmentally sustainable, secure and peaceful world.

Theodora Carroll-Foster
Editor

Coordinator
Agenda 21 Unit
International Development Research Centre

ACKNOWLEDGMENTS

As with any document, be it long or short, the ideas, expertise and efforts of a number of people go into its making. This is certainly true for the "Abstracts, Reviews and Commentaries" of Agenda 21 by IDRC staff, who have contributed much of their invaluable expertise and time to this Agenda 21 review and analysis. A List of all the Reviewers and Commentators is attached, so that readers who are interested in a particular chapter or topic will have the opportunity of knowing where knowledge about particular subjects resides within IDRC. To each person, many thanks for all the work you did, especially given all your other workloads. Proofing documents is not an easy task, but Sara Cardona, Mónica Dankers, Sheryl Davidson and Brenda Lalonde kindly undertook to review every sentence. Your inputs and feedback were most appreciated. And special thanks to Claire Brière, who had the daunting task of constantly incorporating editorial changes and re-formatting the bulky document.

SECTION 1

SOCIAL AND ECONOMIC DIMENSIONS

CHAPTER ONE

PREAMBLE TO AGENDA 21

REVIEW

Humanity stands at a defining moment in history. We are confronted with a perpetuation of disparities between and within nations, a worsening of poverty, hunger, ill health and illiteracy, and the continuing deterioration of the ecosystems on which we depend for our well-being. However, integration of environment and development concerns and greater attention to them will lead to the fulfilment of basic needs, improved living standards for all, better protected and managed ecosystems and a safer, more prosperous future. No nation can achieve this on its own; but together we can, in a global partnership for sustainable development.

This global partnership must build on the premises of General Assembly resolution 44/228 of 22 December 1989, which was adopted when the nations of the world called for the United Nations Conference on Environment and Development, and on the acceptance of the need to take a balanced and integrated approach to environment and development questions.

Agenda 21 addresses the pressing problems of today and also aims at preparing the world for the challenges of the next century. It reflects a global consensus and political commitment at the highest level on development and environment cooperation. Its successful implementation is first and foremost the responsibility of Governments.[1] National strategies, plans, policies and processes are crucial in achieving this. International cooperation should support and supplement such national efforts. In this context, the United Nations system has a key role to play. Other international, regional and subregional organizations are also called upon to contribute to this effort. The broadest public participation and the active involvement of the non-governmental organizations and other groups should also be encouraged.

---

[1] When the term Governments is used, it will be deemed to include the European Economic Community within its areas of competence.

CHAPTER TWO

INTERNATIONAL COOPERATION AND RELATED DOMESTIC POLICIES

Responsible Officer: Philip English

ABSTRACT

1. OVERALL CRITIQUE OF AGENDA 21 CHAPTER

- Reasonable summary of key international economic issues.
- Basically about economic relations and policies.
- Section on domestic economic policies is weak due to wide range of topics covered.
- No mention of agricultural policies. (See other chapters).
- Absence of international political issues, presumably for diplomatic reasons.
- Only briefest mention of social policy and democratic government.

2. KEY CONCLUSIONS ARISING FROM CHAPTER

- "Economic policies of individual countries and international economic relations both have great relevance to sustainable development."
- Key areas for action are:
  a) Trade liberalization;
  b) Making trade and environment mutually supportive;
  c) Providing financial resources and dealing with debt problem; and
  d) Making macroeconomic policies conducive to environment and development.

3. RESEARCH AND/OR IMPLEMENTATION POSSIBILITIES/OPPORTUNITIES

- The improvement of commodity markets, export diversification.
- The relationship between trade and the environment.
- Policies to attract investment capital and reduce or avoid debt problems.
- Search for growth-oriented solutions.
- The design and implementation of national economic policies.
- Information systems on commodity markets and trade control measures.
- Promotion of entrepreneurship and small-scale enterprise.
- Structural adjustment and its social and environmental consequences.
- Incorporation of social and environmental costs in resource pricing.
- Public administration and decision-making.
- Social policy.

4. ON-GOING AND/OR NEW PARTNERSHIPS FOR IDRC

- UNCTAD and the G24: trade, environment, macroeconomic policy.
- GRADE (Peru): taxation and the environment.
- PIDS (Philippines), ACTS (Kenya): structural adjustment and environment.
- TDRI (Thailand): macromodelling and environment.
- TSC (Costa Rica): national accounting and fisheries.

5. SUGGESTED NICHES FOR IDRC

- Economy and the environment, especially trade-related.
- Capacity building for development of national economic policies, especially those related to international economic relations.
- Reform of the international economic system, to the extent that the best Third World economists are available.
- Resource pricing and reform of the national accounts, if the field is not already too crowded.
- Training in environmental economics.

6. OTHER COMMENTS

- This Chapter emphasizes much of what the Centre has been doing for many years.
- The degree of attention paid explicitly to the environment is not great, and not much different than its current weight in Centre programming in this general area.

REVIEW 2

KEY CONCLUSIONS IN THE CHAPTER

WHAT IS THERE

Main Conclusions

"Economic policies of individual countries and international economic relations both have great relevance to sustainable development." (p.2)

Key areas for action are:
- Trade liberalization;
- Making trade and environment mutually supportive;
- Providing financial resources and dealing with the debt problem; and,
- Macroeconomic policies conducive to environment and development.

Agreements Reached for International and National Action
None.

Politically Significant Issues
- International commodity agreements are emphasized even though some governments in the North (eg. US) seem to have decided that these are no longer worth discussing.
- There is a clear statement of support for further trade liberalization, which many groups, particularly in the environmental field, have serious trouble with.

WHAT IS NOT THERE

The Chapter focuses, to a surprising extent, on economic relations and policies. There is only the briefest reference to social policy and to democratic government. However, the former is mentioned in more detail in later chapters. The latter may have been downplayed to make the document more politically acceptable. There is no reference to international political relations. For example, the arms trade and drug trafficking are not mentioned. Technology transfer is also not mentioned, but this is handled in another Chapter.

OVERALL CRITIQUE

Substantive Content

There are no major shortcomings. The discussion is a very fair summary of the key economic issues at the international level. The last section on domestic economic policies is a bit weaker, as it tries to cover a wide range of topics, and it is not always clear what the relationship is with international cooperation. Everything mentioned is reasonable, but others could have been added, notably agricultural policies. This is probably because these are more fully treated elsewhere in Agenda 21.

Design of the Chapter as an Organizing Framework

There is no major problem with the chapter as an organizing framework, with the provisos indicated above about missing material presumed to be in other chapters, or omitted for political reasons.

RESEARCH REQUIREMENTS, CAPACITY BUILDING ETC.

EXPLICIT PROPOSALS IN THE CHAPTER

- Strengthen national capabilities to achieve better functioning commodity markets, greater diversification of the commodity sector, better management of natural resources, and for the gathering and utilization of information on commodity markets;
- The Secretary-General of the UN is requested to strengthen the Trade Control Measures Information System managed by UNCTAD;
- Elaborate adequate studies for the better understanding of the relationship between trade and environment for the promotion of sustainable development;
- Strengthen policies to attract direct investment, avoid unsustainable levels of debt, and foster the return of flight capital to developing countries;
- Work towards growth-oriented solutions for developing countries with serious debt-servicing problems;
- Build capacity in the design and implementation of national economic policies, with specific reference to public administration, central banking, tax administration, savings institutions and financial markets, and the promotion of entrepreneurship.

IMPLICIT PROPOSALS DERIVED FROM THE CHAPTER

- There is a whole range of implicit proposals, covering everything in the fields of international economics and macroeconomics. Specific reference is made to entrepreneurship and small-scale enterprise promotion and improved public administration and decision-making (including reduced corruption).
- Brief reference is made to social policy, and the incorporation of social and environmental costs in resource pricing.
- Mention is also made of the need to ensure that structural adjustment programs do not have negative impacts on the environment and social development.

GAPS AND ALTERNATIVE APPROACHES

None.

NICHES FOR IDRC

GENERAL

Opportunities that Fit Normal Programming
- Most of the economic policy research funded by the Economic and Technology Policy program would fall squarely within the priorities in this chapter. The exceptions would be in the areas of technology policy and agricultural policy research, but the former is covered by Chapter 34, and much of the latter in other Chapters.

New Opportunities
- The most obvious example is trade and the environment, which as been already identified for new attention.

Unusual or High-Risk Opportunities
- The incorporation of social and environmental costs into resource pricing is another possibility. It is high-risk because several other groups are already involved to varying degrees, and it is likely that eventually a series of international norms may be established, such as for national accounts. Thus, there is the possibility that any principles developed by IDRC-funded research might be surpassed by the work of others.

REGIONAL SPECIFICITY
None.

KEY PARTNERS/OTHER ACTORS
Canada
Various.

Other Countries
Various.

RECOMMENDATIONS

WHICH NICHES ARE BEST FOR IDRC PROGRAM?
The strongest niche lies in building local capacity to develop national economic policy (the fourth key area discussed in this chapter, along with the domestic policies that relate to the other three areas). There is also room to support work in the area of international economic relations, especially with the best Third World economists. (However, there is more competition in this field, with various international organizations investing considerable resources to tackle these problems.) IDRC could continue to help highlight Third World interests and perspectives on these international issues.

ARE ADJUSTMENTS NEEDED AT IDRC IN ORDER TO FILL THESE NICHES?
Program Organization
None.

Process and Project Cycle
None.

Structure/Staffing
None.

ARE THERE CROSS-CUTTING ISSUES THAT ARE NOT ADEQUATELY REFLECTED IN ANY OF THE ABOVE?
None.

COMMENTARY 2

Name of Commentator: Hartmut Krugmann

1. GENERAL COMMENTS ON THE CHAPTER

- This Chapter focuses on economics and largely ignores other dimensions (social, environmental). Essentially, a plea is made for free trade and liberal economic policies, within the framework of the prevalent world economic/financial order and on the basis of neoclassical economic thought. Dogmatic (unproven or unrealistic) assumptions) include:
    a) That "an open ...trading system that ...leads to the optimal distribution of global production in accordance with comparative advantage is of benefit to all trading partners (p.4);
    b) Countries/regions being integrated into the world economy and the international trading system benefit from this process (e.g. Eastern Europe or developing countries) (p.5).;
    c) More trade and more liberal trade is good for all involved (throughout the Chapter);
    d) Reducing trade barriers/restrictions everywhere is good for all trade partners (throughout);
    e) A need for removing biases against exports and for discouraging inefficient import substitution;
    f) Environmental regulations can address the root causes of environmental degradation without ("unjustified") restrictions on trade;
    g) Environmental standards valid for developed countries may have unwarranted social and economic costs in developing countries (implying environmental double standards?).
- The Chapter does not see or address any of the following apparent or likely contradictions/trade-offs:
    a) "Genuine cooperation and solidarity" (p.2) without questioning the prevalent world order which is based on relative power, among other things, and tends to discriminate against the weaker "players" across and within countries;
    b) Liberalization of trade and the Uruguay Round of GATT versus a "non-discriminating and equitable trading system" (p.5);
    c) "Promote sustainable growth on an environmentally sustainable basis" (p.17);
    d) Promoting free trade versus incorporating/maintaining environmental standards.
- The Chapter does not recognize or appreciate:
    a) Any ecological limits to economic growth;
    b) Any need to change consumption/production patterns (left to a separate chapter);
    c) Any desirability of relative self-sufficiency in food or other essentials;
    d) Any distinction between protective measures to safeguard social/environmental standards versus protection of inefficient industries;
    e) Effects of free trade on international wage levels and the well-being of the working class.
- Presumably some of the above-mentioned notions and assumptions are a result of political compromises made to ensure that AGENDA 21 is endorsed by all countries in North and South.

2. OVERALL COMMENTARY ON THE FIRST REVIEW OF THE CHAPTER

- The above points expand/modify to a considerable extent what the reviewer states under the section "Key Conclusions". I do not agree with the reviewer that "there are no major shortcomings to note".

3. MAJOR POINTS AGREED/DISAGREED WITH, AND REASONS

- Unlike the reviewer, I have major problems with the Chapter as an organizing framework, even though I realize that political factors may have contributed to the way the issues are conceptualized and some missing aspects may be addressed in later chapters.
- I agree with the reviewer that there are "new opportunities" for IDRC in the area of trade, environment and sustainable development. "Natural resource accounting" fits this category. IDRC is also well placed to sponsor research that address the above-mentioned trade-offs (among economic–social–environmental variables).

4. MINOR POINTS AGREED/DISAGREED WITH, AND REASONS

- None.

5. POSSIBLE ON-GOING ISSUES OR CONCERNS FOR IDRC

- To make an effective contribution to operationalizing "sustainable development" and to inform about the underlying assumptions and implications of meanstream thinking as contained in this Chapter, IDRC must not lose its ability to encourage/sponsor research into alternative approaches to areas and issues such as trade and environment, structural adjustment policies, etc. On the other hand, IDRC may increasingly be called upon to actively collaborate with partners that are more closely tied to the economic and political status quo. Responding to these two simultaneous demands will be a challenge.

6. POSSIBLE IMPLICATIONS FOR IDRC

- As above.

CHAPTER THREE

COMBATING POVERTY

Responsible Officer: Daniel A. Morales-Gómez

ABSTRACT

1. OVERALL CRITIQUE OF AGENDA 21 CHAPTER

- An overview of poverty as an encompassing phenomenon preventing sustainable livelihood.
- Provides a discussion framework, but falls short of addressing the issue in depth.
- Regarding poverty, suggests actions and entry points for strategic planning, research and grass-roots work. Specifics are left to interpretation.
- Adds little to current knowledge about poverty, being a web of generalities and a high level of abstraction.
- Relies on the redistribution-with-growth (RWG) approach of the 1970s. Attempts to link development sustainability, environment and poverty eradication, but fails to raise key factors of underdevelopment and poverty (political ideology, class structure, and capital accumulation).
- Assumes conceptual affinities between governments, international and national organizations on key issues and development goals.

2. KEY CONCLUSIONS ARISING FROM CHAPTER

- Not geared to draw specific conclusions, but a framework for discussion.
- Poverty is stressed as a "complex multidimensional problem" that impedes sustainable development, and is rooted in various national and international factors.
- The eradication of poverty can only be addressed as a "shared responsibility of all countries."
- There is need to better manage environmental resources to achieve sustainable livelihood, through a shared, integrated, and effective "anti-poverty strategy."

3. RESEARCH AND/OR IMPLEMENTATION POSSIBILITIES/OPPORTUNITIES

- Creating options to earn sustainable livelihood.
- Implementing policies focusing on integrated human development.
- Targeting poverty-stricken areas.
- Creating national plans with emphasis on human capital investments. Cross-cutting research and intervention options include: (a) empowering key target groups, respecting cultural integrity, developing learning and knowledge networks, and establishing popular participation; (b) creating national capacity by reducing inequalities, managing actions and resources, creating opportunities for productive employment, facilitating technology and human resources development, and delivering services to satisfy basic needs; (c) introducing integrated policy measures and legal means for health (primary and maternal health care, and sanitation), services management (land, food, water), and education (basic/primary learning and professional training); (d) gathering data and information for policy-planning and evaluation of poverty alleviation/eradication programs; and (e) promoting cooperation in planning, financing, implementing and evaluating anti-poverty strategies.

4. ON-GOING AND/OR NEW PARTNERSHIPS FOR IDRC

- Links with other donors, regional branches of the UN system, Provincial governments, NGOs and private sector organizations in Canada.
- Networks of information on key target groups, successful experiences, and alternative mechanisms for the implementation of poverty eradication strategies in policy-planning in health, social and education.

5. SUGGESTED NICHES FOR IDRC

- Strengthen IDRC's **capacity to support research for sustainable development under the present Program structure**.
- Set up an **integrated thrust on research for poverty eradication**, to assist poor countries in developing or re-assessing cross-cutting government plans and policies to combat poverty.
- Create a **global research consortium on State decentralization**, aimed at establishing a global network on decentralization experiences in areas of policy-planning, decision-making delegation, and management systems of accountability.
- Sponsor an **international task force on the dimensions of poverty in the context of a new world order**, to research alternative scenarios for sustainable development strategies.

6. OTHER COMMENTS

The Chapter downplays the **political–economic** dimension of poverty or the interplay between politics and economics regarding the causes, manifestations and solutions of poverty. This omission leads to treating poverty and its eradication as an homogenous phenomenon and a "natural" state of developing countries that can be overcome through income generation and economic growth strategies.

REVIEW 3

KEY CONCLUSIONS IN THE CHAPTER

This Chapter stresses the centrality of poverty as a "complex multidimensional problem" that impedes the achievement of sustainable development. It recognizes that poverty is rooted in national and international factors for which there is no single or global solution. It argues that the eradication of the manifestations of poverty — including hunger, inequity in the distribution of wealth, and unfavourable conditions for human development — can only be addressed as a "shared responsibility of all countries".

To combat poverty, countries must integrate development and environment concerns so as to have a positive impact on the fulfilment of basic needs. Development policies, must focus on increasing the production of goods, and on addressing the sustainability of natural and human resources, bringing "resources, production and people" together as the pillars of an "anti-poverty strategy".

WHAT IS THERE

Main Conclusions

The Chapter is not geared to draw specific conclusions. Its purpose is to set a framework for guiding later discussions. The eradication of poverty is "a basic condition for ensuring sustainable development". Its achievement requires international and intra-national cooperation, governmental action at various fronts, financing and cost evaluation of country-specific measures, and the building of national capacities to undertake the task.

The purpose of the Chapter is not only to recognize the need to manage environmental resources better to achieve sustainable livelihood, but to urge a shared, integrated, and effective "anti-poverty strategy". In the spirit of this Chapter, sustainable development is a much broader issue that the protection of natural resources or the physical environment. The achievement of sustainable development goals implies dealing simultaneously with "cross-cutting measures", including demographic, health and education issues affecting key social actors (women, youth, indigenous people and local communities), in a context of democratic participation and improved governance.

Agreements Reached for International and National Action
The Chapter does not formally present "agreements" reached for action. It highlights, however, as an urgent matter, the need to take "enabling actions", nationally and internationally, to "support locally driven and country-specific approaches" that will "contribute to the integrated promotion of sustainable livelihoods and environmental protection".

Consensus is expected around inter-related objectives: the creation of opportunities to earn sustainable livelihood; the implementation of policies promoting adequate levels of funding for strategies on integrated human development; the targeting of poverty-stricken areas with sound and sustainable environmental management approaches, and the creation of national development plans with emphasis on human capital investments. These objectives should promote grass-roots, sustained and sustainable economic growth based on development policies that simultaneously address resources management and poverty eradication. However, it should be noted that the concept of "Sustained economic growth" is incompatible with the concept of "Sustainability".

At the country level, actions must focus, "in particular, in the areas of basic education, primary and maternal health care, and the advancement of women". Programs must be geared to empowering various groups and levels of society, facilitating the participation of social actors, and setting the "best possible conditions" for sustainable development over the long-term. The aim is to do so respecting cultural integrity and taking into account ethical considerations.

National governments should cooperate with international, non-government and local community organization. Internationally, the United Nations system and its partners must set poverty alleviation as a priority, assisting governments, promoting technical cooperation, and strengthening existing UN structures.

Politically Significant Issues
There is a number of potentially conflictive areas for donors seeking to take a leading role in the achievement of the objectives proposed by this Chapter:
- The added emphasis on environmental sustainability and natural resources management in the implementation of anti-poverty strategies, may lead to a disproportionate diversion of the already limited capacity of developing countries to respond to the basic needs of their populations. Having to comply with new international demands in setting their resource management and industrialization plans, developing countries may become more dependent upon the priorities of donors and lenders than in the past. This in turn may increase even more the conditionality of aid flows by Northern-set agenda.
- The success of the proposed approach to poverty eradication relies, theoretically, on an efficient international system of cooperation, monitoring and accountability, capable of assuming such roles effectively. However, the current UN system is in a deep institutional crisis. This opens the scenario to an even greater economic and political pressures from the G-7 countries, particularly the US, over sustainable development strategies in the South.

- A weakened UN system, East–West political uncertainty in the global scenario, and the politically symbolic nature of the Agenda 21, make the monitoring and evaluation of concrete poverty strategies almost unfeasible. This has serious potential implications for independent-minded donors (such as IDRC) which now struggle to define themselves according to the Agenda 21 objectives. Their reputation and accountability over the long-term may be weakened in the eyes of their Southern partners.
- The estimated costs of implementing the objectives for poverty eradication (and for the Agenda 21 as a whole) are simply non-affordable by the community of donors and by national governments. This could mean either the inability of donors to meet the demands for more resources from developing countries, or the diversion of scarce resources (of donors and within countries) from basic needs to other areas which are politically more acceptable in the short-term, but less effective over the medium and long-term.

Consideration of these issues could help the Centre decide how far it should go in re-allocating its limited resources and in re-visiting the priorities of its current Programs.

WHAT IS NOT THERE

The Chapter downplays the **political–economy** dimension of poverty: the interplay between politics and economics as regards to the causes, manifestations and solutions of poverty. This omission hinders the strategic identification of the ultimate sources of deprivation. This, in turn, leads to treating poverty and its eradication as an homogenous phenomenon and a "natural" state of developing countries that can be overcome through income-generation and economic growth strategies. Overall, the Chapter misses the key political dimension of strategic decision-making and thus minimizes the potential of its recommendations.

The notion of poverty itself is not explicit. The Chapter uses a concept of poverty which claims to be multidimensional in nature but, at the level of practice, is driven by economic criteria. The emphasis thus revolves around a narrow market-oriented notion of economic growth as the basis for sustainable development. Only superficial references are made to the social, cultural and axiological causes and expressions of poverty, or to the obstacles that may impede the implementation of anti-poverty strategies.

Similarly, poverty is treated in abstraction from the predominant political and economic dynamics of current Western notions of growth and development. The understanding of the causal relations between poverty and leading economic forces, including the role of the market, is almost absent from the Chapter.

Only vague references are made to the legal, institutional and policy-planning links between of poverty and public policy options which deal with them in a sustainable manner. This contributes to an overall vagueness in addressing policy directions that help to identify viable integrated strategies for poverty alleviation or eradication.

The Chapter ignores almost completely the impact of wars and armed conflicts as one of the main causes of poverty in the developing world, often linked to international economic and political interests. It fails to emphasize the responsibility of arms-producing countries in helping to sidetrack resources away from poverty eradication programs. Similarly, it fails to call the attention of governments to the single most important obstacle to implement effective anti-poverty strategies: **military spending**.

OVERALL CRITIQUE

Substantive Content

The Chapter presents a broad overview of poverty closely linked to the achievement of sustainable livelihood. It provides a general framework for discussion, but falls short of pointing out the depth of the issue.

Among the alternatives to deal with poverty, the Chapter suggests various actions, setting possible entry points for strategic planning, research and grass-roots work. These are left to the interpretation of the reader, weakening the translation of the recommendations into actual policy implementation.

Substantively, the Chapter adds little to the existing development wisdom about poverty. It is entangled in a web of generalities, politically correct statements and motherhood suggestions of doubtful use except at a very high level of abstraction. This may bring little comfort to developing country policy-makers and practitioners, to key poverty stricken groups, and to destitute communities looking for more practical guidance for setting specific strategies and programs to combat concrete manifestation of poverty.

The Chapter relies on the redistribution-with-growth (RWG) approach of the late 1970s, which was the theoretical basis for the World Bank approach to poverty eradication in the 1980s. This approach emphasizes: greater participation by the poor in growth, increasing the access of the poor to productive assets, raising the return on the assets of the poor, expanding income generating opportunities, and empowering the poor through mobilizing their talents in community actions. These principles of RWG are explicitly outlined in the Chapter.

In an effort to move ahead and bring to the forefront a link between the sustainability of development, environment and the eradication of poverty, the Chapter fails to raise some key underlying factors of underdevelopment and poverty, e.g. political ideology, class structure, and patterns of capital accumulation. It seems to assume conceptual affinities between governments, and international and national organizations around key development issues and goals their impact on poverty, including the notions of development sustainability and environmental management. The Chapter does not, for example, address in its full dimension the debt burden which increased poverty twofold in the Third World in the last decade, and had a severe impact on the management of natural and human resources.

By suggesting that the eradication of poverty must be rooted in principles of greater equity, empowerment, share responsibility, and international cooperation, in isolation from the prevailing relations of economic power of a changing international order, the Chapter ignores pervading issues of inequality in the distribution of wealth preventing the achievement of these goals. Structural issues of inequality, international dominance, and conflicts between social factions at national levels are also absent.

Design of the Chapter as an Organizing Framework

With the exception of the emphasis on environment and resource management, the Chapter's ideas are not different from similar past international attempts to bridge the gaps between the developing and the developed world. The Chapter falls short of providing an innovative and viable framework for poverty eradication in the context of Agenda 21.

The Chapter should begin by proposing an operational definition of poverty from a political-economy perspective. This should be followed by identifying feasible multidimensional avenues requiring priority action in financial decision-making, policy-planning, and the coordination of practice at the grass-roots. The objectives should be set in measurable terms, over the medium and long-run, and with achievable targets overtime. Key agencies should be identified to take responsibility for addressing specific areas of poverty eradication according to their comparative advantage and experience, thus avoiding duplication.

RESEARCH REQUIREMENTS, CAPACITY BUILDING ETC.

The Chapter touches on the key development issue of the late 20th Century, and provides a theoretical raison d'être for current international aid efforts. Most donor agencies and international organizations place the elimination of poverty among the ultimate goals of their aid strategies and programs. As such, the possible implications of this Chapter are critical to these institutions' attempts of projecting themselves into the next century within the scope of their mandates.

The Chapter does not formulate specific proposals. It suggests lines for action. The Chapter does not categorize directly possible line of actions in terms of requirements for capacity building, training or research. Most of the suggestions, however, can be seen as sources to draw directions in terms of these or other requirements for institutional action.

EXPLICIT PROPOSALS IN THE CHAPTER

The Chapter makes a number of suggestions directly related to its objectives: creating opportunities to earn sustainable livelihood, implementing feasible policies focusing on integrated human development, targeting poverty-stricken areas, and creating national development plans with emphasis on human capital investments.

These suggestions are geared towards covering a variety of cross-cutting sectorial interventions, involving a range of actors at various levels, and using region and country-specific approaches. Specifically, the "proposals" focus on:
- Developing means for the empowerment and participation of key target groups. This implies respect for cultural integrity, developing networks for learning and sharing of knowledge, and establishing popular mechanisms to facilitate these actions;
- Creating national capacity to develop sustainability by establishing conditions to reduce inequalities, setting measures for managing actions and resources, creating opportunities for productive employment including the informal sector, developing market infrastructures and credit systems, facilitating technology and human resources development, and setting systems for the delivery of universal services to satisfy basic need;
- Introducing integrated policy measures and culturally appropriate legal mechanisms that — respecting basic human rights — may help to satisfy basic needs, particularly in health (primary health care, maternal health, and sanitation), services management (land, food, water), and education (basic/primary learning and professional training);
- Setting means for gathering data and information for policy-planning and evaluation of poverty alleviation/eradication programs; and,
- Promoting international and regional cooperation in the planning, financing, and implementation and evaluation of anti-poverty strategies.

Donors and international agencies with multi-sectoral programs of work (such as IDRC) are better suited to deal with the implications of this Chapter. The proposals present a complex terrain for exploration in areas such as grass-roots development, advocacy, financial services, research, and human resources development, to list a few. It is unlikely that a single donor will have the technical capacity or the resources to cover all of them effectively. This would require each donor to assess its own comparative advantage before responding to these proposals.

IMPLICIT PROPOSALS DERIVED FROM THE CHAPTER

At one level, implicit proposals are related to a call for a more comprehensive approach to deal with poverty, in terms of for its understanding, solutions, and coordination of efforts. At another level, proposals can be based on groups to be targeted, specific areas of social activity to be tackled, and requirements to make specific options feasible and effective.

Some of the more explicit suggestions can be adopted, and adapted, to define aid programs for poverty alleviation or poverty eradication. They can be applied to define programs of work in sectoral and multidisciplinary research with specific entry points in key areas of basic needs. The training of human resources, in technical areas and for development management, becomes central to empowerment strategies and to institutional capacities. The need for a more direct role of governments and communities in policy (formulation, implementation and evaluation) is also implicit throughout of the Chapter.

GAPS AND ALTERNATIVE APPROACHES

Since this Chapter attempts to outline a broad framework for more problem/area-specific discussions in other parts of Agenda 21, few specific gaps can be identified. Some aspects, however, could benefit from a fuller treatment:
- The multi-dimensions of poverty shows an urgent need for a better understanding of the complexities of multi-disciplinary research (research on research). This must answer the question about how to make the results useful at both the policy and the practice level.
- The cross-cutting nature of poverty calls for new types of analyses that capture the political-economy dimension of sustainable development strategies and its implications for policy and planning. This requires a stronger emphasis on the technical side of policy research (research on the policy-planning processes).
- The call for greater attention to the evaluation of poverty alleviation and eradication programs, requires re-assessing the value of existing planning and evaluation methodologies (methodological research).
- The suggestion that anti-poverty strategies must be country-specific suggests the need for research on new forms of priority identification for multi-sectoral planning.
- The need to address directly poverty issues which are politically sensitive, including governments' military spending and the role of developed countries in contributing to the maintenance of national military establishments.

NICHES FOR IDRC

The niches for IDRC vis-à-vis Agenda 21, and this Chapter in particular, should be identified within the context of the IDRC Act, and the "principles and practices that will guide our actions and choices over the next several years" set by Strategy 91. **This implies seeing how the concerns, issues, and priorities of Agenda 21 fit into the constitutional framework of the Centre, rather than finding ways to see how IDRC fits into the Agenda proposed by UNCED.**

In both the Act of Parliament and in Strategy 91, the elimination of poverty is the ultimate goal providing meaning and direction to the actions of the Centre. Different from other donor organizations, IDRC defines the content of its programs according to the priorities and actions identified by developing countries. By **definition** the Centre is suited to address one of the central claims of this Chapter: that solutions to tackle poverty must be country-specific and by implication defined according to their own cultural integrity.

GENERAL

Opportunities that Fit Normal Programming

With only few exceptions, all the explicit and implicit proposals in this Chapter fit into the current programming of the Centre. Efforts to adopt a more multi-disciplinary approach in supporting research and research-related activities can further assist IDRC to address the multidimensional complexity of poverty, making research an instrument in the design of "cross-cutting measures" to deal with poverty issues.

From the perspective of research on policy and practice, Programs in both the Social and Health Sciences Divisions address directly the basic human needs dimensions required to be tackled through any integrated anti-poverty strategy. Areas of research on basic health care systems, productive income generation and income distribution strategies, basic primary education and technical training, approaches for more effective human capital investments, integrated human development and social policies, provision and assessment of basic services, understanding of the policy-planning processes of poverty eradication measures, and issues of improved governance, are dealt with by the two Divisions.

The Environment and Natural Resources Division responds to the main stream concerns of this Chapter on the management and resources sustainability and environmental policy, which are integral to the understanding of sustainable livelihood. Programs in the Corporate Affairs and Initiatives Division address the proposals on human resources development, the promotion of knowledge networks between communities, and the involvement of technical expertise in a context of greater cooperation with developing countries (and the Canadian constituency). The Information Sciences and Systems Division responds to the needs for research on data and information gathering for policy and practice, and for the required systems and technologies to make this knowledge available to policy-makers and practitioners.

The Centre has, therefore, the capacity and program structure to respond selectively to the priorities of Agenda 21 as regard to Combating Poverty. The key challenge to IDRC is the development of a capacity to work in an integrated fashion, both among the corporate Programs and between them and the regional offices.

New Opportunities

The new opportunities offered by this Chapter are many. In the context of the current Centre's Programs the possibilities of facing these new opportunities do not rest on the creation of new program areas or in the re-grouping of ongoing activities under new labels. The task at hand is rather to revise, with a clear sense of direction, the current Program emphases.

The new opportunities suggested by this Chapter and by Agenda 21 must be met with a corporate conviction that what the Centre does today is precisely geared towards the central concern of this Chapter: eradicating poverty to make development sustainable.

New areas which the Centre may wish to integrate explicitly into its program strategy are research on:
- The legal structures and systems that accompany cross-sectoral poverty policies;
- Culturally viable anti-poverty measures;
- The new ethics for sustainable development that will contribute to define the "new world order;"
- The viability and political effectiveness of empowerment actions;
- The development and assessment of accountability mechanisms; and,
- Evaluation methods and mechanisms for the assessment of policy and practice in sustainable development strategies.

Unusual or High-Risk Opportunities
The current direction of the Centre and the broad agenda proposed by this Chapter make possible to identify various "high-risk" opportunities:
- Developing politically acceptable and scientifically reliable methodologies for multi-disciplinary research. This may require changing accepted styles of operation and investing resources, both human and financial, in activities which may not be perceived as leading to "concrete products" in the short-term;
- Developing a balanced relationship between a Canadian constituency and developing country partners. The issue here is how to bridge gaps and build networks of knowledge, without falling into models of pure technical assistance or shift radically our primary audience;
- Establishing effective means of leverage in the international community of donors with limited resources.

KEY PARTNERS/OTHER ACTORS
Canada
The issues raised in this Chapter provides an excellent opportunity for the Centre to work with the large community of NGOs and private sector organizations in Canada, dealing with anti-poverty approaches in terms of design, delivery and assessment of programs. This can add a new dimension to the work of IDRC by developing networks of information on key target groups, successful experiences, and alternative mechanisms for the implementation of poverty eradication strategies.

Technically, Canadian universities can provide important assistance to developing country institutions and researchers in training human resources. Provincial governments also represents key potential partners in areas related to the decentralization of anti-poverty programs, and policy-planning in areas such as health, social and education policies. Similarly, private sector initiatives bring together an important set of actors that the Centre can consider in future activities.

Other Countries
The experience and existing networks of institutions place the Centre in a unique position among international organizations to carry out activities suggested by this Chapter. Specifically, the Chapter suggests closer links with agencies of the UN system. For IDRC, this could mean an additional effort to have closer collaboration with regional and country-base branches of the UN system.

RECOMMENDATIONS

WHICH NICHES ARE BEST FOR IDRC PROGRAM?
Given the objectives set by this Chapter the main niche for IDRC role vis-à-vis Agenda 21 is the strengthening of **its capacity to support research** for sustainable development in relation to poverty eradication strategies. Among international organizations and donors, IDRC has the truly unique mandate to focus on **research** which not many other organizations have.

At a more specific level, the following options are worth considering:
- Through each of its regional offices, the Centre can move in a pro-active way to set an **integrated thrust on research for poverty eradication**. This activity can be targeted to assist the poorest countries in a region to develop or re-assess cross-cutting government plans and policies to combat poverty. In addition to selected national organizations, key partners in this initiative could be other donors, regional organizations and selected Canadian institutions.

- In response to the emphasis on empowerment as a condition to efforts aimed at combating poverty, the Centre can create a **global research consortium on State decentralization**. This activity can be aimed at establishing a global network on decentralization experiences in developing countries, focusing on areas of policy-planning, mechanisms for decision-making delegation, and management systems of accountability.
- To assess the impact of poverty on sustainable development plans for the next century, the Centre can create and sponsor an **international task force on the dimensions of poverty in the context of a new world order**. This task force can be mandated to research alternative scenarios within which international aid for poverty eradication must occur over the next decade. It purpose will be to play an advisory role to other donors and international organizations and to serve as a sounding board for their sustainable development strategies.

ARE ADJUSTMENTS NEEDED AT IDRC IN ORDER TO FILL THESE NICHES?

No major program adjustments are required to fill these niches if time is given to the Centre's Divisions to establish their new structures. Adjustments in program emphases, priorities and administration may be required provided that a clear corporate direction is set for the Centre according to its mandate and new mission.

Despite the claimed political and development importance attributed today to Agenda 21, addressing the objectives of this Chapter implies to accept with confidence that the new course established for IDRC pre-Agenda 21, provides the appropriate space and the right opportunities to make a contribution in combating poverty. Adjustments in processes, procedures and technical resources must be made as much as they are required to fulfil the constitutional goals of the Centre. This, however, must be seen primarily as the response to the natural needs and the evolution of IDRC as a healthy organization.

CHAPTER FOUR

CHANGING CONSUMPTION PATTERNS

Responsible Officer: T. Carroll-Foster

ABSTRACT

1. OVERALL CRITIQUE OF AGENDA 21 CHAPTER

- An extremely weak chapter, and mundane. Implies (rightly) that the economic issue is very important.
- Recognizes that consumption patterns are a problem, but uses conventional approaches to try to resolve issue.
- Lacks analysis of relationships between poverty, wealth, role of population, and environment.
- Lacks recognition of need for overall limitations on consumption, growth concepts, population, etc. and does not appear to distinguish clearly between "growth" in the conventional economic sense and "sustainable development".
- Emphasizes change mainly through greater economic efficiency, with the environment treated as an appendage of economics.
- Lacks cross-referencing with other chapters and topics.

2. KEY CONCLUSIONS ARISING FROM CHAPTER

- Chapter acknowledges that existing consumption patterns are unsustainable.
- Consumption growth patterns must be revised without visiting more burdens on the poor or limiting opportunities for the growth of Third World countries.
- Proposals for research are either too limited or mundane, and are being done by others, or too all-encompassing and over-whelming, or outside IDRC's mandate.

3. RESEARCH AND/OR IMPLEMENTATION POSSIBILITIES/OPPORTUNITIES

- Research into the impacts of existing or emerging consumption patters in developing countries, with a focus on specific sectors, groups or regions and the resultant implications for sustainable development.
- Research that is focused on national policies and strategies, but not solely from an over-consumption perspective.

4. ON-GOING AND/OR NEW PARTNERSHIPS FOR IDRC

- NGOs, Research institutions, Women's organizations, Business councils, many of which IDRC has already worked with.

5. SUGGESTED NICHES FOR IDRC
- The Chapter per se did not indicate specific niches for IDRC.
- Within IDRC's overall programming the awareness of the role and inter-relationships which population, poverty, wealth/over-consumption play in threatening the further disintegration of the environment should be made both explicit and implicit.

6. OTHER COMMENTS
None.

REVIEW 4

David Brooks

KEY CONCLUSIONS IN THE CHAPTER

WHAT IS THERE

Main Conclusions
- Existing patterns of global consumption are unsustainable;
- These patterns must be revised but without adding to the burdens of developing countries nor limiting their opportunities for economic development;
- Unsustainable consumption is related both to poverty and to population, but is primarily seen as stemming from the high rates of use in the industrialized countries.

The chapter is divided into two sections:
- Unsustainable Patterns of Production and Consumption;
- National Policies and Strategies to Encourage Change.

The latter is mistitled as it focuses mainly on policies and strategies to encourage greater economic efficiency (with environment treated as a dimension of economics) and little on change (behavioral, attitudinal, societal, etc.).

Agreements Reached for International Action
None. Also no need for new financial resources was identified.

WHAT IS NOT THERE

There is practically nothing in the Chapter that emphasizes the need for overall limits of or limitations on consumption, scale, etc. A few sentences imply recognition of these limits but nothing more.

There is next to no analysis of relationships in the Chapter, hence practically no indication of how poverty, on the one hand, and wealth, on the other, link to consumption, nor the role of population and demographics in both developed and developing countries.

OVERALL CRITIQUE

Substantive Content

An extremely weak Chapter, which is also mundane. Yet it implies (correctly) that the subject is critically important to sustainability.

Overall, the Chapter attempts to emphasize the problem of consumption, but through conventional approaches.

Design of the Chapter as an Organizing Framework

The design of the Chapter is quite appropriate, but it needed to be both more forceful and more explicit about needed changes, and to emphasize the linkages among poverty and population for poor countries, and wealth and population for richer ones. Moreover, it failed to be explicit that this Chapter is linked to each of the other Chapters in Agenda 21.

RESEARCH REQUIREMENTS, CAPACITY BUILDING ETC.

EXPLICIT PROPOSALS IN THE CHAPTER

The proposals for research as stated follow into two categories. Some are mundane (e.g.: "Expand or promote databases on production and consumption . . ."). Others are overwhelming (e.g.: "Assess the relationship between production and consumption, environment, technological adaptation and innovation, economic growth and development and demographic factors").

IMPLICIT PROPOSALS DERIVED FROM THE CHAPTER

Analysis of the global dimensions of environment, and of those aspects stemming from wealth are either too large for or beyond the mandate of IDRC. The Centre's focus must be on consumption patterns of developing countries and their implications for sustainable development. From this perspective, past work on demographics, resource accounting, and the linkages between economic deprivation and environmental degradation are highly relevant.

GAPS AND ALTERNATIVE APPROACHES

Experience suggests that research into the impacts of consumption in developing countries is better approached from an alternative perspective:
- To the extent that the research focuses on the consumption patterns themselves, it is preferable to work with specific sectors, groups or regions rather than to try to generalize;
- To the extent that the research focuses on national policies and strategies, work should be on those directly (and for their value), not from an over-consumption perspective.

NICHES FOR IDRC

Without denying the critical importance of this area, there is not an explicit niche for IDRC. At one level, there is need to be aware of work in this field, and of changing perceptions, values and policies. At the other level, there is need to incorporate some notion of reducing natural resource throughput into all of IDRC's work.

RECOMMENDATIONS

This is one chapter that IDRC can put to one side. However, the explicit — and even more the implicit — conclusions that population, poverty and wealth are all threats to the environment, hence to sustainable development, must play a role in all programming.

COMMENTARY 4

Name of Commentator: Gary McMahon

1. **GENERAL COMMENTS ON THE FIRST REVIEW OF THE CHAPTER**
   - See below.

2. **OVERALL COMMENTARY ON THE FIRST REVIEW OF THE CHAPTER**
   - While I agree with the general conclusions of the first review, it was a bit too critical of the substance of the Chapter. It is not clear what are the alternative approaches to the global problem other than the "conventional" ones.
   - Nevertheless, I agree that there are no major obvious niches for IDRC that come out of this Chapter other than the link between poverty and environmental degradation, which probably fits much better in other chapters of the agenda.

3. **MAJOR POINTS AGREED/DISAGREED WITH, AND REASONS**
   - The reviewer says that Part B on national policies and strategies to encourage change focus mainly on economic efficiency; I do not agree with this. A large part of this section has to do with changing values through government example, pricing policies, and reinforcing (environmentally correct) values.
   - The reviewer also notes that the Chapter should be more explicit about the links between poverty and population as well as between this chapter and others. It should be noted that right at the beginning of the Chapter it states that it should be read in conjunction with Chapter 5 on Demographic Dynamics and Sustainability.
   - I agree with the reviewer that the main issue is the scale of consumption in the West, although I do not see obvious solutions (or IDRC funded research projects) on this issue.
   - The Chapter does not address rising consumption levels and patterns in the newly industrializing or industrialized countries.

4. **MINOR POINTS AGREED/DISAGREED WITH, AND REASONS**
   - None.

5. **POSSIBLE ON-GOING ISSUES OR CONCERNS FOR IDRC**
   - As above.

6. **POSSIBLE IMPLICATIONS FOR IDRC**
   - As noted.

CHAPTER FIVE

DEMOGRAPHIC DYNAMICS AND SUSTAINABILITY

Responsible Officer: François M. Farah

ABSTRACT

1. OVERALL CRITIQUE OF AGENDA 21 CHAPTER

- Little emphasis on the social and cultural contexts.
- Regional/sub-regional variations are looked at exclusively from a developmental "economy-driven" perspective.
- Reproductive patterns and population movements are seen as individual choices and opportunities for enhancement of socio-economic status from within specific political, ethnological, and socio-cultural contexts.
- Two policy perspectives needed addressing: changing family dynamics and reproductive behaviours to achieve sustainability, and local and indigenous strategies for preserving revitalizing natural resources.

2. KEY CONCLUSIONS ARISING FROM CHAPTER

- Indisputable interactions between growing population pressure and the alarming depletion of natural resources. "Critical ecological zones", i.e., densely populated and demographically rapidly growing areas, will degenerate further due to high population growth rates and arbitrary spatial distribution.
- Population dynamics, as a multi-faceted problem, should be addressed through research, policies and strategies involving attitudes, economic, social and cultural values or processes related to demographic phenomena (e.g. fertility, family planning, migration, women's status and reproductive behaviour).

3. RESEARCH AND/OR IMPLEMENTATION POSSIBILITIES/OPPORTUNITIES

- Research and research-related activities (training, building data-bases, setting up inter-disciplinary, multi-institutional research/expert networks, etc.) are needed for the **integration** of demographic dynamics/processes into sustainable development strategies/policies.
- Research is needed to develop measurements and tools to: assess/monitor demographically induced depletion of resources; assess policy and program actions, the strengths and weaknesses of implementing institutions; and assess the quality, performance and decentralization of various population programs and measures.
- Research is needed on: training programs to strengthen political skills; women's empowerment processes and needs within social and cultural contexts; and the interactions between migration and land use.

4. ON-GOING AND/OR NEW PARTNERSHIPS FOR IDRC

- Priorities are identified at a macro-level and include the formulation and implementation of policies and programs. Partner institutions should be capable of conceptualization, problem-solving approaches, and decision-making.

- In Canada, partners could be university-based, government and/or non-government research groups; NGOs involved in community development; and the Canadian business community (for possible technical and technological transfer).
- Outside Canada, partners could be international development agencies, indigenous, and national university, or NGO-based research and development institutions, and experts working in interdisciplinary, multi-institutional frameworks.

5. SUGGESTED NICHES FOR IDRC

- Research on integration processes between population dynamics and depletion of natural resources. The promotion of a worldwide research initiative aimed at the development and the dissemination of a Population-Induced Natural Resources Exhaustion Monitor (PINREM). PINREM encompasses most research areas in the Chapter; is a strategic instrument for policy design and implementation; helps to validate reliable instruments for monitoring success or failure of policies; and represents a mechanism for improving the networking capabilities of government and institutions within non-government between Canada and the world.

6. OTHER COMMENTS

- PINREM can be easily integrated within the Centre's current structure, as an existing program or a special initiative. It will be a world leader in its field and provide great national and international visibility for Canada and the Centre.

REVIEW 5

KEY CONCLUSIONS IN THE CHAPTER

Demographic dynamics have been mainly addressed from a statistical perspective. National and international agencies concerned with population matters have largely concentrated on gathering demographic statistics, and carrying out quantitative analyses or surveys of demographic phenomena (particularly fertility, birth control and migration). These were mainly justified by the lack of demographic data in most developing countries, the need of those countries to master their population dynamics, and primarily, to control and slow down their rapid population growth.

The most significant change in perspective as shown in this Chapter is the prominently recognized relationship and interactive processes between growing population pressure and the alarming depletion of natural resources. Many environmental trends, such as tropical deforestation, desertification, soil erosion, declining air quality and contaminated water sources, tend in fact to occur in geographically concentrated, densely populated, and demographically rapidly growing areas. Such "critical ecological zones" (to borrow the UN term) will most likely degenerate still further with sustained high demographic growth rates and an arbitrary and disorganized spatial distribution of the population. The challenge that population growth poses to sustainable development is multi-faceted and concerns both increasing numbers, i.e., population dynamics and change, and more complex demographic patterns which involve attitudes, economic, social and cultural values and processes related to different demographic phenomena such as fertility, family planning, migration, women's status and reproductive behaviour, etc. The significant change is in shifting the focus from simply counting people to measuring the impact of their dynamics on the environment with a view to proposing policy alternatives and requirements aimed at a more sustainable future.

WHAT IS THERE

Agenda 21 identifies three major program areas:
- Generating and disseminating elements of policies;
- Formulating population–environment integrated policies; and,
- Implementing demographically balanced and environmentally sound development policies and programs. All three areas focus on the links between demographic trends and factors and the environment. They also involve a wide spectrum of research ranging from building and strengthening national databases, to the development of measurement of population-related damages to the environment and sustainability; from the analysis of demographic processes to that of appropriate and feasible population policies and programs aimed at preserving a more sustainable future.

The agreements reached clearly emphasized the key role of the interactive processes between population dynamics and sustainability in all environment-related development research and policies. **Given such emphasis it would be difficult, if not absurd, to imagine an Agenda 21 Organization with little or no focus on population issues.** Even more so since a significant number of IDRC Board members, who are likely to be chosen from UN affiliated agencies and circles, are likely to be particularly sensitive to and keen on, promoting population studies.

The issues identified in this Chapter have serious political implications to the extent that many of them simply deal with reproductive values and behaviours and most often with locally developed and culturally integrated survival strategies. In many developing, rapidly growing, poorly managed societies, the delicate decision on what resources to sustain first human communities or the environment, is usually made, deliberately or otherwise, in favour of the former at the expense of the latter. To reverse this trend one needs to address structural, well-established and deeply rooted patterns and dynamics which involve economic, social, political and cultural determinants associated with human reproduction.

It also requires serious, sustained and coherent political and financial commitment, assessment of prior policy and program actions, broad mobilization of individuals and communities and a minimum of women's empowerment to be promoted from within the social and cultural context.

WHAT IS NOT THERE

Little is said about the experiences learned from or the urgent need to evaluate previous population policies that have been implemented with little or no success over the last three decades. With an additional environment component to population policies, or an additional population component to environmental policies, the risk that such policies fail is even higher and hence the need to build on previous experiences is urgent and relevant.

Human beings and dimensions, and quality of life are vaguely defined and give rise to contradictory interpretations depending on the social, political or religious context.

OVERALL CRITIQUE

Demographic dynamics are heavily shaped by two basic factors: reproductive patterns and population movements. Both involve the inherent nature of individual choices, perceived opportunities for promotion and socio-economic status' enhancement, and political and socio-cultural context. While the Chapter recognizes the "human" dimensions as "key elements" that should be adequately integrated in "comprehensive policies for sustainable development" it pays little attention to context. Regional and sub-regional variations are looked at from a "developmental" perspective which is basically tantamount to globally defined economic development. (The same attitude proved to be inconclusive in previous implemented population policies and programs.)

A chapter on population dynamics is indubitably indispensable and a priority in a comprehensive and feasible Agenda 21. The tone, however, should reflect the need to deal with population dynamics from two basic policy perspectives: changing family dynamics and reproductive behaviours to achieve a sustainable demographic growth, and enhancement of local and indigenous strategies of preserving and revitalising the available natural resources. Serious local and international research and development endeavours should aim at integrating the second perspective into each and every social context so that it becomes socially and culturally internalized. Scenarios similar to those well known in the field of commercial marketing could be developed, adapted and applied to different situations.

RESEARCH REQUIREMENTS, CAPACITY BUILDING, ETC.

Most activities proposed in the Chapter are basically explicit proposals for an extensive research agenda and program for all of the three areas identified. Research and research-related activities are such as building databases; training; setting up inter-disciplinary, multi-institutional research and expert networks; identification of priority areas for action; developing, validating and evaluating appropriate strategies and programs; development of scales, measurements and indicators; etc. They are all concerned with the interaction between demographic processes, natural resources and life support system, and the integration of demographic trends and factors into national, environmentally sound, sustainable development policies. IDRC and like-minded donors have here an unprecedented opportunity and a great challenge to take.

The emphasis in this Chapter in terms of research, is placed on the **end** objective of the **integration** of demographic dynamics and processes into sustainable development strategies and policies. This would indisputably involve, however, implicit research on dynamics and processes per se, which is by itself, an immense research program to the extent that it involves a myriad of substantial and methodological questions and issues. Implicit also is the need for research on adequate measurements and tools to assess and monitor demographically induced resources depletion such as deforestation, desertification, soil erosion, etc., so that policies put forward and implemented, could be assessed, adjusted and improved against a reliable and adequate framework.

Research should primarily be done on assessments of prior policy and program actions; the strengths and weaknesses of institutions implementing population programs; and, the quality, performance and decentralisation of differing population programs and measures.

Research is required on the development of adequate training programs to strengthen the political skills necessary to ensure a better integration of population concerns into sustainable development strategies.

Research is also required on women's empowerment from within specific social and political contexts coupled with appropriately mounted programs aimed at enhancing women's sensitivity to low fertility and to healthy environment.

Also required are comparative studies of migration and land use which could be utilised to isolate the sequence of events: policy changes, population growth and migration and studies of the causes and consequences of rural out-migration from densely settled areas.

NICHES FOR IDRC

GENERAL

It is difficult to identify research opportunities that "fit normal programming" since demographic dynamics, trends and factors simply disappeared as research areas from the Centre's recently implemented structure. For IDRC, Agenda 21 breathes new life into population concerns and stresses the urgent need to reconsider the research priority order so that the Centre would be more in line with Agenda 21's spirit and resolutions.

Most research areas identified in the Chapter and that stressed in II.c above represent new opportunities for the Centre.

OF PARTICULAR IMPORTANCE IS RESEARCH ON:
- Family dynamics and reproductive patterns and their impact on the natural resources;
- Migration and land use; causes and consequences of rural out-migration from densely settled areas;
- Analysis of the relationships between women's status enhancement, women's perception of environmental risks and fertility decline;
- Development of adequate measurements and tools and reference frameworks against which, to assess and monitor population-related depletion of natural resources; and,
- Assessment of population policies and programs and evaluation of the potentials of integrating demographic dynamics and processes into sustainable development strategies and policies;

The widely recognized magnitude and gravity of the population-induced natural resources depletion, the momentum gathered at the Rio Conference and the promising mandate of IDRC as an Agenda 21 Organization, offer an unprecedented opportunity to consider **the patronage and the promotion of research on the development and the dissemination of a Population-Induced Natural Resources Exhaustion Monitor (PINREM)**. PINREM encompasses most of the research areas and ideas proposed in the Chapter and in sections above. In terms of process it presents the Centre with an inter-disciplinary, comprehensive research program which would extend beyond the dawn of the twenty first Century. It also represents an ingenious mechanism of gathering, mixing up and exchanging disciplines and resources from both fields of population and the environment and enhances networking opportunities and capabilities of government and non-government institutions. It gives rise to developing and validating reliable instruments and technology that help monitor changes and success or failures of policy implementation. Given its scope and potential applications, PINREM is most likely to rally significant moral, technical and financial support from third world governments, international donors and many UN agencies. It will eventually serve as a strategic instrument for policy design and implementation in both fields of population and the environment, at all decision making levels, local, regional and international. It will finally have a tremendous impact in terms of national and international visibility for the Centre.

Few pioneering comparable approaches in the field of social sciences such as the Social Trends Monitor in the United Kingdom, have proved to be feasible and conclusive and have had a wide range of policy applications in both public and private sectors. Further in-depth arguments in favour of the Monitor can be developed and expanded should the Centre express interest in taking the lead on such a pioneering world wide initiative.

REGIONAL SPECIFICITY
Rapidly growing populations and their corollary in terms of natural resources depletion has been observed in most of Sub-Saharan Africa, South Asia, Latin America and the Middle East. Evidence on that can be easily found in Central America, the Philippines, Nigeria, Rwanda/Burundi, Sudan and other places where variations in local rates of population increase largely explain observed variations in local rates of deforestation. Other strong statistical association between population growth and deforestation for example may be found in regions such as West Africa and North Africa where a mosaic of cleared and forested land characterizes the landscape. Such a regional specificity could be further discussed as part of a broader programming. (Selected readings on the relationships between demographic dynamics and its impact on the environment are given in Appendix A).

KEY PARTNERS/OTHER ACTORS

Most priorities identified in this Chapter are situated at the macro level and concern basically the generation of policy ingredients and formulation and implementation of integrated policies and programs. While this is an end objective by itself, achieving such an objective will dictate a more subtle approach on the part of the Centre aimed at identifying institutions and human resources:
- Capable of conceptualizing, carrying out and analyzing problem-solving research projects; and,
- Likely to act as a driving force with decision-making circles and leaders towards influencing the policy making process and ensuring an appropriate translation of research findings into policies.

In Canada, partners can be primarily found in university-based government and non-government research institutions as well as Canadian groupings involved in development sectors related to Agenda 21's identified topics and priorities. In addition, partnership could and should be extended to the Canadian business community at large as many technical or technological applications (e.g. remote-sensing techniques, technologically advanced devices, databases management systems, etc.) or experiences in the broadly defined private sector would help design and implement more cost-effective and worthwhile programs.

As to our partners outside Canada, the Centre is invited to work as need be with a variety of players and actors on the international development scene such as the differing UN specialized agencies, donor organizations, international and regional networks, etc. For recipient developing countries, the Centre will need to promote inter-disciplinary, multi-institutional, mixed teams of researchers and decision makers at both community and central levels in a way in which research is closely tied to action and policies. This would obviously involve university-based researchers and research institutions, and most importantly, administrative officials in both government and non-government agencies. Recent Centre experiences show that this approach is feasible, achievable, and very promising.

RECOMMENDATIONS

WHICH NICHES ARE BEST FOR IDRC PROGRAM?
- An opportune and inordinately promising niche for an IDRC Program is the promotion and the development of research on the development and the establishment of PINREM (as described above).
- Another niche is research on the development of environmentally driven evaluation frameworks and "yardsticks" of population policies and programs. The definition of population policies and programs here goes beyond technically designed family planning programs to encompass the research areas described above.

ARE ADJUSTMENTS NEEDED AT IDRC IN ORDER TO FILL THESE NICHES

Program re-organization adjustments will eventually be needed as the recently implemented Centre strategy did very little to emphasize the effect of demographic dynamics and population distribution and movements on the natural resources depletion. To be consistent with Agenda 21's spirit and clear recommendations, and to meet growing national and international expectations about the leading role of IDRC in that domain, the Centre has little choice but to introduce an obvious population program component into its reorganization. The substance, extent, mandate, scope and shape of such a program will be largely determined in terms of the linkages and the interactions between demographic dynamics and processes and depletion of natural resources rather than in terms of research on the dynamics and the processes per se.

In addition to its usual procedural program delivery, the Centre is invited to consider the promotion of networking initiatives and undertakings where IDRC could play a key catalytic, leading, and quite visible role involving other international actors and players in both donor and recipient world wide communities. PINREM for instance, lends itself to such a networking approach and may very well serve as a prototype for other Centre-related internationally driven applications. This, of course, calls for appropriate skills and expertise in the area of demographic dynamics and processes; a significant degree of sensitivity to and familiarity with, environmental issues and concerns; and, "entrepreneurial" skills and expertise in networking, project development and risk-taking.

The proposed changes in IDRC's focus, reach, and vocation; the prospective Board composition in terms of members' profile, background, interest and institutional affiliation; the concerns expressed and the topics proposed in Agenda 21; all of that compels the Centre to alter, perhaps not insignificantly, its structure and staffing procedures. Initiatives such as those discussed earlier in this paper, call for more entrepreneurial, multi-purpose functioning, PR-acclimated and less "territorial" or turf-minded profile on the part of program staff. It also calls for more flexibility in the Centre's project development and initiatives promotion procedures.

APPENDIX A

SELECTED READINGS

Bilsborrow, R. (1987). Population pressures and agricultural development in developing countries: a conceptual framework and recent evidence. *World Development* (Boston, Massachusetts), vol. 15, No. 2, pp. 183–203.

Collins, J. (1988). *Unseasonal Migrations: The Effects of Rural Labour Scarcity in Peru*. Princeton: Princeton University Press.

Conway, M. (1977). Circular migration in Venezuelan frontier areas. *International Migration* (Geneva), vol. 15, No. 1, pp. 35–42.

Ehrlich, P., and A. Ehrlich (1990). *The Population Explosion*. New York: Simon and Schuster.

Hardjono, J. (1986). Spontaneous rural settlement in Indonesia. In *Spontaneous Settlement Formation in Rural Areas*, vol. 2, *Case Studies*. Nairobi: United Nations Centre for Human Settlements, pp. 50–69.

Hellden, U. (1984). Drought impact monitoring: a remote sensing study of desertification in Kordofan, Sudan. Lunds (Sweden): Lunds Universitets Naturgeogrfiska Institution, in cooperation with the Institute of Environmental Studies, University of Khartoum.

Horowitz, M., and P. Little (1987). African pastoralism and poverty: some implications for drought and famine. In *Drought and Hunger in Africa*, M. Glantz, ed. Cambridge: Cambridge University Press, pp. 59–84.

Ibrahim, F. (1987). Ecology and land use changes in the semi-arid zone of the Sudan. In *Lands at Risk in the Third World*, M. Horowitz and P. Little, eds. Boulder, Colorado: Westview, pp. 213–229.

Kelley, A. (1988). The economic consequences of population change in the third world. *Journal of Economic Literature* (Nashville, Tennessee), vol. 26, No. 4, pp. 685–728.

Lele, U., and S. Stone (1989). Population pressure, the environment, and agricultural intensification. *Managing Agricultural Development in Africa*. Discussion Paper No. 4 Washington, D.C.: World Bank.

McNicoll, G. (1990). Social Organization and Ecological Stability under Demographic Stress. Research Division Working Papers, No. 11. New York: The Population Council.

Muscat, R. (1985). Carrying capacity and population growth: definition, cases, and consequences. In *Rapid Population Growth and Human Carrying Capacity: Two Perspectives*, D.J. Mahar, ed. Staff Working Paper No. 690. Washington, D.C.: World Bank. pp. 1–40.

N'diaye, S., and A. Sofranko (1990). Population pressures and farmers' adoption of conservation practices in the Buberuka Highlands of Rwanda. Paper presented at the meeting of the Rural Sociological Society, Norfolk, Virginia, 8–11 August.

Okafor, F. (1987). Population pressure and land resource depletion in southeastern Nigeria. *Applied Geography* (Guildford, England), vol. 7, pp. 243–256.

Pingali, P., and H. Binswanger (1987). Population density and agricultural intensification: a study of the evolution of technologies in tropical agriculture. In *Population Growth and Economic Development: Issues and Evidence*, D. Johnson and R. Lee, eds. Madison: University of Wisconsin Press, pp. 27–56.

Preston, D. (1987). Population mobility and the creation of new landscapes. In *Environment, Society, and Rural Change in Latin America*. D.A. Preston, ed. London: Longman, pp. 195–208.

Repetto, R. (1986). Soil loss and population pressure in Java. *Ambio* (Stockholm), vol. 15, No. 1, pp. 14–18.

Rudel, T. (1989). Population, development, and tropical deforestation: a cross-national study. *Rural Sociology* (Bozeman, Montana), vol. 54, No. 3, pp. 327–388.

Rudel, T., and S. Richards (1990). Urbanization, roads and rural population change in the Ecuadorian Andes. *Studies in Comparative International Development* (New Brunswick, New Jersey), vol. 25.

Shaw, P. (1989). Rapid population growth and environmental degradation, ultimate versus proximate factors. *Environmental Conservation* (Geneva), vol. 16, No. 3, pp. 199–208.

Slade, M. (1987). Natural resources, population growth, and economic well-being. In *Population Growth and Economic Development: Issues and Evidence*, D. Johnson and R. Lee, eds. Madison: University of Wisconsin Press, pp. 331–369.

Talbot, L. (1986). Demographic factors in resource depletion and environmental degradation in East African rangeland. *Population and Development Review* (New York), vol. 12, No. 3, pp. 441–456.

Tallon, F. (1988). L'autosuffisance alimentaire et le problème démographique au Rwanda. *Famille, santé, développement* (Dakar), vol. 13, pp. 6–12.

World Resources Institute (1990). *World Resources, 1990-91*. New York: Oxford University Press.

CHAPTER SIX

PROTECTION AND PROMOTION OF HUMAN HEALTH

Responsible Officer: Maureen Law

ABSTRACT

1. OVERALL CRITIQUE OF AGENDA 21 CHAPTER

- The Chapter is entitled "The Protection and Promotion of Human Health", but little is on the promotion aspect.
- The focus is on a top-down health services delivery model rather than an integrated and empowering approach to health care.
- There are no philosophical underpinnings, (e.g. equity, people-centred, participatory strategies), nor new political challenges or incentives for either the North or the South to change the way they now operate.
- The basis for action sections are good and almost all relevant subject areas are emphasized in the activities presented, except: family planning, occupational health, alcohol and tobacco related diseases, and problems related to war, refugees, and street children.

2. KEY CONCLUSIONS ARISING FROM CHAPTER

- Health and (sustainable) development are intimately connected.
- Inter-sectoral (including business) efforts are required to link health, environmental and socio-economic improvement.
- Multi-disciplinary research, methodology development, capacity-building and training are all supported.

3. RESEARCH AND/OR IMPLEMENTATION POSSIBILITIES/OPPORTUNITIES

- Of the 33 proposals mentioned in the Chapter, the Health Sciences Division highlights the following:
  a) Development of new approaches to planning and managing health systems;
  b) Development of a multi-disciplinary research approach and inter-sectoral research framework;
  c) Integration of research, training and capacity-building especially in such neglected areas as health systems and occupational health;
  d) Promotion of national, inter-country and inter-regional exchange of information;
  e) Environmental health research, including behavioural research;
  f) Development of epidemiologic monitoring systems;
  g) Development of cost-effectiveness analysis and environmental impact assessment methods; and
  h) Exploration of methods for implementing flexible pragmatic solutions, with emphasis on preventative measures.

4. ON-GOING AND/OR NEW PARTNERSHIPS FOR IDRC

- In Canada: a) the HSD/SSD with people/organizations in telecommunications, remote sensing and geographic information; b) people/groups working in Canada's health system because of its multi-cultural nature, the mix of public and private sectors and its decentralized structure; c) people involved with indigenous self-government, the Healthy Cities program and NGOs; and d) specific organizations: CIDA, H&WC, CSIH, CPHA, CUCHID, etc.
- In other countries/regions: SAREC, GTZ, Rockefeller Foundation, Ford Foundation, ODA, and the EEC.
- International Organizations: WHO, PAHO, UNEP, UNICEF, UNDP, ILO, and the World Bank.

5. SUGGESTED NICHES FOR IDRC

- Research into the multi-cultural, socio-economic, environmental, historical and political elements of developing country health.
- Building the capacity of developing countries to predict, elucidate, and intervene against, the health effects of environmental changes; and to research the health risks inherent in the physical/biological/working environments, peoples' behaviour and reaction to risks.
- Research into the health issues which arise from social instability and extreme social change, e.g. forced migration, environmental stress and urbanization.
- Research into the physical, chemical, biological, and psychosocial factors associated with production activities in the agricultural, domestic, and industrial sectors.
- Linking with the Micronutrient Initiative and focusing on research into such areas as: micronutrient malnutrition, malnutrition infection complex, food safety/quality, food security, infant/child feeding, sanitation, diarrhoeal diseases, and women's role.
- Research on issues such as performance and financing of health services and development of health information systems.
- Research on the health sector and other sectors (e.g. agriculture, industry, education, environment) that have significant impact on the health status of populations.

6. OTHER COMMENTS

Health is an essential and central element in environment and sustainable development. The issues in Chapter 6 have explicit and implicit links to many of the other chapters. The Chapter virtually ignores the linkages between population and health. This chapter would be more useful if it promoted a more modern notion of international/community health and sustainable development, and served to galvanize an integrated approach along the theme of Sustainable and Supportive Environments for Health. The comparative advantage for IDRC is to promote this notion of international health by through understanding the determinants of health and human development, and researching societal responses to health and human development needs.

REVIEW 6

KEY CONCLUSIONS IN THE CHAPTER

WHAT IS THERE

Although the major conclusions in this Chapter are sound, there are omissions and major discrepancies between the basis for action sections and the proposed activities.

Main Conclusions
- Health and (sustainable) development are intimately interconnected;
- Inter-sectoral (including business) efforts are required to link health, environmental and socio-economic improvement;
- Multi-disciplinary research, methodology development, capacity building and training are all supported. A heavy and diversified research agenda is proposed;
- There is recognition of country-specific needs and conditions;
- Monitoring systems and decision making models are necessary; and,
- WHO should coordinate countries to develop priority action plans derived from cooperative planning by various levels of government, NGO's and communities within five program areas:
  - Rural Primary Health Care;
  - Communicable Disease Control;
  - Protection of infants, youths, women, and indigenous peoples (vulnerable groups);
  - Urban Health; and,
  - Environmental Health Risks.

Agreements Reached for International and National Action
- No obvious agreements were reached but the Chapter endorses a number of goals agreed by various UN agencies and member governments including the Plan of Action for Implementing the World Declaration on the Survival, Protection and Development of Children in the 1990s. (Agenda 21, Chapter 6: p.12); and,
- The Chapter specifically mentions internationally agreed targets for specific disease eradication or reduction.

Politically Significant Issues
- The lack of emphasis on population growth and family planning as issues for health, sustainable development or environment;
- The applicability of international standards to developing countries, (e.g. environmental pollution standards, occupational health and safety standards);
- The constructing/strengthening of relationships between the public and the private (business) sector;
- The downplaying of the health risks associated with economic productive activities (occupational health); and,
- The financing and cost of implementation of the proposed activities.

WHAT IS NOT THERE
- There are no philosophical underpinnings (e.g. equity, people-centred, participatory strategies) nor new political challenges or incentives for either the North or the South to change the way they now operate;

- There is little emphasis on understanding the behavioral, cultural and economic contexts which determine environmental health risks and sustainability of development;
- There is no mention of war, refugees, street children and migration in the context of protection and promotion of health;
- There is no mention of food security and environmental degradation;
- Health in the working environment (agricultural, industrial, and domestic) is downplayed; and,
- There is no mention of alcohol, or of tobacco-related disease, despite direct health and environmental effects (e.g. land use for tobacco crops in developing countries and deforestation for curing).

OVERALL CRITIQUE

Substantive Content
- Agenda 21, Chapter 6, seems to point to bio-medical, clinical and technological fixes as the major vehicle for sustainable health, yet there is a wealth of evidence that these are not important determinants of health. Historically, most improvements in the health of populations have not coincided with medical or technological breakthroughs, but with hygiene and public health efforts promoted through social and political commitment. The Chapter still has a tendency to champion a top-down health services delivery paradigm rather than an integrated and empowering approach to health care. Nevertheless, the basis for action in this chapter is good and mention is made of almost all relevant subject areas with the exception of those listed above. The main conclusions are sound yet the substantive content (activities) are not consistent, e.g. family lanning appears in the basis for action section but not in the activities, similarly nutrition (and micronutrient deficiency) despite being environmentally related, are given inadequate attention.
- The Chapter appears to forget Principle 1 of the Rio Declaration which states that **Human beings are at the centre of concerns for sustainable development. They are entitled to a healthy and productive life in harmony with nature.**
- There is a heavy and unrealistic dependence on centrally planned and delivered services as opposed to community-based strategies.
- Although the Chapter is entitled, "The Protection and Promotion of Human Health", little is found on the promotion aspect.
- A wide and extensive research agenda is presented but prioritization is not attempted.
- There is no mention of Essential National Health Research.

Design of the Chapter as an Organizing Framework
- This Chapter recognizes the notion of interdependencies, but lacks an overall conceptual framework illustrating the complex set of interrelated factors impacting upon the health of people and communities. If we were organizing Agenda 21, a chapter on health would be both central and essential and would connect to health in other chapters of the Agenda where appropriate. Such a Chapter on health would try to promote a more modern notion of international/community health and sustainable development which would serve to galvanize an integrated approach along the theme of Sustainable and Supportive Environments for Health. These environments would include not just the physical but also the socio-cultural-economic and health system environments.

RESEARCH REQUIREMENTS, CAPACITY BUILDING, ETC.

EXPLICIT PROPOSALS IN THE CHAPTER
There is a broad range of research explicitly called for in the Chapter. The numbers assigned to each proposal relate to Table 1 (found on the last page of this review).

Proposals That Cut Across All Chapter 6 Program Areas
- Development of new approaches to planning and managing health systems.
- Multi-disciplinary research approach and inter-sectoral research framework.
- Integration of research, training and capacity building and the training/education of environmental and health officials at all levels.
- Studies to optimize dissemination of research results.
- Technology transfer and promotion of national, intercountry and interregional exchange of information.

Primary Health Care
Research subjects — food safety, safe water supply, sanitation, health education, immunization, essential drugs, and family planning.

Development of:
- Health education programmes focusing on the role of women.
- Appropriate health technologies and integration of these technologies into health infrastructures.
- Strategies, including reliable health indicators, to monitor progress and evaluate effectiveness of health programs.
- Mechanisms for sustained community involvement in environmental health.
- Environmental health research, including behavioral research on ways to increase coverage and utilization of health services.
- Research into traditional knowledge of preventive and curative practices.
- Exploration of new ways to finance the health system.

Disease Control
- Intervention research to develop disease control policies and evaluate efficiency of alternative approaches.
- Studies on the effects of cultural, behavioral and social factors on control policies.

Development of:
- Epidemiologic monitoring systems for data collection on the distribution of communicable diseases and the institutional capacity to respond.
- Improved vaccines and new disease control technologies.

Protecting Vulnerable Groups
- Research on infants, youth, women, indigenous people, the very poor, elderly and disabled.
- Expansion of social research on the specific problems of these groups.
- Exploration of methods for implementing flexible pragmatic solutions, with emphasis on preventive measures.
- Promotion of organizations representing and composed of vulnerable groups.

Urban Health
Development of:
- Decision-making models to assess costs and health and environmental impacts of alternative technologies and strategies.
- Better methods for the collection of national and municipal statistics based on practical, standardized indicators.

Environmental Risks

Development of:
- Cost/effect analysis and environmental impact assessment methods through cooperative international programs.
- Urban air pollution control strategies and technologies.
- Water pollution control technologies on the basis of health risk assessment.
- Mechanisms to control pesticide risks.
- Solid waste disposal technologies.
- Strategies for improving health conditions in human settlements.
- Environmental monitoring systems for surveillance of environmental quality and health status.

Research into:
- Indoor air pollution reduction including incentives and technologies.
- The effects of uvB radiation on human health.
- The combined health effects of exposure to multiple environmental hazards, including long term exposures to low levels of pollutants.
- Placing environmental health in the curricula of secondary schools and universities.

IMPLICIT PROPOSALS DERIVED FROM THE CHAPTER

The section on vulnerable groups has a limited explicit research agenda, but the universe of research demanded by the health circumstances of children, youth, women, indigenous peoples, and urban life in developing countries is implicit.

GAPS AND ALTERNATIVE APPROACHES

As the "Gaps" in this chapter have been sufficiently covered in the sections "What Is Not There" and "Overall Critique" the focus of this section will be on Alternative Approaches.

The HSD has taken the alternative approach of a multi-method, cyclical research paradigm aimed at sequentially attempting: i) to understand the determinants of health and human development; and, ii) research the societal responses to health and human development needs. Priority is given to participatory research.

NICHES FOR IDRC

GENERAL

Opportunities that Fit Normal Programming
We have supported research in all explicit and implicit topics identified in Chapter 6 (See attached Table 1).

New Opportunities
- Development of new tools for impact assessment studies.
- Greater emphasis on inter-sectoral approaches.

Unusual or High-Risk Opportunities
None.

REGIONAL SPECIFICITY

As required.

KEY PARTNERS/OTHER ACTORS

Canada
- Aspects of Canada's health system, i.e. its multicultural nature, the mix of both the private and public sectors and its decentralized structure, can be used as models for developing countries. Partners will include people/groups working in Canada's health system.
- Important partners might also be those involved with indigenous self-government, the Healthy Cities Programme, and NGOs.
- In partnership with IDRC's Information Sciences Division, HSD could use Canada's comparative strengths in the telecommunications, remote sensing and geographic information systems sectors on the problems of environment, public health and sustainable development. People/groups in these sectors could become partners.
- Examples of specific partners might include: CIDA, H&WC, CSIH, CPHA, and CUCHID.

Other Countries
- Country/region specific partners might include: SAREC, GTZ, Rockefeller Foundation, Ford Foundation, ODA, PAHO and the EEC.
- Examples of international organization partners are: WHO, UNEP, UNICEF, UNDP, ILO, and the World Bank.

RECOMMENDATIONS

WHICH NICHES ARE BEST FOR IDRC PROGRAM?

- After careful review of Agenda 21 Chapter 6, and the PrepComm documents feeding into it, the HSD feels the niche areas for IDRC are:
    - **Towards a new international health** — research into the multi-cultural, socio-economic, environmental, historical and political elements of developing country health.
    - **Environmental change and health** — building the capacity of developing countries to predict, elucidate, and possibly intervene against, the health effects of environmental changes and to research the health risks inherent in the physical/ biological environments, peoples' behaviour and reaction to the risks, and the working environments.
    - **Culture, social change and health** — research into the health issues which arise from social instability and extreme social change, e.g. forced migration, environmental stress and urbanization.
    - **Production activities and health** — research into the physical, chemical, biological, and psychosocial factors associated with production activities in the agricultural, domestic, and industrial sectors.
    - **Nutrition** — linking with the GMI and focusing on research into areas such as micronutrient malnutrition, the malnutrition infection complex, food safety and quality, food security, infant and child feeding, sanitation, diarrhoeal diseases, and the role of women.
    - **Resource Allocation and health care management** — research on issues such as performance and financing of health services and development of health information systems.
    - **Policy for health** — research on the health sector and other sectors (e.g. agriculture, industry, education, environment) that have significant impact on the health status of populations.

ARE ADJUSTMENTS NEEDED AT IDRC IN ORDER TO FILL THESE NICHES?

Program Organization
No.

Process and Project Cycle
No.

Structure/Staffing
Lack of health sciences expertise in some regional offices.

ARE THERE CROSS-CUTTING ISSUES THAT ARE NOT ADEQUATELY REFLECTED IN ANY OF THE ABOVE?

There are health issues cutting across the entire Agenda 21 document. Issues of key importance to human health, and not adequately discussed in this chapter, may be found in:
- Chapter 3 Combating Poverty
- Chapter 5 Demographic Dynamics and Sustainability
- Chapter 7 Human Settlement Development
- Chapter 14 Sustainable Agriculture and Rural Development
- Chapter 16 Biotechnology
- Chapter 18 Freshwater
- Chapter 20 Hazardous Wastes
- Chapter 21 Solid Wastes
- Chapter 24 Global Action for Women Towards Equitable and Sustainable Development

TABLE 1. NICHES FOR IDRC: OPPORTUNITIES THAT FIT PROGRAMMING

CHAPTER 6 PROGRAMME AREAS / HSD AREAS of ACTIVITIES	Rural Primary Health Care	Communicable Disease Control	Protection of Vulnerable Groups	Urban Health	Environmental Health Risks
International Health	1, 2, 4*	1, 2, 4, 13	1, 2, 4, 17, 20	1, 2, 4, 22	1, 2, 4, 23, 33
Environmental change and Health	2, 3, 6, 7, 11	2, 3, 13, 15, 16	2, 3, 17, 20	2, 3, 21, 22	2, 3, 24, 25, 26, 27, 29, 30, 31, 32
Social Change, Culture and Health	2, 6, 9, 10, 11	2, 14	2, 17, 18, 19, 20	2, 21, 22	2, 23, 28
Production Activities and Health	2, 7	2	2, 17, 19, 20	2	2, 24, 26, 33
Nutrition	2, 3, 6, 11	2, 3, 13	2, 3, 17, 19, 20	2, 3	2, 3, 26, 28
Resource Allocation and Health Care Management	1, 2, 3, 5, 7, 8, 12	1, 2, 3, 5, 13, 15	1, 2, 3, 5, 17, 18	1, 2, 3, 5, 21	1, 2, 3, 5, 23, 29, 33
Policy for Health	1, 2, 3, 4, 7, 8, 9, 12	1, 2, 3, 4	1, 2, 3, 4, 17, 20	1, 2, 3, 4, 21, 22	1, 2, 3, 28, 33

* The numbers refer to the research topics found in Chapter 6 as listed in Section II Explicit Proposals in the Chapter.

CHAPTER SEVEN

PROMOTING SUSTAINABLE HUMAN SETTLEMENT DEVELOPMENT

Responsible Officer: Luc Mougeot

ABSTRACT

1. OVERALL CRITIQUE OF AGENDA 21 CHAPTER

- A long chapter with 8 program areas, unevenly detailed and weakly strategized. Some programs are basic, sectoral, problem-related (shelter, infrastructure, energy and transport, construction); others are process-oriented (settlement and disaster management, land-use planning, human relations development).
- Purpose and process are separated - aims and means are not clearly linked; interventions not purposeful and accountable, and funding needs not well targeted and credible.
- Key issues are detailed in other chapters (water supply in 18 and waste management in 21). Cross-referencing program areas of chapters would help identify opportunities or strategies for dealing with more than one problem at a time.

2. KEY CONCLUSIONS ARISING FROM CHAPTER

- Most proposed program areas lack focus and interrelationships, and do not draw upon past lessons learned.
- Text on shelter is not new: settlement management and land-use planning (e.g. data systems) should aim at specific problems, but the effectiveness of intermediate centre growth policies is highly debatable, as is tourism to reduce urban concentration and regional disparities: High occupancy motorized public transport will remain priority in major Third World cities, but energy issues are largely ignored.

3. RESEARCH AND/OR IMPLEMENTATION POSSIBILITIES/OPPORTUNITIES

- Opportunities exist in most program areas, with linkages in the areas of shelter, infrastructure, disaster, energy and construction:
    a) Shelter: access to alternative non-owner housing in central districts; minimizing urban population displacement due to urban renewal, upgrading, etc.; SME credit to housing for home-based business.
    b) Infrastructure: reducing poor districts' dependence on conventional equipment/service provision (treat, reuse, recycle wastes, effluents, discharges to produce food, goods, energy).
    c) Energy/transport: structural solutions for energy conservation by built environment (siting, orientation, layout, design, materials, features for lighting, heating, cooling, etc.).
    d) Disaster prevention/mitigation: preventing causes of human vulnerability as opposed to only coping with hazard impacts; appropriate local and sublocal organizations with techniques and knowledge to understand, react and anticipate risks, argue, participate in, monitor and evaluate socially and economically attractive joint interventions with public and private sectors.

4. ON-GOING AND/OR NEW PARTNERSHIPS FOR IDRC

- Shelter: global Habitat International Coalition network on urban evictions.
- Waste: South American SUR network on local waste management in mid-sized cities plus other LAC and North African projects and African proposals on waste-agriculture links.
- Water: Latin American Urban Hydrogeology network and South American project on urban groundwater supply. Hazards: Central American CSUCA (now FLACSO) network on urban hazard prevention; creation of permanent LA working group and proposals from OAS-CERESIS and U of Manitoba and NE Brazil network.

5. SUGGESTED NICHES FOR IDRC

- Clear niches on issues which are missing in the Chapter or newly emerging, (e.g. shelter, infrastructure, energy, disasters), through a strategy which links research to training and policy-making, with local and sublocal organizations as the main implementors and beneficiaries.

6. OTHER COMMENTS

REVIEW 7

KEY CONCLUSIONS IN THE CHAPTER

WHAT IS THERE

The objectives of program areas and activities proposed in this Chapter are: to improve the social, economic and environmental quality of human settlements and living and working environments of urban workers and urban poor, on the basis of partnerships in eight (8) programs areas on:
- Shelter provision;
- Human settlement management, sustainable land-use planning and management, integrated provision of environmental infrastructure;
- Energy and transport systems;
- Planning and management of disaster-prone areas, construction industry activities; and,
- Resource development and capacity building.

Chapter 7 uses ill-defined concepts, vaguely identified objectives and activities, repetitive statements on financing and cost evaluation, and vague wishes on generic human resource development and capacity building. Summary charts could have helped visualise a global strategy, with its problem system and main entry points for intervention. The same could have been done for each Chapter.

NICHES FOR IDRC

Shelter Provision (highly selective support from IDRC)
The Chapter's objectives and activities are not terribly new. IDRC funded a lot in the 1980s and future funding should be highly selective.

- A missing issue in Chapter 7 and niche for IDRC: Alternative forms of access to non-owner housing. For instance, Agenda 21 perpetuates the rapidly fading dream of home ownership in metro areas, when the Third World reality is that governments will be less able to subsidize public housing, infrastructure, facilities, as well as transportation to still largely concentrated, centrally located, employment districts. Innovative policies are required to tolerate, support and promote other modalities of access to housing, such as rental and shared housing in central districts, through restoration, adaptation, expansion of lots and buildings to such modalities, along with central urban renewal of historic or old industrial-warehousing districts. IDRC has supported one small network and is funding small projects in various regions, with published results.

- New issue present in the Chapter, and a niche for IDRC: Minimization of urban population displacement.
  Issues 7.9 (b) and (g): One concern is now emerging in urban development and infrastructure: the forced displacement of populations due to site, rights-of-way, and a real impact requirements of urban expansion, redevelopment, and public infrastructure. Because of population densities in major Third World metro areas, as opposed to rural areas, and the lack of alternatives to most of those displaced, minimal displacement will become a growing social concern or "hot issue" when devising and implementing measures intended to improve the urban living and working environment. Remarkably little use has been made of lessons learned or taught by existing extensive records of large-scale development projects.

- 7.9 (c) is a case where micro-entrepreneurial credit schemes could and in fact are being used, for instance in Honduras, for (female) beneficiaries to adapt, equip, or expand their homes to accommodate better home-based businesses. Credit to production indirectly helps to improve household living environments.

Human Settlement Management

- This is an instrumental program area with much potential but in Agenda 21 it is so all-inclusive that it loses purpose. It could be promoted with more effective results if it were specified through linking it directly to other problem programs and Agenda chapters relevant to cities.
- As a selective niche for IDRC it could be developed according to sectoral or problem-oriented priorities, because human settlement management is an instrumental program, and a means to reaching solutions or achieving targets on sectoral programs.
- The creation of urban data systems should be tailored to concrete project needs, not promoted at large. Of the three activities listed the more explicit is practically a carbon copy of the World Bank Urban agenda (urban poverty reduction), 7.16 (b).
- A missing issue in this Chapter, but an opportunity for IDRC:
  Reduced dependence of poor urban districts on conventional infrastructure: Under 7.16 (c) innovative city planning strategies item (i) should also consider incentives to reduce dependence on centrally-managed or municipally-funded services. This would include the need for developing local solutions, such as treatment, reuse and recycling of used waters and solid wastes. In this sense 7.16 (d) is probably the more important of all activities for IDRC involvement. (It ties in with Chapters 18 and 21.) The need is to generate socially acceptable and economically attractive activities from wastes, discharges, effluents which will reduce demand on supply and service provision and increase local returns on consumption. (In fact in many cities, people have opposed the installation and management of such services by municipalities, e.g. water distribution in Quito or hand pumps and latrives in Bangladesh.).
- On 7.19 support to research on intermediate urban centres as a means to deconcentrate urban growth does not seem to be a good niche. An evaluation of the much publicized Mexican policy funded by IDRC shows that much of it happened due to rising diseconomies of agglomeration in Mexico City with little directly imputable to government development efforts in intermediate centres. Results are hard to identify and occur in the long term.

- Implicit issue in this Chapter, and a niche for IDRC: urban agriculture: This section refers to food production and small-scale activities directly relevant to local income-generation and thus urban agriculture. It can influence land use development, so as to anticipate and mitigate future urban environmental problems associated with urban growth. IDRC has funded research and is considering further proposals on urban agriculture in intermediate cities of various regions.
- Tourism is proposed in the Chapter as a solution to urban concentration and regional disparities of a country. There is a need for country reviews showing this to have happened on a substantial scale. Tourism at large has been perceived as having contributed little to and often has conflicted with natural environmental conservation, let alone sustainable and equitable social environment.
- Link between the shelter provision program the urban eviction issue: Under 7.20 (b) a major challenge is to convert city centres to viable economic functions, at the same time that urban renewal is being conducted with minimal local population displacement.
- Means and implementation: Since bureaucrats and technocrats are a highly mobile population, a strategy largely under 7.23 depending on educating and training these might have to reach large numbers and still produce few results.
  Local community leaders and NGOs must also be informed about legislation and regulations, and trained adequately in techniques and methods to recognise the extent and limits of their responsibilities and capabilities or demand and argue for assistance from the private and public sectors.
- Section 7.24 provides a starting point from which develop and specify a strategy for the urban agenda.

Sustainable Land-Use Planning

In general all activities proposed under 7.30 are very good;, have been supported by IDRC; and, should be supported selectively to achieve impact in specific problem areas, such as disasters, water, waste, etc.

- This should be linked with the shelter provision program: 7.27 assumes that access to land for urban settlement is infinite or boundless and that ecologically fragile areas are only found in rural areas. Access to land is increasingly difficult by physical expansion due to cities' in ability to provide adequate transportation and services. Residential use must be densified in central districts in an affordable and sustainable way, as well as job patterns. This relates to the non-owner housing issues under the shelter program area and home-based businesses.
- Link this with other chapter program and Agenda Chapters: 7.28 suggests that environmentally sound physical planning would help to account for disaster reduction, local employment generation and waste and water management in suburban areas.
  Efficient and accessible land markets will be insufficient to meet community development needs, even if land registers and transaction procedures are improved. In fact, governments could use these as reasons for adversely affecting the poorer districts.

Provision of "Environmental" Infrastructure
- This is a program area with a rich potential for influencing land-use planning, generating employment, improving environmental quality and decentralizing urban management. The text closely draws on the WB metro area management program. The "integrated approach" should be defined.
- The list of principles under 7.41 is very good and many principles are relevant to disaster reduction strategies. Under (c) it should be "adapt" instead of "adopt". Under (d), the limits for cost-recovering and subsidized servicing to target groups will not be enough, as discussed under 7.16 (c).

Energy and Transport Systems
- Under energy in 7.51 (ii) one aspect not discussed is linking this with programs on land-use, infrastructure and energy efficiency. Where applicable, it should account for hazards so as to structurally reduce vulnerability to extreme geodynamic events. This entails the development of

"passive solutions" for greater energy efficiency and conservation by the built environment (siting, orientation, layout, design, materials). Few centres have conducted energy audits of settlements in developing countries. A number of incentives and regulations could be used for higher income groups to improve private housing energy efficiency and for governments to do the same with public housing programs. Training informal sector builders and suppliers should also be addressed.

- Under urban transport, in 7.52 (a) integrated land-use and transport planning to reduce transport demand also links well with disaster reduction. Under 7.52 (c). Most large Third World cities still have fairly centralized employment districts, while most working class residential areas are far away. Cycleways and footways clearly and largely will be insufficient to move large volumes of daily travellers from home to work good time. High-occupancy motorized public transport will continue to be a priority and greater attention to the interface between official mass transit systems and feeding/competing informal passenger enterprises will be important to reduce, congestion, health risks, and costs.

But IDRC has limited experience and would require a major investment to achieve significant impact in an area where other donors have already a lead.

IDRC could address some aspects of the energy and transport issues selectively, as they relate to other priority areas.

Disaster-Prone Areas (selective, GPI approach and objective specific IDRC support)
- This is an area where IDRC has established project experience, can draw from Canadian expertise; has worked on a wide spectrum of activities in disaster management in major world regions; is networking on an interdisciplinary perspective and at level of intervention which research groups; and, where NGOs are increasingly pressing for governmental policies to account for.
- This is the longest program section of the Chapter. But the order of the three main activities should be: post-disaster reconstruction, pre-disaster planning and development of culture of safety. IDRC's priority should be on the middle category, because research groups working on this consider 7.62 (a) as an entry point to activities under 7.61. Under the culture of safety, IDRC has been and is supporting point (a). In addition to in-depth audits of specific events, it is necessary to identify sectoral responsibilities and press for adjustments and interventions accordingly.
- The section on pre-disaster planning is well written. In (b) methods must be developed for local communities to hold developers accountable for increasing risks and vulnerability generated by activities potentially harmful to the communities, and for these communities to demand sectoral provisions leading to an avoidance or reduction of such adversities. In (d) items (i), (ii) and (iii) should not be confined to industrial-based disaster areas only which reduce the field for improvement to a very small category of total realm of disasters. Finally, mitigative and preventive activities should be promoted.

Construction Industry
- In an urban strategy this could be a major entry point for involving private sector with problem-program activities on shelter, energy (7.69 (c)) and disasters (7.69 (d)). For instance, construction companies in Costa Rica recently were found to support the retrofitting of existing health facilities and the implementation of more stringent construction norms for future facilities.
- In point (f) the emphasis is on increasing the affordability of materials, through credit and bulk procurement which could increase vulnerability rather than reduce it. Emphasis must also be placed on developing local productive capacity.

Human Resource Development
No comments.

Opportunities that Fit Normal Programming

In terms of where IDRC should put its money, through selectively contributing to largely non-physical development program areas, IDRC's impact would probably be greater. This would be because its share of total international funding will be larger when total funding is smaller, but also because non-physical program activities should frame and guide physical development activities for greater overall impact.

COMMENTARY 7

Name of Commentator: Denis Massé

1. **GENERAL COMMENTS ON THE CHAPTER**
   - None.

2. **OVERALL COMMENTARY ON THE FIRST REVIEW OF THE CHAPTER (Agree, Disagree and Reasons)**
   - The first review adequately covers and assesses the main elements presented in this Chapter, particularly with regard to IDRC's mandate and options. I would add that the problematic is truncated, with the pervasive socio-economic and political obstacles to improvement being generally ignored or, in those few instances where alluded to, not pursued. Also, a technocratic bias is evident with a strong emphasis on education, training, finances, and technology development and transfers.

3. **MAJOR POINTS AGREED/DISAGREED WITH, AND REASONS**
   - I agree with the reviewer's main conclusion that the Chapter fails to define strategies, while concepts remain poorly defined and objectives vaguely identified. I would stress, in addition, that the document discusses rather briefly and superficially -when at all- the causes of the problems identified, such as was pointed out by the reviewer regarding the program for Disaster Relief (see point #6 in review). The principal merit of the Chapter is perhaps to report globally and officially, with relatively straightforward language, urgent needs found in human settlements, even though the effectiveness of this "call to action" may seem dubious.

4. **MINOR POINTS AGREED/DISAGREED WITH, AND REASONS**
   - Items 7.18 and 7.19 of the Chapter suggest that policies be geared primarily to the development needs of intermediate cities. The reviewer does not recommend IDRC support for such research, on the ground that results are hard to identify and occur in the long term (see section 2.) This reason is **not** sufficient to justify resisting an observable trend towards intermediate-city research and development. It has been noted that most of the Third World's urban population live in urban centres with fewer than half a million habitants, and less than 3% of the Third World population live in mega-cities of 10 or million inhabitants or more. The environmental problems of intermediate cities are also generally similar in number and intensity to those found in larger agglomerations (see J. Hardoy and D. Satterthwaite, Environmental Problems in Third World Cities: An Agenda for the Poor and the Planet, London: IIED, 1992).

5. POSSIBLE ON-GOING ISSUES OR CONCERNS FOR IDRC

- The Chapter has for its basic premise that "(...) settlements in the developing world need more raw material, energy, and economic development simply to overcome basic economic and social problems." The acute and blatant inequality in the distribution of existing resources in most developing countries, which may largely explain the existence of these basic problems as well as represent the main obstacle to their solution, is apparently not mentioned in the Chapter. If such an omission occurs in an inter-governmental official document like this one, broad-based and durable solutions to the plight of the urban poor are unlikely. This raises questions, as to whether *social equity*, as one of IDRC's three corporate themes, can comfortably fit into this agenda.

6. POSSIBLE IMPLICATIONS FOR IDRC

- I agree with the reviewer that IDRC is well ahead of Agenda 21 with regard to strategy, and more so perhaps in terms of conceptualization and problem definition. Once again, the main contribution of the Chapter is to focus the attention of stake-holders in development on a set of urgent needs which may have been only partially recognized or dealt with previously.

CHAPTER EIGHT

INTEGRATING ENVIRONMENT AND DEVELOPMENT IN DECISION-MAKING

Responsible Officer: R. Spence

ABSTRACT

1. OVERALL CRITIQUE OF AGENDA 21 CHAPTER

- Covers a lot of ground relevant/important to specific/sectoral issues. After distillation, coverage basically good.
- Main problem is lack of conceptual frameworks/views on how environmental issues can be integrated with other public concerns (various levels) and public decision-making, and how tradeoffs and complementarities (notably with economic growth) can be managed.
- Result is a scatter-gun set of recommended activities within the 4 major areas. All activities seem appropriate, but lack a sense of priorities, probable difficulties, likely effectiveness.

2. KEY CONCLUSIONS ARISING FROM CHAPTER

- Integrating environmental concerns with other aspects of development policy/planning/management is essential, and doing so requires much strengthening of data/information/systems, methods, institutions and mechanisms at all levels, policies/laws/regulations/economic instruments themselves, dissemination/ participation/awareness, and the requisite training and HRD.
- The 4 main areas are:
    a) Integrating environment in policy, planning and management;
    b) Providing an effective legal and regulatory framework;
    c) Effective use of economic instruments and market/other incentives; and
    d) Establish integrated environmental and economic accounting (IEEA) systems.

3. RESEARCH AND/OR IMPLEMENTATION POSSIBILITIES/OPPORTUNITIES

- 35 specific research and implementation thrusts are identified (see Review for details); only a few are earmarked for any (UN) agencies.

4. ON-GOING AND/OR NEW PARTNERSHIPS FOR IDRC

- **Conceptual frameworks and environmental economics** (with Canadian academic institutions, sources of expertise in international organizations, other-country academic institutions).
- **Community-to-international resource management mechanisms** (with specialized national and international agencies).
- **Environmental law and regulatory systems** (with Canadian universities — expertise — CIDA and international donors — funding).
- **Environmental technology** (with Canadian universities, Canadian enterprises (cases) and specialized international organizations).

5. SUGGESTED NICHES FOR IDRC

- Conceptual frameworks, integration methods, "sustainable development economics," related education/training, economic instruments and market mechanisms for global and transboundary issues, competitiveness, trade, international cooperation, economically liberalizing countries.
- Local/appropriately decentralized natural resource management systems including IK, women's roles; at other extreme — regional/transboundary planning and management mechanisms.
- Establishing cooperative training network for sustainable development law, regional centres of excellence, support for countries' establishment of judicial and administrative systems.
- Exploring effective economic instruments and market mechanisms for development/transfer, diffusion/adaptation of environmentally sound technologies, and ways of creating guidelines and mechanisms for diffusion of relevant information technologies to developing countries.

6. OTHER COMMENTS

- Early attention to integration concepts/methods will reduce blunders and wastage. Why are environmental issues/concerns/costs not now integrated into private and public decision-making? This entails looking at theories (market failure/externalities/common property), institutional processes, etc.

KEY CONCLUSIONS IN THE CHAPTER

WHAT IS THERE
Main Conclusions

This Chapter contains "life, the universe and everything;" the challenge is to select from a massive menu. The main points:

- Integrating environment in policy, planning and management
    - Applied research of environment and development interactions;
    - Conduct national reviews of policies/plans/budgets, and adopt national strategies for sustainable development;
    - Annual environment and development monitoring reviews, including adopting indicators of economic/social/environmental changes;
    - Transparency/access/dissemination/awareness/participation for environment implications of economic and sectoral policies;
    - Environment data, analytical methods (multiple goal, beyond projects to policies and programs);
    - Natural resource management systems including indigenous knowledge, women's roles; and,
    - Delegating responsibility to the lowest appropriate level;
    - Regional/transboundary planning and management mechanisms;
    - Interdisciplinary approaches throughout education systems; and,
    - Training of policy-makers, planners, managers - and strengthening cross-sectoral/issue government institutions.

- Providing an effective legal & regulatory framework
    - Disseminate information on effective/innovative measures, including coordination/consolidation of data bases, reference sources;
    - Regular assessment of laws/regulations (all government levels);
    - Training of officials who design, implement, monitor, enforce laws and regulations — postgrad, in-service, etc.;
    - Establish cooperative training network for sustainable development law, and regional centres of excellence;
    - Support establishment of judicial and administrative systems;
    - Strengthen compliance/enforcement mechanisms, monitoring, public participation; and,
    - National monitoring of follow-up to international instruments.

- Effective use of economic instruments and market/other incentives
    - Remove/reduce environmental negative subsidies, reform economic and fiscal incentives, establish pricing consistent with sustainable development;
    - Explore effective economic instruments and market mechanisms for:
        i) Energy, transportation, agriculture & **forestry, water, wastes, health,** tourism, tertiary services;
        ii) Global and transboundary issues; and,
        iii) Development/transfer, diffusion/adaptation of environmentally sound technologies;
    - Also for economically liberalizing countries, including technical support and centres of excellence;
    - Create inventory of effective economic instruments and market mechanisms;
    - Research on:
        i) The role of environmental taxation;
        ii) The implications of economic instruments/incentives for competitiveness, trade, international cooperation;
        iii) Social and distribution implications of various instruments;
        iv) Practical implications of pricing (that internalizes environmental costs);
        v) Implications of resource pricing for resource exporters; and,
        vi) Methodologies for valuing environmental costs.
    - Enhance "sustainable development economics," including review/strengthening of higher education curricula, training sessions for government officials, coop and private sector training.

- Establish integrated environment and economic accounting (IEEA) systems:
    - Statistics Office of UN to distribute widely "Handbook on IEEA", develop/test/refine methods, coordinate national training, strengthen technical cooperation among countries, etc.;
    - Department of Economic and Social Development of UN Secretariat to support introduction of IEEAs, better environment/economic/social data collection in cooperation with other UN agencies, national accounting agencies;
    - Governments identify/correct resource related pricing distortions;
    - Governments encourage corporations to implement environmental accounting methods and report environmental information;
    - Donors support strengthening of national statistical agencies and data collection, UN Statistics Office provide technical support;
    - Develop/agree upon guidelines and mechanisms for diffusion of relevant information technologies to developing countries; and,
    - Train integrated data analysts and users/decision-makers.

Essentially, the Chapter argues that integrating environmental concerns with other aspects of development policy/planning/management is essential, and doing so requires much strengthening of data/information/systems, methods, institutions and mechanisms at all levels. Also are needed: policies/laws/regulations/economic instruments dissemination/participation/awareness, and the requisite training and HRD. Overall the coverage and approach are good, and the level of detail as good as might be expected.

Agreements Reached for International and National Action
None indicated in the Chapter, with the exception of actions by UN agencies.

Politically Significant Issues
The effective use of economic instruments and market mechanisms contains a lot of sensitive issues. The Chapter, however, takes a pragmatic rather than ideological approach — to explore, encourage and adopt as appropriate. Research supporting reform of subsidies and incentives will be controversial, but can/should not be avoided.

There are many basic (at least perceived) conflicts/tradeoffs between environmental and other development objectives. Integration will face resistances. A prominent case, perhaps, is institutional changes in governments where vested interests (e.g. Ministries) will fight for turf. Another is getting corporations to adopt environmental accounting and report transparently to everybody.

WHAT IS NOT THERE
No substantive issues missed or downplayed. What is missing (perhaps understandably) (see below) is a conceptual framework linking and prioritizing activities presented on a scatter-gun basis.

OVERALL CRITIQUE
Substantive Content
Accepting the design of the Chapter as given, there are no basic complaints about the content and approach.

Design of the Chapter as an Organizing Framework
I would devote some initial thought to (conceptually) distinguishing "decision-making" which is amenable to individualistic/private/ economic management from that which is fundamentally collective/public. This in turn enables more separation between public measures to improve private decision-making, and (public) measures to improve public decision-making. This lends much immediacy to enhancing sustainable development economics and developing analytical methods for "integration". In short, the Chapter reflects a widespread lack of clarity about why environmental concerns are not presently (much) integrated into development decision-making, and how they could be. Without more clarity on this, big blunders and much wastage will occur as all directions are tackled at once.

RESEARCH REQUIREMENTS, CAPACITY BUILDING ETC.

IMPLICIT PROPOSALS DERIVED FROM THE CHAPTER
The development of good conceptual frameworks and methods for integrating environment in private and public decision-making is crucial, and is covered only in bits in the Chapter. Give this a **lot** of priority and attention.

GAPS AND ALTERNATIVE APPROACHES

Except for the conceptual framework(s) mentioned above, the coverage is good. There is more than enough here.

NICHES FOR IDRC

GENERAL

For simplicity "activities" are marked as N1 (Niche 1), N2 and N3 according to the 3 categories listed below. "R" (e.g. N1R) indicates possible IDRC support on a regional or country specific basis, as opposed to general/global, though not in one region/country but not others. A lot of niches emerge, so the ones that seem most important for IDRC are marked in bold. More work is needed to group and assess these niches, but a first approximation (with suggested partners/actors) is as follows:

- Conceptual frameworks and environmental economics (with Canadian academic institutions, sources of expertise in international organizations, other-country academic institutions).

N2 The development of good conceptual frameworks and methods for integrating environment in private and public decision-making;

N2 Enhance "sustainable development economics," including review/strengthening of higher educational curricula, training sessions for government officials, cooperative and private sector training;

N2 Applied research of environment and development interactions;

N1 Environment data, analytical methods (multiple goal, beyond projects to policies and programs);

Explore effective economic instruments and market mechanisms for:

N2 Global and transboundary issues; and,

N2 The implications of economic instruments/incentives for competitiveness, trade, international cooperation;

N1R Explore effective economic instruments and market mechanisms for economically liberalizing countries, including technical support and regional centres of excellence.

- Community-to-international resource management mechanisms (with specialized national and international agencies) — **governance**.

N1R Natural resource management systems including indigenous knowledge, women's roles, and delegating responsibility to the lowest appropriate level;

N1R Regional/transboundary planning and management mechanisms.

- Environmental law and regulatory systems (with Canadian universities — expertise — CIDA and international donors — funding).

N2R Establish cooperative training network for sustainable development law, and regional centres of excellence;

N2R Support establishment of judicial and administrative systems.

- Environmental technology (with Canadian universities, Canadian enterprises (cases) and specialized international organizations).

N2 Explore effective economic instruments and market mechanisms for development/transfer, diffusion/adaptation of environmentally sound technologies;

N2 Develop/agree upon guidelines and mechanisms for diffusion of relevant information technologies to developing countries.

Opportunities that Fit Normal Programming
See above.

New Opportunities
See above.

Unusual or High-Risk Opportunities
See above.

REGIONAL SPECIFICITY
Noted above.

KEY PARTNERS/OTHER ACTORS
Noted above.

RECOMMENDATIONS

WHICH NICHES ARE BEST FOR IDRC PROGRAM?
The issues best suited to IDRC Program are indicated above. There are genuinely **many** niches in this subject area, and suggest that the indicative list under I above now needs examination by those more versed in environmental issues. There is much judgement in selecting from this long and interesting menu.

ARE ADJUSTMENTS NEEDED AT IDRC IN ORDER TO FILL THESE NICHES?

Program Organization
Basically no.

Process and Project Cycle
Basically no.

Structure/Staffing

Would need more environmental/resource economists, closer interaction between ENRD and SSD, and more legal expertise in or available to regional offices.

ARE THERE CROSS-CUTTING ISSUES THAT ARE NOT ADEQUATELY REFLECTED IN ANY OF THE ABOVE?

Except for the conceptual frameworks point, none to mention at present.

COMMENTARY 8

Name of Commentator: Rohinton Medhora

1. **GENERAL COMMENTS ON THE FIRST REVIEW OF THE CHAPTER**
   - The review contains detailed and thoughtful comments, with judicious conclusions and suggestions.

2. **OVERALL COMMENTARY ON THE FIRST REVIEW OF THE CHAPTER**
   - I agree, particularly given that comments are based on a chapter that, as the reviewer correctly notes at the outset, contains "everything but the kitchen sink", and is, therefore, very general and loose.

3. **MAJOR POINTS AGREED/DISAGREED WITH, AND REASONS**
   - Agree that:
     a) The proper integration between law, economics, environment and decision-making needs to be properly planned, or immense wastage and duplication or cross-purpose of efforts will result;
     b) Reality dictates that "turf wars" between ministries and functionaries may make a mockery of efforts to re-organize the decision-making process.
   - However, the review does not bring out one aspect that struck me about this Chapter, which is that its overall flavour and direction seems to be more geared towards "advice" to LDCs, than to DCs. References in the Chapter to UN, World Bank, sustainable development, emerging economies of Eastern Europe, need for market-based policies, etc. may strike bureaucrats/decision-makers in OECD countries as meaning that all of this does not apply to them. Perhaps this is implied in the comment that the Chapter is too general, but should this not be stated more explicitly?

4. **MINOR POINTS AGREED/DISAGREED WITH, AND REASONS**
   - Just one minor disagreement:
     a) As a minor semantic point, (and, again, as a result of an overly general approach to the issue), I would have criticized the Chapter for its organization. First, there is no indication of how important the four sub-themes of the Chapter are, relative to each other. I would argue that developing an integrated environment and economic accounting system (theme D in the Chapter) comes before the others — sensible policy must be based on sensible numbers. Second, theme A is a wishy-washy introduction that could well have been a conclusion to the more substantive and relevant areas of themes B and C — namely, the legal framework/property rights, and market-based policy approaches.

5. POSSIBLE ON-GOING ISSUES OR CONCERNS FOR IDRC

- Converting this (necessarily?) general and political document into a meaningful research program that IDRC could pursue requires a careful — and ruthless — winnowing of the numerous issues raised in it. Prioritizing and analyzing the issues involves a sober examination of the many important and fascinating areas of study raised. Rush jobs, one page summaries, and cute posters are not the best ways to deal with the matter.

6. POSSIBLE IMPLICATIONS FOR IDRC

- There is a modest but growing literature on regulation, the use of market-based policy instruments, and proper accounting methods in the presence of negative externalities. This is a "hot" field, for which the expertise does not exist in many LDCs. Promoting research and education in this area would be of immense value to local policy officials — both in formulating policy, and in dealing with bilateral and multilateral donors, who are likely to add environmental issues to the conditionality debate. This type of local capacity-building is entirely within the mandate of IDRC.

SECTION 2
CONSERVATION AND MANAGEMENT OF RESOURCES FOR DEVELOPMENT

CHAPTER NINE

PROTECTION OF THE ATMOSPHERE

Responsible Officer: Stephen Tyler

ABSTRACT

1. OVERALL CRITIQUE OF AGENDA 21 CHAPTER

- Politically controversial. Language and issues dominated by a Northern perspective: i.e. global emissions due mainly to fossil fuel whose use must be constrained to prevent irreparable damage to global atmospheric systems.
- Solutions: transfer of advanced emissions controls and energy efficiency technology from North to South, with the adoption of supportive economic and energy policy instruments.
- Questions left unaddressed: how to estimate and allocate the economic costs and benefits of emission reduction technologies; disproportionate share of the emissions burden attributable to industrialized nations; immediate urban air quality and health concerns in developing countries and the adoption of strategies to address these.

2. KEY CONCLUSIONS ARISING FROM CHAPTER

- Main issue is atmospheric emissions due to increasing energy use and industrialization (linked to Convention on Climate Change).
- All nations advised to take measures to support introduction of alternative energy supply sources and more efficient energy use technologies, with emphasis on modern transportation and industrial sectors.
- References to research, training and capacity-building as implementation mechanisms.
- All countries are called to ratify the Montreal Protocol (and amendments) to phase out the use of CFCs.
- Additional scientific effort and international data sharing required to record, model and forecast atmospheric processes and transboundary air pollution.

3. RESEARCH AND/OR IMPLEMENTATION POSSIBILITIES/OPPORTUNITIES

- Areas recommended for research include industrial processes, emission controls, transportation technology and urban transportation planning. Training and capacity-building needed in atmospheric sciences and energy technologies. More interesting range of research issues (for IDRC) which are directly related but not discussed:
    a) Economic valuation and allocation of costs and benefits;
    b) Development of institutions for regional collaboration;
    c) Structure/policy relevance of shared scientific data bases; and
    d) Relevance of Northern technology to developing countries.

4. ON-GOING AND/OR NEW PARTNERSHIPS FOR IDRC

- IDRC has a few established relationships with likely recipients or collaborating donors. Considerable Canadian expertise in energy and resource economics exists in the public and private sectors, including consulting community and such universities as Ottawa, Calgary, Dalhousie, Simon Fraser.
- New relationships needed to enable IDRC to influence:
    a) Scientific and technological research agendas of Northern institutions; and
    b) Utilization of results by development agencies and by developing countries.
- Sympathetic partners: Stockholm Environment Institute, International Institute for Environment and Development, International Institute for Energy Conservation, Tata Energy Research Institute and possibly the East–West Centre at University of Hawaii. The World Bank is interested and active. Developing country expertise: Brazil, Thailand, China, Mexico.

5. SUGGESTED NICHES FOR IDRC

- The technology and hard science issues should be left to others.
- IDRC should concentrate on economic evaluation and analytical methodology research, information management issues, and structure of international linkages (technology transfer, cost and benefit-sharing, institution development).
- A potentially useful role for IDRC would be linking Northern research agencies and donors with Southern institutions and policy researchers to clarify the research agenda for the South. A starting point might be drawing up the energy work of the Energy Research Group (ERG) previously convened by IDRC.

6. OTHER COMMENTS

- High profile. Not presently an IDRC strength, but an issue which is difficult to ignore.

REVIEW 9

KEY CONCLUSIONS IN THE CHAPTER

The contents of the Chapter are closely related to the Climate Change Convention. The Chapter is *not* about atmospheric science. It is mainly about energy use, and responds to the central dilemma that increasing energy use is essential to socio-economic development and improved human welfare, yet current fuel and technology choices are causing unprecedented and potentially irreversible changes to the life-supporting characteristics of the planet's atmosphere.

This Chapter is crucial for developing countries because they are the source of most of the increase in energy demand anticipated over the next century. The Chapter addresses issues of technology choice in transportation and industrial processes, both areas in which major investments will be required in developing countries. The politically-charged issues of ozone depletion and trans-boundary air pollution (e.g. acid rain), also covered here, have already generated a lot of attention from developing countries. This chapter of Agenda 21 recommends measures for developing countries which will be very costly to implement (but potentially catastrophic to ignore).

WHAT IS THERE

Main Conclusions
The Chapter presents recommendations on 4 program areas:
- Improving scientific understanding of atmospheric changes and their implications, principally through research and international collaboration;
- Redirecting development activities in terms of energy supply systems, efficiency of energy utilization, transportation, industrial technology, and land use to reduce atmospheric emissions;
- Preventing stratospheric ozone depletion; and,
- Reducing emissions which have trans-national effects, monitoring and modelling their impacts, and mitigating these.

The Chapter suggests programs (1) and (4) can be addressed primarily through scientific research activities, better collection and sharing of data. Governments are called on to "promote" international scientific collaboration, training of developing country specialists, and establishment and utilization of international data bases. In the case of trans-boundary pollution, governments are also urged to establish or strengthen regional agreements on pollution control, monitoring, and evaluation.

The most important program area is the second one. The Chapter recommends the adoption of "economically viable", new, and alternative sources of energy supply, and of improvements in the efficiency of energy utilization, in all applications. It recommends the efforts of all governments be directed to removing barriers to changes in energy technology. It suggests the development of integrated energy and environmental assessment methodologies, coordinated regional energy planning procedures, consumer awareness and information programs. Similarly, more efficient and less polluting transportation technologies, modes and systems are recommended, as well as urban and regional settlement planning strategies which reduce the environmental impacts of transport.

Under the rubric of industrial development the Chapter recommends the adoption of "cost-effective" pollution controls, new technologies, industrial processes and materials to reduce emissions. The agreements on terrestrial and marine resource utilization are even less concrete, and are intended to address the interaction of extensive land and sea utilization (e.g. paddy rice, algae growth) which have identifiable but poorly-understood feedback roles in global greenhouse gas balances and other global atmospheric processes. Technological and/or methodological research is explicitly called for in several articles, as are technology transfer and capacity-building in developing countries, in relation to each of these fields.

The program (#3) on preventing stratospheric ozone depletion comes down to a call for ratification of the Montreal Protocol and its 1990 amendments and implementing mechanisms.

Agreements Reached for International and National Action
The Chapter calls for lots of "promoting" and "encouraging" and "enhancing" "as appropriate" of course, but gives no firm commitments to actually do much. Governments agree they should ratify the Montreal Protocol and amendments. (See also the Climate Change Convention.)

Politically Significant Issues
A sampling of the minefields:
- Developing countries have been identified as the main sources of growing, incremental energy use, but the South pins the origin of the problem on the North who, by squandering to date the planet's cheap energy sources in order to enrich themselves, have brought everybody else to the brink of a global atmospheric crisis.

- Canada is well-known to be the most energy profligate country in the world (both on a per capita and per $GDP basis, although not per ha.) which puts it in a poor position to lead, especially given the political sensitivities. (Canada has **not** adopted most of the policies recommended in this Chapter.)
- The technologies which could give effect to the Chapter's recommendations are known, and the policies which would support their introduction are obvious, but the costs are the subject of considerable debate. The fundamental question is how to effect an equitable international allocation of financial and technological responsibility. The U.S. says it has already done its share domestically but is willing to sell its clean technology at favourable terms on condition it retains intellectual property rights. The developing countries say they are already paying for the wasteful energy use of developed nations (especially the U.S. and Canada) and are now being asked to pay much more. The Global Environmental Facility (GEF) is an inadequate response to these problems.
- Although the main problem is fossil fuels, the vigorous protests of the Gulf States and of China and India (the world's largest producers and users of coal) resulted in the curious anomaly that in the entire chapter the term "fossil fuels" appears **only** in the exclusionary clause which then recommends special consideration be given to those states which depend on fossil fuels for their income, or which might have difficulty switching to alternative sources of energy.
- India and China have resisted signing the Montreal Protocol to protect stratospheric ozone until an agreement is reached with developed countries on the compensation that their industries will be paid to use more costly substitutes for CFCs.
- Among the sources of transboundary air pollution specifically identified for the attention of signatory governments: "deliberate or accidental destruction of natural resources". The evident intent is to cover not only the Kuwaiti oil fields but also the Amazon rainforest.
- The arguments presented in this Chapter are often cited by the Canadian and international nuclear industry to justify more exports of this controversial technology to the Third World.

WHAT IS NOT THERE

In order to secure widespread international endorsement of Agenda 21, this Chapter could not include any discussion of the allocation of costs of technology transfer, energy pricing policies, energy efficient and renewable energy technologies, industrial process and materials technologies etc. (but all are referred to). There is no discussion of implementing, monitoring, or evaluation mechanisms, or incentives for the type and scale of international collaboration which is explicitly and implicitly called for. Every recommendation is hedged by qualifiers like "economically viable" but there is no discussion of the economic issues: e.g. what is a valid environmental cost of energy utilization and how should it be measured and accounted for in an evaluation of economic viability?

There is also no discussion of the immediate costs of air pollution on human health, although these costs are demonstrably very high in the cities of the Third World already, and becoming rapidly much worse (e.g. estimates for Bangkok are that all children lose an average of more than 4 IQ points prior to the age of 7 due to atmospheric lead levels). The World Bank estimates that up to 5% of all deaths in developing country urban centres can be attributed to complications resulting from air pollution. The incidence of disease and mortality falls disproportionately on the poor.

OVERALL CRITIQUE

Substantive Content

The content of this Chapter is probably among the most controversial in the entire document. The most striking aspect of this Chapter is that it takes a very strongly Northern perspective. The atmospheric protection problem is seen as a "global" one, which requires international action. By contrast, the air pollution in Third World cities is a local issue and not addressed here. The problem is defined in terms of emissions and the main methods which are seen as appropriate to reduce these are technical and economic fixes. Technological solutions have achieved a great deal in the North, where ambient air pollutant levels have declined steadily in the past two decades in spite of continued growth in vehicle fleet and use. But questions which the South might ask (such as: relative scale of energy use in the North vs. South; dependence of South on North for technological innovation; ownership and access to polluting vs. clean technologies; social incidence of air pollution costs) are nowhere included.

Design of the Chapter as an Organizing Framework
While the Chapter raises a large number of very important issues, it gives direction for action on such a broad front (while leaving the specific implementation details so general and vague) that it seems unlikely to yield any concrete results. It succeeds, however, in attracting attention and raising the profile of a subject that cannot be quietly ignored.

RESEARCH REQUIREMENTS, CAPACITY BUILDING ETC.

EXPLICIT PROPOSALS IN THE CHAPTER

- Research, training and capacity-building all figure prominently in the explicit recommendations of the Chapter:
- Research on "natural processes affecting and being affected by the atmosphere, as well as critical linkages between sustainable development and atmospheric changes, including impacts on human health, ecosystems, economic sectors and society";
- More atmospheric observation stations;
- International development and utilization of accessible scientific data bases;
- Development of methodologies to identify threshold pollutant levels;
- Capacity-building in atmospheric sciences in developing countries;
- "Research, development, transfer and use of improved energy-efficiency technologies and processes...";
- "Research, development, transfer and use of environmentally sound energy systems...";
- Development of "institutional, scientific, planning and management capacities" in energy efficiency and environmentally-sound energy supply, specifically in developing countries;
- Transfer of clean transport technologies, including training;
- Systematic collection of data on transportation emissions and development of an international transport data base;
- Development of new urban transportation planning strategies to reduce the demand for travel;
- Transfer clean industrial technologies and capacity to manage and use them;
- International assessment of scientific, health, and socio-economic implications of ozone depletion;
- Observe and assess systematically the sources and extent of transboundary air pollution;
- Strengthen capabilities of developing countries to measure model and evaluate transboundary air pollution;

Capacity-building and human resource development are cited as two of the means of implementation of this Chapter.

IMPLICIT PROPOSALS DERIVED FROM THE CHAPTER

Not specifically addressed in the Chapter:
- The Chapter refers throughout to "economically-justified" and "cost-effective" technologies but dodges the issue of how to do the sums. This could be an instructive avenue of research: social costing of environmental externalities in the case specifically of developing countries;

- Incentives for implementing efficient technologies: What is required? What works? (taxes, fees, financial guarantees?);
- Several different international data sets are referred to. The structure, management and access of these data bases to ensure maximum advantage to developing countries should be investigated;
- Technology transfer figures prominently in this chapter. The broader economic and policy issues of trade, investment and intellectual property rights are related. More specifically, investigations of the allocation of costs and benefits to North–South technology transfer under varying circumstances (sale, licensing, etc.) would be of interest;
- Mechanisms for identification and sharing of international environmental benefits derived from developing country investments.

GAPS AND ALTERNATIVE APPROACHES

The strategies which are envisioned in this Chapter all have to do with the transfer of new and improved technologies from the North to the South. This is **not** the type of relationship which empowers. Issues like: development of advanced indigenous technologies and the international linkages of energy technology decision-making need to be made more explicit. Issues of technology adaptation and commercialization of research results are related here. South–South collaboration could be fruitful.

Research is a key element in the recommendations. Thus, the setting of the international research agenda in this field is important, as many millions of dollars will be committed by other agencies than IDRC. IDRC can influence these by helping to set the agenda in ways which will most benefit developing countries. The challenge is to ensure that research will generate results which can be meaningful to development policy makers, which are timely relative to their needs, and which can be implemented under their constraints. Access to international scientific and policy-related databases could be strategic.

Other areas needing research:
- Research should be undertaken on the management of urban transportation systems (broadly defined, including streets, bicycles, pedestrian movements);
- Institutions for regional negotiation, collaboration and agreement on atmospheric protection;
- Relative merits of standards- or technology-driven air quality regulations in the developing country context;
- Feasible mechanisms for introducing and fostering technological change under the constraints of developing countries;
- Constructive roles for the North in fostering technological innovation within countries of the South;
- Endogenous and exogenous factors affecting the adoption of new technologies: investment, economic growth (in the OECD, for example, energy use in manufacturing declines in proportion to manufacturing investment, not rising energy prices, over past 20 years).

NICHES FOR IDRC

It makes little sense for IDRC to become involved in the technology end of the energy business, or in atmospheric science. These are high-cost and already well-endowed by many other North-based agencies. This whole chapter has already captured the attention of research agencies in the North. This is part of the problem, as the research agenda and solutions risk being dominated by a perspective which not all countries in the South are happy with. I see the main task for IDRC being to build linkages and credibility with some of these mainstream Northern research institutions with the dual objectives of a) interpreting technical research to evaluate policy implications and prospects for implementation in developing countries, and b) influencing the Northern research agenda and definition of the problem.

GENERAL
Opportunities that Fit Normal Programming
There are no programs within which these initiatives could all sit comfortably. Some **might** find a home in places like:
- IS — Structure and management of international scientific data bases to ensure access for developing countries;
- Science and Technology Management (CAID) — generic issues of technology transfer and adaptation, stimulating technological innovation in the South, commercialization incentives.

New Opportunities
ENRD:
- Economic analysis: e.g. social costs of environmental externalities, implications of alternative transportation systems, allocating emissions costs to different sources/technologies;
- Institutions for regional negotiations on atmospheric emissions;
- Incentives for adoption of clean technologies in developing countries;
- Mechanisms for international sharing of costs/benefits of environmental improvements;
- Urban transportation planning: environmental considerations, integration with physical plans, participatory frameworks, low-cost solutions and strategies.

Unusual or High-Risk Opportunities
Since this Chapter is given higher priority in the North than in the South lends developing countries some influence in suggesting its implementation. The North will be putting a lot of research money into this area. The challenge will be in assuring that the proposed research actually yields constructive and innovative results or alternatives for developing countries. IDRC could play an influential role as a "broker" between the scientific or policy research institutions of the North and South. For example:
- Helping to clarify the research agenda;
- Identifying the policy issues in order to guide technology research and timing;
- Setting the potential for technology transfer firmly within the bounds of realistic possibilities given the constraints of developing countries.

REGIONAL SPECIFICITY
Asia: May be a good place to support policy-related research due to rapid urban growth, magnitude of problems in India and China, technological capacity (but weak on economics, which is where IDRC can contribute). The international technology transfer issues will vary considerably by region.

KEY PARTNERS/OTHER ACTORS
Canada
Canada has a poor track record when it comes to policy implementation, but has competent people who understand the issues and analytical techniques. These exist in such places as the University of Waterloo (energy and urbanization), Ottawa, Dalhousie, Simon Fraser (resource economics and policy), and various other institutions and government departments, as well as in the consulting community.

Other Countries
World Bank, Stockholm Environment Institute, International Institute for Environment and Development, International Institute for Energy Conservation, Thailand (Office of Prime Minister recent experience with energy efficiency planning), Brazil, China (ITEESA), TERI (India), East–West Center (University of Hawaii).

RECOMMENDATIONS

WHICH NICHES ARE BEST FOR IDRC PROGRAM?

IDRC should concentrate on economic evaluation research, information management, and the structure of international linkages (such as technology transfer, sharing of costs, etc.). A potentially very useful role for IDRC vis-à-vis this issue is working with other Northern research agencies and donors to help clarify the research agenda.

ARE ADJUSTMENTS NEEDED AT IDRC IN ORDER TO FILL THESE NICHES?

Program Organization

This activity would need to be carefully coordinated, but could be undertaken jointly across divisions as appropriation an integrated basis.

Process and Project Cycle

The major activity suggested here deviates substantially from IDRC's normal research project style. More staff time would be required, including allowance for staff-led "research", position papers, attending international conferences, donor and research agency meetings in North and South, with relatively less output (i.e. projects funded) and more attention to ideas, collaboration and influencing research priorities of others.

Structure/Staffing

This could not be done without (modest) new staffing and at least exploratory new program funding.

ARE THERE CROSS-CUTTING ISSUES THAT ARE NOT ADEQUATELY REFLECTED IN ANY OF THE ABOVE?

See above.

COMMENTARY 9

Name of Commentator: David Brooks

1. **GENERAL COMMENTS ON THE CHAPTER**

2. **OVERALL COMMENTARY ON THE FIRST REVIEW OF THE CHAPTER**
   - The reviewer has done an excellent review of this Chapter. I agree with his thrust and conclusions. The following notes are intended to supplement the comments.

3. **MAJOR POINTS AGREED/DISAGREED WITH, AND REASONS**
   - The first couple of sentences in point I of the review deals with the dichotomy between the title of the Chapter (atmosphere) and its subject matter (energy).
   - From the perspective of research and programming, the greatest weakness of the Chapter is the lack of attention to the need for energy conservation and efficiency in developing countries. (This in no way contradicts his point about the Northern perspective of the Chapter.) Developing countries need increased supplies, but that should not be taken to imply that they should not also emphasize demand moderation. (The only place this is specifically emphasized for developing countries is with respect to greater efficiency in the power sector, which is really a supply technology.)

- The second greatest weakness is the failure to emphasize and clarify distinctions between energy efficiency as an economic approach and as an environmental approach. The two can go in parallel, but not necessarily. The reviewer has treated this at length, and I agree with each point.

4. MINOR POINTS AGREED/DISAGREED WITH, AND REASONS

- I disagree with the reviewer's comment with respect to Canada as the most "energy profligate" country. Part of the reason is statistical and part related to our structure of industry. Further, energy conservation programs here were a world model until recent government initiatives destroyed them.
- At the end of the Chapter, "new and renewable" is defined differently here from at the 1977 conference, when tar sands and some other questionable sources were also included. (In one of its less altruistic moods, Canada argued unsuccessfully that nuclear power was "new and renewable".)
- Re. ozone, some Third World spokespeople see the Montréal Protocol as the beginning of a new round of gross imperialism. (See the article by Bidwai from *The Nation* of 22 June 1992.)

5. POSSIBLE ON-GOING ISSUES OR CONCERNS FOR IDRC

- See below.

6. POSSIBLE IMPLICATIONS FOR IDRC

- As the reviewer states, there is much too much here to be taken on. Our response should have two parts:
    a) First, IDRC should read this Chapter into its general response to Agenda 21, so that capacity-building, technology transfer, institutional development, etc. — for energy in particular — become part of its program activities.
    b) Second, IDRC should pick off one (or possibly "two") specific focus (foci) for future research activities. Urban energy use (notably the opportunity for conservation and efficiency) is of particular importance and brings together many of IDRC's strengths. This cuts across all economic sectors and brings the economics/environment dilemma to the fore (as well as taking on the issue of mega-cities in the developing world). Finally, research on urban energy makes no sense unless it culminates in policy.
    c) The question is: should IDRC dive into research on environmental economics or allow it to slide into other activities. It is premature to take this decision now, and inappropriate to decide it within the context of a single chapter.
    d) Finally, IDRC should make its own operations as energy and materials efficient as possible; indeed, it should be a model. Its internal conservation programs are well behind the state of the art, including both those that involve staff (e.g., excessive use of throw-aways) and those that involve capital (e.g., whole floor lighting because one person is at work). IDRC needs to revitalize the formerly active team that was working out options — but this time with management support!

CHAPTER TEN

INTEGRATED APPROACH TO THE PLANNING AND MANAGEMENT OF LAND RESOURCES

Responsible Officer: Hartmut Krugmann

ABSTRACT

1. OVERALL CRITIQUE OF AGENDA 21 CHAPTER

- This chapter is quite comprehensive, but has a top-down technocratic flair. The importance of a bottom-up participatory plan/management (involving NGOs) could have been emphasized more strongly.
- Operational aspects of integrated land management were left to other sectoral chapters but should have been addressed here.
- Importance of research is recognized; but only the research on **what** is to be planned and managed, not the planning/management process itself.
- Chapter stresses technological and institutional capacity-building, but does not mention explicitly research capacity-building.
- Integration with chapter 8 ("Policy ....") would have broadened the overall approach to all natural resources, not just land resources.

2. KEY CONCLUSIONS ARISING FROM CHAPTER

- Dealing with land pressures and conflicts requires an integrated approach to land use and management, which allows linking sectoral, environmental and socioeconomic aspects, and identifying trade-offs and complementarities).
- Integration should occur: (a) across different environmental, economic and social factors; (b) across different components of natural resource system.
- **Actions** should be taken in the following areas: policies/policy instruments; planning and management systems; awareness building; public participation; information systems; regional cooperation; scientific understanding of land resource systems; testing findings through pilot projects; education/training; technological capacity; institutions.

3. RESEARCH AND/OR IMPLEMENTATION POSSIBILITIES/OPPORTUNITIES

- There are **research** (and related **capacity-building**) possibilities/opportunities on: (un)successful cases of integrated land management; institutional design; innovative cases of institutional coordination; interdisciplinary systematic analysis combining environmental, economic and social aspects; policy formulation; appropriate tools for planning/management such as data acquisition, use, interpretation (e.g. GIS and remote sensing), impact and risk assessment, cost-benefit analysis, and natural resource accounting; and all the other areas mentioned under "**actions**" in the previous paragraph.
- There are **implementation** possibilities/opportunities in the following areas: pilot project design and implementation; training and education; capacity-building in technology use/adaption; and in the strengthening of institutions.

4. ON-GOING AND/OR NEW PARTNERSHIPS FOR IDRC

- There are a variety of possible Canadian and other partners (universities, NGOs, private and public (research) institutes, donors). Many promising partnerships already exist in Canada and Third World Nations, at different levels.

5. SUGGESTED NICHES FOR IDRC

- Most of the research opportunities/possibilities listed above fit under normal IDRC programming.
- There are new opportunities in the area of **regional integration** which is a new area to IDRC (it figures in the EARO and WARO strategies).
- The areas listed above under "**implementation**" would be unusual for IDRC although they are "normal" as far as their research dimension are concerned.
- It would be novel for IDRC to carry out pilot projects, as opposed to only undertaking research on pilot projects.

6. OTHER COMMENTS

REVIEW 10

KEY CONCLUSIONS IN THE CHAPTER

WHAT IS THERE
Main Conclusions

- Main thrust
  This Chapter is devoted to the reorganization and strengthening of the **decision-making structure** (including existing policies, planning, and management procedures and methods) to facilitate an integrated approach to land resources. It is stressed in the Chapter that the operational aspects of planning and management are not dealt with here but in other Chapters (e.g. Forests, Desertification, Biological Diversity, etc). This Chapter is closely related to chapters 8 ("Policy-Making for Sustainable Development"), 37 ("Building National Capacity for Sustainable Development"), and 38 ("Strengthening Institutions for Sustainable Development").

- Main issues and conclusions
  - An integrated approach to land use and management is needed in order to effectively deal with increasing pressure on land, and resolving competition and conflicts, resulting from expanding human requirements and economic activities;
  - An integrated approach helps to minimize conflicts; make the most advantageous trade-offs (and identify important complementarities); link environmental with socio-economic aspects; and, thus make appropriate choices for sustainable development;
  - The essence of the integrated approach is based on the coordination of sectoral planning and management activities concerned with land use and land resources;
  - Integration is envisaged as taking place at two levels: (a) across different environmental, economic and social factors, and (b) across different components of the environmental and natural resource system;

Agreements Reached for International and National Action
The chapter suggests activities/action in the following areas:
- Developing supportive policies and policy instruments;
- Strengthening planning and management systems;
- Promoting application of appropriate tools for planning and management;
- Raising awareness;
- Promoting public participation;
- Strengthening information systems;
- Fostering regional exchange and cooperation;
- Enhancing scientific understanding of the land resources system;
- Testing research findings through pilot projects;
- Enhancing education and training;
- Strengthening technological capacity; and,
- Strengthening institutions.

No concrete agreements for specific (national or international) action are mentioned.

Politically Significant Issues
In all of the above areas of activity/action, **governments at the appropriate level** are supposed to take the initiative (in collaboration with other actors). (This may be in part because Agenda 21 is a UN document and the UN operates mainly at the government level). On the other hand, in many developing countries (especially in Africa where civil societies are generally very underdeveloped) governments may not be the most suitable agents for effecting change or facilitating processes of change. The initiative may have to be taken by other actors such as different kinds of NGOs. This aspect carries obvious political sensitivity.

WHAT IS NOT THERE
Although non-governmental groups (in the civil society and private sector) are mentioned as collaborators, their role is underemphasized and underestimated. For example, under "Raising Awareness", it is proposed that governments ("at the appropriate level") launch awareness-raising campaigns to alert and educate people on integrated land management issues and the role that individuals and social groups can play. What about the awareness-building role of NGOs? The same applies to "Promoting Public Participation" where NGOs may be better equipped than governments to work with local constituencies.

Areas of activity (viii) and (ix) emphasize the importance of research. However, the research topics mentioned relate only to **what** is to be managed (e.g. land capability, ecosystem functions, and interactions between land resources and social, economic and environmental systems). Nothing is said explicitly about research on the management system, structure and process itself.

Similarly, there is no explicit reference to evaluative research of past approaches to and experiments in land management, in order to inform future action.

The "Capacity-building" section refers to strengthening technological capacity and strengthening institutions, but it does not mention Strengthening Research Capacity.

OVERALL CRITIQUE

Substantive Content
The whole chapter has a top-down technocratic flair, as though it was written by a central manager.

Leaving the operational aspects of integrated land management to other chapters (addressing sectoral concerns) may be misconstrued as implying that operationally there is no difference between integrated and sectoral management. The operational aspects should be addressed up-front.

Design of the Chapter as an Organizing Framework
This Chapter could easily be integrated with Chapter 8 ("Policy-Making for Sustainable Development") by broadening Chapter 8 and calling it "Policy-Making, Planning and Management for Sustainable Development". An integrated approach to resource use and management (not just land resources but **all natural resources**) would then become one of the dimensions of policy, planning and management for sustainable development, under part I of Agenda 21 (Social and Economic Dimensions) and thus would set the stage for the whole of part II (Conservation and Management of Resources for Development), i.e. apply to any of the resources discussed in part II.

As it stands, the present Chapter is unnecessarily curtailed in scope by referring only to land resources and by excluding operational aspects. Moreover, the Chapter does not fit easily within part II, as it is the only Chapter not dealing with a specific resource. Merging it with Chapter 8 could remove these limitations.

RESEARCH REQUIREMENTS, CAPACITY BUILDING ETC.

EXPLICIT/IMPLICIT PROPOSALS IN THE CHAPTER
Starting from the broad issues and conclusions listed above:
- Research (interdisciplinary) is needed:
    i. On cases where an integrated approach (to land use) has effectively (or not) dealt with increasing pressure on land and/or resolved competition and conflicts; and, where such an approach has made it possible to deal with difficult trade-offs, identify complementarities and make appropriate choices;
    ii. On experiments of institutional design to do the above;
    iii. On past cases (i.e. lessons learned) and present institutional experiments concerning the coordination of sectoral planning and management;
    iv. On cases/experiments where integration of environmental, economic and social dimensions and/or of different components of the natural resources system has/has not taken place, and with what implications for sustainability. Such interdisciplinary empirical research could be complemented by modelling efforts.
- Capacity-building and Training is needed:
    i. On how to adapt/design institutional processes to facilitate an integrated approach to land use and management (national and local level training);
    ii. In how natural resource systems work and interact with human societies and communities (general environmental awareness/education as well as specialized tertiary-level education and training);
    iii. In how to conduct and use relevant interdisciplinary research.

In regard to the suggested 12 areas of activities/action (listed above), there is a need for:

i. Broad policy research and capacity-building relating to: policy formulation at different levels, taking into account a variety of environmental, economic and social factors; regulatory frameworks and approaches; economic incentives; and, institutional mechanisms, including decentralization/local government.

ii. Research and capacity-building in planning and management methods and systems capable of: integrating environmental and developmental imperatives; coordinating sectoral plans; and, building on traditional management methods and systems. Research/capacity-building in compiling land use and land potential inventories is a related requirement.

iii. Research/capacity-building in relevant techniques of: data acquisition, analysis, use and interpretation (e.g GIS and remote sensing); impact and risk assessment; cost–benefit analysis; and, national resource accounting.

iv. Research broadly in the area of environmental education and awareness building, as well as related training of teachers, trainers, writers, curriculum developers, etc.

v. Research on and capacity-building in participatory decision-making and implementation processes, procedures, programs, projects, etc.

vi. Research, training and capacity-building concerning relevant information systems, coordination/integration of existing sectoral data systems, provision of information to particular segments of the population and special groups (communities, women, etc), and community-based/managed natural resources information systems.

vii. Research and capacity-building in regional information exchange, coordination and integration relating to integrated land use and management, including information systems and network-building.

viii. Research on land resource systems and their sustainability, particularly assessment of land potential, ecosystem functions and interactions, interactions between land resources and human societies, and development of sustainability indicators. Also research on capacity-building in disciplines relevant to these areas and issues, as well as in interdisciplinary inquiry.

ix. Research and capacity-building in pilot project design and implementation.

x. Training and education, and research in training/education methods and approaches.

xi. Capacity-building in technology transfer and use, and related research.

xii. Capacity-building in terms of strengthening institutions (adjustment of institutional mandates, coordinating mechanisms between institutions, strengthening of decision-making capacity). Also research on how such capacity-building might best be done, including research capacity-building.

GAPS AND ALTERNATIVE APPROACHES

The points under "What is not there" that relate to research/capacity-building, refer to things that have not been made explicit. So they should be given more emphasis; but they can be derived indirectly from the Chapter.

Concerning possible alternative approaches, see above for the suggestion to integrate this chapter with Chapter 8.

NICHES FOR IDRC

GENERAL

Opportunities that Fit Normal Programming

All requirements listed above seem to fit under normal programming, particularly those representing research requirements. As for the training requirements listed there, those related to implementation, as opposed to analysis, may be classified under new or unusual opportunities.

From the list on p. 77, the following items fit under normal programming:
(i), (ii), (iii), (iv), (v), (vi), (vii), (viii).

New Opportunities
Item (vii), in part, affords new opportunities, as far as the regional integration dimension concerned. This is a topic which is quite new to IDRC — it figures in WARO's and EARO's new regional strategies.

Unusual or High-Risk Opportunities
Items (ix), (x), (xi) and (xii) would be unusual for IDRC in their aspects of implementation. (In terms of their research dimension only, these items fall under "normal programming".)

In the case of (ix), it would be unusual/novel for IDRC (even though within the possibilities afforded by the Act of Parliament creating IDRC) to carry out pilot projects, beyond supporting research on how to design and implement pilot projects.

REGIONAL SPECIFICITY

Most, if not all, areas of work identified above seem to be relevant to most developing regions, although there may be differences in the degree of relevance.

KEY PARTNERS/OTHER ACTORS

Canada
There should be a variety of possible partners among universities, NGOs and private (research) institutes.

Other Countries
Same as above.

RECOMMENDATIONS

WHICH NICHES ARE BEST FOR IDRC PROGRAM?
Most or all of the research areas highlighted above are good niches for IDRC as they require integrated interdisciplinary approaches and can (in most cases) build on existing IDRC expertise. Aside from ENRD, SSD and ISSD have much to offer here (decision-making processes as socio-institutional processes and important role of information systems, respectively).

ARE ADJUSTMENTS NEEDED AT IDRC IN ORDER TO FILL THESE NICHES?
Not really. IDRC is well equipped to occupy these niches.

ARE THERE CROSS-CUTTING ISSUES THAT ARE NOT ADEQUATELY REFLECTED IN ANY OF THE ABOVE?
No.

CHAPTER ELEVEN

COMBATING DEFORESTATION

Responsible Officer: R.D. Ayling

ABSTRACT

1. OVERALL CRITIQUE OF AGENDA 21 CHAPTER

- Not a chapter on **combating** deforestation: it is strong on planting trees, but weak on conserving forests.
- Only a brief passing reference to landless farmers and need to halt shifting cultivation by addressing social/ecological causes.
- Indifferently linked to other economic sectors, especially agriculture (no mention of agroforestry); weak reference to desertification, biodiversity, water resources.

2. KEY CONCLUSIONS ARISING FROM CHAPTER

- Four program areas: a) institutional and human resource strengthening; b) global information needs (planning, policy development, assessment, economic information); c) "green activities" e.g. industrial/non-industrial plantations, efficient use of fuelwood and energy, urban forestry (brief mention of need to establish protected areas, buffer and transition zones); d) "capture of forest values" and promoting of efficient utilization, value-added and secondary processing, non-timber products, eco-tourism.
- No agreements reached, only activities suggested; no concrete proposals.

3. RESEARCH AND/OR IMPLEMENTATION POSSIBILITIES/OPPORTUNITIES

- Important issues neglected but program area subjects offer opportunities in "rehabilitation forestry" and resource valuation.
- Opportunities with national programs for analysis of constraints to multisector economic planning, feasibility studies on private sector involvement, analysis of research problems/human resource needs, identification/development of low-input, environmentally sound biotechnology, analysis of integrating forestry into national accounting.

4. ON-GOING AND/OR NEW PARTNERSHIPS FOR IDRC

- Chapter weak on international and regional cooperation/coordination but partners would include Canadian agencies (CIDA and key NGOs, universities).
- Other partnerships would be through liaison with ITTO, IUCN, TFAP.

5. SUGGESTED NICHES FOR IDRC

- Support for analytical research/studies linked to policy influencing.
- Unique role in leading other donors in neglected areas of research (e.g. within CGIAR system, with key international actors/programs such as ITTO, TFAP).
- Supporting/establishing regional networks (NGOs, NRS).

- Identifying strong national players and providing long-term support in areas of the Centre's interest.
- Supporting key organizations (developed/developing country) with expertise/proven track records.

6. OTHER COMMENTS

- In spite of the generalities of the Chapter and missing key elements, there are areas of opportunities to have major impact (e.g. support for Model Forests with Forestry Canada; Biodiversity Convention including forestry; CG's CIFOR forest policy program development). There is a need to sharpen focus and select **key ecosystems** and potential solutions rather than only a country focus and one-off activities.

REVIEW 11

KEY CONCLUSIONS IN THE CHAPTER

WHAT IS THERE

Main Conclusions

The "conclusions" are presented in four Program Areas, each preceded by a brief preamble justifying action. These Program Areas are:

- **Institutional/Human Resource Strengthening** — related to the development of "rational and holistic approaches" to sustainable forest development, including the development of programs, plans, policies and projects on management, conservation and sustainable development;
- **Rehabilitation Forestry or "Greening Activities"** — mainly concerned with the promotion of planting activities (including urban forestry and industrial/non-industrial plantations) although some mention is made of establishing protected areas, buffer and transition zones, the conservation of genetic resources and the need to improve planning and management of existing forests for multiple benefits;
- **Capturing Forest Values** — developing methods to determine social, cultural, economic and biological values, promoting improved and efficient utilization of industries and secondary processing, recognizing and promoting non-timber products, promoting the efficient utilization of fuelwood and energy and promoting "ecotourism"; and,
- **Global Information** — increasing the capacities for planning, assessment and systematic observations for integrated forest planning, including improving economic information on forest and land resources.

Agreements Reached for International and National Action

No agreements were reached. The program Areas suggested activities.

Politically Significant Issues

Support for international organizations, such as the FAO, ITTO and others as suggested, should be possible, with the Centre continuing to champion the cause of its traditional beneficiaries as its principal motive for involvement. The Tropical Forestry Action Programme (TFAP), although "currently being implemented in more than 80 countries", does not have the universal support and endorsement, as implied, of all countries nor even of all actors in all countries. Activities within the TFAP should be approached with consideration.

WHAT IS NOT THERE

The "philosophy of forestry" is missing. For instance, the concept that forests, particularly tropical forests, hold the germplasm for future problem resolution, and that all forests are the "lungs of the earth".

The Chapter neglects the ultimate causes of deforestation, i.e., poverty and landlessness in the South, and excessive consumerism in the North. This is a major omission and considerably weakens the document.

The Chapter is strong on planting trees but weak on conserving forests.

Forests are indifferently linked, if at all, to other sectors of the economy, particularly agriculture. There is little mention of agroforestry, for example.

Forest problems and proposed "program areas" are divorced from other interrelated issues such as desertification, fragile ecosystems, water resources, terrestrial biodiversity, land-use activities (including tenure issues and poverty).

There is an obvious need to provide concrete proposals to give substance to the activities promoted, especially by demonstrating in specific areas "on-ground" practices in Canada. More serious thought should be given to implementing and forming international working groups.

OVERALL CRITIQUE
Substantive Content

- **This is not a chapter on "combatting deforestation"**. It is an outline of action on management of forestry activities and planting programs, and even includes "urban forestry".
  It is a chapter on curative activities, not preventative ones. As such, it is a document which has managed to ignore much of the forestry developmental literature of the last ten years, especially in the areas of social and community forestry. It proposes activities such as the development of industrial and non-industrial plantations, the development of national plans for planted forests, and suggests activities to promote the efficient use of fuelwood and energy — the latter a subject which has been particularly explored at length by most, if not all, donors. Most of these activities, whether village woodlots, government plantations, improved woodstoves, have been largely ineffective in reversing or even reducing tropical forest loss. Many are simply uneconomical and/or socially harmful. These are, for the most part, discredited activities. To present them as something new shows either considerable ignorance or at best, only partial understanding of tropical deforestation.
  Time and time again, it has been shown (at least in Africa) that government-run plantations are unsustainable. The only way to increase tree cover is through farmer/landowner planting, i.e.; introduction of trees on farms. Agroforestry is not mentioned as even a possible "cure" for deforestation.
- Little is said about preventing deforestation. There is only one brief and passing reference to landless farmers. Program B suggests the need to limit and aim to halt "destructive shifting cultivation by addressing the underlying social and ecological causes". Nothing is said no proposed about the consumerism of developed countries which is a major driving force behind tropical deforestation, or about the rising wealthy and middle-class in Third World countries which evince the same consumcrism.
- Again, (see *Statement of Principles*), the significant development opportunities offered by tropical forests in strengthening national economies, in poverty alleviation, and in food security have not been emphasized. The global significance of tropical forests for biological diversity conservation is somewhat neglected. Although these humid/sub-humid forests only cover some 10% of the

earth's land area, they may contain more than half the world's terrestrial species. As noted previously, the separation of issues, such as biodiversity and desertification relating directly to forests and to their sustainable management, reduces the urgency for action.
- In spite of the neglect or minimization of these important issues, the four Programs present opportunities for Centre support. Programs B and C ("Rehabilitation Forestry" and "Capturing Forest Values") are more substantial with clear researchable issues.

Design of the Chapter as an Organizing Framework
- This is a vital chapter of Agenda 21 and should have had more substance and prominence. However, the individual lead paragraphs, the "Basis for Action", are useful but suffer from specific details.
- Programs A and D ("Institutional/Human Resource Strengthening" and "Global Information") are obviously related and could have been combined.
- The "boundaries" between the Program Areas are not firm although the development of each is similar and thus useful for comparison. However, the sections on international and regional cooperation and coordination are weak and lack specifics.
- The financial implications are useful only in that they offer comparison between Programme Areas. No basis for the figures or specifics on funding sources are presented. There is some confusion between the various areas of "activities" and "means of implementation".

RESEARCH REQUIREMENTS, CAPACITY BUILDING, ETC.

EXPLICIT PROPOSALS IN THE CHAPTER
None.

IMPLICIT PROPOSALS DERIVED FROM THE CHAPTER

In line with the *Statement of Principles*, much is suggested as to what national governments and the international community should or could do. There are no operational plans presented for implementation of any of the suggested program components. However, there are clear opportunities for Centre activity, particularly in institutional and human resource development and in well-focused studies of the role of forests in national economies. Some of these include:
- Analysis of the constraints to integrated multisector economic planning, including the forestry sector;
- The identification of research problems/solutions and human resource needs in national forest management systems;
- Studies on ways to encourage private sector involvement in resource management;
- Feasibility studies and the development of operational plans for rehabilitation forestry;
- The identification/analysis of low-input, environmentally sound biotechnology to enhance productivity;
- Analysis of integrating forestry into national economic accounting.

GAPS AND ALTERNATIVE APPROACHES

Some key activities include:
- The development of effective public educational programs, particularly for the young and in developed countries, identifying clearly the relationships of consumerism, "life styles" and tropical deforestation;
- Quantification of, through case studies, the role of forests in poverty alleviation and food security;
- Support for research to identify/analyze principal causes of deforestation in key ecozones;
- The provision of effective support to international organizations and mechanisms which are directly concerned with tropical deforestation and biodiversity reduction, such as the ITTO, IUCN, and FAO's Tropical Forestry Action Program.

NICHES FOR IDRC

The Centre has had considerable influence with several international organizations out of proportion to its financial support. These include the Consultative Group on International Agricultural Research (CGIAR), the most important and prestigious organization of donors in the areas of international agricultural and forestry research. Others include the International Union of Forest Research Organizations (IUFRO) and the International Labour Organization. Opportunities exist to maintain these important linkages and to develop new ones, particularly with the International Tropical Timber Organization (ITTO), the FAO's Tropical Forestry Action Program, and the Commonwealth Secretariat.

The Centre has been effective in human resource development, providing support for graduate level training as well as limited support to training and research institutions. Support has been tied to specific projects and has not been as effective as it could have been. IDRC's niche will be to identify clearly those educational pathways it wishes to follow, to concentrate its efforts and resources, and to provide sustained support (PhD; post-graduate) to promising individuals.

The Centre has the opportunity to be a major catalyst among donor agencies in environment and natural resources issues. The energies of its professional staff need to be channelled effectively to maximum advantage. This includes additional administrative streamlining and decentralized decision-making.

GENERAL

Opportunities that Fit Normal Programming

- Support/influence key international organizations such as the CGIAR centres (ICRAF, IBPGR and others involved in natural resource management, and especially the CG's newest entity on forestry research — CIFOR) (all Program Areas);
- "Greening activities" through the promotion of well-focused agroforestry and social forestry interventions, particularly through networking, policy and economic analyses, and "leverage" activities (Program B);
- The development of methodologies to determine the full value of forests, including social, cultural, economic and biological valuation (Program C);
- Feasibility studies on national accounting systems to consider economic/non-economic values of forests (Program C);
- Research on indigenous knowledge systems, especially related to sustainable forest management;
- Research on non-timber products (eg; medicines, bamboos, rattans, forest foods), considering sustainable resource management, product handling/marketing, resource control mechanisms and community returns.

New Opportunities

- Focused support for individuals/institutions in resource accounting, environmental impact analysis, social forestry, policy analysis, including university-level degree programs, short courses and training workshop;
- Support for the early involvement in the formulation of national forestry action plans through the TFAP, as well as support for implementation, analyzes, evaluation and training;
- Promotion of the testing/evaluation of ITTO's *Criteria for the Measurement of Sustainable Tropical Forest Management*;
- Support for feasibility studies (by nationals) and implementation activities of alternatives to deforestation (buffer and transitional zones, forest reserves, etc.);
- Support for germplasm analysis of important ecosystems, including sustained support for *in situ* conservation;

- Promotion of the identification and/or development of sustainable forest management models, particularly where this support can be networked regionally or globally;
- Support for the analysis of information needs of developing countries for the development of plans/programs on sustainable resource management, and support or establish international information systems.

Unusual or High-Risk Opportunities

The previous opportunities imply full public sector involvement and general consensus in all aspects of resource decision-making. That this is seldom the case, even in developed countries, suggests that many activities involving resource conservation/utilization trade-offs, environment/development conflicts, have the potential for high risk. Government plantations, for example, have, in some instances, removed forest cover in order to plant high-value species, thereby denying the poor access to produce (fuelwood, food, fodder from natural woodlands) which they consider important.

REGIONAL SPECIFICITY

See *Statement of Principles*.

KEY PARTNERS/OTHER ACTORS

In addition to others described in this section in the *Statement of Principles*, collaboration with the Centre's Information Sciences Division should be developed. There are also a number of potential Canadian partners with expertise in forest/land-use information systems (e.g., Ontario's Ministry of Natural Resources).

RECOMMENDATIONS

WHICH NICHES ARE BEST FOR IDRC PROGRAM?

Given the Centre's limited human and financial resources, more impact will be possible through well-focused interventions with a limited number of international organizations/mechanisms and national programs. Unless attracting and retaining additional technical expertise is possible, the Centre should continue to support analytical research as opposed to biological research as suggested in the Chapter. The development of harvesting and management technologies, research to improve forest-based industries, the promotion of urban forestry and "eco-tourism", should not be given serious consideration.

The Centre can, however, have maximum influence and effect by indicating **immediate** support for the following:
- The development/implementation of the forest policy program of the CGIAR's newest centre, CIFOR, and the support of CIDA for Canada to be one of three sponsoring members of CIFOR;
- Identification of opportunities within the CGIAR to influence and coordinate activities on natural resource management and germplasm conservation;
- Analysis of constraints/resolution of IARC–NAR collaboration;
- Creating the means for effective liaison with ITTO, TFAP, IUCN and other key international players;
- Support for the Commonwealth Secretariat's Forestry Initiative on sustainable forest models;
- Creating a "critical mass" of Centre officers to form an interdisciplinary team, with the responsibility and resources to implement Chapter 11.

ARE ADJUSTMENTS NEEDED AT IDRC IN ORDER TO FILL THESE NICHES?

Program Organization

There are too many "GPIs" within ENR, too few participants, and considerable overlap in some areas. Activities should become strongly focused, and issues such as sustainable forest management, biodiversity, water resources, desertification, resource economics, etc. should be planned and implemented by a team.

Process and Project Cycle (see Statement of Principles)
See above.

Structure/Staffing
Additional professional officers are required, especially in biological sciences, in order for the Centre to retain credibility with other donors and with recipients.

COMMENTARY 11

Name of Commentator: Eglal Rached

1. **GENERAL COMMENTS ON THE CHAPTER**

- An excellent review. The author rightly notes major discrepancies in the Chapter, particularly as they relate to the poor coverage of major causes for deforestation, and the curative vs preventive bias. The review provides a good critique of recommended activities and their anticipated ineffectiveness, and stresses the poor coverage of subjects like agro-forestry, biodiversity, link with agriculture and role of poverty and problem of landless in deforestation. Minor other critiques can be made:
  a) The Chapter does not mention the importance of land tenure in forest degradation;
  b) It does not cover the problem of effective implemention of existing laws and regulations;
  c) There is a bias toward developed countries forest management style (recreational, public awareness, public relations, etc.) which may not be appropriate for developing countries;
  d) It limits problems of deforestation to humid and tropical areas, does not integrate mountainous forests in dry/semi-dry areas;
  e) There is an absence of activities relating to impact assessment and monitoring of reforestation programs.

2. **OVERALL COMMENTARY ON THE FIRST REVIEW OF THE CHAPTER**

- I agree with all statements, except perhaps the one relating to agro-forestry. While it may be true that on privately owned land the best solution may be agro-forestry, this does not apply to common or state-owned land.

3. **MAJOR POINTS AGREED/DISAGREED WITH, AND REASONS**

- Complete agreement with the comment that this is not a chapter on "combatting deforestation" but rather on reforestation and afforestation.
- Very few specifics on prevention, which is known to be much less expensive and more "diversity friendly" than reforestation programs. What will happen to the neglected, remote but yet relatively untouched forests while donors and governments are busy replanting forests with a very limited number of tree species.
- Agree with statement that the Chapter does not address the consumerism of developed countries. Although consumerism is not necessarily a bad feature (it favours export markets), little is said/done about international market prices, quotas, etc.
- Fully agree with the statement relating to the importance of integrating biodiversity, desertification and deforestation.

- Agree with the need for the Centre to concentrate on focused interventions based on analytical research.

4. MINOR POINTS AGREED/DISAGREED WITH, AND REASONS
- To my knowledge little biological research work on reforestation with multiple/native species has been undertaken. This is perhaps an area to be considered for biological research.

5. POSSIBLE ON-GOING ISSUES OR CONCERNS FOR IDRC
- Well covered in the review's section discussing unusual or high risk opportunities.

6. POSSIBLE IMPLICATIONS FOR IDRC
- Agree with author's comments about the need for the Centre to concentrate interventions. The careful selection of issues and partners is recommended.

CHAPTER TWELVE

COMBATING DESERTIFICATION AND DROUGHT

Responsible Officer: Eglal Rached

ABSTRACT

1. OVERALL CRITIQUE OF AGENDA 21 CHAPTER

- Recognition of importance of land degradation in arid and semi-arid areas, but lacks clear focus, problem diagnosis and priorities. More thorough diagnostic of desertification problems and clearer distinction between and among dryland degradation processes would assist in the identification of appropriate responses and management strategies.
- Lacks focus: programs cover micro to macro management issues, drought relief, areas vulnerable to desertifications and desertified lands.
- Generally more attention to corrective than preventive ones — does not emphasize the precautionary approach.
- Except in rare cases, Chapter suggests little research is required: a wrong assumption in many areas.
- Lacks provision for environmental assessment and impact assessments.
- Too much focus on UN organizations, and not enough on other types of organizations.

2. KEY CONCLUSIONS ARISING FROM CHAPTER

- There is a need to combat desertification and drought, qualified as a major environmental problem threatening vast areas of the globe and large human and animal populations. To do so, action is required on 6 fronts:
    a) Strengthening knowledge bases and information tools for monitoring desertification rates and processes.
    b) Combatting land degradation through intensified soil conservation, afforestation and reforestation activities.
    c) Eradication of poverty and promotion of alternative livelihood systems in marginal areas.
    d) Development of comprehensive anti-desertification programs at the national level and integrating them in national development and environmental plans.
    e) Formulation of drought preparedness and drought relief schemes.
    f) Promotion of popular participation and environmental education.

3. RESEARCH AND/OR IMPLEMENTATION POSSIBILITIES/OPPORTUNITIES

- Research on soil conservative technologies, participatory research in community management of natural resources, in-situ conservation of biodiversity, agro-forestry and afforestation techniques for rangelands.
- Land use planning, development of land-use models based on local practices for improvement of soil and biodiversity conservation, drought and salinity resistant plants and shrubs.
- Research on networking data bases from various sources and of different scales, and research on integrating socio-economic variables with bio-physical data.

- Research to understand desertification processes and segregate among and between causes of desertification, especially at the local level.
- Research on production systems involved, indigenous knowledge, land tenure and communal management of resources.
- Research on alternative income generation technologies, and their economic, environmental, social and equitable sustainability.
- Capacity-building in information sciences, conservation technologies, planning and systems management.

4. ON-GOING AND/OR NEW PARTNERSHIPS FOR IDRC

- On-going partnership with national institutions such as Universities (Egypt, Jordan, Morocco), and Institutions (Algeria, Tunisia), with international organizations (ICARDA, ACSAD)
- New promising partnerships with ORSTOM, Observatoire du Sahara, Ciheam, Ibsram, Icraf, Acct, as well as World Bank, USAID and UN organizations.
- Large expertise in Canada, particularly in information sciences, land use modelling and planning, and experience in soil conservation under drought conditions in Western Canada (although not entirely relevant).

5. SUGGESTED NICHES FOR IDRC

- Close match with ENR program interests in sustainable management of rangelands and rainfed croplands, importance of community participation, need to develop alternative income opportunities in marginal areas.
- IDRC can play an active role in most programs, except drought relief and refugees problems. A strong focus could be on local management issues, preventive measures, and integration of different program components, also rangelands and rainfed croplands. Less emphasis on salinization under irrigation.
- Good capability in Information Sciences (remote sensing, GIS, networking, linking socio-economics with geo-physical variables) to support desertification initiatives.
- Strength in policy research and capacity-building.

6. OTHER COMMENTS

- None.

REVIEW 12

KEY CONCLUSIONS IN THE CHAPTER

WHAT IS THERE

Desertification is described as land degradation in arid, semi-arid and dry sub-humid areas resulting from various factors, including climatic variations and human activities. It is a major environmental problem threatening vast areas of the globe and affecting large human and animal populations.

Priority for combatting desertification is placed on preventive measures for areas that are not yet or are only slightly degraded. However severely degraded areas are not be neglected.

To combat desertification and drought, this chapter proposes six comprehensive programs aimed at fragile ecosystems prone to desertification (rangelands, marginal rainfed cropland and irrigated cropland). These are:
- Strengthening the knowledge base and developing information monitoring systems for regions prone to desertification and drought, including the economic and social aspects of these ecosystems;
- Combating land degradation through intensified soil conservation, afforestation and reforestation activities;
- Developing and strengthening integrated development programs for the eradication of poverty and promotion of alternative livelihood systems in areas prone to desertification;
- Developing comprehensive anti-desertification programs and integrating them into national development plans national national environmental planning;
- Developing comprehensive drought preparedness and drought-relief schemes, including self-help arrangements, for drought-prone areas and designing programs to cope with environmental refugees
- Encouraging and promoting popular participation and environmental education, focusing on desertification control and management of the effects of drought.

The estimated total annual cost for the Chapter's initiatives is approximately 10 billion dollars (1993–2000), with participation from national, international and regional organizations.

WHAT IS NOT THERE

Does not emphasize research and needs to investigate what is feasible, which technologies are available, which technology need to be developed or adapted, etc.

Lacks provision for measuring impact of recommended anti-desertification measures on environment, socio-economics, etc.

Chapter concentrates on Middle East and Africa. No mention of other continents.

Too much concentration on Governmental and International agents. Nothing on role of private sector.

OVERALL CRITIQUE

Substantive Content

The definition of "desertification" is too broad. The term desertification is used to describe the whole spectrum of marginal areas from those already desertified to areas prone to desertification. It also includes lands decertified by salinization. The diagnosis of the causes of desertification are not precise: "(they) result from various factors, including climatic variations and human activities". The broadening of the term robs it of much diagnostic value, and makes it difficult to properly prioritize and select areas and/or approaches where scarce available resources may be utilized the most efficiently.

"Desertification" could better be described as "a process by which land degradation ultimately results in the creation or expansion of deserts", or "as the extreme case of land degradation". This definition has the advantage of directing more attention to land degradation, and focusing more on preventive measures than on corrective ones.

Figures on desertification provided in the introduction need more substantiation and may be overestimated. The two main reasons for this are:

- Questionable baseline scientific information and overreliance on early estimates from the Sahelian Region, (reliance on very thin network of meteorological sites, extrapolation from one region during period of prolonged drought, in many cases reliance on unsubstantiated guesses of government officials)
- No basis for distinguishing between the effects of prolonged drought conditions (short lasting effects) and actual desertification Long lasting): Recent combined remote sensing/ground truthing studies indicate that in some areas which had been labelled decertified only a few years earlier lands became again biologically active when rainfall resumed.

The point here is not to say that desertification is not a global issue. Rather it highlights the need for a more thorough diagnostic of the problem and a clearer distinction between and among dryland degradation processes in order to identify appropriate responses and management strategies.

Moreover, it also highlights the importance of addressing the issue at a micro-management level, rather than globally. A thorough diagnosis of the problem at this scale may mean that work is more required in other fields such as women, community participation, sustainable production systems, etc.

The scope of presented programs is, in my opinion, too broad: On one hand, as indicated above, it recommends to cover lands degraded at various levels, on the other it wishes to cover areas such as drought relief and designing programs to cope with environmental refugees. Again here the chapter would benefit from more focus.

In general programs are presented separately, without provision for required linkages/interactions between and among their components (for example between popular participation/poverty alleviation/soil conservation)

All programs are to be implemented at all levels (local, national, regional and international). More specificity is required and provision for linkages between these levels is required.

Although there is a complete program of poverty alleviation, little is said about equity, or gender issues.

Although desertification caused by salinization is included in the chapter, little activities are specifically directed towards this aspect.

Design of the Chapter as an Organizing Framework.
This Chapter could be more clearly be called: "Managing Fragile Ecosystems: Sustainable development of arid and semi-arid lands".

Programs are generally well-organized and cover information needs, technology, policy, poverty issues and training. Research needs are generally poorly covered, as is the problem of coordination between programs. Program five (drought preparedness and drought relief) mainly focuses on drought relief and coping with refugee problems. Should those issues be considered within Agenda 21? Perhaps only the drought preparedness component should be retained, then placed within the second program (related to soil conservation and sustainable production systems).

There is a large degree of overlapping between objectives in a number of topics, particularly on information systems, and the development of sustainable alternative technological packages and production systems.

For a research organization like IDRC, the organization of programs is disorientating: research-related activities are explicitly or implicitly found under different headings: "Data and information", "Scientific and technological means", International and regional cooperation and coordination". Pooling research requirements under one heading would be helpful.

RESEARCH REQUIREMENTS, CAPACITY BUILDING ETC.

EXPLICIT PROPOSALS IN THE CHAPTER

- Strengthening the knowledge base and developing information and monitoring systems.
  Linking, integrating data from various sources and levels (local, national, regional and international) and ensuring compatibility is not a simple issue. No standards are presently available and considerable research will be required on information systems and data standards, integrating different data sources, monitoring technologies/systems and their requirements, etc. In addition to a good training program for information professionals.

  IDRC has been working, to some extent, at integrating socio-economic with geo-physical variables. This is again another field where considerable research is required, and a difficult one.

  Activities include a review and study of the "means for measuring ecological, economic and social consequences of desertification and land degradation, and integrating these studies internationally into desertification and land degradation assessment practices". This is an important area of research, particularly in view of generating the political will and the financial means at the national level to prevent land degradation. Research on the contribution of marginal lands to national economies, culture and environment would be very useful.

  As stressed in the overall critique, there is an imperative need to diagnose causes of desertification, at the local level. This is not included in suggested activities and should be given high priority. Remote sensing and ground truthing. Long term monitoring.

  As relates to capacity building, there is no mention of training and education of local staff.

- Combating land degradation through inter-alia intensified soil conservation, afforestation and reforestation activities.
  Explicit research areas:
  a. Development of land-use models, based on local practices for the improvement of soil and biodiversity conservation practices;
  b. Development, testing and introducing appropriate drought resistant, fast-growing and productive plant species.

  More research is required than that explicitly suggested. Some of these elements are included under other headings (scientific means or International cooperation), in particular activities related to technology development and dissemination and indigenous knowledge. Research needs should be more explicitly spelled out. The development of data bases on state of knowledge would be an essential first step.

  It is often suggested that the problem of desert expansion is one of economics and ethics rather than of science. Research on economic et anthropogenic factors influencing land degradation should be included.

  Need to stress inter-disciplinarity.

Research also needed on afforestation and reforestation: what is impact (socio-economical and environmental) of present afforestation schemes, how could they be improved.

- Developing and strengthening integrated development programs for the eradication of poverty and promotion of alternative livelihood systems:
  Explicit research areas:
    a. Socio-economic baseline studies to have good understanding regarding, particularly resource and land tenure issues, traditional land-management practices and characteristics of production systems;
    b. Inventory of natural resources and their state of degradation, based primarily on knowledge of local population;
    c. Dissemination of info on technical packages;
    d. promote exchange and sharing of info on development of alternative livelihoods with other agro-ecological regions; and,
    e. Undertake applied research in land use. (This should go under preceding objective).

  Research needed on generating/transferring appropriate alternative income generating technologies for these areas. Concern about environmental consequences of implemented industries. Concern about equity, social acceptability.

  Capacity building in participatory research.

- Developing comprehensive anti-desertification programmes and integrating them into national development and environmental plans:
  Explicit areas:
    a. There are surprisingly few research activities which are specifically related to the area of policy and planning. The suggested study area is to undertake applied study on the integration of environmental and development activities into national development plans.

- Drought preparedness and drought relief schemes
  As indicated above, I mainly see the role of IDRC in the area related to drought preparedness (water harvesting, reducing water demand by improving water utilization, etc.)

IDRC certainly has a niche there, we have been working hard on some of these issues in the past (rangelands, water harvesting, etc.) and have acquired good knowledge and contacts. New elements are presently being developed, particularly those related to information sciences modelling, linking socio-economics and natural sciences, and income generation in marginal areas. More will need to be done in the latter, and more also on several areas related to networking and capacity building.

The Chapter is quite relevant to MERO, WARO and SARO, it also has some importance in other regions (China, India, Peru and Chile).

International partners listed are limited. Other partners in Canada : CCRS, Water specialists, remote sensing and GIS community. Other International partners: ORSTOM (France), IBSRAM, ACCT, ACSAD, ICARDA, ICRAF, World Bank, USAID, and UN organisations.

COMMENTARY 12

Name of Commentator: R.D. Ayling

1. GENERAL COMMENTS ON THE CHAPTER

- This is another "combatting" chapter of Agenda 21, with more cures than preventions as noted in critique.
- A good review of a somewhat vague and unfocused chapter, with an abstract excellent and more critical than the review itself; review is reasonably strong and forceful with useful insights for several pages, then "running out of time and steam at the end".
- Could have had more criticism of: the all-encompassing nature of the Chapter, particularly for an issue (desertification) which may or may not be "real"; also of distinct Africa/Middle East slant with subsequent neglect/disregard for other regions; downplaying by chapter's authors of central role that inappropriate/ineffective land-use policies play in "desertification"; quality of leadership role played by international actors such as existing UN agencies & others.

2. OVERALL COMMENTARY ON THE CHAPTER

- Any criticisms of the review are related only to the author's time constraints.
- A good review and in full agreement; however, review requires finishing, i.e.; consideration and details on implications (if any) on present and future Centre programming and partnerships. Weakness of chapter's thoughts on poverty alleviation not stressed, nor is Chapter's reliance on revamping/remodelling current international agencies attacked, as the answer to "desertification".
- Agenda 21's separation of related issues (desertification and drought, deforestation, land and water resources) only briefly noted.

3. MAJOR POINTS AGREED/DISAGREED WITH, AND REASONS

- Complete agreement with commentary, especially recognition that Chapter's definition of "desertification" is too broad and thus authors "rob of it much diagnostic value", making it difficult to prioritize activities. Use of this vague, all-inclusive definition also diverts attention to underlying causes of land degradation, i.e.; inappropriate land-use practices (including failure to initiate real land reform) but also government disruption, disruption/erosion of traditional land management practices. As such, it further allows the authors of chapter 12 an easy way out, i.e.; to ignore poverty, landlessness and inequities. "Desertification" is not due to "various factors including climate variations", but to land abuse and to social, economic and political factors permitting this abuse. The impact of demographics is poorly addressed.
- Full agreement on recognition that the issue of "desertification" may be suspect, unsubstantiated, and overestimated; is founded upon weak baseline data, over-reliance of early estimates, extrapolations and guesses; state of this weak knowledge base persists in spite of repetitive UNEP monitoring; much of this weakness may stem from existing definitions of "desertification".
- Agreement with observation on the overlapping of the objectives of the Chapter's different programs, and the poor coverage of research.

4. MINOR POINTS AGREED/DISAGREED WITH, AND REASONS

- I agree with the author of the review that the Chapter should have been "Managing Fragile Ecosystems: Sustainable Development of Arid and Semi-Arid Lands" (this would have included sections on water, soils, forests, biodiversity, etc. — perhaps UNCED should have focused more on ecosystems instead of splitting resource sectors).

5. POSSIBLE ON-GOING ISSUES OR CONCERNS FOR IDRC

6. POSSIBLE IMPLICATIONS FOR IDRC
- IDRC should not concentrate on desertification, but focus on supporting research on the development of rational land-use plans, including strengthening indigenous CPR management, and land tenure reform.

CHAPTER THIRTEEN

SUSTAINABLE MOUNTAIN DEVELOPMENT

Responsible Officer: Hugo Li Pun

ABSTRACT

1. OVERALL CRITIQUE OF AGENDA 21 CHAPTER

- It recognizes the importance of Mountain ecosystems as sources of water, energy and biological diversity. Over 50% of the world's population is affected by the increasing deterioration of mountain ecologies and connected watershed areas.
- The need for an integrated approach for conserving, upgrading and using the natural resource base of land, water, plant, animal and human resources is also recognized.
- Concepts, ideas, objectives and strategy proposed are sound. A more holistic approach is needed to better link policy and technological research, environmental concerns, and objectives within existing R&D institutions.
- The document could have been organized better by defining subprograms by ecoregions and main themes, and establishing goals.

2. KEY CONCLUSIONS ARISING FROM CHAPTER

- Need to strengthen existing institutions at all levels to generate multidisciplinary knowledge on mountain ecosystems through integrating technologies and policies.
- Promote policies for the use and transfer of environmentally-friendly technologies and farming and conservation practices.
- Build-up knowledge and understanding on mountain ecosystems by creating mechanisms for cooperation and information exchange.
- Diversify mountain economies by creating other income/employment opportunities.

3. RESEARCH AND/OR IMPLEMENTATION POSSIBILITIES/OPPORTUNITIES

- Surveys of the different forms of use of natural resources.
- Research on land/water management related to agricultural practices.
- Establish bio-physical and meteorological monitoring of key indicators for sustainability.
- Strengthen the role of international research and training institutes, and NGOs.
- Promote networking among institutions of all types.

4. ON-GOING AND/OR NEW PARTNERSHIPS FOR IDRC

- Canada: strengthen the partnership with Canadian universities, ie: Forestry and Highlands: Laval, Lakehead, York, U. of Toronto; Semi-arid lands, soils and pastures: McGill, UBC, Saskatchewan, Alberta. Common property and minorities: Simon Fraser, York, Manitoba, etc.
- International organizations: the CG system (CIP, CATIE, CIAT, IRRI, ICIMOD, IBSRAM, ICRAF).
- National programs, universities and NGOs in Asia, Latin America and Africa.
- Other donors: SDC, CIDA, AID, IFAD, ORSTOM, GTZ, World Bank, etc.

5. SUGGESTED NICHES FOR IDRC

- Support: holistic/participatory studies in selected ecoregions; networking; coordination among institutions and donors; research on diversification of sources of income/employment; studies to learn from development projects and provide feedback to R & D; environmental impact studies for development projects; and use information generated in projects to propose policy interventions and development schemes.

6. OTHER COMMENTS

- Given the need to concentrate resources and achieve sustainable and long-term impacts a more integrated effort between Centre Programs/Divisions is needed. The ecosystem identity allows the selection of cases for the integration/implementation of combined actions of a series of cross-cutting themes including: combating poverty, sustainable agriculture, biological diversity, and indigenous people, among others.

REVIEW 13

KEY CONCLUSIONS IN THE CHAPTER

The Chapter recognizes the **tremendous importance of mountain ecosystems** as sources of water, energy and biological diversity, as 10% of people of the world live there and over 50% of the world population is affected in various ways by mountain ecology and the degradation of watershed areas.

The Chapter recognizes the need for **using an integrated approach** for conserving, upgrading and using the natural resource base of land, water, plant, animal and human resources.

Two programs are recommended: One for the **generation of knowledge about ecology and sustainable development** of mountain ecosystems, and the other for **promoting integrated watershed development and alternative opportunities.**

The objectives are sound for the first program: they include diagnosis, maintenance and generation of databases to facilitate integrated management of resources, participatory research on sustainable technologies and agricultural practices, networking for communications and clearing-house, coordination.

The objectives for the second program are more ambitious: the development of appropriate land-use planning by the year 2000 to prevent soil erosion; to increase biomass production and maintain ecological balance; to promote income-generating activities and improve infrastructure and social services especially for local/indigenous communities; and, to develop arrangements to mitigate effects of natural disasters.

The programs need to be closely interrelated. In the document the process of generation of knowledge is separate from the diffusion and application of knowledge. A systems approach is needed to look at both processes, so that generated knowledge can be used for development programs, and be based on on-going development experiences. Also research is needed to assess the impact of changes in one ecosystem or watershed on neighbouring ones (downstream effects).

WHAT IS THERE

Main Conclusions

There is a need to:
- Strengthen existing institutions or establish new ones at local, national and regional levels to generate multidisciplinary land/water ecological knowledge on mountain ecosystems;
- Promote policies to provide incentives for the use and transfer of environment-friendly technologies and farming and conservation practices;
- Build-up knowledge bases and understanding by creating mechanisms for cooperation and information exchange among institutions working on fragile ecosystems;
- Encourage policies that provide incentives to farmers and local people to conserve and regenerate the resource base;
- Diversify mountain economies by creating /strengthening tourism;
- Integrate forest, rangeland, wildlife activities to maintain mountain ecosystems;
- Prevent soil erosion and promote erosion control;
- Establish watershed development committees or task forces to coordinate integrated services to support local initiatives in animal husbandry, forestry, horticulture and rural development at all administrative levels;
- Support NGOs assisting local organizations and communities in the preparation of projects that would enhance participatory development of local people;
- Undertake income-generating activities in cottage and agro-processing industries; and,
- Emphasize the participation of women, indigenous people and communities in all those activities.

Agreements Reached for International and National Action

General agreement to undertake the following is indicated:
- **Coordination of regional and international cooperation** and facilitation of exchange of information between specialized agencies, donors, governments, regional, national and non-governmental institutions working on mountain development.
- **Strengthening the role of international research and training institutes** such as the CG system, and regional institutions (ICIMOD, IBSRAM).

WHAT IS NOT THERE

A more holistic concept is required. For example, in the document environmental issues are separated from socio-economic ones. Sustainable development will need to consider the promotion of economic sustainability and stability, the equitable distribution of costs and benefits, the rational use and conservation of natural resources, and the preservation of the environment. Those factors need to be interrelated otherwise developing countries will not be able to protect the environment while poverty and inequity prevail.

Human resource development is also dealt with on a restricted basis: for both environmental issues and indigenous mountain populations. **Environmental concerns should be promoted at all levels** (decision-makers, researchers, development agents, managers/utilizers of resources) and with the holistic approach before mentioned.

Therefore, the following steps should be taken:
- **Creation of awareness.** Considerable progress has been achieved among developed country populations, some research managers in international organizations, and some researchers in developing countries. However, the vast majority in developing countries still have not achieved that level of awareness, as more pressing needs exist. A better strategy is to incorporate environmental concerns within existing R & D structures/organizations, and translate them into specific plans/

programs. The creation of separate institutions/programs will tend to dilute the use of resources or separate/isolate environmental efforts from other development activities.
- **Definition of methodologies and actual implementation of specific cases** on the use of holistic approaches. Defined methodologies are needed for those holistic approaches as well as the documentation of experiences and the development of new concrete cases.
- **Diffusion of experiences.** Successful cases or positive lessons learned will need to be distributed widely to create further commitments, give credibility to holistic approaches, and broad impacts.
- **Broadered Scientific Research Capacity.** The recommendation on strengthening scientific research capacity is too restricted. It emphasizes meteorology, hydrology, forestry, soil sciences and plant sciences. It leaves out other disciplines, such as social sciences, ecology, animal sciences, and systems analysis, among others, that are critical for sustainable development of mountain areas.

OVERALL CRITIQUE

Substantive Content

In general, the objectives and proposed activities make sense. The right ideas and concepts are there. What is lacking is the more holistic view, and the how to do it. The Chapter before is just the starting point, moving into specifics. The document assumes, especially in the program to promote integrated development, that many environmental-friendly technologies and practices are already known, and the policies to make them feasible. If that is the case, why are they not used widely? This requires an evaluation, under specific field conditions.

Activities related to data and information gathering include only monitoring and inventory types. They should also include the generation of new information on policies and practices and their impacts on the environment and the well-being of local populations.

Design of the Chapter as an Organizing Framework

The document is quite general. It includes a general description of programs, objectives, activities, and means of implementation. It lacks goals (targets to be achieved over time), and needs better organization (maybe subprograms according to ecosystems or ecoregions or main themes).

RESEARCH REQUIREMENTS, CAPACITY BUILDING ETC.

EXPLICIT PROPOSALS IN THE CHAPTER

Research:
- Surveys of different forms of soils, forest, water use, crop, plant and animal resources of mountain ecosystems;
- Research on land/water management in relation to technologies and agricultural practices in mountain ecosystems;
- Establishment of meteorological, hydrological, and physical monitoring analysis in mountain regions;
- Building inventories of forms of soils, forests, water use, crop, plant and animal genetic resources; and,
- Identification of hazardous areas more vulnerable to disasters.

Capacity building:
- Launching training programs in environmentally appropriate technologies;
- Support for higher education for environmental studies;
- Strengthening of the role of international research and training institutes in applied research relevant to watershed development;

- Strengthening of existing institutes or establish new ones to generate a multidisciplinary land/water ecological knowledge on mountain ecosystems; and,
- Promotion of networking.

IMPLICIT PROPOSALS DERIVED FROM THE CHAPTER

Research:
- Existence of appropriate agricultural technologies and practices;
- Existence of appropriate environmental and economic policies.
  Under most conditions in most developing countries, research is needed to bring about an appropriate combination of policies and technologies that contribute to economic sustainability and stability, equity, and the preservation of the environment.

Capacity building:
- Existence of appropriate methodologies for holistic, complex research;
- Awareness and readiness of researchers in developing countries to undertake holistic research; and,
- Institutional capacity and stability to undertake long-term research and development.
  Since all the above are not always available in many developing countries, it would be necessary to work with selected groups of institutions that could play catalytic/role models and promote more efforts through networking.

GAPS AND ALTERNATIVE APPROACHES

- A more holistic perspective for research.
- Better linkages between research and development efforts.
- Increased capacity for the application of policies and technologies that contribute to preserve/enhance the environment through specific research studies. Need to base development on research results.
- Build environmental concerns into on-going research, training and development efforts, including both existing institutions and networks.
- Better focussed programs based on specific mountain/ecoregions.
- Develop specific cases on those ecoregions.

NICHES FOR IDRC

GENERAL

Opportunities that Fit Normal Programming
- **Support specific research projects on selected mountain ecosystems following a systems approach.** This would require multidisciplinary, holistic and participatory efforts that address sustainability from the bio-physical and socio-economic points of view. These projects could include diagnosis, identification of needs and aspirations of the population, evaluation of actual practices on the environment, evaluation of alternative practices, impact of present policies, formulation of alternative policies, in situ conservation of biodiversity, production to utilization research linked to impact on the environment.
- **Networking of institutions in developed and developing countries.** This would need building environmental concerns and understanding, holistic perspectives and policy studies into existing networks.

New Opportunities
- **Influencing specific regional and global research agendas** to promote sustainable development;

- **Promoting regional and global collaboration** for the sustainable development of mountain ecoregions;
- **Supporting and promoting innovative approaches in holistic research**: specific case studies in selected ecoregional systems (expanded, more macro view of farming systems by studying interactions of farms in a watershed or region, their relation to externalities, and impact on the environment);
- **Supporting research on linkages/impact of practices across ecosystems** or watersheds;
- **Supporting research on alternative sources of income/employment** for people living in mountain areas, *interalia*: ecotourism, aquaculture, agroindustries, handicrafts, promotion of more intensive systems in better endowed areas;
- **Supporting studies to learn from development** projects, and provide feedback to other R & D initiatives;
- **Supporting environmental impact studies** for development projects; and,
- **Linking policy and technology research.**

REGIONAL SPECIFICITY

- There is a relatively greater institutional and human resource capacity for holistic research on mountain ecosystems in Latin America and Asia than in Africa.
- Although similar ecologies results and experiences could be extrapolated from the bio-physical perspective, their application would have to be evaluated from the socio-economic perspective, including of cultural differences. For example, mountain eco-regions in Latin America and Asia are of higher altitude and are more fragile given the increased pressure for their exploitation.
- The relative differences in maturity of political institutions across regions need to be considered when formulating policies and regulations.

KEY PARTNERS/OTHER ACTORS

Canada
- Forestry and highlands: Laval, Lakehead, York, University of Toronto.
- Semi-arid lands, soils and pastures: McGill, UBC, Saskatchewan, Alberta.
- Common property, tenure, indigenous minorities: Simon Fraser, York, St Mary's, Manitoba, Queens.
- Food processing: Manitoba.
- Agricultural systems: Guelph, Manitoba.

Other Countries
- Asia: ICIMOD, IRRI, IBSRAM
- Latin America: CIP, CATIE, CIAT
    - Peru: FUNDEAGRO, IEP, Bartolome de las Casas, GRADE
    - Bolivia: IBTA, CEBIAE, ILDIS
    - Colombia: U. de los Andes, FEDESARROLLO
    - Ecuador: FUNDAGRO, INSOTEC, CAAP
- Africa: ILCA, CIMMYT, ICRAF

RECOMMENDATIONS

WHICH NICHES ARE BEST FOR IDRC PROGRAM?

- Influencing specific regional and global research agenda to promote sustainable development. To do this, and maintain credibility the Centre should:
    - Show specific/concrete results produced from Centre-supported efforts in the short, medium and long-term; and,
    - Demonstrate the capacity for generation of collaborative efforts (networking at different levels: globally, regionally, and locally), and their usefulness.
- Supporting projects in concrete cases in selected mountain ecoregions. Work should be built from on-going efforts in Latin America and Asia, due to the already generated institutional and research capacity, the needs, contacts and probability of impact. Some of those projects will need to be highly integrated/larger ones to understand the whole-complexity and evaluate a wider range of issues (bio-physical, socio-economic, political), and alternatives (policy-related, technological, services and infrastructure). Others could be smaller and address more specific concerns on topics previously mentioned (under new opportunities).

ARE ADJUSTMENTS NEEDED AT IDRC IN ORDER TO FILL THESE NICHES?

Program Organization

Given the need to concentrate resources, **more integration should be promoted among Centre Programs/Divisions, and between the global and regional initiatives**. The number of global initiatives should be reduced to concentrate resources in key cases in specific ecoregions.

Process and Project Cycle

Process could be sped-up by agreeing on the global initiatives, and the key cases and ecoregions. To develop some of the more complex projects **team work** will be needed, as well as a longer development process. **Delegation of responsibility and establishment of accountability** at the proper level will be necessary. Less turf protection and more institutional identification/team work will be necessary.

Many of the projects will need to be long-term (5 to 15 years). In those cases, specific intermediate outputs will need to be established to monitor progress. Evaluation indicators should be agreed during project development between PO's and recipients.

Structure/Staffing

Changes are not so necessary if appropriate functioning mechanisms are established that allow team work, agility, and adequate level of funding.

ARE THERE CROSS-CUTTING ISSUES THAT ARE NOT ADEQUATELY REFLECTED IN ANY OF THE ABOVE?

This Chapter is highly interrelated to several others, most notably, the ones on : Combating poverty, demographic dynamics, sustainable human settlement, land resources, sustainable agriculture, biological diversity, freshwater resources, strengthening role of major groups, indigenous people and communities, and others.

The ecosystem identity allows the integration and implementation of combined, concrete actions of the cross-cutting themes.

COMMENTARY 13

Name of Commentator: Claire Thompson

1. GENERAL COMMENTS ON THE CHAPTER

- A solid chapter with reasonable goals.
- "Participation" is a theme throughout, but seems appended; document still reads as a top-down approach (i.e. "governments...should..."), although commendable to see emphasis on cooperation between governments and regional and international organizations (from South and North).
- Little direct linkage made in the Chapter to other relevant chapters and themes ("Combatting Poverty", "Biodiversity", equity...).
- Left with impression of "damage control" - little focus on socio-economic structures feeding process of degradation (e.g. commercialization...).
- Recognizes "integrated" approach to natural resource management, but leaves interpretation open and undefined.

2. OVERALL COMMENTARY ON THE FIRST REVIEW OF THE CHAPTER

- A thorough review with good synthesis of the Chapter.
- Analysis/critique is well-developed, although a little "scattered" for reader (possibly due to structure of review format itself).
- Does not discuss "top down" bias in chapter, although IDRC's role in reaction to this is implied through mention of IDRC's activities linking government and community sectors.

3. MAJOR POINTS AGREED/DISAGREED WITH, AND REASONS

- Agree: process of generation of knowledge viewed separately from that of diffusion and application of knowledge. The physical separation of these two in the text is replicated in the substance.
- Agree: overall approach/process is not "holistic", i.e. does not integrate the bio-physical with the socio-economic. However, I would probably place even more emphasis on this critique, bringing cultural issues into play as well. How can research methodologies and applications be "holistic" if the process by which these are arrived at is not (i.e. if it is led by governments and international organizations "in consultation" with community groups)?

4. MINOR POINTS AGREED/DISAGREED WITH, AND REASONS

- None.

5. POSSIBLE ON-GOING ISSUES OR CONCERNS FOR IDRC

- How to effectively input research results from community and grassroots sector into policy-making at government, regional and international levels? How to ensure this issue reaches the agenda of those carrying out the two major objectives of this Chapter?
- Mechanisms for influencing specific regional and global research agendas to ensure a "holistic" process in developing the agendas and in approaching the research.

6. POSSIBLE IMPLICATIONS FOR IDRC

- None.

CHAPTER FOURTEEN

PROMOTING SUSTAINABLE AGRICULTURE AND RURAL DEVELOPMENT

Responsible Officer: Ronnie Vernooy

ABSTRACT

1. OVERALL CRITIQUE OF AGENDA 21 CHAPTER

- There is no statement on what sustainable agriculture or rural development is and how these two concepts relate to each other.
- Sustainable agriculture here is oriented towards increasing production on land already in use and avoiding further encroachment on marginal land. It minimizes questions of production choices (key issue: food versus export crops/commodities), and distribution choices (access to markets, access to information/technology, and prices).
- Food production is not very explicitly linked to the questions of distribution and consumption, especially between developed and developing countries.
- The twelve programs identified are not well linked or organized viz. agrarian reform and planning, diversification of farm and non-farm employment, education, and integrated pest management.

2. KEY CONCLUSIONS ARISING FROM CHAPTER

- The major objective of this program is to increase food production in a sustainable way and enhance food security.
- Priority is given to maintaining and improving the capacity of the higher potential agricultural lands, as well as to conserve and rehabilitate lower potential lands.
- For each of the twelve program areas forms of international cooperation (with the help of the FAO, World Bank, IFAD, CGIAR, and through GATT) and national action are proposed.
- Throughout the Chapter, participation of local people, villages and communities and institution/organization building receive a lot of attention.

3. RESEARCH AND/OR IMPLEMENTATION POSSIBILITIES/OPPORTUNITIES

- Basic and applied research concerning soil conservation and rehabilitation, sustainable water management, conservation and sustainable use of plant genetic and animal genetic resources, integrated pest management (all in the domain of low input sustainable agriculture).
- Policy-oriented research, from the international (FAO, World Bank) to the national (ministries) and regional levels.
- Research with a strong participatory aspect, involving farmers (men and women) and other groups related to agriculture and food production-processing, the execution of research and plans, and implementation and monitoring/evaluation.
- Research on issues of rural energy use which is closely related to sustainable agriculture.

4. ON-GOING AND/OR NEW PARTNERSHIPS FOR IDRC
- New partners: NGOs including key women's associations with a strong farmer oriented program; and/or farmers' organizations in close cooperation with research centres and universities.

5. SUGGESTED NICHES FOR IDRC
- Strengthening the internal capacities of rural people's organizations; incorporating gender issues into research, training, and planning; testing and developing (new) participatory methods; development of on-farm and off-farm income generating activities; training of key actors involved in agriculture such as entrepreneurs, women, bankers, managers and traders, in sustainable agriculture and related activities.

6. OTHER COMMENTS
- The twelve programs could be re-defined and re-organized, by taking the farm-level and improving farming systems (including distribution and consumption; management; farmers' organizations; and gender) as starting points and relate those to programs of land conservation (or soil conservation), water for sustainable food production, conservation and sustainable utilization of plant genetic resources and animal genetic resources, integrated pest management, and sustainable plant and nutrition. In addition, the program on rural energy transition should be integrated.
- The institutional context, which includes agricultural policy making (planning, implementation and evaluation) and institution building could be re-defined.
- Research, education and training is a third entry point. It will be impossible to develop sustainable agriculture without farmers who demonstrate that it is a viable alternative. Therefore, farmers (women and men) and farms as organizing/management units should be at the core of this program.

REVIEW 14

KEY CONCLUSIONS IN THE CHAPTER

WHAT IS THERE

Main Conclusions

Given the increasing demand for food (especially in developing countries where population growth is highest), the Chapter states that the major objective of this program is to increase food production in a sustainable way and enhance food security.

Priority is given to maintaining and improving the capacity of the higher potential agricultural lands. In addition, it is necessary to conserve and rehabilitate lower potential lands.

Support is needed from the rural people, national governments, the private sector and international agencies.

To realize these goals, twelve program areas are proposed as a basis for action.

Agreements Reached for International and National Action
For each of the twelve program areas, various forms of international cooperation (with the help of the FAO, World Bank, IFAD, CGIAR, and through GATT) and national action are proposed.

Throughout the Chapter, the participation of local people, women, villages and communities and institution/organization building receive a lot of attention.

Politically Significant Issues
- Developed versus developing countries:
   In the Introduction it is stated that, to realize the goals of this program, "major adjustments are needed in agricultural, environmental and macro-economic policy, at both national and international levels, in developed as well as developing countries".

   Throughout the Chapter the emphasis is put on the situation in developing countries. There are no specific comments on the situation in developed countries, nor on how the situation in the developing countries relates to the situation in developed countries.

- Focus on policy formulation; neglect of implementation:
   There is a strong emphasis on the need to develop alternative policy plans and programs, which is a good point. However, very little is said about the aspects and problems related to implementation (for example, bureaucratic structures, links between governments and NGOs, responsibilities, incentives and sanctions, monitoring and evaluation).

- Technology versus new forms of organization/management:
   Throughout the chapter there is no detailed statement on the relation between the introduction of new technologies (considered a key tool) and actual or new forms of organization/management. These questions are almost continuously separated from each other.

WHAT IS NOT THERE

- There is no statement on what sustainable agriculture/rural development is and how these two concepts relate to each other.
- Sustainable agriculture should not only be oriented towards increasing production on land already in use and avoiding further encroachment on land that is only marginally suitable for cultivation. It should also address questions of production choices (key issue: food versus export commodities), and distribution choices (access to markets, prices).

OVERALL CRITIQUE

Substantive Content
- The problem of food production should be more explicitly linked to the questions of distribution and consumption, looking at the relation between the situations in developed and developing countries.
- Related to this, there is a lack of internal logic among the twelve program areas. Agrarian reform and planning, diversification of farm and non-farm employment, education, and integrated pest management are not necessarily the **same kind of tools** to use, nor is it clear how they could or should **relate to each other**.
   This critique of course affects the strongness/weakness of the organizing framework of the chapter.

Design of the Chapter as an Organizing Framework

The issues of sustainable agriculture and rural development are very important and do merit special attention. However, the twelve are programs could be re-defined and re-organized:

- One could take the farm-level and improving farming systems (including distribution and consumption; management; farmers' organizations; and, gender) as a starting point and relate this to the programs of land conservation (maybe better: soil conservation), water for sustainable food production, conservation and sustainable utilization of plant genetic resources and animal genetic resources, integrated pest management, sustainable plant and nutrition -programs e) until j). In addition, one could integrate the program on rural energy transition (k) into this point.
- A second entry-point could then be the institutional context which includes agricultural policy making (planning, implementation and evaluation), and institution building.
- A third entry point would be research, education and training.

RESEARCH REQUIREMENTS, CAPACITY BUILDING ETC.

EXPLICIT PROPOSALS IN THE CHAPTER

- To review and reformulate if necessary national and regional (if existent) agricultural/food policies on the basis of criteria of sustainability (14.8).
- To collect national baseline information on the status of natural resources relating to food/agricultural production (14.10; 14.38; 14.47).
- Research on agro-ecological zones (14.31; 14.41).
- To establish and strengthen networks that focus on the interaction between agriculture and the environment (14.11).
- To train local economists, planners and analysts in realizing policy reviews (14.14) and elaborate plans (14.42).
- To train farmers and rural communities; and, bankers, managers, entrepreneurs and traders in rural servicing and small-scale agro-processing techniques (14.32).
- To collect data on social innovations developed by governments, local communities and NGOs for improved rural development (14.19).
- Testing participatory developments methods, training and education (14.20), concerning farm technology development and transfer (14.22; 14.50) and indigenous ecological knowledge (14.22 and 14.28).
  Note: There is no explanation of what is meant by "indigenous knowledge".
- Research on plant and animal genetic resources (14.62; 14.71); plant nutrition (14.90).
- Research on rural energy transition strategies (14.99).

IMPLICIT PROPOSALS DERIVED FROM THE CHAPTER

- None mentioned.

GAPS AND ALTERNATIVE APPROACHES

Maybe it is better to focus on sustainable agriculture. If we wish to relate sustainable agriculture explicitly to rural development (as in the title of the chapter), we need a sound conceptual framework to do this (which right now is missing). "Rural development" is such a broad concept...

Sustainable agriculture is as much a priority for so-called developing countries as it is for developed countries. This asks for a strong comparative approach that links situations and problems in both categories of countries.

It will be impossible to develop sustainable agriculture without farmers who demonstrate that it is a viable alternative. I think therefore that farmers and farms as organizing/management units should be at the core of this program.

NICHES FOR IDRC

GENERAL

Opportunities that Fit Normal Programming
There are many relevant opportunities as far as I am able to judge (given my short time at IDRC), for example, related to the fields of low-input sustainable agriculture and community management of biodiversity.

New Opportunities
Here, I will indicate opportunities that I consider important given my field experiences and knowledge. (I do not know if and to which degree IDRC is already involved in projects that focus on these issues):
- Strengthening of the internal capacities of rural people's organizations.
- Incorporate gender issues in research, training, and planning.
- Testing and developing (new) participatory methods.
- Development of on-farm and off-farm income generating activities.
- Training of key actors involved in agriculture such as entrepreneurs, bankers, managers and traders, in sustainable agriculture and related activities.

Unusual or High-Risk Opportunities
- None mentioned.

REGIONAL SPECIFICITY
- None mentioned.

KEY PARTNERS/OTHER ACTORS

Where possible, farmers' organizations/groups should be involved in research, education and planning (projects).

RECOMMENDATIONS

Sustainable agriculture should occupy a central place in the sustainable production systems program and that socio-economic, gender and cultural aspects should receive as much as attention as technical ones (technology only works if people make it work).

COMMENTARY 14

Name of Commentator: Hugo Li Pun

1. GENERAL COMMENTS ON THE CHAPTER

- Strongly agree with the suggestion that this should be a central topic for the Sustainable Production Systems program.
- Also with the general conclusions on the need to maintain and improve the capacity of the higher potential agriculture lands, and conserve and rehabilitate lower potential lands.
- The twelve programs suggested could be comprised in:
  a) Agricultural policy and planning;
  b) Sustainable farming systems;
  c) Biodiversity and sustainable use of genetic resources.
- The explicit proposals in the Chapter make sense.
- In promoting interactions between agriculture and the environment, it is better to strengthen existing networks and institutions.

2. OVERALL COMMENTARY ON THE FIRST REVIEW OF THE CHAPTER

- I agree with many of the conclusions on the Chapter.
- Sustainable agriculture is a major challenge for both developed and developing countries. The relations between the agricultural sectors of both have to be understood as policies in developed countries, and resulting outputs and exports have strong implications for developing countries.
- The approach to tackling sustainable agriculture issues has to be holistic, including understanding the bio-physical and socio-economic factors involved, and finding feasible alternatives.

3. MAJOR POINTS AGREED/DISAGREED WITH, AND REASONS

- In selecting entry points, I propose to use ecoregional approaches. This would allow the selection of representative locations where resources to study and develop sustainable agriculture and promote rural development could be concentrated.
- Based on diagnostic studies conducted at those sites, identify main constraints and propose alternatives to be tested.
- In pursuing such efforts, ensure that truly participatory approaches and methods are used to involve people in finding solutions to their own problems, ensure equitable participation and distribution of benefits among different sectors in society (women, the aged, native groups), incorporate local knowledge when feasible, involve NGOs and local governments, look for more integrated approaches (mixed systems, search for off-farm income/employment opportunities including agroindustries), and preserve the resource base, etc.

4. MINOR POINTS AGREED/DISAGREED WITH, AND REASONS

- None.

5. POSSIBLE ON-GOING ISSUES OR CONCERNS FOR IDRC

- Based on the work that the Centre has been supporting in farming systems, its experiences could be promoted and disseminated to ensure that evolving issues are taken into account.

- Work should be conducted at least at two levels of analysis: the farm and farming systems and the group of farms (watershed, ecoregion). At present most experiences supported by the Centre have been at the farm/farming system level or even at lower hierarchies (crops, animals, trees).

6. POSSIBLE IMPLICATIONS FOR IDRC

- Strong support should be provided to on-going networks to help in:
    a) The creation of awareness among national programs;
    b) The definition/fine-tuning of methodologies;
    c) The development of cases/studies;
    d) The training of researchers in more holistic approaches;
    e) Promoting stronger linkages between international centres, local programs and NGOs;
    f) Promoting stronger linkages between R & D efforts.
- New networks may need to be created following ecoregional approaches. The Centre could play a catalytic role to help the CG system in the implementation of those approaches based on its experiences on a wide range of subjects involved in sustainable agriculture, and based on its contacts and influence or reputation within the international community.

CHAPTER FIFTEEN

CONSERVATION OF BIOLOGICAL DIVERSITY

Responsible Officer: Sam Landon

ABSTRACT

1. OVERALL CRITIQUE OF AGENDA 21 CHAPTER

- Emphasizes the utility function of biodiversity; human actions are recognized as the main cause of biodiversity loss, while the most important consequence of biodiversity decline is identified as impeded human development.
- Inadequate recognition of ecological function of biodiversity and no recognition of the intrinsic value of biodiversity:
    a) Result in weakening statements about the importance of indigenous knowledge and management;
    b) Represent a missed opportunity to give wide currency to an idea which may be key to a necessary reorientation of humans' relationship with nature.
- Approach of the Chapter is fundamentally flawed as it treats "Biological diversity as a reductionist concept":
    a) This approach focuses on the ultimate objective of conserving genetic/species diversity whereas a preferable alternate approach would be to switch the ultimate objective to one of conserving/enhancing the healthy functioning of ecosystems;
    b) To achieve the goal of this alternate approach, i.e. healthy ecosystem functioning, the integration of the management of the various components of the ecosystem is necessary.

2. KEY CONCLUSIONS ARISING FROM CHAPTER

- Principle purpose of Chapter is to document general international agreement on the importance of biodiversity and to support the stronger Convention on Biological Diversity. As such, it serves its purpose, recognizing the main areas in which work is needed to improve the conservation of biological diversity, advocating a bottom-up, national approach with international support.
- Calls for "urgent and decisive action to conserve and maintain genes, species and ecosystems, with a view to sustainable management and use of biological resources.
- Calls for action at the national level with international cooperation necessary to augment national capacities and support national strategies:
    a) Integration of strategies for biodiversity conservation within all relevant sectors of national economies;
    b) Strategies to be based on country studies of biodiversity.
- Underlines the "bottom-up", participatory approach.

3. RESEARCH AND/OR IMPLEMENTATION POSSIBILITIES/OPPORTUNITIES

- Explicit proposals in the chapter call for:
    a) Country studies;
    b) Research on traditional methods and indigenous knowledge;
    c) Biotechnology generation, transfer and adaptation;

d) Promotion of cooperation in scientific and economic understanding of biodiversity;
   e) Developing measures and arrangements to implement the rights of countries of origin of genetic resources;
   f) Technical and economic/socio-economic research on biodiversity;
   g) Policy-relevant research on conservation and utilization of biodiversity;
   h) Ecological research; environmental education;
   i) Supporting information exchange/scientific networks;
   j) Human resource/capacity building; and
   k) Research on biodiversity effects of development projects.
- Implicit proposals suggest research on the conservation of domesticated species *in situ*.

4. ON-GOING AND/OR NEW PARTNERSHIPS FOR IDRC

- This Chapter is subordinate to the Convention on Biological Diversity. (Please see comments on the Convention.)

5. SUGGESTED NICHES FOR IDRC

- See point 3 above. (Please see comments on the Convention.)

6. OTHER COMMENTS

- Politically charged issue, with developing countries asking for improved access to biotechnology while the developed seek continued access to genetic resources: there are expectations about the potential of biotechnology and the potential market value for genes. This tend to negate the intrinsic worth of other species generally.
- UNCED Secretariat estimates annual average cost of implementing the activities of this Chapter to be about $3.5 billion with $1.75 billion coming from the international community on grant or concessional terms.

REVIEW 15

Brian Belcher

KEY CONCLUSIONS IN THE CHAPTER

WHAT IS THERE

Main Conclusions

Human actions (habitat destruction, over-harvesting, pollution and the introduction of weed and pest species) are recognized as the main causes of loss of biodiversity. The most important consequence of biodiversity decline is identified by the chapter as the threat of impeded human development. The Chapter calls for "urgent and decisive action to conserve and maintain genes, species and ecosystems, with a view to the sustainable management and use of biological resources." Much of the action required will be at the national level. International cooperation will be necessary, but such cooperation will largely be to augment national capacities and strategies. The principal purpose of this chapter seems to be to document general international agreement on the importance of biodiversity and to support the stronger Convention on Biological Diversity. Emphasis is on the utility function of biodiversity.

The UNCED Secretariat estimated that the average total annual cost (1993–2000) of implementing the activities of this chapter to be about $3.5 billion, including $1.75 billion from the international community on grant or concessional terms.

Agreements Reached for International and National Action

The action called for in Chapter 15 is seen mainly as the responsibility of national governments "with the cooperation of the relevant United Nations bodies and, as appropriate, intergovernmental organizations". Emphasis is placed on the need for the development and implementation of programs of action at the national level, and the integration of strategies for biodiversity conservation within all relevant sectors of national economies. These strategies are to be based on country studies ("or other methods") of biodiversity, its importance, potential, threats to, etc. *In situ* and *ex situ* conservation methods are seen as twin pillars of biodiversity conservation, but with ex situ only as a supplementary method for particular species. A series of activities is outlined, designed to promote biodiversity conservation and restoration in damaged ecosystems, private lands, areas adjacent to protected areas, etc.

Politically Significant Issues

The issue of biodiversity conservation is quite highly charged politically. The negotiations were coloured by a deep schism between developed and developing countries. The former have been pushed by their electorate to do something about biodiversity losses (e.g. rainforest destruction/elephant poaching). The developing countries have recognized the pressure on the developed countries' politicians and took a hard line, wanting payment for conservation.

The issue is complicated by elevated expectations about the potential of biotechnology and concomitant (probably unrealistic) assumptions about potential market value for genes, with the likely owners of these commodities (the developed and developing countries respectively) jealously guarding access by the other. The developing countries fought hard for commitments from the developed countries for improved access to biotechnology, as quid pro quo for continued access to genetic resources.

The document contains a liberal sprinkling of politically correct rhetoric about consulting with indigenous people, learning from traditional methods of biodiversity conservation and sustainable biological resource use, and recognizing the particular role of women.

The wording of the Chapter was changed drastically during the last negotiating session in order to underline this "bottom-up" approach.

WHAT IS NOT THERE

The chapter focuses mainly on the utility value of biodiversity; the provision of goods and services for human benefit which depend on the variety and variability of living things. There is some, though probably inadequate, recognition of the ecological function of biodiversity, and no recognition of the intrinsic value of biodiversity. This omission makes statements about the importance of indigenous knowledge and management ring hollow. More importantly, it represents a missed opportunity to give wide currency to an idea which may be key to a necessary re-orientation of man's relationship with nature.

Otherwise, as a document subordinate to and supportive of the Convention on Biological Diversity, the chapter is general in its coverage of the topic and relatively inclusive.

OVERALL CRITIQUE

Substantive Content

Chapter 15 is a general, supporting document. It effectively serves its purpose, recognizing the main areas in which work is needed to improve the conservation of biological diversity and advocating a bottom-up, national approach with international support.

Design of the Chapter as an Organizing Framework

"Biological diversity" is very much a reductionist concept. It is a product of the same kind of thinking or view that spawned reductionist science, classical economics and many of the problems that Agenda 21 seeks to address. From this perspective, the approach of the Chapter appears to be fundamentally flawed.

A viable, and perhaps preferable, alternative approach might have been to orient chapters around ecosystem sustainability, with subdivisions based on varying kinds and levels of human intervention. This would shift the focus from an ultimate objective of conserving genetic/species diversity to one of conserving/enhancing the **healthy functioning of eco-systems**.

Obviously the human economy is a major component in most eco-systems. The most logical approach to achieving the goal of healthy eco-system functioning would be the integration of the management of the various components of the eco-system. Thus, within agro-ecosystems for example, access to genetic resources, access to modern techniques for genetic modification, integrated pest management and effective policy structures, etc., would all be important components in an effective management approach. The health and resilience of tropical forest eco-systems depends on the diversity of the flora and fauna present, resource harvesting regimes, land-use practices, and so on. An organization of this kind would unify many of the concepts which, under the current organizational framework, are treated as overlapping components of separate issues. The integration urged by the Chapter would then flow naturally from the objectives.

Obviously, radical change is much more difficult to achieve than incremental, evolutionary change. The issue of biodiversity conservation has achieved a high level of public recognition, in part due to the negotiations around the Convention and this chapter. For this reason alone the treatment of biodiversity as a stand-alone issue makes sense. It is a highly complex issue, with considerable overlap with many other issues, (some of which are covered as separate chapters of Agenda 21 and as conventions). Hopefully the strong emphasis on the national approach and on the integration of biodiversity issues within the broader policy environment will be acted on.

RESEARCH REQUIREMENTS, CAPACITY BUILDING ETC.

EXPLICIT PROPOSALS IN THE CHAPTER

- 15.4(e) country studies - role for CIDA and IDRC.
- 15.4(g) research on traditional methods and indigenous knowledge.
- 15.4(h) biotechnology generation, transfer and adaptation.
- 15.4(i) promotion of cooperation in scientific and economic understanding of biodiversity.
- 15.4(j) development of measures and arrangements to implement the rights of countries of origin of genetic resources.
- Technical and economic/socio-economic research on biodiversity (15.5(c).
- Policy-relevant research on conservation and utilization of biodiversity.
- Ecological research.
- Environmental education.

- Support for information exchange/scientific networks.
- Human resource/capacity-building.
- Research on biodiversity effects of development projects.

IMPLICIT PROPOSALS DERIVED FROM THE CHAPTER

- Research on the conservation of domesticated species *in situ*.

NICHES FOR IDRC

GENERAL

This chapter is subordinate to the Convention.

CHAPTER SIXTEEN

ENVIRONMENTALLY SOUND MANAGEMENT OF BIOTECHNOLOGY

Responsible Officer: Bill Edwardson

ABSTRACT

1. OVERALL CRITIQUE OF AGENDA 21 CHAPTER

- Biotechnology and its potential impact on the environment are significant enough to deserve a chapter.
- No attempt to priorize the needs of or specific opportunities for the South regarding the application of biotechnology; all possible areas are listed, many overlap with other chapters.
- Emphasizes research and application of modern biotechnology (genetic engineering etc.), but overlooks opportunities for traditional biotechnologies.
- More useful to lead with Section E (Establishing enabling mechanisms for the development and the environmentally sound application of biotechnology) as the major organizing framework. Into this could be incorporated an activity on priorization of needs or opportunities for biotechnology in developing countries among the multiple topics listed in sections A,B,C.

2. KEY CONCLUSIONS ARISING FROM CHAPTER

- Biotechnology can contribute to all aspects of environment and development, specifically in increasing availability of food, feed and renewable raw materials, improving human health and protection of the environment.
- Funding of several billions of dollars is estimated to be required, as well as mobilization of international, national agencies, scientists, private sector, farmers, etc. in executing the extensive list of activities presented.
- The dominant role of Multinational Corporations in Biotechnology research, technology access was not included; intellectual property rights (IPR), and its significance as a limiting factor to the diffusion and access of technologies was not covered(yet included in Biodiversity chapter).
- Public acceptance of biotechnological products or applications is becoming a major factor in market success, safety and regulation.

3. RESEARCH AND/OR IMPLEMENTATION POSSIBILITIES/OPPORTUNITIES

- Product development and research for the development of enterprises based on biotechnology or biotechnology products, in both agrofood and health fields.
- Applications of biotechnology in the environmental protection area in developing countries.
- Methodology for priorization and selection of activities where impact would be achievable in the medium-term.
- Research and training on risk assessment and biosafety regulations and for support to LDC positions at international fora on biosafety procedures.
- Screening of biodiverse materials for useful, marketable characteristics and where biotechnology could be advantageously applied.

4. ON-GOING AND/OR NEW PARTNERSHIPS FOR IDRC

- Creation of new and dynamic partnerships among researchers, institutions, private companies, entrepreneurs, banks, government departments within developing countries and between North and South. This would require international and national championing and brokering for progress to occur, roles which the Centre could play in bringing together the necessary partners (including donors) to integrate all of the various components and activities for sustainable biotechnology enterprise development and environmentally sound application of its products in developing countries.
- Within Canada, collaboration with CIDA, NRC, Canadian Institute of Biotechnology, ISTC, universities, private companies, private consultants, Ag Canada, provincial government programmes.
- Abroad with development banks, multi-agency consortia and NGOs.

5. SUGGESTED NICHES FOR IDRC

- Brokering with other agencies, private sector, researchers, etc. on product development and enterprise development.
- Prioritization activities to identify specific developing country opportunities.

6. OTHER COMMENTS

- The selection among niches would depend in part on decisions made on which role the Centre decides to play in this field, and the subsequent allocation of funding and staffing.
- The Centre's Biotechnology Committee (involving staff working or interested in biotechnology at the Centre) could act as working group to develop initial opportunities for brokering.
- Centre staff resources should be augmented with 1 or 2 specialists with experience in research and applications of modern biotechnology, preferably related to environmental protection/remediation (waste treatment, pollution control, utilization of waste etc.), as well as experience with brokering, technology partnerships. These specialists could be involved as consultants/advisors assigned to the Biotechnology Group. Alternatively this experience could be tapped as part of a partnership agreement with other institutions.

REVIEW 16

KEY CONCLUSIONS IN THE CHAPTER

WHAT IS THERE

Main Conclusions
- Biotechnology can contribute to all aspects of environment and development, specifically to increasing the availability of food, feed and renewable raw materials, improving human health and protection of the environment.
- The safety of biotechnology products or processes should be assured through international agreement on principles to be applied on risk assessment and management.
- Funding of US$20 billion/year (from 1993 to 2000) is estimated to be required, as well as the mobilization of international, national agencies, scientists, private sector, and farmers, etc. in executing the extensive list of activities presented in the 5 program areas.

Agreements Reached for International and National Action
- None

Politically Significant Issues
- The dominant role of Multinational Corporations in Biotechnology research, technology access and intellectual property rights was not included, due principally to the strong lobbying of the US.
- The issue of public acceptance of biotechnological products or applications is becoming a major factor in market success, safety and regulation.

WHAT IS NOT THERE
- There is no mention of the issue of intellectual property rights (IPR) and its significance as a limiting factor to the diffusion and access of technologies, processes and products.
- The role of the multinationals in controlling the transfer of technology is not discussed.
- The high capital requirement for biotechnology research is not mentioned, yet this is a major constraint for developing countries wanting to enter this field.
- There is no distinction made between biotechnology **tools** (e.g. genetic engineering techniques) and biotechnological **processes** (the production of products using biotechnology), The latter implies all of the downstream activities related to access, application, utilization of biotechnology by farmers, industry, legislators, consumers etc. The former relates to techniques for researchers.
- Developing countries' opportunities may immediately lie with biotechnological processes, particularly those which do not rely on the need for fundamental work on DNA modification, e.g. tissue and cell culture, enzymatic processes, fermentation, selective extraction.

OVERALL CRITIQUE
Substantive Content
- A comprehensive and extensive list is provided of all the possible areas where biotechnology could be applied (e.g. agriculture, forestry, fisheries, environment, health products.) There is no attempt to prioritize needs or specific opportunities for developing countries.
- The orientation is towards research and application of modern biotechnology (genetic engineering, etc.) with less emphasis on opportunities for traditional biotechnologies.
- Some key elements are lost in the lists, e.g. the need for acceleration of technology acquisition, assessment of comparative costs and benefits of different technologies for a given purpose, training of scientists which includes management training as well as training of managers for multidisciplinary projects, and creation of public awareness of benefits and risks.

Design of the Chapter as an Organizing Framework
- Biotechnology and its potential impact on the environment are significant enough to deserve a separate chapter.
- The organization of the chapter is weak, as it lists all the possible areas where biotechnology could be applied, many of which overlap with other chapters, such as sustainable agriculture, biodiversity, deforestation, protection of human health, management of wastes, etc.
- It might have been more useful to lead with Section E (Establishing enabling mechanisms for the development and the environmentally sound application of biotechnology) as the major organizing framework. To this could be incorporated an activity on prioritization of needs or opportunities for biotechnology in developing countries among the multiple topics listed in sections A,B,C.
- Section D on biosafety is well done.

RESEARCH REQUIREMENTS, CAPACITY BUILDING, ETC.

EXPLICIT PROPOSALS IN THE CHAPTER

This chapter envisages an extremely extensive program of biotechnological research and development applied to agriculture, fisheries, forestry, human health, pollution control, industry, as well as safety and policy. In addition major requirements for training and technology transfer are presented. The total ball park budget is US$20 billion dollars per year (from 1993 to 2000), with about US$200 million per year from "the international community on grant or concessional terms." Thus the program presented would exceed all of IDRC's annual budget. Almost all of the areas presented could fit with the activities of the ENR, HS, SS, and CAI Divisions.

IMPLICIT PROPOSALS DERIVED FROM THE CHAPTER

- None mentioned.

GAPS AND ALTERNATIVE APPROACHES

Given the barriers to access and application of modern biotechnology for developing countries, the complexity of activities and the high cost of research, the environmentally sound application of biotechnology demands specific attention to creating new and dynamic partnerships among researchers, institutions, private companies, entrepreneurs, banks, government departments within developing countries and between developed and developing nations. This will require some international and national championing and brokering for progress to occur. IDRC may wish to take on this role for one or two specific opportunities. This aspect is not mentioned in the chapter.

NICHES FOR IDRC

GENERAL

Opportunities that Fit Normal Programming
- The extensive list of activities in Sections A and B could fit well with current ENR and HS Division Programs. Many of these activities relate to application of biotechnology tools to agricultural, forestry and fishery production. Given the reduced emphasis on agricultural, forestry and fishery production research at IDRC, biotechnology applications in these areas should not be considered, except as identified through particular GPIs. However product development and research for the development of enterprises based on biotechnology or biotechnology products, in both agro-food and health fields could be supported.
- Similarly, the opportunities for biotechnology applications in the environmental protection area should be seized as an area which has received relatively less attention to date and where there are major needs and opportunities in developing countries. Again these could fit with ENR and HS Programs.
- The focus should be on problems to be solved or opportunities for sustainable development rather than on aspects of the technology itself. This implies a multidisciplinary approach, something that IDRC is well placed to promote across its Divisions. In addition there is a need for prioritization and selection of activities where impact would be achievable in the medium-term, consistent with our funding levels. SS could lead these activities in collaboration with ENR, HS and CAI.

New Opportunities
- Product development and enterprise development activities mentioned above will require considerations of additional topics beyond those currently considered by IDRC, such as identification of niche markets of no interest to MNCs, rapid access and acquisition of technologies, bioprocessing and processing equipment development, enterprise structures, enterprise management and financing,

involvement of private sector, marketing development, biosafety and enabling policy environments. These considerations could be beyond the capabilities of the Centre to handle alone. As mentioned above, this will require the development of project championing and brokering capabilities, roles which the Centre could play in bringing together the necessary partners (including donors) to integrate all of the various components necessary for sustainable biotechnology enterprise development and environmentally sound application of its products in developing countries.

- Biosafety issues are extremely important for the application of biotechnology both from the point of view of the prevention of risks and in order to gain public acceptance. IDRC will need to develop guidelines for its own funded research in this area. In addition the Centre could facilitate research and development in developing countries on risk assessment and biosafety regulations and for support to LDC positions at international fora on international biosafety procedures. Again the Centre's main role here could be as broker to bring parties together.

Unusual or High-Risk Opportunities

- As developing countries have an inherent market advantage through access to a greater proportion of the world's biodiversity, a long term program could be considered to screen materials for useful and marketable characteristics and where biotechnological tools or processes could be advantageously applied. Some MNCs have already initiated this, but few if any developing countries have the funds, staff or facilities to do this. The Centre could perhaps promote collaboration among international botanic groups, universities, IBPGR, etc. to move beyond taxonomy to include economic and environmental aspects and so perhaps kick-start some new development opportunities in developing countries. This could be an activity for ISS, ENR, HS and CAI.

- The financing of new enterprises in developing countries, particularly high risk ones, such as those applying biotechnology, will likely be problematical. The Centre could experiment with other donors or indeed banks and international venture capital agencies in consortia or in collaboration with consortia to be set up in developing countries in order to establish enterprises and market their products. There is already some discussion being initiated in Canada on this. The Centre's role again could be to broker or support the development of brokers who could facilitate such activities and to document the experience and impact.

REGIONAL SPECIFICITY
- None specified.

KEY PARTNERS/OTHER ACTORS
Canada
CIDA, NRC, Canadian Institute of Biotechnology, ISTC, universities, private companies, private consultants, Agriculture Canada, provincial government programs.

Other Countries
- None indicated.

RECOMMENDATIONS

WHICH NICHES ARE BEST FOR IDRC PROGRAM?
The selection among niches would depend in part on decisions made on which role the Centre decides to play in this field, and the subsequent allocation of funding and staffing. Activities above, with prioritization activities could be accommodated within existing programs. These would not necessarily lead

to a leadership or brokering role for the Centre, which would be needed for niches described above. Such a role could be taken by the Centre at this time for product development, enterprise development and financing activities mentioned above; many developing countries are exploring how to get biotechnology applications going and several donors, development agencies as well as the private sector in developed countries are looking for opportunities to link together to make things happen and to take advantage of each individual entities particular capabilities.

ARE ADJUSTMENTS NEEDED AT IDRC IN ORDER TO FILL THESE NICHES?

Program Organization

It could be useful to utilize the Centre's Biotechnology Committee, which incorporates the staff working or interested in biotechnology at the Centre, as a working group to develop initial opportunities for brokering (Centre-wide GPI?). An operational budget should be assigned, part of which could be employed to hire in expertise or contract out services to individuals or agencies as required. This group could also coordinate all other biotechnology activities in the individual Divisions, in order to ensure consolidation of efforts across all the activities necessary to follow through to impact. The group should be assigned authority to operate an entrepreneurial and agile approach so as to be able to catalyse and foster opportunities and activities as they arise as befits a broker and project champion.

Process and Project Cycle

Brokering activities and enterprise projects may be more effectively managed on a preplanned phasing cycle, where the activity and its projected budget over a number of phases is agreed to in advance, but that appropriations for each phase are only committed based on results. This would maintain momentum and allow for rapid adjustment to changes as they happen.

Structure/Staffing

Centre staff resources should be augmented with 1 or 2 specialists with experience in research and applications of modern biotechnology, preferably related to environmental protection, waste treatment, pollution control, utilization of waste, etc.), as well as experience with brokering technology partnerships. These specialists could be involved as consultants/advisors assigned to the Biotechnology Group. Alternatively this experience could be tapped as part of a partnership agreement with other institutions.

As mentioned earlier above, a Centre-wide team approach may be more effective than individual Divisional activities.

ARE THERE CROSS-CUTTING ISSUES THAT ARE NOT ADEQUATELY REFLECTED IN ANY OF THE ABOVE?

- Training at all levels (technical, research and project management, extension etc.) is mentioned as an essential activity throughout the chapter, but is not presented as an area for IDRC focus, due to the high cost and numbers involved. The Centre may wish to negotiate with other donors to ensure that appropriate human resource development activities are provided, in order that to permit sustainable implementation of Centre-funded project results and recommendations.

- The involvement of beneficiaries and the public in providing input on project design and progress, as well as concerns about safety and impact have not been adequately covered.

CHAPTER SEVENTEEN

OCEANS AND THEIR LIVING RESOURCES

Responsible Officer: T. Carroll-Foster

ABSTRACT

1. OVERALL CRITIQUE OF AGENDA 21 CHAPTER

- Provides good summary of key points, but also is a very general document, which needs more specific definition.
- In some instances, places priorities on environmental protection first and sustainable development second, which may not be in accordance with Third World states' priorities.
- Paper is quite global in concept. More regional specificity would be useful.
- Acknowledges that new approaches are needed but does not provide concrete details on to achieve these.

2. KEY CONCLUSIONS ARISING FROM CHAPTER

- Recognizes that the marine environment is a critical element of global life and is under considerable pressure. It offers a positive asset for sustainable development.
- Some proposed program areas will require new approaches to management and development.
- A more integrated approach to the oceans and their resources, more and better planning, and broadly-based participation to achieve consensus on approaches and priorities are needed.
- High level policy planning and coordination, plus national guidelines for integrated coastal zone management are needed.

3. RESEARCH AND/OR IMPLEMENTATION POSSIBILITIES/OPPORTUNITIES

- The Chapter outlines 7 somewhat overlapping program areas: marine environmental protection;
- Integrated management and sustainable development of coastal areas; sustainable use/conservation of marine living resources of the high seas, and of those under national jurisdiction; addressing critical uncertainties for the management of the marine environment and climate change; strengthening international/regional cooperation and coordination; and the sustainable development of small islands.
- Environmentally safe technology development, including development of endogenous scientific and technological capabilities.
- Establishment of and support for centres of excellence in integrated coastal and marine resource management.
- Specific research on indicator development (e.g. socio-economic and environmental indicators for coastal zone management.
- Human resource development and capacity-building.

4. ON-GOING AND/OR NEW PARTNERSHIPS FOR IDRC

- DFO, provincial ministries, Canadian sustainable fisheries development group, selected Canadian universities, NGOs.
- LDC institutions and researchers, to be identified and selected.

5. SUGGESTED NICHES FOR IDRC

- Take the leadership role in the Oceans sector left open by the demise of ICOD.
- Focus on small islands' sustainable development and management.
- Some of the items noted under point 3 above, especially focused capacity-building and identification of specific approaches to integrate management.
- Integrated management and sustainable development of coastal areas.
- Sustainable use and conservation of marine living resources under national jurisdiction.
- Strengthening international and region cooperation and coordination.

6. OTHER COMMENTS

- Evidently this Chapter was one of the more contentious due to concerns of countries over the UNCLOS (Law of the Sea) which has not been signed by many countries (Canada included), and is a push for a new Law of the Sea that also covers the High Seas and their fisheries.

REVIEW 17

Brian Davy

KEY CONCLUSIONS IN THE CHAPTER

WHAT IS THERE

Main Conclusions

The marine environment is a critical element of global life and offers a positive asset for sustainable development.

The chapter is subdivided into 7 often overlapping program areas requiring new approaches to marine and coastal area development. These are as follows:

- Integrated management and sustainable development of coastal areas, including exclusive economic zones;
- Marine environmental protection;
- Sustainable use and conservation of marine living resources of the high seas;
- Sustainable use and conservation of marine living resources under national jurisdiction;
- Addressing critical uncertainties for the management of the marine environment and climate change;
- Strengthening international, including regional, cooperation and coordination;
- Sustainable development of small islands.

These areas require new approaches to management and development; however, there are few details on what approaches should be followed, except to note that current approaches are inadequate. Most of the conclusions centre on a more integrated approach, more planning and the use of broadly based participation to achieve consensus.

Agreements Reached for International and National Action

Listed below are some samples, to give some guidance for the recommendations to follow. (It would be worthwhile to verify just how strong the agreements for action are.)

- States to establish/strengthen a high level policy planning body or national coordinating body for this sector;
  States to establish national guidelines for integrated coastal zone management using existing experience, and a global conference to exchange experience to be held in 1994
- Not available
- States to assess high seas potentials and develop profiles of all stocks (target and non-target);
  States to cooperate...etc. through existing organizations and if these do not exist then set them up and all interested states should join; details on existing organizations such as International Whaling Commission, IATTC, etc., given as examples that all concerned states should join and support.
  States to convene an intergovernmental conference on straddling stocks and highly migratory fish stocks. The PrepCom for this meeting will be in St. Johns Newfoundland (likely in 1993). To date there is little interest in putting the broader sustainable fisheries development approaches on the table again at that conference, particularly those program areas which are a higher priority for LDC's.
- States should cooperate to assess and develop sustainably resources within their national zone.
  This section includes explicit statements that this section is the one where most developing countries need cooperation and financial assistance (Note: there are very few specific statements of LDC needs in the text). This section has been and should continue to be a topic of major IDRC support.

Politically Significant Issues

According to the Canadian delegation at Rio and the PrepComs, the Oceans session was one of the most contentious sessions as well as the session of most interest to Canada.

Some concerns include the position of countries on UNCLOS (UN Law of the Sea). Many countries have not signed, including Canada, but favour the direction of this Convention; others like USA are very opposed and will not sign. In Canada, as well as others, there is an increasing push for a new Law of the Sea that covers the High Seas which have no real management system in place at present. The High seas fisheries was the main Cdn area of interest at Rio but appears to have less LDC (particularly LLDC) interest.

This same section includes the contentious whaling issue but as far as I am aware this is not a serious developing country concern.

WHAT IS NOT THERE

- Nothing obvious.

OVERALL CRITIQUE

Good summary of key points; parallels many of the conclusions already covered under AQUA GPI. The main problem is that this chapter tries to cover the waterfront completely and therefore ends up being very general. As noted above, there are few specifics on what new approaches are needed.

Substantive Content
Coverage very general and needs more specific definition; this could be an important role for IDRC to work with LDC's to obtain such information. Our experience with networks and workshops puts IDRC in an advantageous position to pursue this aspect.

Design of the Chapter as an Organizing Framework
The program areas listed as sections of this Chapter are reasonable despite the fact that they overlap. The problem is the difficulty in obtaining the cross-cutting themes.

Some of the priorities seem to favour environmental protection first and sustainable development later. Not all developing states would agree with this. These priorities need verification with LDC and especially LLDC states as their urgent priorities may be more development-related.

RESEARCH REQUIREMENTS, CAPACITY BUILDING ETC.

EXPLICIT PROPOSALS IN THE CHAPTER
- Integrated management and sustainable development of coastal and marine areas including EEZs
- Environmentally safe technology development with development of endogenous scientific and technological capabilities.
- Support for "centres of excellence" in integrated coastal and marine resource management.
- Specific research on indicator development (e.g. socio-economic and environmental indicators for coastal zone management)
- Human resource development and capacity-building are critical needs with inputs required at all levels and via national and international inputs. Unfortunately, the suggested capacity-building seems too broad to allow donor focus. IDRC should continue to advocate linkage of training to research support as in the past.

IMPLICIT PROPOSALS DERIVED FROM THE CHAPTER
IDRC should develop a series of criteria on what its overall priorities for Agenda 21 support will be.

GAPS AND ALTERNATIVE APPROACHES
- None mentioned.

NICHES FOR IDRC

GENERAL

Opportunities that Fit Normal Programming
Most IDRC research support should focus on sections a), d), and f). These three chapters are the areas of major LDC need and IDRC already has established projects, programs and networks in these sections. The main constraint is the limited resources available.

Research on new technology and methods to achieve the integrated broadly based approach within the above are opportunities to be pursued.

New Opportunities
Section (b) on marine environmental protection is important but should not be a focal point unless significant new resources are available to IDRC.

Section (g) on sustainable development of small islands may be a new niche approach for IDRC for significant impact.

Unusual or High-Risk Opportunities
Not much of a role for IDRC in section c) on the high seas unless the focus is on topics where Canada has a major concern, some of which are shared with developing countries. If this were the case, there is a significant opportunity for research to develop a new Law of All the Seas, not just one for the 200 mile zone around each country.

Section (e) on climate change is also a possible topic for IDRC but given likely available resources, support is not a high priority.

REGIONAL SPECIFICITY
Most of the Chapter is global in concept. The next stages will involve more regional specificity. In terms of IDRC regions, ASRO and SARO already have expressed interest and selected specific aquatic ecosystems in various stages of definition and development as IDRC research foci. This process should be reviewed and broadened under the suggested eco-regional approach.

KEY PARTNERS/OTHER ACTORS
Canada
Canada has considerable interest (much of the present interest in Canada is on the high seas fishery "the cod wars off the Maritimes") and capability in this sector (Department of Fisheries and Oceans, Provincial ministries, selected Canadian universities, and NGOs can all be tapped). IDRC has a contact group interested in this sector.

Other Countries
There is need to identify and work with selected LDC institutions and researchers to further refine their priorities and interest in follow-up to Agenda 21. As some of the issues for suggested research involve items of political sensitivity, priority countries should be those with strong political will to follow and support the activities of Agenda 21. This activity will require sustained local support over at least the next 10 years to achieve any real impacts. Measurable outputs can be obtained in the short term if partners are chosen well most are identified already). New resources will be the key to significant impact, and the need for more time.

There is an opportunity now to push for a greater awareness of Agenda 21 among other donors interested in this sector. SIFR offers an excellent mode of action to do this.

RECOMMENDATIONS

WHICH NICHES ARE BEST FOR IDRC PROGRAM?
- See views on IDRC niche above.

ARE ADJUSTMENTS NEEDED AT IDRC IN ORDER TO FILL THESE NICHES?
Program Organization
The 2 chapters on aquatic resources (chapters 17 & 18) are admittedly rough outlines but their size, scope of coverage (2 of 40 chapters) and need for concerted action suggest that IDRC should allocate more resources to these topics.

With the apparent dismantling of ICOD (by shifting this Centre to CIDA), IDRC should seize the new opportunity offered by Agenda 21 to take a stronger leadership role in the Oceans sector. The small islands focal point mentioned above, is one possible entry point that ICOD had focussed on to some extent. This could be expanded to include an increase in support for integrated management and sustainable development of coastal areas and the living resources within these areas.

Process and Project Cycle
Canada has been working to develop a stronger Canadian position on this topic. Obviously timing of IDRC efforts following Rio and Agenda 21 could be crucial to tap the strong Canadian interest in this topic. IDRC, hopefully, will pursue the Oceans issue to follow up on the vacuum left by the dismantling of ICOD.

Structure/Staffing
The small islands focal point would require increases in staff and funding to pursue the outline that is given here.

ARE THERE CROSS-CUTTING ISSUES THAT ARE NOT ADEQUATELY REFLECTED IN ANY OF THE ABOVE?

Community development, environmental pollution, and institutional development approaches need to be better defined and inserted into the action text that follows. *(In fact, an overall matrix for all the Agenda 21 chapters to reflect the cross-cutting nature of most of the issues would be desirable.

As discussed in the GPI preparations, the next steps require focussing, more focussing and more focussing. It is necessary to develop criteria across all the Agenda 21 topics that will guide our approach to this topic. Some initial suggestions are:
- Assessment of national support/action for parts or all of the Agenda 21 document;
- Assessment of other donor interest and priorities;
- Definition of IDRC priorities (focus on applied research; capacity-building only where linked to this research support; support primarily to national programs rather than UN or other international bodies; the merits of an eco-regional subdivision as a way to achieve a critical mass of support in certain focal points?)

COMMENTARY 17

Name of Commentator: Andrew McNaughton

1. **GENERAL COMMENTS ON THE CHAPTER**
   - I agree with the reviewer that the Chapter covers "most of the waterfront". IDRC focus will be determined by existing programs, effective demands of recipient institutions, subregional (country) priorities, and eco-regional or other thematic criteria (e.g. community-based resource management) and interaction of "global" and "regional" priority setting.

2. **OVERALL COMMENTARY ON THE FIRST REVIEW OF THE CHAPTER**
   - None.

3. MAJOR POINTS AGREED/DISAGREED WITH, AND REASONS

- Agree with the focus on a) Coastal Zones, d) Resources Under National Jurisdiction, and f) International Cooperation. IDRC has momentum and good connections including Asian, Latin American and Canadian. Sections a and d mostly overlap. For g) Small Island States, suggest limiting to Caribbean only (i.e. not South Pacific or Indian Ocean) plus inter-regional linkage to Asian archipelagic states' programs (Indonesia, Philippines). Need for strong inter-donor communication on all of these, e.g. SIFR and other fora.
- Agree about maintaining linkage of capacity-building with applied research support, but draw in other donors (especially CIDA and Development Banks) for training programs. Support national HRD and institutional needs assessment activity in research and planning.
- Agree that the LDC priority re. conservation vs development requires attention, in context of other cross-cutting North–South issues, e.g. aid-trade.

4. MINOR POINTS AGREED/DISAGREED WITH, AND REASONS

- None.

5. POSSIBLE ON-GOING ISSUES OR CONCERNS FOR IDRC

- Suggest IDRC explore state of play and possible IDRC niche re. Global Conference on Coastal Zone Mgmt.
- Resource economics as a basis for policy decisions is necessary but generally weak everywhere including aquatic resource sector. It needs a long-term sustained HRD program.

6. POSSIBLE IMPLICATIONS FOR IDRC

- None.

CHAPTER EIGHTEEN

FRESHWATER RESOURCES

Responsible Officer: T. Carroll-Foster

ABSTRACT 18

1. OVERALL CRITIQUE OF AGENDA 21 CHAPTER

- Substance is limited. Lacks adequate detail, especially quantitative, on the significance of the problem.
- Fails to discuss the extent to which water resources development contributes to economic productivity and social well-being.
- Fails to discuss the fact that freshwater is likely to be a key future development constraint.
- Overall poorly organized, with little new information, much overlapping, lack of connection with Chapter 17 (Oceans) and cross-referencing with other chapters, and many simplistic approaches. A new framework is needed.

2. KEY CONCLUSIONS ARISING FROM CHAPTER

- The subject matter and the Chapter are very important and merit serious IDRC and other donors' inputs.
- Water may be the most critical element for sustainable development. Water demands are increasing rapidly — 70–80% for irrigation, 20% for industry, but only 6% for domestic consumption (and basic needs).
- In-depth, well-defined research is needed in various areas, and much greater and better community involvement in water use issues is critical. This would entail including education and awareness-raising about conservation. Also the development of suitable economic instruments in terms of integrated water resources development and management.
- Suggested research generally too heavy on water modelling and upstream research regarding water resources assessment.
- 3 concurrent objectives regarding the protection of water resources, water quality, and aquatic resources need to be pursued — maintenance of ecosystem integrity, public health protection and human resources development.
- Although Chapter states that by year 2000 all states should achieve targets of 40 litres of water per urban resident and 75% on-site sanitation facilities and solid waste disposal, the lack of details necessitate more in-depth analysis, research and low-cost technologies development and implementation.
- There is a need to relate the high priority given to food security by most states to the need for greater priority being given water for sustainable food production and rural development (presently quite a low priority) — a contradiction.
- Overall there seems to be an acceptance that water resources management should be carried out at the catchment basin or sub-basin level.

3. RESEARCH AND/OR IMPLEMENTATION POSSIBILITIES/OPPORTUNITIES

- Research on many different aspects of integrated water resources development and management, including community involvement on water use issues; also water resources assessment, with less emphasis on water modelling and upstream research.
- Protection of water resources, water quality and aquatic life (see: Mar del Plata Action Plan), which integrates ecosystem integrity, public health protection, and human resources development.
- Continuation of research into drinking water supply, sanitation, and solid waste disposal, including low cost technologies for rural and urban sustainable development.
- Water for sustainable food production and rural development research would include rain-fed and irrigated agriculture, livestock water supply, inland fisheries/aquaculture, agro-forestry, water-related adaptive research, etc.
- Research on the impacts of climate change on water resources.

4. ON-GOING AND/OR NEW PARTNERSHIPS FOR IDRC

- See Chapter 17 Review.

5. SUGGESTED NICHES FOR IDRC

- Most of those items noted under 3. above with the exception of the last — impacts of climate change, which would entail extensive research related to IPCC, IGBP and similar programs.
- Specifically: research at catchment-basin or sub-basin levels would tie into ENR's eco-regional approach; research on interactive databases, forecasting methods and economic planning models for water resource management; technological research on new/alternative sources of water supply; development of global hydrologic models; cooperative research, including on complex aquatic systems; identification of critical areas, capacity-building needs and models, and technology transfer; and continuation and dissemination of research on low cost water supply and sanitation for low income/high density urban settlements.

6. OTHER COMMENTS

- None.

REVIEW 18

KEY CONCLUSIONS IN THE CHAPTER

WHAT IS THERE

Main Conclusions

Seven (7) program areas listed:

- **Integrated Water Resources Development and Management**
  Water may be the most critical element for sustainable development. Water demands are increasing rapidly with 70–80% needed for irrigation, 20% for industry and only 6% for domestic consumption (no LDC breakdown given or future time frame for these % are given). The approach suggested is first priority should go to meeting basic human needs and the safeguarding of ecosystems; beyond this water users should be charged appropriately. General targets for the year 2000 and 2025 for costed national action programmes are given under the listed program areas.

Research is needed on a variety of topics; only the general ideas are indicated as the specific details need definition. Community involvement on water use issues are critical. The concept of pushing action to the lowest possible level of organization needs to be better implemented (a possible IDRC entry point). This approach should include education and awareness raising on issues such as conservation. Development of suitable economic instruments is a key need in much of this work.

- **Water Resources Assessment**
  Most of the suggested research seems too heavy on water modelling and other more upstream research.

- **Protection of Water Resources, Water Quality and Aquatic Resources**
  See Mar del Plata Action Plan for information on the consequences of various users of water on the environment.

  3 concurrent objectives will have to be pursued: maintenance of ecosystem integrity, public health protection and human resources development. (A long list of activities is given but few specific research details).

- **Drinking Water Supply and Sanitation**
  Few research details given.

- **Water and Sustainable Urban Development**
  By the year 2000 all states to achieve the targets of: at least 40 litres of water per urban resident and 75% to have on-site or community facilities for sanitation, establish discharge standards and 75% solid waste disposal in an environmentally safe way(?? no details given).

  Continuation of previous research on low cost technologies needed.

- **Water for Sustainable Food Production and Rural Development**
  This topic does not have the priority that it deserves given the % users of water resources given above and the high priority accorded to the achievement of food security by most countries.

  Research related to rain-fed and irrigated agriculture including livestock water supply, inland fisheries/aquaculture, and agro-forestry are indicated. Specific items include research on critical areas for water related adaptive research; capacity strengthening, and technology transfer as part of an integrated sustainable approach is indicated.

- **Impacts of Climate Change on Water Resources**
  Extensive research is needed related to IPCC, and IGBP and similar programs; however, I would not recommend this as an IDRC niche.

In all sections, there seems to have been acceptance that water resources management should be carried out at the level of the catchment basin or sub-basin. This should be noted for IDRC as it argues that IDRC follow a similar approach and identify selected catchment basins for focal points for support. This would tie in nicely with the suggested ENR eco-regional approach as well.

Agreements Reached for International and National Action
None specifically but many items that "states could do"; no specific section on International and regional cooperation and coordination as in Chapter 17.

Politically Significant Issues

Transboundary water resources (e.g. lakes and rivers shared by riparian states) are important (and will be increasingly so in the future) in many regions, e.g. Africa. Many donors and international agencies have avoided work on this topic because of the political nature (i.e. need for sharing and joint management of these resources). It is likely that with the increasing need for water, these resources will become areas of increasing conflict....some already are flash points leading to threats of military action. Integrated management measures related to balancing need and historical ownership issues with a future sustainable transboundary development plan are needed.

WHAT IS NOT THERE

As noted above the section on water for sustainable food production and rural development should be a higher priority for support.

OVERALL CRITIQUE

Substantive Content

The substance is limited. More detail, preferably quantitative, on how significant is the problem would help this Chapter. One issue noted but not followed up on is the extent to which water resources development contributes to economic productivity and social well being. This issue needs further research to make its case more forcibly particularly when arguing for more resources to attack this problem. The present case is built more on generalities and emotion then on clear facts. Freshwater is likely one of the key future development constraints but the case here is not clearly and logically presented.

Design of the Chapter as an Organizing Framework

This chapter is very important and merits serious IDRC and other donor input. However, the chapter sections seem to be poorly organized with a great deal of overlap, little new information, and an abundance of simplistic approaches that seem to be based more on the need to fill in the section headings than to develop a suitable operational framework. More effort is needed to develop a new framework and an IDRC niche in combination with other interested donors.

RESEARCH REQUIREMENTS, CAPACITY BUILDING ETC.

EXPLICIT PROPOSALS IN THE CHAPTER

- Research on interactive databases, forecasting methods and economic planning models for water resource management are needed. Technological research on new or alternative sources of water supply are also suggested.
- Development of global hydrologic models is needed.
- Cooperative research is suggested but no details; research on complex aquatic systems.
- Research on low cost technology.
- Continuation of research on low cost water supply and sanitation for low income and high density urban settlements.
- Identification of critical areas, capacity building and technology transfer.
- Extensive research related to existing international programs.

IMPLICIT PROPOSALS DERIVED FROM THE CHAPTER

- None mentioned.

NICHES FOR IDRC

GENERAL

Opportunities that Fit Normal Programming
This is important topic needs integrated approaches. This is a niche that IDRC could fill as well as if not better than most donors.

New Opportunities
As noted above research on transboundary water resources is one item that should be considered for IDRC support.

Unusual or High-Risk Opportunities
- Not apparent.

REGIONAL SPECIFICITY

Difficult to assess now until more specific details established above.

KEY PARTNERS/OTHER ACTORS

Canada
Canada has considerable expertise in this area. The AQUA GPI draft outline lists a number of possible collaborating institutions. See Chapter 17 comments.

Other Countries
(See comments on Chapter 17.) IDRC has a number of good mechanisms in place to pursue this topic.

RECOMMENDATIONS

WHICH NICHES ARE BEST FOR IDRC PROGRAM?
- As indicated above.

ARE ADJUSTMENTS NEEDED AT IDRC IN ORDER TO FILL THESE NICHES?

Program Organization
IDRC could play a key role in integrated water resources management.

Involvement in the transboundary water resource issue would be more effective if more resources (funding and staff) were available. Otherwise we run the serious risk of not putting a critical mass into any one topic to achieve the desired impact.

Process and Project Cycle
- None.

Structure/Staffing
- See above.

ARE THERE CROSS-CUTTING ISSUES THAT ARE NOT ADEQUATELY REFLECTED IN ANY OF THE ABOVE?

There are a variety cross-cutting issues related to environmental concerns (resource accounting and other evaluative mechanisms for watersheds, EIA etc), forestry and other land use activities in watersheds, disease transmission throe water borne vectors, etc. Also information systems support, mainly in terms of interactive databases, is required (see Chapter 40). Follow-up is needed to define cross-cutting views and to integrate them into the next steps.

Linkages with Chapter 17 on the Oceans need to be explored more in terms of IDRC programming. Some are noted in this Chapter, e.g. related to urban water needs/supply in areas of high population concentration which are most often coastal areas. Other obvious links are the connections via the hydrological cycle, global climate change, and atmospheric pollution.

Research on Research

Since most of the Agenda 21 approach requires integration and coordination mechanisms as the first priority, IDRC should explore different means to carry this out at the various levels requiring action. Specific multidisciplinary "on the ground" applied research programs may be the best way to achieve this. Successful "hands on" research projects will be the most effective promotional mechanism for this concept.

In addition to the specific research points noted above, IDRC should consider research on the role of research in Agenda 21, identification of gaps in the present agenda, new approaches to achieving sustainable development, and other more general issues related to creating the best enabling environment for action on Agenda 21. For instance, in terms of the role of research, some problems do not require new technology or research for their solution, but rather funds and political will.

Targets

The other general issue relates to setting of specific targets. This is needed to accelerate change and IDRC should think carefully how to encourage this in conjunction with national institutions and other donors.

COMMENTARY 18

Name of Commentator: J. Hea

1. GENERAL COMMENTS ON THE CHAPTER

- A long chapter consisting of a non-exhaustive description of freshwater topics and without sufficient reference to related issues in other chapters. I agree with the reviewer that a new framework is needed to better address the environmental challenges posed under freshwater resources.

2. OVERALL COMMENTARY ON THE FIRST REVIEW OF THE CHAPTER

- I agree with the reviewer that freshwater resources are a vital concern to IDRC and international donors. Areas of concern cover the spectrum from drinking water, public health, food security to the preservation of wetlands. Because of this importance, the Chapter should be more focused and some measure of quantitative analysis should be provided.

3. MAJOR POINTS AGREED/DISAGREED WITH, AND REASONS

- I agree with the overall assessment and identification of gaps by the reviewer.

4. MINOR POINTS AGREED/DISAGREED WITH, AND REASONS

- The reviewer is perhaps too critical of the Chapter, which could be reorganized into a clearer set of themes and description of methods. Because of the scope of the subject, it should be made clear that descriptions are illustrative only as points of departure to UNCED's objectives.

5. POSSIBLE ON-GOING ISSUES OR CONCERNS FOR IDRC

- Freshwater resource projects can be very large scale and likely will require partnerships.

6. POSSIBLE IMPLICATIONS FOR IDRC

- Many of the topics in the Chapter fall under the AQUA GPI while others are more multidisciplinary both within and between IDRC divisions. The importance to global climate change activities should be assessed.

CHAPTER NINETEEN

ENVIRONMENTALLY SOUND MANAGEMENT OF TOXIC CHEMICALS

Responsible Officer: Pierre Zaya

ABSTRACT

1. OVERALL CRITIQUE OF AGENDA 21 CHAPTER

- Very short-sighted approach; mentions only casually the crucial issues. Based on the usual assumptions:
  a) The North knows best, and it will teach the others to be just as good;
  b) Large chemical companies are making a mess but it is necessary, so let's all try to live with the consequences without asking questions ("environmentally sound management of chemicals").
- A large part of the Chapter only promotes the continuation of the work of existing committees of international institutions.
- No provisions are made for helping LDCs to define what are their problems in relation to toxic chemicals, and to make cost/benefit analysis of the various alternatives.

2. KEY CONCLUSIONS ARISING FROM CHAPTER

- A considerable number of international bodies are already involved in work on chemical safety: they have formed the International Program on Chemical Safety (IPCS). Its efforts should be strengthened, in collaboration with the FAO, the OECD, the European Community, etc.
- Six programs are proposed; the program called "Strengthening of national capabilities and capacities for management of chemicals" represents more than 92% of the budget estimate for the Chapter.

3. RESEARCH AND/OR IMPLEMENTATION POSSIBILITIES/OPPORTUNITIES

- Research and data gathering for assessment of chemical risks, including review of previously accepted pesticides.
- Networking between different international and national institutions to exchange information on chemicals and to reach consensus on:
  a) Harmonization of classification and labelling of chemicals (especially pesticides);
  b) Monitor and assess the illegal traffic in toxic and dangerous products and its environmental, economic and health implications.
- Capacity building and training for:
  a) Evaluation of hazards and related information exchange on toxic chemicals;
  b) Developing and strengthening risk assessment capabilities at national and international level.
- Establishment of related government policies, regulatory and non-regulatory measures.

4. ON-GOING AND/OR NEW PARTNERSHIPS FOR IDRC

- If the Centre undertakes activities related to this Chapter, Environment Canada should be involved, as well as Universities researchers with expertise in the field and specialized Centres such as the Canadian Centre for Occupational Health and Safety (Hamilton).

- The Chapter also envisages the participation of most developed countries into this activity, as well as international organizations (UNEP, ILO, WHO, FAO, OECD, EC).

5. SUGGESTED NICHES FOR IDRC
- Practically all the activities included in this Chapter could fit in the existing structure of IDRC. Indeed, some activities, such as the work on Pesticide Regulation in LDCs (Keystone Dialogue) could constitute an interesting addition to the activities indicated.

6. OTHER COMMENTS
- There does not seem to be a niche *specifically* for the Centre in tackling the problems of toxic chemicals. It is in itself a problem of the North, which is already studied by numerous other international organizations and committees.
- The related problems of the LDCs should be addressed more generally in another context, together with (inter alia) Chapters 8 (Environment and Decision Making), 20 (Hazardous Wastes), 21 (Solid Wastes and Sewage) and 22 (Radioactive Wastes), into a "Capacity Building in Environment" Initiative.

REVIEW 19

KEY CONCLUSIONS IN THE CHAPTER

WHAT IS THERE
Main Conclusions
- Two of the major problems are:
    - lack of sufficient scientific information for the assessment of risks.
    - lack of resources for assessment of chemicals for which data is available.
- A considerable number of international bodies are already involved in work on chemical safety: they have formed the International Programme on Chemical Safety (IPCS). Its efforts should be strengthened, in collaboration with the FAO, the OECD, the European Community, etc.
- Six programs are proposed; their relative importance can be judged by the amount (million $) attributed to each:

Expanding and accelerating international assessment of chemical risks	30
Harmonization of classification and labelling of chemicals	3
Information exchange on toxic chemicals and chemical risks	10
Establishment of risk reduction programmes	4
Strengthening of national capabilities and capacities for management of chemicals	600
Prevention of illegal traffic in toxic and dangerous products	No figure given
Enhancement of cooperation related to several programmes	No figure given

Agreements Reached for International and National Action
The "objectives" of each program probably represent a wish list rather than a formal agreement. However, the following have been noted:

- Achievement by 2000 of full participation and (possibly mandatory) implementation of the Prior Informed Consent (PIC) procedures in the **London Guidelines for the Exchange of Information on Chemicals in International Trade**, possibly through GATT.
- By the year 2000, national systems for environmentally sound management of chemicals, including legislation and provisions for implementation and enforcement, should be in place in all countries to the extent possible.

Politically Significant Issues
- The program "Strengthening of national capabilities and capacities for management of chemicals" is certainly the most "empowering", from a LDC point of view. It is also the most costly and therefore the most likely to be dropped.
- Most of the knowledge is in the North and particularly with large (mostly transnational) companies.
- When knowledge about toxic chemicals is available in LDCs, it is probably hard to find by those who would need it.
- There are profits to be made by taking advantage of the ignorance and negligence of LDC governments in the matter of banned or restricted chemicals.
- Disclosure of safety information about chemicals (right-to-know programmes) might endanger the commercial confidentiality of the chemical manufacturer.

WHAT IS NOT THERE
"Community right-to-know programs" are mentioned in a couple of places, but they are lost among the rest and certainly not emphasized.

OVERALL CRITIQUE
Substantive Content
- The approach is very short-sighted on the whole and mentions casually the crucial issues.
- It is based on the usual assumptions:
    - The North knows best, and it will teach the others to be just as good.
    - "Environmentally sound management of chemicals": large chemical companies are making a mess but it is necessary, so let's all try to minimize the consequences.
- Although it does not represent the greatest part of the estimate allocated, a great part of the chapter is dedicated to the continuation of the work of the existing committees of international institutions.
- No efforts are made to help the LDCs define what their problems are in that matter.

Design of the Chapter as an Organizing Framework
Toxic chemicals do represent a problem, but this problem can only be solved satisfactorily if it is analyzed in the context of each country. In each case, the costs and benefits must be balanced.

There is a large overlap between programs within this Chapter. I would see most of the activities described in this chapter lumped with those of Chapter 20 (Hazardous Wastes), 21 (Solid Wastes and Sewage) and 22 (Radioactive Wastes). All these are particular applications of what should be done under Chapter 8 (Environment and Decision Making).

RESEARCH REQUIREMENTS, CAPACITY BUILDING ETC.

EXPLICIT PROPOSALS IN THE CHAPTER

- Research and data gathering for assessment of chemical risks.
- Review of previously accepted pesticides whose acceptance was based on criteria now recognized as insufficient, their possible replacement.
- Networking between different international and national institutions to exchange information on chemicals and to reach consensus on:
  - Chemical risks for several hundred chemicals.
  - Harmonization of classification and labelling of chemicals (especially pesticides).
  - Interpretation of technical data.
  - Monitor and assess the illegal traffic in toxic and dangerous products and its environmental, economic and health implications.
- Capacity building and training for:
  - Evaluation of hazards and related information exchange on toxic chemicals.
  - Developing and strengthening risk assessment capabilities at national and international level.
- Establishment of government policies, regulatory and non-regulatory measures for:
  - Risk reduction based on accepted producer liability principle.
  - Product labelling.
  - Substitution of some chemicals.
  - Phasing out of some toxic chemicals.
  - Prevention of accidents, preparedness and response.
  - Reduce dependence on the use of agricultural chemicals.
  - Adoption of community right-to-know programmes.
  - Prevention of illegal import and export of toxic and dangerous products.

IMPLICIT PROPOSALS DERIVED FROM THE CHAPTER

None.

GAPS AND ALTERNATIVE APPROACHES

The problem is not really what is absent, as the lack of coherence and unity: everything is mentioned at least once. But the emphasis is certainly on the discussions at the level of the governments, and preferably, of the international organizations (UNEP, WHO, OECD, etc). Nowhere can one get the impression that the groups concerned (workers in chemical factories, peasants using pesticides) might have a say in the decisions and management of toxic chemicals.

The emphasis should be on:
- Capacity-building for developing and strengthening risk assessment capabilities at national and international level.
- Consultations with the people concerned: users and populations put at risk by the chemicals; for establishing the cost benefit analysis.

NICHES FOR IDRC

GENERAL

Opportunities that Fit Normal Programming
Practically all the activities included in this Chapter could fit in the existing structure of IDRC. Indeed, some activities, such as the work on Pesticide Regulation in LDCs (Keystone Dialogue) could constitute an interesting addition to the activities indicated.

New Opportunities
If it is decided to include this particular topic into a more general "Capacity Building in Environment" Initiative, then this could be called legitimately a new opportunity.

Unusual or High-Risk Opportunities
None.

REGIONAL SPECIFICITY
Applies to all regions.

KEY PARTNERS/OTHER ACTORS
Canada
Environment Canada should be involved in this activity. There are numerous scientists in Universities with a lot of expertise in the field, as well as specialized Centres such as the Canadian Centre for Occupational Health and Safety (Hamilton).

Other Countries
As designed, the chapter envisages the participation of most developed countries into this activity, as well as international organizations (UNEP, ILO, WHO, FAO, OECD, EC).

RECOMMENDATIONS

WHICH NICHES ARE BEST FOR IDRC PROGRAM?
There is not a niche for the Centre **specifically** in tackling the problems of toxic chemicals. Other international organizations and committees are already dealing with it.

The problem can be tackled more generally, together with (*inter alia*) Chapters 8 (Environment and Decision Making), 20 (Hazardous Wastes), 21 (Solid Wastes and Sewage) and 22 (Radioactive Wastes), into a "Capacity Building in Environment" Initiative.

ARE ADJUSTMENTS NEEDED AT IDRC IN ORDER TO FILL THESE NICHES?
No.

ARE THERE CROSS-CUTTING ISSUES THAT ARE NOT ADEQUATELY REFLECTED IN ANY OF THE ABOVE?
No.

COMMENTARY 19

Name of Commentator: Aung Gyi

1. GENERAL COMMENTS ON THE CHAPTER

- Within the framework of environmental sound management and sustainable development, Chapter 19 should have been combined with Chapter 20 on hazardous wastes and Chapter 21 on solid wastes to get the overall view of the problems and issues related to toxic chemicals and wastes.
- Chapter 19 is a typical UN document which was based on the work of the UN and other International Organizations; the problems and issues reflected mainly the North's views, and were addressed mainly to national governments and the international organizations to take the necessary actions.
- There were hardly any mention of issues related to the strengthening/empowerment of the communities, including workers, farmers to raise their awareness and capacity to handle and mitigate the toxic chemical problems.
- It also did not cover the "accountability" issue whenever there are negative impacts/consequences on human health and on the environment.

2. OVERALL COMMENTARY ON THE FIRST REVIEW OF THE CHAPTER

- One of the main conclusions was left out under "A. What is there" in the review. The reviewer did not mention specifically the lack of national capabilities and capacities for management of chemicals in the developing countries, which was one of the main conclusions of the document and for which the biggest amount of funds were requested. He touched upon this aspect later.

3. MAJOR POINTS AGREED/DISAGREED WITH, AND REASONS

- I agree with the reviewer in his general conclusion that the document was presented from the North's point of view and no efforts were made to help LDCs define what their problems and their views were in this matter. Important aspects such as "Community right-to-know programs" were mentioned briefly only in a couple of places.
- I also agree that there is no niche specifically for IDRC program to tackle the problems of toxic chemicals as such. There is however a niche for IDRC to build capacities in developing countries to manage toxic chemicals, hazardous wastes, solid wastes and sewage, but not in the area of radioactive wastes. There is IAEA; and most of the countries are also more acutely aware of the danger of this waste than other wastes and precautions were taken normally.
- IDRC could look into the capacity-building in the developing countries in two ways: institutional mechanism establishment or improvement, and empowerment of communities, workers and farmers. I agree that Canada has a lot to offer in this area: scientists in the universities with expertise, Environment Canada, and the Canadian Centre for Occupational Health and Safety.

4. MINOR POINTS AGREED/DISAGREED WITH, AND REASONS

- One minor point: I disagree that the strengthening of national capacities for management of chemicals is the most costly and therefore the most likely to be dropped. The people who drafted the document felt that this was important. There will also be pressure from the LDCs to help build up their capacities to manage chemicals and hazardous wastes through various fora. Therefore I expect that some support will be given by international organizations, UN or otherwise in capacity-building activities in the developing countries.

5. POSSIBLE ON-GOING ISSUES OR CONCERNS FOR IDRC

- The biggest issue is the difference in perception between the North and developing countries in the area of environment and sustainable development in general, and specifically in the area of toxic chemicals and hazardous wastes. IDRC could play a role in bridging the gap in the perception between the North and developing countries.
- Raising awareness, and developing skills of vulnerable communities or groups of people, and strengthening the policy/advisory capacity of government organizations and NGOs, universities, research centres will be on-going issues of IDRC.

6. POSSIBLE IMPLICATIONS FOR IDRC

- Comparatively speaking, the area of toxic chemicals (and for that matter hazardous wastes) is the component which has been less researched in the developing countries. IDRC might have difficulty in general in finding the appropriate institutions, organizations, personnel in the developing countries to do research in this area. IDRC might have to rely on the Canadian institutions to make its efforts more effective.

CHAPTER TWENTY

MANAGEMENT OF HAZARDOUS WASTES

Responsible Officer: Javier Verastegui

ABSTRACT

1. OVERALL CRITIQUE OF AGENDA 21 CHAPTER

- Given frequent political changes, the Chapter gives too much responsibility to governments and states, particularly in education and policy assessment. Only a passive role is given to local populations in developing countries.
- Activities are mostly oriented to legal and control aspects, compared to research, precautionary approaches and remediation and public awareness activities.
- Activities dealing with hazardous wastes produced by big corporations are predominant compared with those related to small-scale enterprises.
- This Chapter should have been merged with Chapter 19 (Toxic Chemicals) and Chapter 22 (Radioactive Wastes).

2. KEY CONCLUSIONS ARISING FROM CHAPTER

- In general, the activities outlined in the four program areas are well structured, including problem identification, monitoring, prevention, minimization, treatment, remediation, R&D, technology transfer, policy assessment, training and capacity building.
- Transboundary movements and international traffic of hazardous wastes are not universally banned in the Chapter, despite some countries (governments) allowing these activities (e.g. dumping of chlorinated insecticides in developing countries).

3. RESEARCH AND/OR IMPLEMENTATION POSSIBILITIES/OPPORTUNITIES

- R&D on hazardous waste management and cost-effective alternatives for productive processes in developing countries, particularly, including reduction, recycling, treatment and disposal technologies at a small-scale enterprises.
- Transfer of environmentally sound and low-waste production technologies to developing countries.
- Promotion and capacity-building development of information, training and technology assessment centres.
- Development and transfer of environmental management systems, including industry audits.
- Assessment, research and training programs for evaluation, prevention, control of health risks related to hazardous waste management.
- Development and dissemination of educational materials concerning hazardous waste management and related health and environmental risks.
- Assessment, implementation and monitoring of policies and legislation to stimulate cleaner production methods, avoid disposal, and prevent traffic of hazardous wastes, following the "polluter pays" and "cradle-to-grave" approaches.
- Assessment of governments and NGOs for developing practical guidelines for the characterization, classification, prevention, minimization, safe handling and disposal of hazardous wastes.

4. ON-GOING AND/OR NEW PARTNERSHIPS FOR IDRC

- Besides IDRC's traditional recipient/beneficiary partnerships (R&D and NGO institutions), two new partnerships are needed: government agencies and people's organizations (associations, cooperatives, etc).
- Regional organizations (like ASEAN, ECOWAS, PACTO ANDINO, etc.) should also be considered as new partnerships.
- New partnerships with United Nations agencies, in particular, WHO, UNEP and UNIDO.

5. SUGGESTED NICHES FOR IDRC

- All opportunities in 3. could be good niches for IDRC, from at a global perspective. R&D in hazardous waste management could be more important for the relatively more industrialized regions (SARO, ASRO, LARO); whereas, regulatory activities could be more important for the less developed regions (WARO, EARO).
- The best niches for IDRC could be:
    a) Assessment of policies for developing countries.
    b) Development of national/regional information centres/networks.
    c) Development of risk guidelines and self-audit manuals for the public and small-scale enterprises, respectively.
    d) Development and transfer of environmentally friendly production technologies.
- Activities/opportunities related to the strengthening of local capacities for policy implementation and control of hazardous waste traffic could be considered as unusual or high-risk opportunities, given their political implications (big corporation lobbies).

6. OTHER COMMENTS

None.

KEY CONCLUSIONS IN THE CHAPTER

WHAT IS THERE

Main Conclusions
Approach includes problem identification, monitoring, prevention, minimization, treatment, remediation, R&D, technology transfer, policy assessment, training and capacity building in the field of hazardous wastes management.

Agreements Reached for International and National Action
Basel and Bamako Conventions on the Imports and Control of Transboundary Movements of Hazardous Wastes and their Disposal (World and African countries, respectively).

Politically Significant Issues
Overall target (d) and objective B.(b) don't exclude the possibility of hazardous wastes imports to developing countries which have not banned them explicitly. IDRC's extensive work with NGOs in some of those countries could be criticized if not dealing against the imports of such wastes.

WHAT IS NOT THERE

Local populations in developing countries are not well considered as actors in the whole processus of hazardous waste management. Only a passive role is considered (20.18.c, 20.27.a.b.c), opposed to the very active role of governments and industry.

OVERALL CRITIQUE

Substantive Content

Activities in the 4 program areas give too much responsibilities to the governments and states, compared to those given to community organizations, NGOs and institutions. Particularly, educational, training and policy assessment activities should prefer broad public, technical institutions and non-governmental organizations rather than ministerial officers.

Most of the activities in the 4 Programme Areas are too related with legal and control aspects, compared to research, remediation and public mobilization activities.

Almost all of the activities are dealing with hazardous wastes produced by big corporations (20.1). Environmental problems derived from hazardous wastes produced or managed by local small and medium industries are not considered with a high emphasis.

Design of the Chapter as an Organizing Framework

This chapter should be merged with chapter 19 (Management of Toxic Chemicals) and chapter 22 (Management of Radioactive Wastes) because they are very related in nature and remediation approaches.

Also, this chapter is quite isolated from chapter 34 (Transfer of Technology). It is important to relate them because there is a growing trend to export not only wastes but also high-polluting plants and technologies from developed to developing countries.

RESEARCH REQUIREMENTS, CAPACITY BUILDING ETC.

EXPLICIT PROPOSALS IN THE CHAPTER

20.13.c, 20.19.f, 20.26.a, 20.26.c: R&D on hazardous waste management and cost-effective alternatives for processes and substances that currently result in the generation of hazardous wastes in developing countries, with particular emphasis on biotechnologies and small and medium industry (related to SED/ENRD mission).

20.13.e: Transfer of environmentally sound technologies and know-how on clean technologies and low-waste production to developing countries (related to CAID and SED/ENRD mission).

20.13.f: Research on treatment, recycling, reuse and disposal of wastes at their source when it is both economically and environmentally efficient for industry to do so.

20.13.g.h.i: Promotion of technology assessment centres, training and information centres, and environmental managements systems, including industry audits, in developing countries.

20.14.b.c.d: Establishment of national and regional information collection and dissemination clearinghouses and networks, extending and strengthening existing systems.

20.22.e: Implementation of training and research activities related to evaluation, prevention and control of health risks, and the treatment and disposal of hazardous wastes.

20.28.a: Development and dissemination of educational materials concerning hazardous wastes and their effects on environment and human health, for use of schools, by women groups and by the general public.

20.42.a.b: Assessment, implementation and monitoring of legislation to prevent the illegal import and export of hazardous wastes to developing countries.

IMPLICIT PROPOSALS DERIVED FROM THE CHAPTER

20.13.b.k: Assessment to governments on stimulating industrial innovation towards cleaner production methods, by means of economic and regulatory incentives, following the "polluter pays" principle and the cradle-to grave approach.

20.22.a: Assessment to governments in order to establish and maintain inventories of hazardous wastes and their treatment/disposal/contaminated sites, in order to assess exposure and risk to human health and the environment, and initiate remedial measures if necessary.

20.22.b.d: Assessment to governments in order to develop practical technical guidelines for the characterization, classification, prevention, minimization, safe handling and disposal of hazardous wastes, using improved health-based criteria.

GAPS AND ALTERNATIVE APPROACHES

The responsibility of most of the above mentioned proposals were assigned to governments. However, they could be well conducted by technical institutions, NGOs and/or community organizations. By this way, a sustainable process of consciousness, training, transfer and assimilation of technology and know-how could be better achieved.

NICHES FOR IDRC

GENERAL

Opportunities that Fit Normal Programming
All explicit proposals mentioned above, where the related IDRC Division or ENRD GPI is mentioned between parenthesis.

New Opportunities
The three implicit proposals mentioned above should be considered as new opportunities for our Division mentioned there (CAID, SSD, HSD, ENRD).

Unusual or High-Risk Opportunities
Many activities considered in Programme Areas C and D, related to the strengthening and harmonizing criteria, regulations and controls for hazardous wastes transboundary movements and trade, should be considered as unusual or high-risk opportunities for our Special Initiatives Program, CAID, and for our Social Science Division.

REGIONAL SPECIFICITY

The chapter deals with a subject of global interest. Nevertheless, R&D for management of hazardous wastes is more related to relatively more industrialized regions as LARO and SARO; whereas, regulatory and control activities is badly needed in less developed regions as WARO and EARO.

KEY PARTNERS / OTHER ACTORS

Canada
Many public, academic and private specialized institutions (list is too long).

Other Countries
Small and medium industries, R&D institutions, NGOs, community organizations, and health agencies in developing countries.

RECOMMENDATIONS

WHICH NICHES ARE BEST FOR IDRC PROGRAM?

Assessment and development of hazardous waste management policies for developing countries.

Development of national and regional information networks.

Development of self-audit manuals to assist SME dealing with hazardous wastes (metal finishing, tanneries, batteries, etc.)

Development and adaptation of environmentally friendly technologies for industrial waste management.

ARE ADJUSTMENTS NEEDED AT IDRC IN ORDER TO FILL THESE NICHES?

Program Organization
No adjustments would be necessary, with the exception of a clear definition in CAID in order to deal with assessment and research on regulatory and controls in the field of Hazardous Wastes.

Structure/Staffing
Within ENRD, it would be interesting to look forward and to introduce a new GPI exclusively oriented to deal with Sustainable Waste Management problems including Hazardous (Chapter 20) as well as Solid Waste Management (Chapter 21). Accordingly, URB and SED GPIs should be released from these areas.

ARE THERE CROSS-CUTTING ISSUES THAT ARE NOT ADEQUATELY REFLECTED IN ANY OF THE ABOVE?

Not apparent.

COMMENTARY 20

Name of Commentator: Sylvain Dufour

1. GENERAL COMMENTS ON THE CHAPTER

- I agree with the general conclusions of the reviewer to the effect that:
    a) Its general thrust relates well to the ENRD mission;
    b) Local populations are not involved enough in the implementation of the Chapter; and
    c) The contents and approach of all waste-related chapters could have been merged.

2. OVERALL COMMENTARY ON THE FIRST REVIEW OF THE CHAPTER

- The Chapter places a lot of emphasis on inventory and looking at essentially background and base line data without necessarily showing how problems will be solved. Undoubtedly this needs to be done, but emphasis must clearly be on the future "industrial revolution" which will be required to occupy the new generation outside the already saturated agrarian economy.

3. MAJOR POINTS AGREED/DISAGREED WITH, AND REASONS

- I disagree (mildly) about what is missing; I would say that over and above the involvement of local communities, awareness-building and advocacy are necessary and should be developed.
- The Chapter does not give even summary definitions of what constitutes hazardous waste and what some of the buzz-words really mean (like "cradle-to-grave" approach).

4. MINOR POINTS AGREED/DISAGREED WITH, AND REASONS

- Regional Specificity: more than regulatory and control activities are needed in West and East Africa — capacity-building, development and implementation of "greener" technologies are two areas where the Centre could have an impact. The relative stage of development of these two regions is such that new capacities are still to be established and that waste-generating activity is going to rapidly increase in the future. It is obviously better (and cheaper) to prevent now than to mitigate later.

5. POSSIBLE ON-GOING ISSUES OR CONCERNS FOR IDRC

- None.

6. POSSIBLE IMPLICATIONS FOR IDRC

- None.

CHAPTER TWENTY-ONE

SUSTAINABLE MANAGEMENT OF SOLID WASTES AND SEWAGE-RELATED ISSUES

Responsible Officer: Gilles Forget

ABSTRACT 21

1. OVERALL CRITIQUE OF AGENDA 21 CHAPTER

- Very top-down, international bureaucracy-oriented approach. Waste-oriented rather than people-oriented: prescriptions for handling and monitoring of wastes takes precedence over the well-being, health and survival of people.
- Sanitation is an obscure component of "solid wastes & sewage related issues".
- No mention of hygiene or hygiene education, their relevance to effective use, operation and maintenance of waste collection/treatment facilities.
- Little emphasis on promotion of inter-sectoral efforts to link waste management to health, nutrition, and socio-economic development of the poor; recycling and reuse of nutrients (treated sewage in agriculture and aquaculture) is down-played; little emphasis is placed on cost recovery and equity issues on the provision of waste services.
- Community management of services and of resource generation activities is down-played.
- No mention of the need to understand the political, cultural and economic local contexts in the introduction of new technologies and associated issues.

2. KEY CONCLUSIONS ARISING FROM CHAPTER

- Environmentally sound waste management must go beyond collection and safe disposal: minimizing wastes, maximizing reuse and recycling, promoting environmentally sound disposal and treatment, and extending waste service coverage.
- A settlements infrastructure and environment program should be launched by the international community and selected United Nations organization to coordinate the activities of all the UN system in this area.
- It is doubtful that the institutionalization of waste management activities amongst sectoral agencies will prove beneficial to the poor. A better option would be to promote the integration of sanitation and hygiene as essential elements in the sustainable management of environmental health risks.

3. RESEARCH AND/OR IMPLEMENTATION POSSIBILITIES/OPPORTUNITIES

- Develop and strengthen national capacities in research and design of environmentally sound technologies to reduce wastes.
- Develop methodologies for country-level waste monitoring.
- Undertake research on the social and economic impact of waste minimization at the consumer level.
- Demonstration and pilot programs to optimize waste minimization instruments.
- Develop and strengthen national capacities to reuse and recycle wastes.
- Expand training programs on water supply and sanitation to incorporate waste reuse and recycling.

- Develop low cost, low maintenance waste-water treatment systems with safe sludge disposal options, industrial waste treatment, and low technology, ecologically safe waste disposal options.

4. ON-GOING AND/OR NEW PARTNERSHIPS FOR IDRC
- Selected environmental businesses.
- Women's organizations and associations.
- Health organizations, NGOs, environmental technology institutions, etc.

5. SUGGESTED NICHES FOR IDRC
- Participatory research on environmental sanitation and hygiene; in-country capacity-building, technology development and dissemination of environmentally sound sanitation technologies.
- Exploration of how communities could work with the various levels of government to ensure minimum levels of service which would contribute to the improvement of their health and the protection of the environment.
- The NGO and informal sector connection should be explored; research on the coordination and cooperation between policy-making, research and development and implementation.
- Social conflict arising from the introduction of infrastructure and cost recovery activities at the community level.
- Research on hygiene behaviour and sanitary risk assessments.
- An increased consideration of cross-cutting issues such as gender, housing, literacy and security in the design of projects.

6. OTHER COMMENTS
- Although there is a clear and vital relation between the conclusions drawn from the activities of the UN Water and Sanitation Decade to waste management, especially regarding the needs to involve people in the decision making, the Chapter did not make use of this information.
- The Chapter proposes regulatory and large scale solutions to the problems which are brought about by overpopulation, over-consumption, and lack of education. Although no one would claim that an international set of rules is not needed, no real attention has been paid to the "on the ground" causes of waste production and mismanagement. This is clearly where IDRC's comparative advantage lies.
- The emphasis on waste management makes it impossible to translate into a clear programme framework for the Centre, which would allow it to respond to the needs of the poor of LDCs.

REVIEW 21

Andres Sanchez

KEY CONCLUSIONS IN THE CHAPTER

WHAT IS THERE

Main Conclusions
Program areas included in this chapter are closely related to those of the following chapters:
- Fresh water resources (chap.18); ii) Human settlement (chap. 7); iii) Health (chap. 6); and, iv) Consumption patterns (chap. 4).

Environmentally sound waste management must go beyond collection and safe disposal of wastes. The root causes of the problem should be addressed by:

- Minimizing wastes through a preventive approach focused on changes in lifestyles and in production and consumption patterns;
- Maximizing waste reuse and recycling;
- Promoting environmentally sound waste disposal and treatment; and,
- Extending waste service coverage (in developing countries in particular).

A "settlement infrastructure and environment programme" should be launched by the international community and selected United Nations organizations to coordinate the activities of all organizations of the United Nations system involved in this area and include a clearing-house for information dissemination on all waste management issues.

Agreements Reached for International and National Action
A number of specific (and less specific) targets are presented for developing and implementing various aspects of national waste management programs, as well as population coverage targets for the provision of waste services (including the treatment and disposal of sewage, waste waters and solid wastes).

Politically Significant Issues
There is a technical issue with possible political ramifications: the chapter (beginning with its title) lacks clarity with respect to the subject it addresses. A definition of **solid wastes** is indeed presented, with the explicit exclusion of hazardous materials and inclusion of human excreta. Unfortunately, the reader has to discover what is meant by "**sewage-related issues**". This seems to include sewage itself (domestic and combined storm/domestic flows), and waste waters (which may refer to industrial and commercial non-hazardous liquid wastes).

On the other hand, there is an existing concept called **sanitation** which is commonly defined as : "the control of all the factors in people's physical environment that exercise or can exercise a deleterious effect on his/her physical development, health and survival". This concept is often used to refer, in particular, to the handling of both sewage and solid wastes (including refuse and human excreta).

The problem is that the chapter does not make clear what is the advantage in using new vague terms for existing concepts and what level of integration and collaboration is being sought with existing international organizations working in this area, such as The Water and Sanitation Collaborative Council. These issues may become important in light of the chapter's proposal for the creation of new organizations and the possibility for duplication of efforts.

WHAT IS NOT THERE
No mention of hygiene, no hygiene education and its relevance to the effective use, operation and maintenance of waste collection and treatment facilities.

Little emphasis on the promotion of inter-sectoral efforts to link waste management, health, nutrition, and the socio-economic development of poor populations.

Recycling and reuse of nutrients (eg., use of treated sewage or excreta in agriculture or aquaculture) is down played.

Little emphasis is placed on cost recovery and equity issues on the provision of waste services.

Community management of services and of resource generation activities is down played.

COMMENTARY 21

Name of Commentator: Danilo Anton

1. GENERAL COMMENTS ON THE CHAPTER

- Chapter 21 largely a wish list of what to do to improve the wastes situation. It is difficult to disagree with the issues raised such as minimizing wastes, maximizing environmentally sound waste reuse and recycling, promoting environmentally sound waste disposal and treatment, extending waste service coverage, and setting "agendas" to meet the main objectives (management, information, cooperation/ coordination, implementation, etc).

- As it has been well put by the reviewer, wastes seem to have precedence over people. Very little is said about the actual people behind the wastes issue. Some of the main players are not even discussed.

- There are three "types" of people affected by the waste activities/policies:
  a) The people actually or potentially using the wastes services (the "users");
  b) The people working in/managing the formal institutions dealing with the issue (often public institutions);
  c) The people working informally in the recycling business ("classifiers").

- The Chapter deals with the first two groups, but not the third, or informal sector, which sees "waste" as a valuable resource, not just something to eliminate. In poor and wealthy cities, many garbage elements, e.g. paper and cardboard, plastic, glass, metals and even organic remains, can be (and actually are) used for economic purposes.

- In Third World countries, as the economic situation deteriorates, more sectors of the population take advantage of this "wastes" resource. An informal garbage recycling system is created and quickly expands.

- The majority of "garbage-recycling communities" lead very difficult lives. They live next to garbage dumps; in slums, without services, in the worst environments of the city; in dangerous flood plains or unstable slopes; in the garbage itself, in contact with flies, mosquitoes, rats, various parasites, etc.; often they must eat garbage, and accumulate garbage in their houses; their children live and play in garbage or heavily contaminated water seeping from garbage.

- Such communities are very common throughout Third World countries. In Ciudad Netzahuatcoyotl in Mexico City, in the coastal slums of Djakarta, in the Brazilian "favelas" and in Calcutta or Bombay, tens of million people (perhaps 100 million, but no firm statistics are available) live directly or indirectly from garbage recycling.

- This "informal industry" competes with municipal garbage collecting services; is often illegal; is carried out in the night or in uncontrolled dumps; and involves not only adults but many children. Normally, these communities do not have normal city services; access to water and electricity is very limited; health controls are practically nil; and their quality of life is extremely poor (due to both low incomes, and lack of services).

- Only minor, indirect references to the informal sector are made in the Chapter: viz. "21.24.b) Providing technical assistance to informal waste reuse and recycling operations;" or "21.25.d) Encouraging NGOs...to mobilize community support for waste reuse and recycling through focused community-level campaigns".

2. OVERALL COMMENTARY ON THE FIRST REVIEW OF THE CHAPTER

- No major disagreement with the Review, although it includes the wastewaters aspects, which are implicit rather than explicit in Chapter.
- Agree with the reviewer's criticisms of the Chapters approach: its "top-down approach"; its "waste-oriented" nature rather than people; its lack of mention of hygiene aspects; and its "little emphasis on inter-sectoral efforts", etc.

3. MAJOR POINTS AGREED/DISAGREED WITH, AND REASONS

4. MINOR POINTS AGREED/DISAGREED WITH, AND REASONS

- Agreement with the need to put people first. This necessitates clear identification of the people to be dealt with:
    a) The informal recycling sector;
    b) The population at large using waste removal systems; and
    c) The people working and managing the wastes institutional system. (See pt. 1 above.)
- Main disagreement with the review is its insufficient emphasis on the "poorest of the poor".

CHAPTER TWENTY-TWO

SAFE AND ENVIRONMENTALLY SOUND MANAGEMENT OF RADIOACTIVE WASTES

Responsible Officer: Sylvain Dufour

ABSTRACT

1. OVERALL CRITIQUE OF AGENDA 21 CHAPTER

- A lack of a thorough description of the extent of the problem, both in terms of environmental effects and of countries affected (for instance, is this much of a problem in small poor countries?).
- A lack of a description of how some people are directly affected by this problem.
- The official view of many of the First World atomic energy agencies is conveyed while ignoring many of the issues raised by environmental monitoring groups (even the most moderate ones). This view leads to the potentially erroneous conclusions that policy-making and promotion of practical measures can be done when, in fact, there appears to be no technical basis from which to promote or formulate policies. The views of developing countries are not apparent.
- The important area of low-level radioactive mine wastes, very common in developing countries, has been completely omitted from the Chapter.

2. KEY CONCLUSIONS ARISING FROM CHAPTER

- There are no significant changes in perspective or conclusions for developing countries. Nuclear applications as described are still very much targetted to industrialized countries, a few newly-industrialized, and some of the very large developing countries (e.g. China, India, Pakistan). Most developing countries remain passive spectators and are sometimes victims of poor practices by the rest of the world.

3. RESEARCH AND/OR IMPLEMENTATION POSSIBILITIES/OPPORTUNITIES

- There is only one "means of implementation" explicitly relating to research: it relates to the health and environmental impact of radioactive waste disposal (par. 22.8(b)).
- There are several implicit research agendas. For instance: technical data for the formulation of safety guidelines; development of better processing and storage techniques for wastes; awareness-building in communities affected by waste problems, etc.

4. ON-GOING AND/OR NEW PARTNERSHIPS FOR IDRC

- Given the cloak of secrecy that often surrounds nuclear technologies, it is not possible to easily determine who the willing "official" partners might be. In some countries with a nuclear power program, it might be possible to identify advocacy groups who could assist at least on the political aspects. It is doubtful any worthy technical collaborators could be found outside of the medical field.

5. SUGGESTED NICHES FOR IDRC

- Research directly related to the issues of radioactive waste management and disposal is likely too expensive and long term for IDRC. It can also be argued that the generators of waste should contribute the bulk of funds for research, either directly or through government taxes. Therefore, there are only very limited options for IDRC.

6. OTHER COMMENTS

- None.

REVIEW 22

KEY CONCLUSIONS IN THE CHAPTER

There are no significant changes in perspective or conclusions for developing countries. Nuclear applications as described are still very much for industrialized countries, a few newly-industrialized and some of the very large developing countries (e.g. China, India, Pakistan). Most developing countries remain passive spectators and are sometimes victims of poor practices by the rest of the World[1]. Finally, the verbs used to present agreements are passive definitions (promote, encourage, respect, etc.), and virtually meaningless from an action standpoint. It will therefore be impossible to objectively evaluate the success of the proposed program, if implemented.

It is difficult to relate issues to developing country concerns because of the lack of elaboration in the background section, which is weak.

WHAT IS THERE

Main Conclusions
The only conclusions drawn in the Chapter are that sound waste management is important (par. 22.2) and that waste management systems are needed in many countries.

Agreements Reached for International and National Action
There seems to be little beyond promotion and encouragements. No specific program is presented.

Politically Significant Issues
The issue of technology transfer could, as usual, be a hot potato. The monitoring of potential agreements on export controls and moratoria could also lead to a confrontation of sorts between developing countries and waste-producing countries.

WHAT IS NOT THERE
The Chapter completely omits the issue of low-level radioactivity found in the mine tailings of some developing countries (e.g. from the exploitation of uranium, bauxite, copper, phosphate, etc.). It is also silent on military testing wastes that often result in environmental contamination.

---

[1] It should be mentioned that the Chapter refers implicitly to civilian uses. Military uses in many developing countries are more important than civilian applications.

The Chapter also takes the view that existing technology for management and disposal of radioactive waste is adequate. This may not be the case in practice as there is a considerable scientific argument that remains unresolved about the long-term viability of so-called permanent storage.

It is impossible to figure out where the financial and cost evaluations come from ($ 8 million; par. 22.7). The whole issue of human resource development and public awareness is also absent.

OVERALL CRITIQUE

Substantive Content
It would have been useful to have a more thorough description of the extent of the problem, the environmental effects and the countries affected.

The official view of many of the First World Atomic Energy Agencies is obvious but many of the issues raised by the environmental monitoring groups are ignored. The views of developing countries are not given.

Design of the Chapter as an Organizing Framework
If Agenda 21 were to be redesigned, the four chapters dealing with wastes should be combined. A more comprehensive technical and politico-economic research agenda developed.

RESEARCH REQUIREMENTS, CAPACITY BUILDING ETC.

EXPLICIT PROPOSALS IN THE CHAPTER
There is only one "means of implementation" explicitly relating to research. It relates to the health and environmental impact of radioactive waste disposal (par. 22.8(b)).

IMPLICIT PROPOSALS DERIVED FROM THE CHAPTER
There are several implicit research agendas depending upon the point of view. For instance: technical data for the formulation of safety guidelines; development of better processing and storage techniques for wastes, etc.

GAPS AND ALTERNATIVE APPROACHES
Research could also be carried out on the alternatives to radioactive materials. This involves first the whole issue of energy demand and consumption (to reduce the need, real or perceived, for nuclear power) and second, the substitution of radionuclides in many scientific and industrial applications (for instance rather than using nuclear densimeters in geotechnical engineering and soil science, scientists could go back to the use of rubber balloons, water columns and other indirect ways of measuring moisture and density).

NICHES FOR IDRC

GENERAL

Opportunities that Fit Normal Programming
None.

New Opportunities
Research to reduce energy demand and improve supply management has an indirect impact on the need for nuclear power and hence on the volume of wastes generated by this industry. This may be addressed under the Consumption Chapter (it is peculiar that there is no Chapter on energy...). The difficulty is that it is not the poorest countries that will, initially, benefit most from research funding.

Unusual or High-Risk Opportunities
Collaboration of Canadians with developing country researchers or policy-makers in the formulation of standards and guidelines for handling low-level radioactive wastes in small quantities.

REGIONAL SPECIFICITY

All regions as defined by IDRC have countries that are active in the nuclear sector and all countries must deal with the issue of low-level waste (mine dumps, discarded medical equipment, etc.).

KEY PARTNERS/OTHER ACTORS

Canada
Atomic Energy of Canada Limited and perhaps a few University Departments could be partners. Public utilities like New Brunswick Hydro, Hydro Québec and Ontario Hydro could be partners in some circumstances.

Other Countries
Given the cloak of secrecy that often surrounds nuclear technologies, it is not possible to determine without a detailed and personalized survey who the willing "official" partners might be. In some of the countries with a nuclear power program, it might be possible to identify advocacy groups who could assist at least on the political aspects. It is doubtful any worthy technical collaborators could be found outside of the medical field.

RECOMMENDATIONS

WHICH NICHES ARE BEST FOR IDRC PROGRAM?
Research directly related to the issues of radioactive waste management and disposal is too expensive and long term for IDRC. Moreover, the generators of waste should contribute the bulk of funds for research, either directly or through government taxes.

ARE ADJUSTMENTS NEEDED AT IDRC IN ORDER TO FILL THESE NICHES?

Program Organization
None.

Process and Project Cycle
None.

Structure/Staffing
None.

ARE THERE CROSS-CUTTING ISSUES THAT ARE NOT ADEQUATELY REFLECTED IN ANY OF THE ABOVE?
None.

COMMENTARY 22

Name of Commentator: Javier Verastegui

1. GENERAL COMMENTS ON THE CHAPTER

- The minimization approach is not given enough emphasis. It is one of the most important ways to deal with the problem of radioactive wastes, as with the management of all other wastes, because, up to now, no reliable methods exist to manage hazardous wastes in a completely safe way.
- Specific plans and proposals are needed to study alternatives for the complete substitution of nuclear power by clean technologies (solar energy, fuel cells, etc.). This would require a world effort in R&D and dissemination.
- Military experiments and potential uses of nuclear energy are not considered in the chapter as a source of regional and world contamination.
- Public awareness about the health hazards and potential risks of radioactive wastes in developing countries is not considered in the "Means of Implementation".

2. OVERALL COMMENTARY ON THE FIRST REVIEW OF THE CHAPTER

- General agreement with the main comments made by the reviewer.

3. MAJOR POINTS AGREED/DISAGREED WITH, AND REASONS

- In particular, agreement with the reviewer's key conclusion about the lack of significant changes in perspective for developing countries.
- Also agreement with "What is not there": Chapter 22 does not consider (a) radioactive mine tailings, (b) military testing wastes; and (c) human resource development and public awareness.

4. MINOR POINTS AGREED/DISAGREED WITH, AND REASONS

- The reviewer suggests that the Chapter regards the existing technology (for radioactive waste management) as adequate; and that only paragraph 22.8(b) is explicitly related to research. Agreed that the unresolved status of long-term viability (the so called "permanent storage") is a major concern, but the Chapter states clearly the need to "promote research and development methods for the safe and environmentally sound treatment, processing and disposal, including deep geological disposal of high-level radioactive waste" (paragraph 22.8(a)).

5. POSSIBLE ON-GOING ISSUES OR CONCERNS FOR IDRC

- Public awareness of local populations about health hazards and potential risks of bad radioactive management methods.
- Determination of the level of radioactive waste contamination in water bodies, soil and atmosphere near radioactive wastes management sites (treatment, processing, disposal).

6. POSSIBLE IMPLICATIONS FOR IDRC

- In some developing countries, even civil uses of nuclear energy are subject to military control. In those countries, potential IDRC support for NGOs studying local contamination levels and developing public awareness programs could be limited.

SECTION 3

STRENGTHENING THE ROLE OF MAJOR GROUPS

CHAPTER TWENTY-THREE

STRENGTHENING ROLE OF MAJOR GROUPS

PREAMBLE

Critical to the effective implementation of the objectives, policies and mechanisms agreed to by Governments in all programme areas of Agenda 21 will be the commitment and genuine involvement of all social groups.

One of the fundamental prerequisites for the achievement of sustainable development is broad public participation in decision-making. Furthermore, in the more specific context of environment and development, the need for new forms of participation has emerged. This includes the need of individuals, groups and organizations to participate in environmental impact assessment procedures and to know about and participate in decisions, particularly those which potentially affect the communities in which they live and work. Individuals, groups and organizations should have access to information relevant to environment and development held by national authorities, including information on products and activities that have or are likely to have a significant impact on the environment, and information on environmental protection measures.

CHAPTER TWENTY-FOUR

GLOBAL ACTION FOR WOMEN TOWARDS SUSTAINABLE AND EQUITABLE DEVELOPMENT

Responsible Officer: T. Carroll-Foster

ABSTRACT 24

1. OVERALL CRITIQUE OF AGENDA 21 CHAPTER

- Recognition that women's involvement is critical to sustainable development.
- Reiteration of previous conventions on the status of women — women must be involved at all levels of policy/decision-making, planning, implementation, etc.
- Proposes some concrete measures to be undertaken by national governments and UN bodies, but ignores similar measures are needed for other groups.
- Fails to analyze/allocate real costs of implementing measures proposed.
- Implementation section is weak. Financial costs are extremely under-estimated.
- Lacks cross-referencing to other chapters, although women's integration is a cross-cutting theme. Fails generally to make linkages to other groups.

2. KEY CONCLUSIONS ARISING FROM CHAPTER

- National governments and UN bodies especially must do more to ensure women are involved in key policy- and decision-making if sustainable, equitable and environmental development is to be achieved.
- Women's full integration into environment and development still remains very politically sensitive (and emotionally charged).
- Chapter targets UN bodies mandated to deal with women (e.g. UNIFEM), but downplays the need for substantive changes in UN agencies that are not women-or socially-oriented (e.g. World Bank, and IFIs).
- Substantial resource allocation to implement the measures proposed will be needed if women's role and status in environmentally sustainable development is to be achieved. Presently financial estimates are low and unrealistic.

3. RESEARCH AND/OR IMPLEMENTATION POSSIBILITIES/OPPORTUNITIES

- Chapter provides 7 specific areas for "research, gender-sensitive data collection and information dissemination":
    a) Women's knowledge/experience in natural resources management/conservation;
    b) Impact of structural adjustment programs on women, e.g. fuel subsidy cuts;
    c) Impacts on women of environmental degradation, armed hostilities, etc.;
    d) Structural linkages between gender relations, environment and development;
    e) Integration of the value of unpaid work into UN System of Accounts and natural resource accounting mechanisms;
    f) Rural and urban training, research and resource centres for women and environmentally sound technologies;

g) Environmental, social and gender impact analyses; and
h) Review of adequacy of UN agencies in integrating/responding to women.

4. ON-GOING AND/OR NEW PARTNERSHIPS FOR IDRC

- IDRC's previous partnerships with various women's Third World organizations, associations and networks.
- Linkages with more Canadian women's organizations, and new, emerging Third World Women's organizations, NGOs and ENGOs, and with universities which have set up chairs of Women's studies or equivalent.

5. SUGGESTED NICHES FOR IDRC

- Most items under 3., except the review of the UN agencies.
- Training in environmental screening, assessments, impacts and sustainable development planning and implementation for women/organizations, and NGOs/ENGOs.
- Environmental and sustainable development capacity-building in its widest/deepest sense for women at all levels.
- Development of gender-sensitive research, data-bases, natural resource accounting systems, and training of women trainers in this area.

6. OTHER COMMENTS

- See Review: Global Action for Women, Chapter 24.

REVIEW 24

KEY CONCLUSIONS IN THE CHAPTER

WHAT IS THERE

Main Conclusions

If sustainable development, which is also equitable and environmental, is to work, greater efforts by national governments, UN bodies, and other organizations will be needed to ensure the involvement of women in key policy- and decision-making at all levels.

National governments will need to undertake effective implementation of the several international agreements and conventions affecting women, e.g. the Nairobi Forward-looking Strategies for the Advancement of Women, which also address women's relationship to and involvement in natural resources and eco-system management, if Agenda 21 is to be successfully implemented.

United Nations bodies — and not only those with a primary focus on women, e.g. as UNIFEM and INSTRAW — will also need to take a more proactive approach to women's integration into programs and decision-making related to sustainable development and Agenda 21.

An in-depth analysis of the real costs of implementing this chapter — likely to be substantially greater than the $40 million estimate of the UNCED Secretariat — will be needed, and financial and technical commitments for such implementation will need to be obtained if substantive achievement is to occur.

Agreements Reached for International and National Action
Under Objectives, 8 proposals were made for national governments, the most specific and pertinent of which are:
- Implementation of the Nairobi Forward-looking Strategies for the Advancement of Women, especially "women's participation in national eco-system management and control of environmental degradation";
- Increased proportions of women decision-makers, planners, technical advisers, etc. in the environment and development fields;
- Establishment of mechanisms to assess the implementation and impact (including contributions and benefits) of development and environment policies and programs on women, by 1995;
- Formulation and implementation of "clear governmental policies and national guidelines" to achieve equality in all aspects of society, especially in the management of natural resources and the environment, including access to resources, credit, agricultural inputs and implements; and,
- Implementation of measures that "ensure women and men the same right to decide freely and responsibly the number and spacing of their children".

Under the Activities section, it was agreed that governments should undertake 12 specific implementation steps. A number of these essentially were reiterations of key calls for action in international conventions or agreements on the status and role of women. The Activities pertaining to women and sustainable development urged the following action:
- Measures to review policies and establish plans to increase the proportion of women as decision-makers, etc. in sustainable development policies and programs;
- Measures to strengthen women's and their organizations' capacity-building for sustainable development;
- Provisions of environmentally sound technologies, accessible and clean water, efficient fulled supply, and adequate sanitation facilities, which have been designed, developed and improved in consultation with women;
- Programs that establish and strengthen health facilities, including women-centered and women-managed reproductive health care and affordable, accessible, responsible planning of family size and services;
- Programs that support and strengthen equal employment opportunities, including equal access to credit, agricultural implements and inputs, land, and other natural resources;
- Programs of consumer awareness that have women's active participation, so as "to reduce/eliminate unsustainable consumption and production patterns, especially in industrialized countries, and to encourage investment in environmentally sound productive activities, and to induce environmentally, socially friendly industrial development"; and,
- Measures to review progress, including an appraisal report and recommendations for submission to the 1995 Conference on Women.

Politically Significant Issues
National governments are again being asked to ratify all conventions pertaining to women, if they have not done so. Ratifying governments are asked to legislate and implement measures to strengthen women's legal capacity to participate fully and equally in decisions on sustainable development. States parties to the Convention on the Elimination of All Forms of Discrimination against Women are asked to review and propose amendments on environment and development elements, such as access to natural resources, by AD2000, and to ask for the development of reporting guidelines by the Committee on the Elimination of Discrimination against Women. Given past delays, intransigence, and reluctance by many governments to allocate adequate levels of resources to women's needs and status, and concomitant political sensitivities, it is likely that the linkage of women and environmentally sustainable development will be politically charged and a number of trade-offs will occur.

One of the more politically significant aspects of this chapter is buried in the middle, under "Areas requiring Urgent Action". It advocates that "countries **should** take urgent measures to avert the on-going rapid environmental and economic degradation in developing countries that generally affects the lives of women and children in rural areas suffering drought, desertification and deforestation, armed hostilities, natural disasters, toxic waste and the aftermath of the use of unsuitable agro-chemical products".

WHAT IS NOT THERE

No linkage is made between this chapter (24) and the other Agenda 21 chapters, and the need to ensure that women, their needs, concerns, role and participation should be integrated throughout the other Agenda 21 chapters, such as Combatting Desertification and Drought (Ch. 12) or Sustainable Agriculture (Ch. 14), rather than be dealt with in an isolated manner.

No linkage is made to other key groups, e.g. the Role of Workers (Ch. 29), Role of Business (Ch.30), the Scientific and Technical Community (Ch.31) or the NGOs (Ch.27), and Indigenous People (Ch.26) and no acknowledgement exists that these groups, over and above governments and UN bodies, also need to undertake measures that ensure the full and equal participation of women in their sustainable development policies and programs.

Armed hostilities is one of the major causes of human suffering and environmental degradation in many countries. This is one of the few chapters that refers to that problem, but it does not elaborate on that issue other than to suggest that some research on the impact of armed hostilities on women should be undertaken.

Means of implementation is non-existent. Cost evaluation and finance required for the implementation of this chapter's activities is completely weak and inadequate. They are also indicative that the UNCED Secretariat neither comprehended the enormity of the problem nor the need to allocate an amount of resources to women's involvement in sustainable development proportionate to their numbers and percentages. The implicit expectation is that governments will come up with actual costs and financial terms once implementation programs are decided upon. Without strong leadership from some source, women's Global Action programs are likely to be woefully under-implemented and under-funded.

While the chapter indicates that the Secretary-General of the United Nations should review the adequacy of all UN agencies, including those with a focus of women (UNIFEM, INSTRAW), in meeting development and environment objectives and in the inclusion of and increase of women in senior decision-making roles, this chapter does not specifically mention the World Bank and regional banks that have major impacts on the environment and on women's lives.

OVERALL CRITIQUE

Substantive Content

This chapter reiterates and emphasizes the importance of women's involvement and participation in sustainable development at all levels. It, in essence, points out that, despite many existing international agreements and conventions that focus on women, much remains to be done to ratify, implement, legislate, and activate policies and programs that not only positively affect women per se but also contribute to environmentally sustainable and equitable development.

The final chapter is considerably stronger than its earlier drafts, in large part because of the considerable work and efforts made by the Canadian delegation, which also ensured that women were integrated to a degree in some of the other chapters.

Compared with some of the other chapters, such as Chapter 27 — Non-governmental Organizations — this chapter is less "wishy-washy" than those and identifies some fairly concrete, positive actions that "should" be taken within specific timeframes (e.g. the 1995, when the UN Conference on Women occurs in Beijing).

Design of the Chapter as an Organizing Framework
Somewhat scanty or incomplete as an Organizing Framework. It does not distinguish between important and less important matters, or set priorities. It does not have an Implementation section or an adequate Costing and Finance section. It states relatively clearly what action should be taken by national governments and UN institutions, as opposed to some chapters that "waffle".

RESEARCH REQUIREMENTS, CAPACITY-BUILDING, ETC.

EXPLICIT PROPOSALS IN THE CHAPTER
The section, "Research, Data Collection and Dissemination of Information"(24.8 (a–g)), sets out 7 specific areas in which countries should develop "gender-sensitive data-bases, information systems and participatory action-oriented research and policy analyses, with the collaboration of women and academic institutions:

- Women's knowledge and experience of natural resources management and conservation;
- The impact of structural adjustment programs on women, especially cut-backs in social services, education, health, food and fuel subsidies;
- The impact on women of environmental degradation, drought, desertification, toxic chemicals, and armed hostilities;
- The structural linkages between gender relations, environment and development;
- The integration of the value of unpaid work into resource accounting mechanisms, using the UN System of National Accounts, to be revised and issued in 1993;
- The development and inclusion of environmental, social and gender impact analyses in policy and program development and monitoring; and,
- The creation of rural and urban training, research and resource centres to disseminate environmentally sound technologies to women, in both developed and developing countries.

The section on "International and Regional Cooperation and Coordination" advocates:
- The need for a review of the adequacy of all UN institutions in meeting development and environment objectives, including women's role, and recommendations for strengthening the organizations' capacities and capabilities to implement Agenda 21 and incorporate women into sustainable development programs and decisions; and,
- A review (yet again!) of the status of women and their numbers in senior policy-level and decision-making posts within the UN system.

IMPLICIT PROPOSALS DERIVED FROM THE CHAPTER
Generally explicit, as indicated above.

Possibly more research is indicated if and when the UN system, governments and non-governmental organizations undertake UNCED follow-up and Agenda 21 implementation and attempt to ascertain how "gender considerations are to be fully integrated into all their policies, programs and activities" (24.11).

Also implicit is the need for an in-depth analysis of what the cost will be to implement the activities outlined in this chapter and where the funds might be accessed.

GAPS AND ALTERNATIVE APPROACHES

Indicated above.

NICHES FOR IDRC

GENERAL

Opportunities that Fit Normal Programming
Everything outlined above appears to have fitted or could fit into IDRC's normal programming in all areas.

New Opportunities
IDRC could re-emphasize the type of work that it has undertaken in the past to ensure that women are fully and equally integrated into all aspects of development and the environment, and undertake to take a leadership role in the involvement of women in research, training, capacity-building, and institution-strengthening with respect to sustainable development.

IDRC might undertake research into the linkages between women, NGOs, Business and other Key Groups, and the effectiveness of their policies and programs to integrate women into their sustainable development initiatives.

Unusual or High-Risk Opportunities
None immediately apparent, unless IDRC decides it wants to tackle the impact on women and the environment of armed hostilities.

REGIONAL SPECIFICITY
None.

KEY PARTNERS AND/OR OTHER ACTORS

Canada
To date national women's organizations in Canada have not been much involved in or linked with development, although many of these have had environment committees and are increasingly becoming concerned with and knowledgeable about sustainable development concepts. Some, in the last five years, have become involved in CIDA-funded projects with Third World women. Some examples of organizations that might be contacted include: the Canadian Federation of University Women, Business and Professional Women, National Action Committee for the Status of Women, Canadian Nurses Association, Canadian Home Economics Association, etc.

Other Countries
Many possible networks and linkages exist in both developing and developed countries, over and above those that IDRC has already liaised and cooperated with.

RECOMMENDATIONS

WHICH NICHES ARE BEST FOR IDRC PROGRAMMING?
IDRC could handle virtually all the research components noted above as none of them are particularly outside IDRC's orbit, with the possible exception of research pertaining to the UN system. But the extent to which it would do so would obviously be subject to human and financial resources being available.

ADJUSTMENTS NEEDED AT IDRC

Program Organization

On-going awareness-creation, training and education about women's role and need to integrate women fully and equally into sustainable development policies, programs, etc. will probably be necessary to ensure that women are not marginalized or side-lined in key programs, and to ensure that women are recognized not only as beneficiaries of programs but also as full, knowledgeable participants who can help achieve environmentally sustainable development.

Process and Project Cycle

With the increasing emphasis within IDRC of addressing issues on an integrated and holistic basis, the inclusion of women should be a sine qua non. However, the reality remains that not everyone necessarily knows how to achieve women's integration and involvement. Training and education should help to ease this problem.

Structure/Staffing

The person responsible for WID/GAD may find her hands more than full without additional back-up from people with WID/GAD knowledge and expertise combined with environmental and sustainable development expertise.

CROSS-CUTTING ISSUES

As noted above, more connection with NGOs, business and industry, trade unions, etc. to ensure that women are effectively integrated into policies, planning, programs, and decision-making at all levels.

COMMENTARY 24

Name of Commentator: Rosina Wiltshire

1. GENERAL COMMENTS ON THE CHAPTER

- In placing the specific objectives of the Chapter within the broader context of the Nairobi Forward-Looking Strategies and relevant UN conventions, this Chapter reinforces the recommendation that the gender issue is both specific and cross-cutting.
- A subsequent review of this Chapter might be done in coordination with the other chapters, such as poverty and demographics, biodiversity, major groups, etc. to draw out the cross-cutting elements.

2. OVERALL COMMENTARY ON THE FIRST REVIEW OF THE CHAPTER

- The Review could be broadened to include implications arising from the broader context noted above.
- Financial estimates are not necessarily low or unrealistic if this basic recommendation for a new conceptualization of development, a more gender equitable allocation, and more efficient use of existing resources is accepted by the international community and national governments.

3. MAJOR POINTS AGREED/DISAGREED WITH, AND REASONS

- (See 2 above.) New partnerships will have to extend beyond the usual nexus between women's organizations and the environment and development NGOs, to UN agencies, donor agencies, the academic community, and even business and industry.

4. MINOR POINTS AGREED/DISAGREED WITH, AND REASONS

- In identifying the need to address the impact of major IMF/World Bank policies such as structural adjustment, the Chapter implies the need for greater transparency and accountability of these agencies.

5. POSSIBLE ON-GOING ISSUES OR CONCERNS FOR IDRC

- The Earth Charter was meant to be the foundation of principles for Agenda 21. IDRC may need to act as a catalyst for strengthening the Rio Declaration as an essential framework for Agenda 21.

6. POSSIBLE IMPLICATIONS FOR IDRC

- This Chapter implies the need for putting a gender lens and an equity lens to every IDRC project and program as well as across projects and programs, and strengthening gender and equity training. IDRC has positioned itself to do this.
- It also implies broadening IDRC's partnership base to include more active collaboration with UN agencies, donors and NGOs, but also being a catalyst because its mandate for research and knowledge creation coincides with the priority areas of action identified.

CHAPTER TWENTY-FIVE

CHILDREN AND YOUTH IN SUSTAINABLE DEVELOPMENT

Responsible Officer: Jean-Michel Labatût

ABSTRACT

1. OVERALL CRITIQUE OF AGENDA 21 CHAPTER

- Participation of youth and children at the local, national and international level of decision-making in programs whose content has yet to be define, is interesting, but vague. It is therefore important to specify what strategies should be put in place to make this participation meaningful. Mere participation cannot replace national economic and social policies aimed at improving the overall conditions of children (presumably within the family and community) before branching out into the national and international arena.
- This Chapter doesn't specify what the North must contribute, sacrifice or change to modify the international situation which contribute directly or indirectly to poverty in the South.

2. KEY CONCLUSIONS ARISING FROM CHAPTER

- **International level**: UN and national governments should promote participation of youth in UN decision-making processes and in national delegations to international meetings. Specific interests of children should be taken into account in the participatory process on environment and development.
- **Country level**: Countries should promote dialogue between the youth community and Government and establish mechanisms that permit youth access to information and the opportunity to present their perspectives on Government decisions. Governments should implement programs for children in health, nutrition, education, literacy and poverty alleviation and promote the empowerment of local populations towards the objective of integrated community management of resources.

3. RESEARCH AND/OR IMPLEMENTATION POSSIBILITIES/OPPORTUNITIES

- Improve the dissemination of relevant information to governments, youth organizations and other NGOs on current youth positions and activities.
- Ensure access for all young to all types of education reflecting their economic and social needs and incorporating the concept of environment awareness and sustainable development.
- Research into social policies and capacity-building that will give children and youth a voice in environmentally-related decision-making that concern them.
- Establish task forces that include youth and youth NGOs to develop educational and awareness programs specifically targetted to the young population.
- Promote primary environmental care activities that address the basic needs of communities.
- These activities implies the need for a multidisciplinary approach dealing with several categories of individuals to whom other chapters are dedicated (women, indigenous people, etc.).

4. ON-GOING AND/OR NEW PARTNERSHIPS FOR IDRC
- UNESCO, Agha Khan Foundation, NGOs and community associations concerned with children and youth; research and academic institutions; government agencies and ministries dealing with social affairs. Inter-regional exchanges of experience could be helpful in developing adequate and appropriate policies to protect youth and children.

5. SUGGESTED NICHES FOR IDRC
- IDRC has always given children and youth an important place in its programming, and has acquired important experience. Its particular niche may be to support research into the links between social participation, participatory research, and training of children as important to sustainable development.
- The "empowerment through knowledge" concept can be applied to children and youth as well as to adults. IDRC could support research into how traditional ways of inserting children and youth into community life might be adapted to fit the need for early awareness of present and future responsibilities with respect to the protection and management of natural resources.

6. OTHER COMMENTS
- This Chapter remains at a very general level and this detracts from its potential impact. It is not sufficiently integrated with other chapters. This risks masking the fact that the problems of youth and children are linked to the problems of the wider society. It does not make an adequate distinction between the different needs of children and youth in industrialized versus Third World countries, or between needs of different categories (street children, urban and rural children, children and youth, etc.).

REVIEW 25

KEY CONCLUSIONS IN THE CHAPTER

WHAT IS THERE
Main Conclusions
No specific conclusions are drawn in this chapter. Recommendations fall under two program headings:
- Advancing the role of youth and actively involving them in the protection of the environment and promoting economic and social development; and,
- Children in sustainable development.

The first program comes from the recognition that youth comprise nearly 30% of the world population and that their involvement in environment and development decision-making and in the implementation of programs is critical to the long-term success of Agenda 21.

This program places the specific question of young people in a more general context, taking into account the recommendations proposed at the international level to ensure that youth are provided a secure and healthy future, an environment of quality, improved standard of living and access to education and employment. This is a way of going beyond the environmental problematic per se, to place the debate at the level of sustainable development.

The second program deals with children who, in many developing countries comprise nearly half the population. They are in both developing and industrial countries highly vulnerable to the effect of environmental degradation, and they are perceived as quite aware supporters of environmental thinking. It is stated that their needs should be taken fully into account in the participatory process on environment and development in order to safeguard the sustainability of actions taken to improve the environment.

Agreements Reached for International and National Action
This chapter contains several main recommendations.
- **The role of youth**
  At the international level, it is recommended that the UN and national governments promote participation of youth in UN decision-making processes and in national delegations to international meetings.

  This should lead to a review and a coordination by the UN and international organizations of their youth programs. There should be also an improvement in the dissemination of information on current youth positions and activities, and in the monitoring and the evaluation of the application of Agenda 21.

  Furthermore, the UN and national governments should promote the United Nations Trust for the International Youth Year and collaborate with youth representatives in the administration of it, focusing particularly on the needs of youth from developing countries.

  At the national level, it is recommended that countries promote dialogue between the youth community and Government and establish mechanisms that permit youth access to information and the opportunity to present their perspectives on Government decisions.

  This participatory objective should be linked to policies which will ensure that 50% of youth (gender balanced) have access to education (secondary or vocational) by the year 2000, that youth unemployment is reduced, and that young people's human rights are protected.

- **Children in sustainable development**
  At the international level the document recommends that specific interests of children be taken fully into account in the participatory process on environment and development and that UNICEF maintain cooperation and collaboration with other organizations of the UN, Governmental and non-governmental organizations to develop programs for children.

  At the country level governments should take active steps to implement programs for children especially in health, nutrition, education, literacy and poverty alleviation. There should be a ratification of the Convention on the Right of the Child (General Assembly Resolution 44/25 of 20 November 1989).

  An effort should be made to "improve the environment for children at the household and community level and encourage the participation and empowerment of local populations including women, youth, children and indigenous people, towards the objective of integrated community management of resources, especially in developing countries". Mobilization of children and their parents through schools and local health centres could "become effective focal points for sensitization of communities to environmental issues".

At the country level one of the key objectives is to "establish procedures to incorporate children's concern into all relevant policies and strategies for environment and development at the local, regional and national levels".

Politically Significant Issues

Children and youth do not vote, and have traditionally held little or no power in the political scene or in public life in general. Their lack of voice is particularly detrimental to them in countries where their well-being is not a major concern of the Government. What we note in many Third World countries is that children and youth are, along with women, the main victims of certain mechanisms of underdevelopment: wars, natural disasters, international economic competition leading to the exploitation of cheap labour, and the neglect of social policies due to worsening economic conditions.

For example, considering the large number of street children in many Third World cities, it is dismaying to learn from Alphonse Tay, of Unesco's Education Program for Street Children, that "Government funding for programs for street and working children is pretty nil since these kids are not considered in national education policies and budget".

One may wonder in certain cases if there is any political will to protect children and youth, particularly when one learns of international rings of traffickers in children as cheap labour, prostitution and even suppliers of organs for rich buyers. These widespread ills appear to be ignored or tolerated by many Third World governments. As mentioned by the ECOSOC Commission on Human Rights, "Large scale criminal organizations dealing in child trafficking all too often enjoy the tolerance of the authorities" (IADL Statement Feb. 1985).

The question is whether anything has changed in the equation, to allow us to believe that the recommendations, many of them embedded in other international resolutions and declarations, now have a better chance of being implemented. The challenge is to define specific strategies in order to implement these agreements, and there is very little of that in this chapter.

Given the above, the Centre will have to be very selective as to the countries with which it works on projects relating to this topic, to ensure that there is a clear political will to protect youth and children from such forms of exploitation. This is important not merely on ethical grounds, but also to ensure that the Centre does not become compromised by a partnership with governments that countenance child abuse and exploitation.

WHAT IS NOT THERE

This chapter addresses the very delicate and complex questions of implementing policies allowing children and youth to participate, at all levels of decision making relating to the implementation of Agenda 21; it remains at a very general level, however, and this detracts from its potential impact.

The idea of participation of youth in decision-making fora brings into focus the more general question of community participation in decision-making. This is particularly appropriate at a time when democratic processes seem to be gaining ground throughout the world. There is a risk at this juncture of falling into a naive approach to the very complex relationship between the macro- and micro-levels of society.

The chapter does not make an adequate distinction between the different needs of children and youth in industrialized versus Third World countries, or between needs of different categories (street children, urban and rural children, children and youth, etc.).

Although the chapter refers to economics, health, etc., it is not sufficiently articulated with other chapters, and this risks masking the fact that the problems of youth and children are linked to the problems of the wider society, and should not be addressed in a piecemeal fashion.

This chapter does not consider adequately the economic role of child labour, and, more generally, the role of children and youth as agents of development; this is related, not only to political factors mentioned above, but also to a more ingrained view that children are passive, dependent objects of programs and policies; in this sense, mechanisms to change the attitudes of adults to children — and which are not dealt with in this chapter — are a necessary preliminary step.

While the starting point of the chapter is clearly youth and children participation, it seems that the actions proposed remain for the most part in a welfare perspective, in order to compensate for the weakness of the social system. In fact, what is needed is a departure from this vision and a perspective that makes children and youth effective actors in development.

OVERALL CRITIQUE

Substantive Content

A lot of the ideas expressed here are taken from recommendations of previous international documents — in most cases either not implemented or obvious failures — thus making them appear as reiterated pious hopes for actions in favour of youth and children. However, although the dominant idea is that of participation of children and youth at the international and national levels is not a new one, the insistence on this issue in the chapter gives it a renewed sense of urgency.

This notion of the participation of youth and children in programs whose content has yet to be defined, is interesting, but vague. Considering the actual lack of power of youth and children at the economic and political levels, the challenge would be to find ways to make sure that their participation in such events as international meetings and the like would not be mere tokenism. It is therefore important to specify what strategies should be put in place to make this participation meaningful, while avoiding the very real risk of reproducing yet again elitist patterns reflecting those of their parents (whose children would participate in international conferences? how can children without access to education profit from access to information and training that would allow them to be effective participants in national and international fora, and so on). Questions of equitable redistribution and access to basic services such as primary education, and of content of educational programs, remain fundamental. This type of research may be of particular interest to IDRC.

Mere participation of a minute proportion of children and youth is not a panacea: it cannot replace national economic and social policies aimed at improving the overall conditions of children (presumably within the family and community) before branching out into the national and international arena.

But decisions concerning children and youth do not depend only on national policy. In traditional societies, children, like youth and women, do have a clear place, function and role, albeit subordinate to the men. They are provided for in terms of essential needs and training for their future adult role in society. The major societal dysfunctions linked to rapid urbanization, wars, and the internationalization of local economies have disrupted traditional patterns and often thrown children and youth into lives of deprivation and misery. In order to improve the situation of this sector of society, it is necessary to address the global context of North-South relations, international conflicts and control over the major economic actors who currently escape national political and legal control.

A corollary question is what the North must contribute, sacrifice or change to correct the fundamental inequities which allow environmental and societal degradation, and what political and economic powers in Third World countries must be put in place to favour sustainable, equitable development. These issues are profoundly political, and have been downplayed in the document.

As the circumstances and conditions of children (and their chances of access to health and education) are so inextricably linked to those of the adults responsible for them, and in particular of their mothers, it is important to insist on policies and programs which improve the situation of women themselves.

It is important to note that the promotion of the interests of youth and children must be appropriate to the cultural context, which is not a static entity. Social change, and specifically changes concerning the status of children, require the involvement of the members of a community, and for this, adequate information must be made available to inform decisions. Furthermore, it would be appropriate to question the relevance of using Western concepts of family, children, youth, etc. in a non-western context.

Design of the Chapter as an Organizing Framework

The structure of the chapter could be revised by first examining the problems of children and youth in developing and industrialized countries, and their underlying causes, at the economic, political and social levels. On the basis of such a diagnostic, strategies to overcome these causes effectively could then be put forward. Obviously, simplistic solutions should be avoided. The participation of youth in the strategy formulation and implementation may be fruitful, but only as a complement to a strong political commitment of different levels of authority to improving their overall conditions. The factors contributing to the current general lack of political will should also be closely examined.

RESEARCH REQUIREMENTS, CAPACITY BUILDING ETC.

EXPLICIT PROPOSALS IN THE CHAPTER

Following are examples of some explicit activities which could generate interesting proposals. They are characterized mainly by an effort to propose a multidisciplinary approach which recognize the complexity of the overall context.

- How to improve the dissemination of relevant information to governments, youth organizations and other non-governmental organizations on current youth positions and activities, and monitor and evaluate the Agenda 21.
- Ensure access for all young to all types of education, wherever appropriate, providing alternative learning structures; ensure that education reflects the economic and social needs of youth and incorporate the concept of environmental awareness and sustainable development throughout the curricula; and, expand vocational training, implementing innovative methods aimed at increasing practical skills.
- Establish task forces that include youth and youth non-governmental organizations to develop educational and awareness programs specifically targeted to the youth population on critical issues pertaining to youth. These task forces should use formal and non-formal education methods to reach a maximum audience. National and local media, non-governmental organizations, businesses and other organizations should assist in these task forces.
- Promote primary environmental care activities that address the basic needs of communities, improve the environment for children at the household and community level and encourage the participation and empowerment of local populations, including woman, youth, children and indigenous people, toward the objective of integrated community management of resources, especially in developing countries.

IMPLICIT PROPOSALS DERIVED FROM THE CHAPTER

As noted above, most activities mentioned in this chapter are not explicit proposals in terms of research and capacity building; rather, they refer to proposals for such actions appearing in other chapters. In order to reach explicit proposals, it would have been necessary to address issues pertaining to strategies and processes required to attain the objectives stated in the document (such as expanding educational opportunities, improving nutrition, fighting poverty, etc.). It is to be noted that many of the "activities" listed are not really activities but rather objectives to be reached.

In this sense, many activities refer implicitly to possible proposals, particularly in terms of research into social policies and capacity-building that would give children and youth a voice in environmentally-related decision-making that concerns them, within the limits discussed above. New structures and processes required for this would entail preliminary research and training consistent with IDRC's mandate. Most obvious are problems linked to education and employment.

The emphasis on promoting "primary environmental care activities that address the basic needs of communities, improve the environment for children at the household and community level and encourage the participation and empowerment of local populations including women, youth, children and indigenous people towards the objective of integrated community management resources, especially in developing countries" implies the need for multidisciplinary research dealing with several categories of individuals to whom other chapters are dedicated (women, indigenous people, etc.).

GAPS AND ALTERNATIVE APPROACHES

By partitioning Agenda 21 into categories of people or agents of change (Chapters 23 to 32), the profound articulation between the various problems on one hand, and the role of economic, political, environmental, social and cultural factors on the other, may be lost from sight. This approach dilutes the fundamental crisis and the radical changes required at the national and international levels to improve the situation.

NICHES FOR IDRC

GENERAL

Opportunities that Fit Normal Programming

The place and role of children and youth have always been of concern to the Centre, and particularly to the HSD and SSD. Thus Agenda 21 provides scope for continuity and focus, rather than a departure from current concerns.

Some opportunities include:
- Research in non-formal education and vocational training.
- Research on educational systems reflecting the economic and social needs of youth and incorporating the concept of environmental awareness and sustainable development.
- Research into practical aspects of sensitizing youth to environmental and sustainable development issues.
- The emphasis on communities, and on reaching children through their parents, provides an opening to conduct research into indigenous knowledge systems, for example with respect to the links of health and nutrition to environmental protection.

Generally speaking, research, institutional and human capacity building are all addressed in this chapter, although not in very specific terms.

New Opportunities
The articulation of issues related to including environmental concerns in education, training and community action, and, more notably to participation of children in decision-making concerning environmental issues may offer a number of very interesting avenues of research, as does the concept of promoting the participation of children in national and international fora. These will entail research not only into policy matters, but into training and capacity-building and the empowerment of youth.

The interest in the participation of youth coincides with the Centre's heightened interest in democracy and decentralization. The type of issues involved would likely emphasize qualitative over quantitative research methods.

Unusual or High-Risk Opportunities
Real participation can bring about changes in the balance of power, among various groups within a given society, and between North and South. Research in this area is highly political and must be recognized as such. It also raises ethical issues of engineering social and cultural change.

A very interesting, yet risky area of research is that related to children living in societies in conflict/at war. To date, IDRC has generally kept away from such areas, for practical reasons; considering the apparent increase in conflict areas, this unofficial position may need to be addressed, particularly given the devastating environmental effects of prolonged conflicts.

REGIONAL SPECIFICITY
In Africa, although climatic factors bring about drought, desertification and famine which affect the most vulnerable segments of society, societal factors, and war in particular, are also extremely important agents of environmental degradation and human misery. Given the magnitude of the problems of the continent, the resolutions and recommendations of this chapter appear insufficient.

KEY PARTNERS/OTHER ACTORS
Canada
See below (other countries)

Other Countries
Unesco, Agha Khan Foundation, NGOs and community associations concerned with children and youth; research and academic institutions; government agencies and ministries dealing with social affairs.

Inter-regional exchange of experience should be helpful in developing adequate and appropriate policies to protect youth and children and provide them with access to health, education and social participation. For example, Latin America has a long experience with studying the problems of street children, a problem which is now gaining more visibility and attracting interest in Africa.

RECOMMENDATIONS

WHICH NICHES ARE BEST FOR IDRC PROGRAM?
The Centre has always given children and youth an important place in its programming, and has acquired important experience. Its particular niche may be to support research into making links between social participation, participatory research, and training of children to assume a more important role in sustainable development. The "empowerment through knowledge" concept can be applied to children and youth as well as to adults.

IDRC could support research into how traditional ways of inserting children and youth into community life might be adapted to fit new realities, and in particular the need for early awareness of present and future responsibility with respect to the protection and management of natural resources in order to give sustainability a chance.

ARE ADJUSTMENTS NEEDED AT IDRC IN ORDER TO FILL THESE NICHES?

IDRC should examine how (and what elements of) Agenda 21 might contribute to overall programming, given that this programming is the result of systematic consultations and analyses of global and regional trends and issues, and not try to match or adopt the organization and contents of this document. For this reason, no particular adjustments are required in terms of organization, project cycle or staffing.

Program Organization
No adjustments are required.

Process and Project Cycle
No adjustments are required.

Structure/Staffing
No adjustments are required.

ARE THERE CROSS-CUTTING ISSUES THAT ARE NOT ADEQUATELY REFLECTED IN ANY OF THE ABOVE?

As stated above, children and youth cannot be considered outside of the wider society and the global economic, social and political context.

COMMENTARY 25

Name of Commentator: Constance Lim

1. GENERAL COMMENTS ON THE CHAPTER

- The Chapter presents many general recommendations for the benefit of youth and children. However, it does not integrate these recommendations into Agenda 21.
- The activities proposed are also so general that they sound more like objectives.

2. OVERALL COMMENTARY ON THE FIRST REVIEW OF THE CHAPTER

- Agreement with the first review of the Chapter. The Chapter is weak in that it does not take into account the wider context of the problem.
- The Chapter does not look at the many causes of the plight of children and youth. Hence its proposals for action are weak. For example, if youth and children are to have more access to education, this means taking action on certain local and international economic forces, and not just providing more educational resources.
- Agree that traditional social and community roles for children and youth must be examined more closely to see how these roles can be adapted for effective change. Otherwise, such actions as promoting dialogue with youth can easily become only token gestures, if youth and children are given no more than a passive role in development strategies.

- Youth and children belong to many different circumstances, but the strategies in the Chapter do not distinguish between these different circumstances. If the different needs of youth and children according to their circumstances are not clearly defined, some of the proposed activities may merely promote an already privileged class of youth and so prolong the existence of non-sustainable systems.
- One point to be noted and emphasized more is that: any strategy for sustainable and equitable development, to be successful, must improve the situation of the majority of children and youth in terms of health, nutrition, education and alleviation of poverty. Inequitable development is perpetuated by inequitable conditions among children and youth.

3. MAJOR POINTS AGREED/DISAGREED WITH, AND REASONS
- None.

4. MINOR POINTS AGREED/DISAGREED WITH, AND REASONS
- None.

5. POSSIBLE ON-GOING ISSUES OR CONCERNS FOR IDRC
- None.

6. POSSIBLE IMPLICATIONS FOR IDRC
- None.

CHAPTER TWENTY-SIX

RECOGNIZING AND STRENGTHENING THE ROLE OF INDIGENOUS PEOPLE AND THEIR COMMUNITIES

ABSTRACT

1. OVERALL CRITIQUE OF AGENDA 21 CHAPTER

- Recognizes the role of indigenous people in sustainable development not previously adequately addressed.
- Emphasizes the importance of implementing sound development policies that recognize, accommodate, promote and strengthen the role of indigenous people and their communities.
- Chapter does not address the more substantive and possibly conflictual issues of the inner workings of indigenous communities and their structure.
- No discussion on how the character and needs of communities influence their approaches to environmental management; class conflicts; the role and use of indigenous knowledge in achieving sustainable, equitable development.
- Over-emphasis on state's role and its responsibility/relationship with indigenous communities.
- Minimal discussion of gender issues.
- Addresses past omissions where sustainable environmental policies were developed without recognizing the existence of indigenous people. Overall, a top-down approach.

2. KEY CONCLUSIONS ARISING FROM CHAPTER

- A need to explore the interplay between strategies that include ecological, political and cultural considerations and how decisions indigenous communities make about environmental issues.
- A seminal role for research by/for indigenous communities who lack power of knowledge. By networking groups and providing them with tools to explore and propose solutions for their problems, there is a stronger opportunity for empowering these communities.
- Both gender and indigenous knowledge must be kept in mind throughout Agenda 21.
- Emphasis should be to work nationally from the grass-roots, and not just through governments.
- Essential to work from a multi-disciplinary, holistic and integrated approach.

3. RESEARCH AND/OR IMPLEMENTATION POSSIBILITIES/OPPORTUNITIES

- IDRC could undertake research that examines in depth the following issues and proposes policies, methods, etc.:
    a) Conflicts within communities (cultural, social, political, economic, religious, legal, etc.);
    b) Issues of internal democratization within communities;
    c) Issues of gender and class, age, and economic resources, etc, and how they influence the values of land and culture;

d) Role of state in its dealings with the indigenous communities. Exploration of community demands can be channelled to government; what systemic infrastructure needs to be built to facilitate more democratic, accountable decision-making;
e) Role of indigenous knowledge; exploration of where and how it is useful;
f) Role of external factors: authoritarian states, economic exigencies, international actors and their effect on resources;
g) Links with other indigenous groups internationally as identified by North/South groups;
h) Capacity-building of institutions; collaboration with other donors and NGOs.

4. ON-GOING AND/OR NEW PARTNERSHIPS FOR IDRC

- In Canada, work with NGOs that collaborate with indigenous people; Assembly of First Nations, university departments or professors working on indigenous issues; native women's groups; smaller grass-roots groups; World Council of Indigenous People; with CIDA, Environment Canada, etc.
- In other countries, identify regional, national and international indigenous organizations that do culturally appropriate research, involve indigenous researchers, and employ a participatory approach. Agencies in the US and Europe; international networks of NGOs and advocacy groups.

5. SUGGESTED NICHES FOR IDRC

- Supportive role as technical advisor and as knowledge mediator with indigenous people.
- Research, consolidation and dissemination of indigenous knowledge.
- Empowering marginalized groups through research into sustainability of traditional culture.
- Support of indigenous people in setting and carrying out their research agenda.
- Training indigenous researchers in research methodologies, approaches, information exchange.
- Providing indigenous communities the opportunity to use and control the research process and its results.
- Funding research that encourages involvement in decision-making, including: participation by women, old and young people, grass roots organizations, and the consolidation of traditional knowledge systems.
- Developing greater power decentralization among communities by working with identified leaders, women's and youth groups in identifying research priorities.
- Involving indigenous people as key sources of expertise, and training them in scientific methods, skills transfer and institutionalized indigenous knowledge.
- Identifying new issues for research now outside IDRC's mandate, e.g. the development of an indigenous scientific community using traditional knowledge and scientific skills. Working more closely with Canadian indigenous organizations linked with international indigenous groups.
- Funding the development of culturally appropriate research methods based on oral, intergenerational indigenous knowledge.

6. OTHER COMMENTS

- Developing research projects that may be used by Canadian and Third World indigenous groups for politically sensitive issues such as land and language claims could be sensitive for IDRC but such programs would help to redress the balance and give the power of knowledge to hitherto neglected peoples and communities. Initially, financial and technical assistance to indigenous people for their own research may be slow to give results but with time results will improve. The commitment to research by indigenous people should be made, and the risks recognized.

REVIEW 26

Yianna Lambrou

KEY CONCLUSIONS IN THE CHAPTER

WHAT IS THERE

Main Conclusions
National and international efforts to implement environmentally sound and sustainable development should **recognize, accommodate, promote, and strengthen** the role of indigenous people and their communities.

Agreements Reached for International and National Action
Some of the goals in the document are already present in the ILO Indigenous and Tribal Peoples Convention (no.169), are being drafted into the Universal Declaration on Indigenous Rights, and were proclaimed **The International Year for the World's Indigenous People** (1993).

Politically Significant Issues
The politics of sustainability may clash with the politics of sustainable equitable development in that equitable resource management may entail conflicts between social groups over the control and use of resources. Conflicts over land and traditional rights over its control and use (such as we find presently in Canada) may escalate to a national level and involve the state and indigenous communities as both seek to influence national policies.

WHAT IS NOT THERE

Since the document comes from a UN framework of thinking, it assumes a degree of social and cultural homogeneity and overall uniformity that is not reflected in reality. It lacks a more nuanced understanding of the interplay of indigenous communities and their conflicts with the state.

OVERALL CRITIQUE

Substantive Content
The chapter lacks an understanding of the need to analyze "**the structure and social life of a community and how its particular character shapes its approaches to environmental management**". This is where IDRC could provide research capacity. There is a lack of recognition for the class interests and the heterogeneous social groups that may function within indigenous communities and their conflicting interests. There is no discussion of the seminal role of indigenous knowledge in the role of achieving sustainable equitable development.

The approach to this issue emphasizes the state's responsibility and assumes that the national states are eager and willing to take this on. It does not recognize the conflictive and historical opposition of the state to its indigenous communities.

Design of the Chapter as an Organizing Framework
Absolutely imperative that Agenda 21 should have a chapter on indigenous people and their communities. This begins to recognize the political, historical omissions of the past and the key role of indigenous people in achieving sustainable equitable development. A discussion of their contribution is a first small step in crossing the Western ethnocentric view of development and acknowledging that an indigenous view of sustainable and equitable development exists, and should be fully heard, not only in romantic terms, but in practical and accountable goals of development.

RESEARCH REQUIREMENTS, CAPACITY BUILDING ETC.

If this chapter's main conclusion is to **recognize, accommodate, promote and strengthen** the role of indigenous people and their communities, the implications for IDRC are clear.

Research and networking with other like-minded donors is needed to recognize primarily who composes these communities, what they need, what are the specific concerns regarding their social and natural resources, how they envisage managing them, and how working relationships be developed between their organizations and national and international decision-making bodies.

The process of empowerment to which Agenda 21 is committed involves local capacity-building (via research and training) to achieve greater participation in decision-making and strategic choices regarding resource management. Development agencies should also recognize that policies need to be developed that take into consideration the specific socio-economic and political circumstances of North and South indigenous groups.

EXPLICIT PROPOSALS IN THE CHAPTER

- Ratification and application of international conventions;
- Adoption or strengthening appropriate policies and legal instruments to protect indigenous people;
- UN, international development and finance organizations, and governments should seek active participation of indigenous people;
- Organization of annual inter-organizational coordination meetings between governments and indigenous organizations;
- Provision of technical and financial assistance for capacity-building;
- Strengthening research and education programmes;
- Encouraging the understanding of indigenous people's knowledge and management experience related to the environment; and,
- Developing with governments national arrangements to consult with indigenous people.

IMPLICIT PROPOSALS DERIVED FROM THE CHAPTER

Based on the above, Agenda 21 begins to address some of the omissions of the past where sustainable environmental policies were developed without consulting or even recognizing the existence of indigenous people.

GAPS AND ALTERNATIVE APPROACHES

An important distinction is how to use and preserve traditional knowledge to manage resources. The use and application of indigenous knowledge however may consciously not always be applied or applicable given other political and economic exigencies of a particular situation. Important to explore the appropriate strategies that include ecological, political and cultural considerations and the interplay between them.

At first glance the Chapter touches upon the important issues of indigenous people and it makes an important contribution to recognising the role they place. However, it gives undue and unfounded importance to the role of governments, assuming a leadership role that is at best historically dubious, and at worst dangerous and oppressive.

NICHES FOR IDRC

GENERAL

Opportunities that Fit Normal Programming

Networking — It is an urgent priority that indigenous groups, both in Canada and in the Third World, seek to enhance and develop solidarity and information links with each other. IDRC should seek to promote these links by bringing groups from both the South and the North to exchange information on indigenous knowledge, land tenure issues, common property, appropriate technologies, biodiversity, ethnobotany, population growth, impact of non-indigenous resource management systems. The aim would be to develop appropriate international policies and strategies that have greater national and international impact for indigenous people. (In the past, IDRC supported networking between the Dene Nation and indigenous groups in Asia and Africa.)

Research — IDRC could undertake research that examines in depth the following issues and proposes policies, methods, ways that are suitable and determined by the indigenous people and their communities:
- Conflicts within communities;
- Issues of internal democratization within communities;
- Issues of gender and class, age, etc. and how they influence values of land and culture;
- Role of the state in its dealings with the indigenous communities. (The state's role in Agenda 21 is erroneously framed as benign.);
- Role of indigenous knowledge and how it may actually function in reality as decisions are made on a variety of criteria, e.g. exploitation, survival. (Indigenous knowledge may sometimes be side-stepped to achieve other ends. Important to research how and where it is most useful; seek entry points other knowledge systems.);
- Examine the role of external factors: authoritarian regimes, economic exigencies, international actors and how they affect land, resources, and decision-making;
- Develop links with other indigenous groups internationally on common concerns as identified by North/South indigenous people;
- Cultural/biological diversity of peoples and plant/animal species; and,
- Explore how indigenous knowledge can be institutionalized within each specific cultural context: constraints and opportunities.

Capacity building — training and consciousness raising about laws, historical inequities, gender issues, leading to greater participation from the grass roots. IDRC is well placed to use its commitment to training and institutional building both in Canada and in the Third World to strengthen the institutions of indigenous people. Through information networks, provide insights to indigenous groups and their communities to how donors work so they can directly access them.

Collaborate with other donors and NGOs working with indigenous groups — Undertake research that involves other agencies in the United States and Europe as well as Asia: Italy, Japan, Norway, Denmark, Sweden, and Germany are examples.

New Opportunities
- Undertake research that involves active participation of grass-roots organizations. Seek to develop greater decentralization of power among the communities by working not only with the identified leaders and well known figures of indigenous communities, but also encourage women's and youth groups to participate in identifying research priorities.
- IDRC should systematically seek to involve indigenous peoples as sources of expertise and not only rely on Western, non-indigenous, outside "second-hand experts".

- Train indigenous peoples in scientific methods and emphasize transfer of skills and expertise. Institutionalize indigenous knowledge.
- Seek to identify issues for research that are not necessarily on IDRC's present mandate but are required for the empowerment of indigenous communities: the development of an indigenous scientific community that relies both on traditional knowledge and newly acquired scientific skills. (The Inuit have undertaken some similar research).
- Work more closely with Canadian indigenous organizations who can serve as links with international indigenous groups, building research capacity and cooperation.
- IDRC should fund the development of culturally appropriate research methods given that indigenous knowledge is mostly oral rather than written, and is transmitted inter-generationally through the relationship with the land and nature. Indigenous culture is indivisible and requires understanding and a research methodology that respects its totality.

Unusual or High-Risk Opportunities
- It may be sensitive for IDRC to develop research projects and information data bases that will be used by indigenous groups in Canada and the Third World for politically sensitive issues such as land and language claims, women's rights, restoration of aboriginal fishing and hunting rights, and self-government, etc. The political nature of these issues should not deter IDRC, particularly in Canada. Research is not politically neutral and is constantly used to oppress or discriminate marginalized peoples. Here is an opportunity to redress the balance and give the power of knowledge to those who will use it directly for their communities' benefit. Research should be rooted in the communities and should involve the direct participation of the people involved in indigenous knowledge systems. This may not always be as easy to carry out particularly at the early stages.

- Financial and technical assistance which is given directly to indigenous people to conduct their own research may be slow to give results or difficult to complete at first. As research capacity is incrementally developed, the output should improve. However, the commitment to research undertaken by indigenous people has to be made, and the risks should be recognized.

REGIONAL SPECIFICITY
None.

KEY PARTNERS/OTHER ACTORS
Canada
- NGOs working with indigenous people in Canada
- The Assembly of First Nations
- University departments or professors working on Indigenous issues
- The Native Women's Association
- Other smaller grass-roots groups
- The World Council of Indigenous People
- CIDA; Environment Canada
- Universities and colleges
- World Council of Indigenous People

Other countries
Identify regional, national and international indigenous organizations that are endeavouring to do research that is culturally appropriate, involves indigenous scientists, and employs a participatory approach, for example:
- Agencies in the US and Europe

- NGOs/ENGOs
- Advocacy groups

RECOMMENDATIONS

WHICH NICHES ARE BEST FOR IDRC PROGRAM?

IDRC is eminently poised to play an important role in this area of indigenous peoples and their communities, particularly in the ENR division which now not only engages in technical research issues of environment conservation but also embraces recognition of the cultural and social implications of sustainable and equitable development. The issue of indigenous peoples is a holistic issue "par excellence" since it combines subtle and compassionate understanding of ethical and cultural values, with technical knowledge about sustaining plant and animal species in a degrading environment. To adequately and responsibly deal with research on indigenous people IDRC needs to assume an imaginative and committed role not only as technical advisor but also as knowledge mediator in a partnership of solidarity and advocacy with indigenous peoples.

IDRC must play a role vis-à-vis indigenous knowledge, the sustainability of traditional culture and the empowerment of marginalized groups through research. We are quickly accumulating experience on the ethics, subtleties and problems of supporting research in this field. IDRC funded an IIRR workshop on Indigenous Knowledge in the Philippines in September 1992. A seminar planned in October (5–7) on Indigenous Knowledge aims to bring together IDRC staff and outside experts to help determine in unison what our institutional research agenda should be. Hopefully, a vision of the intricacies and challenges of working with indigenous people will aid us to refine our priorities.

However, it remains seminally important that IDRC does not lose consciousness of the fact that it is here to play a supporting role to the concerns of indigenous people and in no way set the agenda for them. Its contribution can be in the training of indigenous researchers and in the collaborative definition of research methodologies and approaches giving them the opportunity to exchange information with each other in Canada and in the Third World.

The approach in the Agenda 21 document is top-down, minimizes internal workings and importance of community, assumes an idealized yet un-examined view of community dynamics and interrelationships, ignores the issue of race, and government discrimination against indigenous people. The assumption that governments stand by their aboriginal people has been proven repeatedly false not only in Canada but in most places of the globe. Historically, governments, the state have been agents of oppression, marginalization, poverty, usurpation of lands, military rule, denial of citizenship and loss of livelihood. It is not envisaged that governments wholeheartedly will renew a centuries old relationship of oppression just because a chapter in Agenda 21 designates them as caretakers of aboriginal people. IDRC's role should clearly be on the side of the indigenous communities, playing a truly empowering role by providing the opportunity to appropriate, utilize and control the research process and its results. IDRC should be funding research that encourages involvement in the decision-making, participation by women, the old and young people, and the consolidation of traditional knowledge systems: not to ossify indigenous traditional knowledge but to sustain its roots in a way that will permit indigenous people to absorb external influences as they see appropriately fit.

ARE ADJUSTMENTS NEEDED AT IDRC IN ORDER TO FILL THESE NICHES?

Program Organization

The new structure of ENR and interdisciplinary way of working, not only within the division but also with other divisions, will enhance and encourage a holistic and committed approach to the indigenous peoples involvement in research. However, these links have to be strengthened and made more socialized. It is easy to duplicate and fragment efforts if communication is not shared, or if efforts are duplicated haphazardly.

IDRC needs also to escape in some ways from the UN "inoffensive" mode of trying to please everyone, and instead seek to assume a position of support and commitment to indigenous people that is not only lip-service, but engages them in real and tangible ways as full and active participants in research. The advocacy of the indigenous people should be strengthened by sound technical knowledge which IDRC can help to provide.

Process and Project Cycle

No changes foreseen.

Structure/Staffing

No changes foreseen.

ARE THERE CROSS-CUTTING ISSUES THAT ARE NOT ADEQUATELY REFLECTED IN THE ABOVE?

No.

COMMENTARY 26

Name of Commentator: Gisèle Morin-Labatût

1. GENERAL COMMENTS ON THE CHAPTER

- The Chapter recognizes the role of indigenous people in sustainable development that has not been adequately addressed in the past. It emphasizes the importance of implementing sound development policies that recognize, accommodate, promote and strengthen the role of indigenous people and their communities.
- The overall objectives are consistent with those of IDRC: empowerment of local communities, participation in resource management and other sustainable development strategies.
- The recommended approach of encouraging national governments to promote the participation of indigenous people is coherent with the position taken by Canada, i.e. to place primary responsibility of implementation of Agenda 21 with national governments.
- Indigenous knowledge, mentioned in so many other chapters as an essential ingredient for sustainable development, is only briefly alluded to in this Chapter.

2. OVERALL COMMENTARY ON THE FIRST REVIEW OF THE CHAPTER

- The review is very comprehensive and points to several important omissions in the document, as well as to a certain naive approach with respect to the relationship between national governments and indigenous peoples.

- Other possible areas of research relate to the inequalities (caste, gender, etc.) and inter-ethnic tensions existing within traditional cultures, how these negatively affect equitable development, and how they can be addressed.

3. MAJOR POINTS AGREED/DISAGREED WITH, AND REASONS

- The reviewer highlights the importance of research by indigenous groups and for indigenous communities; of providing them with training and tools to explore solutions to the problems they identify; of working with a multi-disciplinary approach. These points are very important whenever IDRC cooperates with local communities, be they indigenous or not.

4. MINOR POINTS AGREED/DISAGREED WITH, AND REASONS

- The reviewer states that IDRC should be clearly on the side of indigenous communities: this may cause problems in cases of conflict between government and indigenous groups (because IDRC's projects require government clearance) or in case of conflicts between different indigenous groups.
- The reviewer notes the top-down approach recommended in the Chapter and proposes that it be tempered by a community (grass roots) action. Working with community groups exclusively might provoke a negative or hostile reaction from some governments; IDRC might seek to develop mechanisms to facilitate cooperative research involving both governments and community groups.

5. POSSIBLE ON-GOING ISSUES OR CONCERNS FOR IDRC

- The possible areas of research suggested by the reviewer could be addressed by IDRC, through ENR, SSD, ISS and CAID.
- Traditional environmental knowledge, which is recognized as a vital component of sustainable development, is intimately linked with a particular world view. The question of transferability and expansion of knowledge will have to be addressed. Research into the universal principles governing traditional approaches to knowledge acquisition and transfer, that go beyond the cultural specificity, could be encouraged and supported.
- The question of whether indigenous knowledge constitutes an identifiable, separate body of knowledge for communities themselves, should be addressed: is the distinction purely academic? is the bottom line really what knowledge is already there? and what other knowledge is needed within a given community, so that it can participate fully in environmentally-sound development?

6. POSSIBLE IMPLICATIONS FOR IDRC

- In order for IDRC to develop meaningful projects with indigenous organizations, it will have to emphasize capacity-building as a major component, including project identification, negotiation and management.
- Working with indigenous organizations in both Canada and the Third World entails a higher degree of political awareness and implication than usual; this will require learning about the politics of relationships among the major players, and how they relate to national governments.

CHAPTER TWENTY-SEVEN

NON-GOVERNMENTAL ORGANIZATIONS

Responsible Officer: T. Carroll-Foster

ABSTRACT 27

1. OVERALL CRITIQUE OF AGENDA 21 CHAPTER

- A very weak chapter. Does not appear to have been put together with any real inputs from both North and South NGOs or ENGOs (environmental NGOs).
- Despite increasing lip-service from governments and UN agencies about the value of NGOs, the weakness of the Chapter belies the purported value of NGOs.
- The activities proposed are neither innovative nor progressive, and do not relect the capacity and capability of NGOs.
- No cross-referencing with other Agenda 21 chapters.
- Fails to analyze Implementation and Financial needs, and thus negates the existing importance and potential value of NGOs.

2. KEY CONCLUSIONS ARISING FROM CHAPTER

- NGOs are recognized as vital to shaping/implementing participatory democracy.
- Their diverse experience and expertise are seen as important for implementing environmentally sound and socially responsible sustainable development.
- NGOs' global community network should be tapped and strengthened.
- Strengthening/promulgating legislation to support NGOs and their consultative groups will be unacceptable to governments wary of NGOs' independence/influence.

3. RESEARCH AND/OR IMPLEMENTATION POSSIBILITIES/OPPORTUNITIES

- Weak in identifying specific, concrete measures — mainly suggested reviews of ways to enhance UN agencies' mechanisms for involving NGOs in their work.
- Strengthening or promulgating legislation to enable NGOs to establish consultative groups or protect communities and public interest groups through legal action concerning sustainable development. This would necessitate some research being undertaken and capabilities being developed.

4. ON-GOING AND/OR NEW PARTNERSHIPS FOR IDRC

- On-going partnerships with NGOs, ENGOs, women's organizations/networks.
- Consortia and coalitions within Canada (e.g. SAP, CPCU, CCIC, CFUW) and abroad (DAWN, IFUW, TWN, KENGO).
- Research institutions, community colleges, business councils, consulting firms.

5. SUGGESTED NICHES FOR IDRC

- Capacity-building and strengthening of NGOs/ENGOs in sustainable development concepts, planning, implementation and development, and environmental/social/gender analyses/screening/assessments/impacts, including training, training modules, courses and pilot projects, research techniques, data-bases.

- Greater use of NGOs networks for the dissemination of practical research results, and exchange of North–South/South–North information and solutions.
- Cross-training: of NGOs in actual environmental issues and ecology, and ENGOs in social development, and the inter-relationship of both.
- Development of cross-fertilization and collaboration between the two halves of the private sector — business and NGOs — through various mechanisms.
- Assistance to NGOs in developing greater awareness about environment, women and indigenous people, and integrative, replicable pilot projects, and generally developing greater professional capacity and expertise.

6. **OTHER COMMENTS**
- None.

REVIEW 27

KEY CONCLUSIONS IN THE CHAPTER

WHAT IS THERE

(Please note that the acronym "NGOs" includes environmental NGOs, development NGOs, women's organizations, non-profit associations.)

Main Conclusions
- NGOs (variously described as formal, informal, grass-roots movements, self-organized, non-profit organizations which represent groups addressed in Chapter 27,) are now recognized as playing "a vital role in the shaping and implementation of participatory democracy";
- NGO credibility arises from "the responsible and constructive role they play in society";
- The independent nature of NGOs "calls for **real** participation", hence independence is seen as a "major attribute of NGOs and the precondition of real participation";
- NGOs are seen as possessing "well-established and diverse experience, expertise and capacity" in those fields (unspecified) which are also seen as being of "importance to the review and implementation of environmentally sound and socially responsible sustainable development" (ESSD);
- The NGO community is further perceived as having a "global network, that should be tapped, enabled, and strengthened in support of the efforts to achieve the common goals" (of sustainability).

Agreements Reached for International and National Action
No agreements were reached for international action. The chapter mentions 4 specific objectives which governments and international bodies **should** undertake, but no real process or mechanism was put in place to ensure that occurs. Essentially the 4 objectives are rather weak:
- Mechanisms to allow NGOs to play their partnership responsibly and effectively should be developed by governments, international bodies;
- A process to review formal procedures and mechanisms to involve NGOs at all levels (policy-making, decision-making, implementation) should be initiated by the UN system and governments;
- A "mutually productive dialogue" should be established at the national level between **all** governments and NGOs regarding their respective roles in "ESSD", by 1995 (the only specific date mentioned);

- NGOs should be promoted and allowed to participate in the conception, establishment, evaluation of official mechanisms and procedures to review Agenda 21 implementation.

The need for substantial new financial resources for NGOs is largely ignored, if not actually circumscribed by weasel words. For example, while costs are envisaged for enhancing consultative procedures and mechanisms between NGOs and "official organizations", they are portrayed as being "relatively limited and unpredictable". NGOs are then recognized as requiring (or is 'needing' meant?) "additional funding — stated to be "significant but cannot be reliably estimated" — in support of their establishment of, improvement of, or contributions to Agenda 21 monitoring systems", yet Chapter 27 does not actually discuss the direct involvement of NGOs in setting up such systems.

Politically Significant Issues

The main politically significant issue identified is the need for governments to "promulgate or strengthen, legislative measures necessary to enable the establishment of *consultative groups* by NGOs, and to ensure NGOs the right to protect the public interest through legal action". In many societies either or both of these could be dynamite, given that the majority of countries are not overly given to democracy or democratic participation by their citizens, communities, or organizations of any stripe. Note the measures are not directed at NGOs themselves but at consultative groups set up by NGOs or the protection of public interest, not the NGOs per se.

The majority of governments are highly suspicious and wary of NGOs, people's movements, etc. and have, in the past — and present — put up considerable roadblocks, including persecution, to halt the momentum and actions of NGOs. Many governments will need considerable, and strong, persuasion to ensure the existence and independence of NGOs; to allow NGOs to develop and promote consultative groups and meaningful consultation at all levels; to let NGOs into the inner sanctums where decisions are made; and, to give and ensure NGOs the right and ability through legal action to protect the public interest as well as themselves.

WHAT IS NOT THERE

The document is stuck in a 1960s mind-set and is somewhat paternalistic. It does not appreciate the extent to which NGOs (to use this acronym to cover a wide variety of social, people's, environmental, etc. movements and organizations) have evolved and become, in many instances, the visionaries and leaders of Agenda 21 items. It does not attempt to define "partnership" and, despite the sub-title, really does not address the concept of "partners for sustainable development".

It treats NGOs in a monolithic way. It thereby makes the mistake of assuming that the variegated NGOs will have common cause or agenda and will be amenable to being treated in the same way by international organizations or governments. It fails to incorporate any analysis about NGOs, whether North or South, and therefore does not appear to understand how NGOs work; how they relate to communities and societies; how they network locally and internationally; and, develop momentum, action, and change.

It talks about what governments "should" do, but does not really elaborate on the role of the NGOs except by implicit assumptions. It is obvious that the input of NGOs had relatively little substantive impact on this chapter, which was, as is known, an after-thought of PrepCom III, when NGOs protested to the UNCED Secretariat in Geneva that they were not being taken seriously and were not being integrated into either UNCED or Agenda 21 (as also happened with the other "Major Groups").

It lacks logic or analysis in terms of the Means of Implementation, whether Financing and Cost Evaluation or Capacity-building. It fails to analyze the constraints that NGOs must deal with, and how difficult it is for them to become full partners in consultative processes because of the lack of resources available to them on a consistent basis.

OVERALL CRITIQUE
Substantive Content
- Surprisingly, and disappointingly, a very weak section, replete with pablum-type statements.
- Even though NGOs are increasingly given kudos by decision-makers at all levels, the reality is evidenced by this ill-conceived chapter — NGOs are still not taken very seriously — any more than are women or indigenous peoples. This is further evidenced by the lack of attention paid to Costs and Financing and to overall Implementation.
- The Activities proposed that the United Nations system and inter-governmental organizations should undertake can hardly be called innovative or particularly progressive — they appear to be more of the same, and redolent with foot-dragging. In the case of governments, the chapter does not even propose that they should undertake the five identified Activities but only "should take measures to ....". Given the amount of innovation, energy, imagination, and vision shown by the majority of NGOs, the section on Activities does not reflect any of that and can only be regarded as being in a terminal state of palsy.

Design of the Chapter as an Organizing Framework
The design of Chapter 27 follows the generic design of most of the Agenda 21 documents, but it lacks a substantive Preamble and explanation about NGOs and their evolution to this point in time where they should be regarded and included as full partners in protection of the environment and sustainable development. It does not define what "NGO" means and what it includes.

It fails to draw linkages between the different "partners" or to distinguish between them. For instance, it does not mention women, indigenous groups, business and industry, environmental NGOs, wildlife and animal protection agencies, research institutions, civil society organizations, etc.

It makes generic statements as to what measures UN system agencies and governments should undertake, but it mentions nothing about what NGOs are doing, and could or should do (for instance, the development of a series of NGO "treaties" on a number of cross-sectoral and sectoral issues as well as the development of sustainable development and environmental training and the establishment of an NGO Code of Conduct for N & S NGOs).

It does not link this chapter or cross-reference it with other key chapters involving networks, people's movements, partnerships, institution- and capacity-building, etc.

Overall the design needs revamping in order to be more comprehensive and inclusive.

RESEARCH REQUIREMENTS, CAPACITY-BUILDING ETC.

EXPLICIT PROPOSALS IN THE CHAPTER
Overall the proposals as encapsulated in the Objectives and Activities sections are mundane and weak. Maybe with all the political pressures they could not be otherwise. Yet some of the other chapters in Agenda 21 are quite forceful and concrete, and thus indicative of good committee leadership and collaboration.

The most explicit proposals are listed in the Activities section, but these are weakened by the insertion of the phrase that the UN system, inter-governmental organizations and forums, and governments "should **take measures to**" do something rather than actually **do** it. The UN system is expected to undertake the identified activities "in consultation with NGOs", whereas such consultation is not suggested as applicable to those activities proposed for governments.

- The seven activities identified for UN agencies to undertake vis-à-vis NGOs largely amount to reviews of and reporting on ways to enhance individual UN agencies' procedures and mechanisms by which NGOs might participate in policy, decision-making, implementation and evaluation and by which UN agencies might draw on NGO expertise and views for the agencies' purposes or for Agenda 21 follow-up. Overall, the activities are more of the same reviews of NGO participation and access to data/information that have occurred throughout the UN system over the last 20 years. No mention is made of specific activity as related to sustainable development and the environment.
- The five activities — or measures — identified for governments amount to establishing dialogue with NGOs; encouraging partnerships; involving NGOs to carry out Agenda 21 and taking into account their findings; making data accessible to NGOs; and, reviewing government education (in what area, sector? No mention is made of development or environment) programs to identify how NGOs might be included (to do what, with what?)
- The most positive proposals are slipped in under Means of Implementation — Capacity-building where it is mentioned that UN organizations "will need to provide increased financial and administrative support for NGOs", especially Southern, contributing to Agenda 21 monitoring and evaluation, **but** no nominal figures or substantive requirements are attached which thereby weakens the proposal. Governments "will need to promulgate or strengthen legislative measures to enable" NGOs to establish consultative groups or protect public interest through legal action, **but** this proposal does not mention legislative action to establish NGOs themselves and to protect NGOs.

IMPLICIT PROPOSALS DERIVED FROM THE CHAPTER

- None really.
- Basically the scenario is more of the same treatment of NGOs: marginalization or trivialization; lack of recognition of what they can contribute; what their needs are; what their constraints are, not least of which are the vacuous statements by UN agencies and governments alike about including NGOs but in actuality keeping them on the sidelines with little money and other resources allocated to them.
- NGOs will most likely be asked to participate in Agenda 21 follow-up but will not be provided with the wherewithal. Hence NGOs will have to find $$$ and other resources.

GAPS AND ALTERNATIVE APPROACHES

- Gaps — almost everything!
- Alternative approaches — See Niches for IDRC.

NICHES FOR IDRC

GENERAL
Opportunities that Fit Normal Programming
IDRC could continue to:
- Strengthen networks and partnerships between research institutions themselves and, increasingly, with NGOs (including women's organizations and both developmental and environmental agencies) and the private sector, as part of its on-going capacity-building, and enhance those by incorporating training on and research into environmentally-related aspects of development and environmental processes and tools (e.g. EAs and EIAs).

- Enable NGOs to increase their professional capacity for research into and evaluation of the development process in which they typically are engaged, and extend that to a better understanding of local and regional eco-systems and environmental processes, and the resultant consequences for environmentally sustainable development.
- Strengthen environmental education and training on both a North–South basis and South–South basis, but broaden the thrust by more widely disseminating the results of the education, training and lessons learned among research institutions, NGOs, and the private sector.
- Work with the private sector in such areas as urban hydrology, mining, building technology, environmental engineering, biotechnology and food processing, and expand that thrust both sectorally and in terms of constituencies or audiences in the North and South.
- Undertake collaborative activities with various specialized agencies of the UN system, bilateral donor aid agencies, and funding or private philanthropic organizations, but expand the past informal linkages into more formal global partnerships with key institutions, and ensure that both the not-for-profit and profit private sectors are included in the linkages and consultations.

New Opportunities
IDRC could undertake or help to initiate the following:
- Relate NGO Treaties (TNCs, Consumption and Lifestyle, Trade and Sustainable Development, Alternative Economic Models, People's Earth Declaration, etc.) to Agenda 21 Chapters at a Forum where E&D NGOs meet with business/industry, government, women's organizations to develop a pro-active, constructive agenda for the weaker aspects of Agenda 21 (e.g. the NGO chapter, Consumption chapter, etc., plan of action, time-frame and budget to be disseminated to UN agencies and governments for action.
- Using widespread consultation, develop environmental and sustainable development (E&SD) training models for N & S NGOs, including how to scope out and undertake environmental screening, assessments, and impact assessments; pilot test the models; develop comprehensive training system and materials appropriate to specific countries or regions; train NGO leaders and trainers at different levels, and ensure good representation of women and indigenous peoples; monitor and evaluate, so that lessons learned can lead to on-going evolution of training in E&SD, more sustainable projects/programs, and more professionalism among both N & S NGOs.
- Help NGOs to become more professional, accountable and responsible at all levels, including expanding their environmental knowledge and capability, management techniques, policy and economic development capabilities and/or knowledge, and organizational, implementation and evaluative skills so that they can better serve their constituencies, implement genuinely "sustainable" projects or programs, and have positive inputs into and impacts on government policies.
- Develop a mechanism that more widely and effectively disseminates research results, lessons learned, etc. on both a North and South basis (often Northern NGOs are as lacking in solid information as are Southern), and helps to make such results or lessons adaptable to different conditions or environs.
- Work to bring together NGOs and business/industry with a view to finding "common cause" and areas of collaboration and reinforcement for environmentally sustainable development, and to reducing automatic mistrust, mythologies and destructive dissension.

Unusual or High-Risk Opportunities
- Working with NGOs to develop comprehensive environmental and sustainable development principles, policies and strategies that might be used for or incorporated into government and multilateral/bilateral initiatives, and even incorporated into the NGOs' proposed Code of Conduct for NGOs (1991–92).

- Working with NGOs to develop national conservation strategies (NCSs), state-of-the-environment reports (SOERs) on a local, regional or national scale, and appropriate legislation applicable to the governance of and support for NGOs and for the legal foundation to support NCSs and SOERs including their implementation and enforcement.
- Working with NGOs and the private sector to ascertain in what ways research results can be implemented in a widely-based, practical, constructive way (e.g. investments for the application of low-technology).
- Ensuring that NGOs consistently move towards the full integration of women and indigenous peoples in their projects and programs at all levels and in all capacities — or basically put into practice their purported inclusionary principles — and working with NGOs to develop their knowledge and capacity to do so.

REGIONAL SPECIFICITY

Not country- or region-specific, but it should be noted that a number of NGO/ENGO consortia and coalitions now exist worldwide with support with bilateral aid agencies such as CIDA and SIDA. These should be identified with the view of assessing which are the most advanced, responsible and accountable, and which might, therefore, be the best partners for IDRC's work, in addition to individual or independent NGOs.

KEY PARTNERS AND OTHER ACTORS

Canada
- Development NGOs, consortia, coalitions, e.g. CPCU, CCIC, SAP, TWN (See CCIC Directory — NGO Profiles)
- Environmental NGOs
- (See CEN's Directory)
- Women's organizations, including business & professional women's associations (See List of National Women's Organizations)
- Research institutions, universities, community colleges (e.g. Algonquin College)
- Business and industry associations or organizations (e.g. CESO, Business Council on Sustainable Development, Canadian Chamber of Commerce, etc.)
- Federal, provincial, territorial governments
- Local municipal authorities

Other Countries
All of the above, but especially:
- Coalitions and consortia of Third World Development and Environment NGOs (e.g. TWN, South Asian Partnership, KENGO)
- Coalitions and consortia of women's organizations (e.g. DAWN, IFUW,)
- UN agencies (UNEP, INSTRAW, UNIFEM, World Bank)

RECOMMENDATIONS
(See above — Normal, New, and Unusual Opportunities)

WHICH NICHES ARE BEST FOR IDRC'S PROGRAM?
- On-going and new research
- Capacity-building and institution-creation and -strengthening
- Facilitation and development of new networks and linkages including bringing together NGOs and the private sector

ARE ADJUSTMENTS NEEDED AT IDRC IN ORDER TO FILL THESE NICHES?

Program Organization

Nothing major — probably more fine-tuning as a result of knowing the NGO community and its capabilities better.

Process and Project Cycle

As above.

Structure and Staffing

Appears to have been taken in part through the Special Initiatives Program in IDRC, but, if IDRC does become more involved with NGOs and the suggested initiatives or opportunities then some additional staffing will be required.

ARE THERE CROSS-CUTTING ISSUES THAT ARE NOT ADEQUATELY REFLECTED IN ANY OF THE ABOVE?

The major problem in this chapter and other Agenda 21 chapters is the lack of cross-referencing between chapters to illustrate their linkages or impacts. The Guide — "The Global Partnership for Environment and Development" — prepared by UNCED/Geneva (April 1992) provides flow charts that show cross-sectoral linkages (see attached).

COMMENTARY 27

Name of Commentator: C. Smart

1. **GENERAL COMMENTS ON THE CHAPTER**
   - Although recognizing the new importance of the NGOs in development and in Sustainable and Equitable Development (SED) particularly and calling for new partnerships between governments and NGOs based on legal guarantees for their right to exist and to oppose official policy, there is, however, an air of after-thought about the Chapter.
   - Even so, the inclusion of a specific chapter on the role of NGOs and the recommendations to governments to factor them into policy-making and program delivery is a gain on which NGOs can and should build and to which donors must respond.

2. **OVERALL COMMENTARY ON THE FIRST REVIEW OF THE CHAPTER**
   - The Review of the Chapter is well done. Agree with it in all respects.

3. **MAJOR POINTS AGREED/DISAGREED WITH, AND REASONS**
   - As above.

4. **MINOR POINTS AGREED/DISAGREED WITH, AND REASONS**
   - As above.

5. POSSIBLE ON-GOING ISSUES OR CONCERNS FOR IDRC

- The Review sets out a comprehensive range of activities the Centre should consider to forge stronger partnerships with NGOs. The number of activities, contacts, and issues is large and would, if responded to fully, require a sub-program to implement.

6. POSSIBLE IMPLICATIONS FOR IDRC

- Agree with the reviewer that a greater involvement with the NGOs in Canada and the developing countries will require more program staff and resources.

CHAPTER TWENTY-EIGHT

LOCAL AUTHORITIES' INITIATIVES IN SUPPORT OF AGENDA 21

Responsible Officer: Denise Deby

ABSTRACT

1. OVERALL CRITIQUE OF AGENDA 21 CHAPTER

- The Chapter is important in highlighting the key role of local authorities in sustainable development, but is superficial.
- Treats local authorities as homogenous; assumes they will be equal partners despite different sizes, scales, relative power.
- Ignores issues of central–local government relations; ignores difficulties of intersectoral policy planning and implementation; assumes local authorities act in the interests of citizens, are politically neutral.
- Does not discuss mechanisms for or feasibility of popular consultation (many countries do not have such mechanisms; many significant groups in developing countries are informal, illegal or semi-legal).
- Little recognition that environmental degradation results from poverty and unequal access to resources to meet basic needs.
- Does not define what "capacity-building" is required for local authorities.

2. KEY CONCLUSIONS ARISING FROM CHAPTER

- Participation of local authorities is essential to achieve Agenda 21 objectives.
- Local authorities should implement "local Agenda 21s" through consultation with their populations and cooperation with other local authorities.
- International agencies in partnership should increase support for local authority programs.
- Local authorities' programs, policies, laws and regulations to achieve Agenda 21 objectives should be assessed.
- Local authorities should implement programs to include women and youth in decision-making, planning and implementation.

3. RESEARCH AND/OR IMPLEMENTATION POSSIBILITIES/OPPORTUNITIES

- Research:
    a) To assess and improve local authority programs, policies, laws and regulations (not only environmental policies but also economic and social policies, land use, service standards, etc. that are directly related to Agenda 21);
    b) On means of integrating women and youth in decision-making; on the policy implications of causes of environmental degradation at the local level (poverty, unequal access/distribution of resources, etc.); on central-local government relations, decentralization and strengthening of local authorities.

- **Strengthen:**
  a) Community, civic and other organisations' capacity to define their own priorities and strategies in order to participate as full partners in local consultative processes; support institutions working in local authority capacity-building and local environment management; support cooperation and information-sharing among local authorities.

4. ON-GOING AND/OR NEW PARTNERSHIPS FOR IDRC

- **Developing countries:** central ministries of local government, of environment and natural resources, etc.; national and regional associations of local authorities; research institutions; training institutes; universities; NGOs, citizens' groups, other civil society organisations.
- **Canada:** municipal and provincial government departments responsible for planning, environmental and other services; Federation of Canadian Municipalities; CIDA (Management for Change, bilateral programs); universities.
- **International:** International Union of Local Authorities; World Bank; UN agencies (UNCHS and others); other bilateral donors and like-minded agencies.

5. SUGGESTED NICHES FOR IDRC

- Many chapter activities are suited to IDRC's special niche of supporting applied research, information-sharing, and capacity-building and to IDRC's experience in supporting a variety of institutional types (government, non-government and independent research institutions) and in promoting collaboration among these. As a relatively "neutral" agency which supports locally-relevant research, IDRC has much to offer. IDRC could, for example:
  a) Support research by and for local authorities, citizens and other organisations to define "local Agenda 21s"; facilitate the consultative process between local authorities and citizens, organisations and the private sector. Entails building the capacity of key civic, community and other organisations to define their own priorities and needs.
  b) Support key institutions to assess and improve local authority programs, policies, laws and regulations; support intersectoral research and networking by institutions working in local authority capacity-building; research on alternative finance systems and sources for local governments; and on training/human resource development needs.
  c) Support analyses of the actual and potential role of underrepresented groups, particularly women and youth, in decision-making, planning and implementation, and mechanisms for participation at the local level.
  d) Build on and sharpen the focus of support for innovative research on informal and community initiatives which could be developed into environmentally sustainable practices; includes identification of innovations that work e.g. community-based service delivery which meets criteria of participation, cost-effectiveness and sustainable development; community-based land trusts; etc.; decentralization policies, processes, and effects (on local government capacity, the environment, etc.); local/central government relations, and what could be decentralized in order to strengthen the ability of local authorities to meet Agenda 21 objectives, including political and social as well as technical aspects (e.g. democratization, participation).
  e) Promote exchange among local authorities and local authority associations.

6. OTHER COMMENTS

- IDRC support for such activities would facilitate the implementation of activities called for in other Agenda 21 chapters.

REVIEW 28

KEY CONCLUSIONS IN THE CHAPTER

WHAT IS THERE

Main Conclusions
The Chapter presents the following rationale:
- Many of the problems, and the solutions, in Agenda 21 are rooted in local activities; and, local authorities are responsible for implementing national as well as local policies and providing infrastructure, so the participation of local authorities will be a determining factor in achieving the objectives of Agenda 21.
- Local authorities should contribute to the implementation of Agenda 21 through consultation with their populations and through cooperation with other local authorities.

Agreements Reached for International and National Action
This Chapter deals with international, national, and local action.

By signing this chapter, the signatories to Agenda 21 have agreed on a number of actions to support local implementation of Agenda 21:
- Local authorities should develop local "Agenda 21s", through consultation with citizens, organisations, and private enterprises;
- There should be an assessment (the chapter does not indicate by whom) of local authorities' programs, policies, laws and regulations to achieve Agenda 21 objectives;
- UN and other international agencies should form partnerships to increase support for local authority programs;
- Cooperation should be increased among local authorities; and,
- Local authorities should implement programs to include women and youth in decision-making, planning and implementation.

Politically Significant Issues
IDRC support for the activities proposed in this chapter would have to take into account a number of political issues related to local government, which are not discussed in the chapter:
- In most countries national and local governments have different powers and responsibilities. It may be difficult for some national governments to ensure that local authorities implement the actions agreed to in this chapter. Conversely, national governments could end up not taking action on Agenda 21 items, arguing that is the responsibility of local authorities. In supporting the activities proposed in this chapter, IDRC would have to be aware of the extent to which local authorities have jurisdiction in relevant areas.
- Although in this chapter, national governments recognize the need to strengthen local authorities' ability to implement Agenda 21 activities, the relative strength and independence of local governments is often a politically sensitive issue. National (and regional) governments may be unwilling to devolve the necessary powers to local authorities, or authority to collect and manage finances necessary to meet responsibilities, even where national governments have adopted or affirmed policies of decentralisation of authority to local governments. IDRC support for decentralisation in sectors where governments are unwilling to devolve authority could be seen as an unwelcome challenge to national authority or as interference.
- There is also an assumption in this chapter that local authorities act in the best interest of their citizens, that they are politically neutral, and that there are no security risks to the citizens in the implementation of the activities described. This assumption is at best naive, since it does not

recognise that governments may be unwilling to allow participation or that they have interests other than meeting the needs of the public, and at worst dangerous for citizens. Moreover, it could be politically unacceptable for external agencies to insist on activities that appear to have a certain political or ideological basis, such as the kind of democratisation that would be required for citizen participation called for in this chapter.
- There are issues which arise if IDRC is to work more closely with other agencies in support of the activities in this chapter. Researchers and policy makers in the past have often looked to IDRC to support research which provides alternative paradigms, solutions, etc. to those in the development mainstream. For example, a dominant approach to local government strengthening which emphasises improving systems of management and human resources, which has been supported by some multilateral agencies, has been criticised by research and policy-making bodies as being technocratic and neglectful of social and political issues.

WHAT IS NOT THERE
- The Chapter does not discuss mechanisms for or the feasibility of consultation with citizens, organisations and private enterprises. The chapter implies that such mechanisms already exist, or that they can be easily developed. However, in developing countries, many if not most of the significant or affected groups are illegal or semi-legal — e.g. informal sector enterprises, non-governmental organisations, citizens living under squatter conditions or in shelter that falls short of legal standards, etc. Local authorities may turn a blind eye to or even participate in "semi-legal" activities, but there could be significant risks or difficulty in obtaining citizen and private sector participation if semi-legal groups and activities are identified or made more visible.
- The chapter does not say anything about local government finance, which is a key to the planning and implementation of the activities in the Chapter and to sustainable economic, social and environmental planning and program implementation at the local level.

OVERALL CRITIQUE
Substantive Content
- The Chapter does not provide an operational definition of local authorities. As a result, it treats local authorities as homogeneous, ignoring issues of size, scale and relative power. Behind the proposed activities lies the assumption that local authorities can function as equal partners.
- As explained above, the chapter ignores the political feasibility of participation and issues related to local vs. national powers. This calls into question the feasibility of some of the proposed activities.
- The main activities identified are networking among, strengthening of and technical assistance to local authorities. Underlying this approach (which is found in other parts of Agenda 21) is the assumption that knowledge and skills alone can solve environmental problems. There is little recognition that environmental degradation (especially as manifested at a local level) results from poverty and from unequal access to resources to meet basic needs (inequality based on class, gender, etc.). The Chapter does not discuss the role of local authorities in facilitating or inhibiting these processes.
- There is also little attention paid to the needs of people and how these will be included in the design of strategies for sustainable development. For example, the chapter assumes that "the process of consultation would increase household awareness of sustainable development issues". It may, but this approach tends to be based on the assumption that the problems of environmental degradation are due to lack of awareness, which is not always the case particularly among the poor in developing countries. Implementing awareness raising activities alone risks exacerbating burdens on the poor and not addressing the real causes of overuse or misuse of resources.

- This chapter recognises the need for "capacity-building" for local governments, but does not provide details on precisely what kind of "capacity-building" is intended. The function of "environmental management" cannot be isolated; all local authority activities which affect the environment (provision of shelter, water, sanitation, infrastructure; regulations and standards; fees and charges, etc.) have to be considered.

Design of the Chapter as an Organizing Framework

This Chapter is important in drawing attention to the important role of local authorities in development, which has often been ignored in the past. The chapter cannot be considered in isolation; the role of local authorities is significant in most of the Agenda 21 chapters. However, devoting a separate chapter to this highlights the importance of local authorities in Agenda 21 activities, and reflects the interest of certain local authorities in being part of the process.

RESEARCH REQUIREMENTS, CAPACITY BUILDING ETC.

EXPLICIT PROPOSALS IN THE CHAPTER

Most of the activities proposed in the chapter relate to networking, information collection or capacity-building:

Networking activities
- By 1993 the international community should have initiated a consultative process to increase cooperation among local authorities;
- By 1994 representatives of local authorities' associations should have increased cooperation to enhance exchange of information and experience and mutual technical assistance; and,
- The chapter calls for periodic consultations of international partners and developing countries to review strategies and decide on how to mobilise international support.

Activities requiring some research or information collection and dissemination
- By 1996 local authorities should have undertaken a consultative process with their populations to achieve consensus on a "local Agenda 21" for their community. This process is to include obtaining information from citizens and local, civic, community, business and industrial organisations on the best strategies;
- Local authority programs, policies, laws and regulations to achieve Agenda 21 objectives are to be assessed and modified; and,
- UN agencies are called on to strengthen services in collecting information on strategies for local authorities.

Capacity-building/training activities
- The Chapter calls on international and donor agencies to collaborate "to support, extend and improve existing institutions working in the field of local authority capacity-building and local environment management"; and,
- The Chapter calls on support for training and capacity-building as indicated in other chapters.

IMPLICIT PROPOSALS DERIVED FROM THE CHAPTER
- Information gathering and exchange on which to base the activities proposed above.
- One of the activities envisioned is the implementation and monitoring of programs to ensure that women and youth are represented in decision-making, planning and implementation. There is a need for better understanding of current roles of women and youth, culturally- and locally-specific means of integrating them in decision-making, etc.

- Community, civic and other organisations may need assistance to define (and develop the capacity to define) their own priorities and strategies, in order to participate as full partners in local consultative processes.
- The capacity of associations of local authorities to effectively represent their members/constituencies may need to be developed.

GAPS AND ALTERNATIVE APPROACHES

The chapter does not present an analysis of the problems nor a very extensive assessment of solutions needed. Research may well be needed to supplement what is mentioned above, or to investigate assumptions in the chapter, if sustainable development which meets basic needs is to be achieved. This could include research on:
- The causes of environmental degradation at the local level (including poverty, unequal access/distribution of resources, etc.), and their policy implications;
- Existing regulations and legislation, including but not limited to environmental ones — e.g. land use, service standards — and how to improve or change these;
- Informal sector and community initiatives and strategies (how people obtain resources and services) and exploring the potential of integrating or building on these in a sustainable way, without adversely affecting the people involved;
- Constraints to the effectiveness of local authorities in meeting citizens' needs in a sustainable way;
- Central-local government relations, relative powers, decentralisation;
- Political and social as well as technical aspects (e.g. democratisation, participation); and,
- Research for the purposes of empowerment of local groups and individuals, particularly disadvantaged ones.

Such research should focus on the design of locally-appropriate solutions although the information-sharing activities presented in the chapter are important.

NICHES FOR IDRC

GENERAL

Opportunities that Fit Normal Programming

Networking: The activity to promote cooperation among local authorities and local authority associations to exchange information, experience and technical assistance fits IDRC's mandate to support South–South cooperation and information exchange.

Research: Research is explicit or implicit in a number of proposed activities, as explained in the previous section. IDRC through its normal programming could play a particularly effective role. For example:
- IDRC could support research by both local authorities and citizens and other organisations to identify strategies for "local Agenda 21s", perhaps partly in the context of support for other chapters;
- IDRC could be effective in supporting key institutions to undertake the proposed assessments of local authority programs, policies, laws and regulations to achieve Agenda 21 objectives. IDRC could also assist in research and dissemination of information on promising strategies;
- Given its relative objectivity and its experience in supporting locally-relevant research, IDRC could support analyses of the actual and potential role of under-represented groups, particularly women and youth, in decision-making, planning and implementation; and,
- IDRC has a comparative advantage in supporting innovative research which could be taken advantage of in order to investigate other topics identified earlier, particularly under II.C. For example, on:
  - Informal sector and community initiatives and strategies (how people obtain resources and services) which could be developed into environmentally sustainable practices;

- Decentralisation policies, processes, and effects (on local government capacity, the environment, etc.); local/central government relations, existing functions and powers, and what could be decentralised in order to strengthen the ability of local authorities to meet Agenda 21 objectives; including political and social as well as technical aspects (e.g. democratisation, participation);
- Identification of innovations that work — e.g. community-based service delivery which meets criteria of participation, cost-effectiveness and sustainable development; community-based land trusts, etc.;
- Alternative finance systems and sources for local governments;
- Identification of local authorities' training/human resource development needs; and,
- Support for research by local authorities — evaluations of programs, formulation of appropriate policies, etc.

Capacity-building/training: The activity to support and improve institutions working in local authority capacity-building and environmental management fits with IDRC's research and institutional capacity-building mandate. Also, research training and capacity-building are implicit.

Donor collaboration to achieve these objectives: IDRC has experience working in the area of local government strengthening with several of the agencies mentioned (e.g. World Bank, IULA) on which it could build.

New Opportunities

IDRC could assist in facilitating the consultative process between local authorities and citizens, organisations and the private sector to identify strategies for "local Agenda 21s". Specifically, IDRC could support efforts by key civic, community and other organisations to identify/design appropriate strategies. This would entail building the capacity of such institutions to define their own priorities and needs. IDRC could also support research which identifies mechanisms for promoting participation in local authorities. IDRC's experience in supporting a variety of institutional types (government, non-government and independent research institutions) and in promoting collaborative research among these would be useful here. This type of activity could be seen to fit within normal IDRC programming but implies a broader and perhaps more flexible approach.

New opportunities also lie in support for research on issues which are not central to any of IDRC's current program areas, particularly political participation and governance at the local level, or within existing mechanisms, such as support for training and human resource development in addition to research.

Unusual or High-Risk Opportunities

Research, dissemination and implementation of results on a number of politically sensitive issues (relating to political participation, legitimacy of local governments, etc.) would entail high risks, but the pay-offs in terms of equitable development and effectiveness of assistance could be quite high.

REGIONAL SPECIFICITY
None.

KEY PARTNERS/OTHER ACTORS
Canada
- City and provincial governments responsible for city planning, environmental services. etc.;
- Federation of Canadian Municipalities, especially their International Program;

- CIDA (which provides support to local authorities); e.g. its Management for Change and bilateral programs; and,
- Universities with expertise in local government issues.

Other Countries
- International Union of Local Authorities (IULA);
- World Bank;
- UN agencies (Habitat and others);
- Other bilateral donors interested in supporting local governments (e.g. Italy, Netherlands);
- In developing countries, central ministries of local government, of environment and natural resources, etc.;
- Associations of local authorities in developing countries;
- Local authorities in developing countries;
- NGOs, citizens' groups, other civil society organisations; and,
- Research institutes.

RECOMMENDATIONS

WHICH NICHES ARE BEST FOR IDRC PROGRAM?

Given the importance of local authorities and other local actors in policies, programs and activities which are directly related to sustainable (or unsustainable) development, it is crucial for IDRC to give consideration to this chapter. IDRC support for local authorities' actions would facilitate the implementation of activities called for in other Agenda 21 chapters. Clearly, IDRC has a unique mandate and is in a unique position to support research and related activities which will contribute to achieving the goals of sustainable development, participation and effectiveness which underlie this chapter. The issue is how IDRC should approach the matter and to which activities it should allocate resources.

Such choices should be made on the basis of IDRC's strategic and comparative advantage. For example, networking of local authorities is best left to, for example, the structure of IULA. IDRC should collaborate with such organisations but should allocate scarce program funding to some of the innovative research, capacity-building and networking activities described in III above.

ARE ADJUSTMENTS NEEDED AT IDRC IN ORDER TO FILL THESE NICHES?

Program Organization
No significant changes are needed. What is needed is communication among programs working on issues in Agenda 21 that involve decisions or activities at the local level.

Process and Project Cycle
No significant changes needed.

Structure/Staffing
No significant changes needed.

ARE THERE CROSS-CUTTING ISSUES THAT ARE NOT ADEQUATELY REFLECTED IN ANY OF THE ABOVE?
No.

CHAPTER TWENTY-NINE

STRENGTHENING THE ROLE OF WORKERS AND THEIR TRADE UNIONS

Responsible Officer: Gary McMahon (with Don de Savigny)

ABSTRACT 29

1. OVERALL CRITIQUE OF AGENDA 21 CHAPTER

- Weak chapter which pushes for implementation of many of the things which are already on paper and generally ignored with regards to working conditions.
- In many countries trade unions have little influence and will not be big players in the debate but the Chapter does not discuss unorganized labour at all, or the tension between the goals and needs of unorganized and organized labour.
- The emphasis on organized labour also seems amiss, given that the most severe effects on the environment are likely to come from unorganized rural workers and the informal sector.

2. KEY CONCLUSIONS ARISING FROM CHAPTER

- Workers will pay some of the largest costs of the adjustment to sustainable development.
- Important to get trade unions involved in the process right from the start.
- Emphasis should be on tripartite agreements between workers, government, and employers with regards to environmental issues, including occupational health and safety concerns, but tends not to be.

3. RESEARCH AND/OR IMPLEMENTATION POSSIBILITIES/OPPORTUNITIES

- Relation between micro-occupational health and safety and more macro-environmental concerns: viz. research on micro-pollution havens, e.g. when firms transfer to developing countries because of lax occupational health and safety measures rather than weak general environmental laws.
- Analysis of the costs of adjustment to be born by workers when different items of Agenda 21 are implemented.
- Analysis of existing institutional structures with respect to individual labour rights and organized labour rights in developing countries.

4. ON-GOING AND/OR NEW PARTNERSHIPS FOR IDRC

- International Labour Organization, World Health Organization, UNDP.
- CLC, Canadian Occupational Health Centre, Labour Canada, CUSO, Federal and Provincial departments.

5. SUGGESTED NICHES FOR IDRC

- Participatory research with trade unions on interaction between worker health and safety goals and general environmental goals.
- Micro-pollution havens.

- Empirical work on the effects of sustainable development adjustment on workers, organized and unorganized.
- Research on relations between labour institutions/rights and the success of sustainable adjustment programs.

6. OTHER COMMENTS

None.

REVIEW 29

KEY CONCLUSIONS IN THE CHAPTER

WHAT IS THERE

Main Conclusions
- Workers will pay some of the main costs of adjustment to sustainable development.
- Important to get trade unions involved in process right from the beginning.
- Emphasis on tripartite agreement between workers, government, and employers with regards to environmental issues, including occupational health and safety concerns.

Agreements Reached for International and National Action
Promote ratification of relevant conventions of ILO.

Politically Significant Issues
Whole issue of workers' rights, and that the poor will likely pay the adjustment costs.

WHAT IS NOT THERE

- This rather short chapter deals almost exclusively with organized (or organizable) workers.
- It seems likely that the most severe environmental damage occurs due to the actions of workers in the unorganized formal sectors and in the rural areas.

OVERALL CRITIQUE

Substantive Content
- Weak chapter which pushes for implementation of many of the things which are already on paper and generally ignored with regards to working conditions.
- In many countries trade unions have little influence and will not be big players in the debate.

Design of the Chapter as an Organizing Framework
The Chapter deals with problems in an UNCTAD/ILO type of fashion; that is, by decree things will improve. It should be written from a more realistic perspective of the problem: i.e. the lack of workers' rights in general (at least, de facto) in many countries; the fact that the burden of macro-structural adjustment has largely fallen on workers; and, then look at possibilities so that the same does not happen with sustainable development structural adjustment.

RESEARCH REQUIREMENTS, CAPACITY BUILDING ETC.

EXPLICIT PROPOSALS IN THE CHAPTER
- Many of the proposals deal with occupational health and safety issues.
- Another major concern is the need to "teach" trade unions about sustainable development; this is probably better left to the ILO.

IMPLICIT PROPOSALS DERIVED FROM THE CHAPTER
The main implicit proposal is that workers will bear a large part of the cost of sustainable development adjustment.

GAPS AND ALTERNATIVE APPROACHES
See section on niches for IDRC.

NICHES FOR IDRC

GENERAL

Opportunities that Fit Normal Programming
- The Health Sciences Division is quite active in the area of occupational health and safety. In particular, it has funded participatory research with trade unions in hazards identification, monitoring, and control. It seems that this type of work could easily be extended to put more emphasis on the interaction between worker health and safety and general environmental goals. It could also probably include non-organized labour, especially agricultural workers;
- The fear of the creation of micro-pollution havens could also fall into this area; that is, the transfer of firms to LDCs not because of the ability to externally pollute but the ability to have workers involved in unsafe environmental conditions.
- This latter would be an area with a possibility of research jointly funded by HSD and SSD.

New Opportunities
- Much as in the structural adjustment debate, there is a great need for empirical work of the effects of sustainable development adjustment (SDA) on workers, organized and unorganized;
- Of particular importance may be the existing institutional structures with respect to individual labour rights and organized labour rights in developing countries;
- A niche for IDRC could be to look at how these two groups of rights are hindering/adapting to structural adjustment and how this will likely affect the hindrance/adaptation to SDA. For example, it is quite easy to think of ways in which stronger worker rights could make SDA more difficult or easier. In addition, the informal labour institutions which have developed in almost all LDC's will also be critical to the success of SDA; and,
- It seems likely that this type of research would fall mainly into the social policy and economic and technology policy programs.

REGIONAL SPECIFICITY
None.

KEY PARTNERS/OTHER ACTORS
Canada
- Trade unions.

Other Countries
- ILO.
- World Health Organization.

RECOMMENDATIONS

WHICH NICHES ARE BEST FOR IDRC PROGRAM?
- Work should continue along the lines already being followed by the Health Sciences Division.
- Focus on the importance of institutional "rights", how they are changing under structural adjustment, and how they will affect the enactment of SDA.

ARE ADJUSTMENTS NEEDED AT IDRC IN ORDER TO FILL THESE NICHES?
Program Organization
No.

Process and Project Cycle
No.

Structure/Staffing
No.

ARE THERE CROSS-CUTTING ISSUES THAT ARE NOT ADEQUATELY REFLECTED IN ANY OF THE ABOVE?
No.

COMMENTARY 29

Name of Commentator: Daniel A. Morales-Gómez

1. GENERAL COMMENTS ON THE CHAPTER
- The Chapter focuses on the role that workers and their representative organizations can play in SED. The emphasis, is on environment-related issues rather the broader problematic of sustainable development.
- The Chapter provides few new insights. It emphasizes existing conventions often have had little impact on workers' lives and organization.
- The Chapter does not address the underlying issues obstructing workers' political and workplace participation as a means to reach overall economic development. It also ignores the factors determining the extent in which workers and their organizations can influence aspects such as their own technical development, their participation in the management of their work environments, and their sharing of wealth resulting from their work, all of which are critical in terms of strengthening the role workers can play in SED.
- The Chapter seems to limit its recommendations to workers who operate under forms of organized labour. It misses an important sector of the labour force in most developing countries, where small-enterprise workers and workers in the informal sector are disenfranchised and do not benefit from participatory and representative forms of labour organization.

2. OVERALL COMMENTARY ON THE FIRST REVIEW OF THE CHAPTER

- The review identifies the weaknesses of the Chapter as well as the generality of its analysis.
- The review raises the need to identify ways by which to avoid burdening workers with additional pressures that may result from SED and environmental strategies. These could add to the impacts that structural adjustment programs already have had. This is particularly relevant in socio-economic contexts in which workers have little say in the control of the processes of production.

3. MAJOR POINTS AGREED/DISAGREED WITH, AND REASONS

- The review does not sufficiently highlight one of the main recommendations made in the Chapter, which is the need to increase workers' education, training and retraining. This is critical to preparing workers to play an active role in SED.

4. MINOR POINTS AGREED/DISAGREED WITH, AND REASONS

- One important point insufficiently considered in the review is the link between increased workers' participation and poverty alleviation, which goes beyond issues related to the organization of workers' immediate work situation to their role in the development of the society.

5. POSSIBLE ON-GOING ISSUES OR CONCERNS FOR IDRC

- Governments and international agencies allocate substantial educational resources to the technical-vocational education of youngsters, and to on-the-job training and re-training of workers. Research on these issues is often limited and carried out by ill-equipped government departments, without attention to the importance of science development and technological change. Strengthening the research capacity of government centres of technical and vocational training on these issues could be a niche for the Centre in helping to strengthen the role of workers in SED.

6. POSSIBLE IMPLICATIONS FOR IDRC

- Workers as a distinct target group is not often directly addressed by IDRC. The call to strengthen the role of workers in SED opens new opportunities for the Centre to support research that directly addresses issues of workers' participation at the workplace, innovation in self-management, workers' ownership and profit sharing schemes, and other forms of workers organizations, workers' technological training and education, and workers' representation in policies for SED.

CHAPTER THIRTY

STRENGTHENING THE ROLE OF BUSINESS AND INDUSTRY

Responsible Officer: Sitoo Mukerji

ABSTRACT

1. OVERALL CRITIQUE OF AGENDA 21 CHAPTER

- While the Chapter is noteworthy in its recognition of the legitimacy and desirability of industrial and technical activities, the measures it proposes to ensure implementation are weak.
- No serious constraints or inducements are proposed to improve the sustainability of industry.
- Business roles are presented largely as incremental improvements over existing technological and managerial practices, and industry stewardship is expected to be achieved through moral persuasion and private self-regulation.

2. KEY CONCLUSIONS ARISING FROM CHAPTER

- The Chapter proposes two program areas for national, international and private action:
  a) promoting cleaner production, and b) promoting responsible entrepreneurship. However, no additional resources are recommended for these programs.

3. RESEARCH AND/OR IMPLEMENTATION POSSIBILITIES/OPPORTUNITIES

- Responsible business activity implies adoption of cleaner and more efficient production methods, engagement in partnerships to transfer and diffuse technologies and management practices to other firms, and use of relatively transparent pollution accounting methods.

4. ON-GOING AND/OR NEW PARTNERSHIPS FOR IDRC

- The Centre should increase and improve its efforts to respond to the specific technological development needs of Small- and Medium-size Enterprises (SME's). This Chapter considers SMEs as "non-controversial", which lends itself to increased involvement of these SMEs with both the R&D and industrial communities in Canada. The Centre should encourage increased working contact between SMEs in developing countries with the SMEs in Canada, including the medium- and smaller-sized environmental consulting and/or service firms.

5. SUGGESTED NICHES FOR IDRC

- To encourage the transfer of environmentally sustainable technologies, the Centre should increase its activities with those institutions and agencies which are engaged in providing industrial and technical support to SMEs.
- To encourage environmentally sustainable and sound business capabilities the Centre should explore the possibilities of support for institutions engaged in business development, particularly where these are of national or regional in scope.

- To encourage adoption of "best-practice" in management, technology and entrepreneurship the Centre should support projects dealing with the innovative processes including such activities as industrial diagnosis, technology adoption and adaptation, etc.
- To improve understanding of the concept of environmentally sustainable development the Centre should support innovation policy studies which includes the above as key goals.

6. OTHER COMMENTS

- Chapter 30 argues that prosperous and responsible business and industry "are a key part of the solution to the problem of sustainable socioeconomic development. Their roles should therefore be strengthened." Firms are advised to "recognize environmental management as among the highest corporate priorities and as a key determinant to sustainable development."

REVIEW 30

KEY CONCLUSIONS IN THE CHAPTER

WHAT IS THERE

Main Conclusions
- The chapter argues that prosperous and responsible business and industry, "including transnational corporations", are a key part of the solution to the problem of sustainable socioeconomic development. Their roles should therefore be strengthened.
- Firms "should recognize environmental management as among the highest corporate priorities and as a key determinant to sustainable development." Responsibility means adoption of cleaner and more efficient production methods, engagement in partnerships to transfer and diffuse technologies and management practices to other firms, and use of relatively transparent pollution accounting methods.

Agreements Reached for International and National Action
- Two program areas for national, international **and** private action are identified: a) promoting cleaner production, and b) promoting responsible entrepreneurship. No additional resources are recommended for these programs.

Politically Significant Issues
- The chapter reflects uneasiness concerning the role of businesses in sustainable socio-economic development. The qualification "including transnational corporations" is added to the phrase "business and industry" no less than sixteen times in seven pages.
- This represents sensitivity about the image of transnationals in the developing world. **Small-Medium Enterprises are not controversial**.
- The chapter suggests that self-regulation, persuasion, and market forces, followed by regulation, are the ways to bring firms to adopt cleaner production methods. This mixture of carrots and sticks may not convince everyone. Environmentally sustainable development may require stronger policy arrangements at the national and international levels than Chapter 30 suggests.
- The Chapter tends to emphasize voluntary, apparently altruistic firm behaviour — for instance, in the establishment of partnerships, in the transfer of technology to affiliates, etc. — that may not be realistic.

WHAT IS NOT THERE

- Measures to ensure implementation are weak; such measures are to be funded through reallocated resources. No serious constraints or inducements are to be mobilized. Business roles are presented largely as incremental improvements over existing technological and managerial practices, coupled with a greater degree of altruistic behaviour. Chapter 30 does not seem to contain as many proposals for useful action as other chapters of Agenda 21.
- Sustainable" is frequently used as a synonym for "more efficient" or "cleaner." These operational definitions are so wide as to make virtually any improvements in production efficiency a step toward sustainability.
- Section 30.22 recommends that transnational firms accept to transfer environmentally sound technologies to affiliates in developing countries without "extra external charges." Does this mean that some kinds of technology should be available at cost? No proposals are put forward to monitor the conditions under which environmentally improved technologies are diffused through intracorporate channels.
- There is no recognition that much of the present environmental crisis at the global level stems in large part from consumption patterns of the industrialized North. Simply making or increasing the efficiency of these patterns of consumption may not lead to sustainability.
- It does not adequately address the environmental crisis that exists at the local or regional level, and is caused by or contributed to by local small, medium and large enterprises.

OVERALL CRITIQUE

Substantive critique

- It is refreshing and encouraging to see legitimacy attributed to firms and economic and industrial activity. The recognition that economic opportunity can provide significant relief to impoverished groups is important.
- However, the thrust of the argument is to suggest that business and industry, "including transnational corporations," can largely be entrusted to learn to exercise stewardship, responsible entrepreneurship, and leadership with respect to sustainable development. At the same time, it is suggested that getting the prices right with respect to environmental externalities will greatly contribute to movement toward cleaner, more efficient production. The Chapter leans perhaps too heavily on privatization and markets to establish a world regime of environmental governance with respect to the productive sector. It carefully avoids suggesting supra-national public procedures or institutions for establishing rules of the game. For example, the chapter proposes mainly training and information–dissemination roles for international organizations.
- From an innovation policy perspective, the arrangements and measures proposed to encourage the development and diffusion of best-practice, environmentally sustainable technologies and management techniques do not begin to go far enough. IDRC can play an important role here (see below).

Design of the Chapter as an Organizing Framework

- Replace program A, "promoting cleaner production," with "promoting environmentally sustainable production systems." Enlarge the focus from cleanliness to one encompassing cleanliness, efficiency, and sustainability. Incorporate measures for more vigorous technology- and information-sharing cooperative programs at the international level. Include measures for performance targets and monitoring systems for technologies, industrial sectors, and production systems.
- Replace program B, "promoting responsible entrepreneurship," with "promoting environmentally responsible business practices." The section "basis for action" is too exclusively focused on SMEs. It should include a rationale for fostering responsibility among larger firms, "including transnational corporations." Some provision must be made for tracking changes in firm behaviour around the world, and better arrangements to encourage implementation should be found.

- Drop the suggestion that the problem to be solved is the lack of business influence over the behaviour and decisions of governments. Replace with better suggestions for public-private consultation and concerted action, including involvement of consumers and citizens' groups.

RESEARCH REQUIREMENTS AND CAPACITY BUILDING

EXPLICIT PROPOSALS IN THE CHAPTER

The Chapter contains proposals for action in the following areas. Most are based on new kinds of behaviour and new kinds of organizational arrangements, and require that "best practice" be described and diffused:

- Public-private partnerships to implement sustainable development.
- Policy packages to promote cleaner industrial production and sustainably managed enterprises.
- Annual reports by business on environmental performance.
- Voluntary codes of conduct.
- Inter-firm cooperation on the technology of cleaner production and the diffusion of best-practice environmental management.
- Industry-promoted cleaner production policies.
- Environmental awareness initiatives to be taken by individual companies.
- Education and training initiatives to be taken by international organizations and governments.
- Expansion of the information-diffusion roles of international scientific and technical organizations.
- Establishment of venture capital for sustainable development projects and programs, and more financial support for entrepreneurs engaged in sustainable development activities.
- Transfer of environmentally sound production technology to affiliates of transnational firms.
- Industry-led national councils on sustainable development, and better industry advice.
- International organizations on environmental issues.
- More industry-funded R&D on environmentally sound technologies, and more international agency support for technology and management for sustainable development in developing countries.
- Business should place greater emphasis on the ethics of health, safety, and environmental sustainability.

IMPLICIT PROPOSALS DERIVED FROM THE CHAPTER

- That existing activities be reorganized so that present resources can be allocated to the above activities. This implies a degree of concentration and follow-up of Agenda 21.
- That there be some monitoring procedure of worldwide initiatives taken in response to Agenda 21, and some evaluation of their effectiveness.

GAPS AND ALTERNATIVE APPROACHES

- See above.
- That there be better independent means of tracking performance of technologies, sectors, groups of firms, or of individual firms with respect to environmentally sustainable business practices.

NICHES FOR IDRC

GENERAL

Opportunities that fit Normal Programming

- The Chapter illustrates the need for continuing and enhanced activities by IDRC to meet the needs of developing countries for environmentally-friendly, sustainable technologies for industries. The Chapter should not be read in isolation; it relates strongly to the section dealing with technology transfer (Chapter 34). IDRC should continue to seek cooperation and collaboration with the

Canadian public and private sector where appropriate and possible. Both of these chapters strongly suggests that IDRC take a much harder look at the needs of developing countries for industry development as a priority.
- Referring to specific points above, IDRC should increase and improve its efforts in:
  - Public-private partnerships;
  - Policy packages for sustainably managed enterprises;
  - Help countries to develop standards;
  - Provide training for venture capital arrangements in cooperation with Canadian private sector;
  - Transfer of environmentally sound technologies;
  - Industry assistance and advice; and,
  - Support projects which propose to expand the research front-both in cases of development of products and processes as well as policy.

New Opportunities
- **SMEs.** The Chapter presents IDRC with new opportunities to increase and improve its efforts to respond to **the specific technological development needs of Small- and Medium-sized Enterprises** in the developing countries (with concomitant social benefits such as employment and better income distribution). SMEs are considered "non-controversial" in the chapter and this lends itself to increased involvement of SMEs with both the R&D and the industrial communities in Canada. New efforts should be promoted to bring SMEs in developing countries in closer working contact with Canadian SMEs. (Increased private sector awareness of IDRC's roles and potential could ensue.)
- **SME.** Technological support agencies. IDRC should increase its activities with those institutions and agencies which are **engaged in SME industrial and technological support** in developing countries. These agencies can be both entry points into networks of SMEs in developing countries and the fulcrum point for activities designed to bring about changes in those SME communities. They are particularly valuable agents of technology transfer. They lend themselves to increased collaboration and cooperation with both the industrial support organizations in Canada and the Canadian SME community, leading to increased Canadian visibility for IDRC.
- **Business Development.** Environmentally sustainable and sound (best-practice) business capabilities are stressed in the chapter. IDRC should explore possibilities of support for **institutions or organizations in developing countries engaged in business development**, particularly where these are national or regional in scope. Collaboration with Canadian counterparts and the business community in general should be stressed and increased.
- **Innovation Management.** The chapter repeatedly emphasizes the importance of **"best-practice" in management, technology and entrepreneurship.** IDRC should support initiatives designed to bring about improved capabilities by supporting projects dealing with the innovative processes including such activities as, for example, industrial diagnosis, technology needs determination, technology sourcing and acquisition, technology adoption or adaptation, etc. "Management of Innovation" activities would provide a unique set for IDRC within international development agencies.
- **Innovation Policies for Environmentally Sustainable Development.** Agenda 21 calls for governments and industry associations to collaborate to develop and apply policy packages to encourage sustainable development. This will require a great deal of support in terms of capacity building, training, and network development. It will also require support for basic social science research on the factors influencing the development and adoption of environmentally sustainable production systems. Finally, it will require active experimentation to develop sustainable, policy-relevant collective action encompassing public and private actors at the international, national, sectoral, or local levels.

Unusual or High-Risk Opportunities

Although some of the activities above might be viewed as being part of the "normal" spectrum of IDRC endeavours, if IDRC were to devote **dedicated efforts** towards the capture and utilization of best-practice technologies in such an integrated and holistic manner, such activities would be "unusual" in the sense of being exceptional or excellent. By doing this, IDRC could unfold a unique set of activities and create an unusually effective role for itself in support of developing countries.

REGIONAL SPECIFICITY

Activities such as those outlined above would not be regionally specific, except to the extent that the types of activities engaged in would be predicated upon the presence or absence of specific regional expertise or systems.

KEY PARTNERS/OTHER ACTIONS

Canada

- Activities suggested are predicated upon systematic efforts to **involve the Canadian SME community** in Third World development. Experience has shown that the SME community is interested in developing viable, small, new and sustainable markets for its technologies and expertise and because of enlightened self-interest is interested in industrial cooperation and collaboration. Also establish contact with such business groups as: BCNI; CFIB, etc.
- Activities are also predicated upon desirability of engaging **industry-support agencies in Canada** in cooperative and collaborative endeavours with their counterparts in the developing countries. Organizations such as Association of Provincial Research Councils, individual Research Councils, Industrial Research Assistance Program (IRAP) of National Research Council, IRAP network partner agencies, Centres of Technological Excellence throughout Canada, Provincial Ministries of Science and Technology, provincial Science Councils and Private Industry Associations could all profitably be involved. Funding of activities could be sought from international sources levered by IDRC seed funding.
- There may also be scope to consider involvement with Canadian policy advisory groups in Canada, such as the Roundtable on the Economy and the Environment.

Other Countries

- SMEs;
- SME support agencies;
- R&D institutions;
- SME consortia and associations, including BCSD and ICC; and,
- National, regional and sub-regional governments and agencies.

RECOMMENDATIONS

BEST NICHE FOR AN IDRC PROGRAM

Assistance to **institutions and agencies which support technological development in SMEs in developing countries** should be a niche in which IDRC could function well. The need for improved capacity to identify, source, acquire, transpose, adopt and adapt "best-practice" technologies, S&T policies, management practices and business expertise is well recognized. By engaging in the support of such activities, IDRC would establish itself at the forefront of endeavours in this field. Increasing the ability of developing countries to capture and use technologies would enhance substantially the utilization of research results, including IDRC's.

ADJUSTMENTS
- The **Innovation Management Program** (working title) currently under development in the RUP section of CAID addresses a large number of the issues found in this chapter of Agenda 21. One of the key thrusts of the program will be to support the intermediate level agencies responsible for industrial, technological policy and research results deployment and uptake in industries in developing countries.
- Details of the program, its mission and goals, staffing and funding will be supplied to IDRC management in the very near future.

CHAPTER THIRTY-ONE

SCIENTIFIC AND TECHNOLOGICAL COMMUNITY

Responsible Officer: J. Hea

ABSTRACT 31

1. OVERALL CRITIQUE OF AGENDA 21 CHAPTER

- The questions raised are how the scientific and technological community can contribute to the environment and sustainable development? And how the role of science and technology can be better communicated to decision-makers, governments and the public?
- The term "community" is generic since scientists and other professionals are organized into associations or councils which have sections, committees, panels concerned with environmental issues. In most cases, the associations will be the entry to increased awareness and response to Agenda 21 objectives.
- The need for professional ethics and practice codes should also be referred to under the heading "Scientific and Technological Means" in each chapter of Agenda 21.
- Chapter 31 does not call for agreement by governments but is rather a consultative process. This should be amended to call for a declaration of codes of practice by the scientific and technological community governing the environment and sustainable development.

2. KEY CONCLUSIONS ARISING FROM CHAPTER

- The scientific and technological community must be formally involved in the environment and sustainable development.
- The community should communicate its knowledge to decision-makers and the public.
- Scientists and technologists must retain independence to investigate and to publish.
- There is a need for professionals to adopt codes of practice.
- The process to attain these goals is through consultation between UN, governments, and scientists and technologists.
- Government action is required to create a greater ethical awareness by the scientific and technological community of its responsibilities and improve communications with decision-makers and the public.
- No immediate agreements are proposed but governments are asked to review responsiveness by scientists and technologists to the environment and sustainable development through councils and to communicate findings to the UN. UNESCO could take the lead in collaboration with governments, NGOs and the public.

3. RESEARCH AND/OR IMPLEMENTATION POSSIBILITIES/OPPORTUNITIES

- Identify which professionals in Canada will be part of the consultative process.
- IDRC already judges the merit of proposals on consideration of ethics and this should be formalized to include the codes of practice where applicable for the institutions and professional associations to which researchers belong.

- Make the consultative process on ethics part of all UN activities related to the environment and sustainable development.
- Describe for each Agenda 21 goal which professionals are involved and how to develop personal and corporate values.

4. ON-GOING AND/OR NEW PARTNERSHIPS FOR IDRC

- Participation with UN, governments, scientists and technologists to review issues, membership on panels, and communications with these and the public.

5. SUGGESTED NICHES FOR IDRC

- Active role in consultative process with scientists and technologists in Canada and in developing countries in line with UNESCO's goals when enunciated.
- Capacity-building of institutions which train professionals in environmental ethics.
- Lead in preparing agreements by governments on codes of practice for the environment and sustainable development.

6. OTHER COMMENTS

- Cross-cuts with Chapter 35 on "Science for Sustainable Development".

REVIEW 31

KEY CONCLUSIONS IN THE CHAPTER

The lead questions are:

How can the scientific and technological community contribute to a safe environment and sustainable development and how can the role of science and technology be better communicated to decision-makers, governments and the public? It is recognized that the independence of scientists to investigate and publish must be maintained. A corollary to this right is the need for adoption and international acceptance of ethical principles and codes of practice by the scientific and technological community towards the environment and sustainable development.

The Chapter addresses these issues in two parts:

Part A: Covers steps by governments to review the responsiveness of the scientific community to the environment and sustainable development through a process of consultation including councils, committees and panels of scientists and decision-makers, NGOs, and the public and leading to capacity-building of organizations and professional networks.

Part B: Covers the promoting of codes of practice based on the responsibilities and ethical awareness by scientists. Implementation of Part B has the same approach as Part A: through advisory groups; and, by legal instruments created to ensure that appropriate codes are respected.

WHAT IS THERE
Main Conclusions
The scientific and technological community (engineers, architects, industrial designers, urban planners, other professionals and policy makers) is asked to make a more open and effective contribution to the decision-making process concerning the environment and sustainable development.

Government action is required to help create a greater ethical awareness by the scientific and technological community of its responsibilities and to improve communications with decision-makers and the public. Codes of practice and legal instruments are needed to ensure that these responsibilities are honoured subject to laws and regulations.

Agreements Reached for International and National Action
No immediate agreements are proposed. Governments are asked to review scientific and technological activities to ensure responsiveness to sustainable development through councils, organizations and committees and to communicate findings to the UN and other agencies. UNESCO could take the lead in collaboration with governments, NGOs and the public.

Politically Significant Issues
Professional associations are politically powerful within a society and internationally, i.e. medical, law, engineering, academic and other "liberal professions". Suggestions that they and their members are not ethically committed and sensitive to the environment and sustainable development are likely to be rejected out-of-hand. Goodwill and diplomacy will be required to draft and implement new codes of practice. Fortunately, many associations have already established committees for the environment and the UN and governments will be able to consult with them to effect changes.

There is a need to protect scientists and technologists working for institutions, governments and private companies from employer pressure to skirt environmental regulations by making non-compliance legally risky. Adequate laws, inspectors and enforcement of regulations are needed under a recognized authority, i.e. a Department of Environment.

WHAT IS NOT THERE
The designation "scientific and technological community" used in the chapter is generic. In fact, professionals are licensed by associations, academic institutions, boards and other legal entities. Many professionals work for companies under regulations set for their industry. What is missing is a degree of precision as to the professionals and their associations who compose the "community," their conditions of work, and responsibilities both individual and corporate towards the environment and sustainable development. Such an analysis is a necessary step towards developing ethical codes and personal responsibilities as well as strengthening collective values.

OVERALL CRITIQUE
Substantive Content
The concept of ethical behaviour and standards by professionals in respect to a safe environment and sustainable development is well expressed as is the consultative process between the scientific and technological community and governments, NGOs, and the public. Most people will agree that codes of practice are needed and to be followed they must be enforceable by law. A lead role by UNESCO supported by governments and NGOs is reasonable given the origin of the initiative in the Rio Declaration.

Design of the Chapter as an Organizing Framework

The separation of the program areas into two parts, the first emphasizing communication and cooperation between scientists and technologists, decision-makers, and the public, and the second promoting codes of practice appears sound.

RESEARCH REQUIREMENTS, CAPACITY-BUILDING ETC.

EXPLICIT PROPOSALS IN THE CHAPTER

Proposals in the Chapter call for explicit action by governments to review issues, communicate about science and technology, and cause codes of practice to be implemented.

IMPLICIT PROPOSALS DERIVED FROM THE CHAPTER

These explicit objectives are challenged by the vast scope of Agenda 21 where involvement by the scientific and technological community is literally part of every topic on the environment and sustainable development. As such, ethical and regulatory issues affecting professionals implicitly permeate the entire Rio Declaration. This leads to a need for research on professional involvement, human resource development and capacity-building if these goals are to be reached.

GAPS AND ALTERNATIVE APPROACHES

The scientific and technological community called upon to participate in the adoption of agreements on environment and development under Agenda 21 needs to be identified. It would also be useful to reference the role of these professionals and their associations in key chapters, i.e. Chapter 35 "Science for Sustainable Development". It may be ultimately decided that considerations under the heading "Scientific and Technological Means" in each chapter should subsume professionals and codes of practice.

NICHES FOR IDRC

GENERAL

Opportunities that Fit Normal Programming
IDRC as a research organization has supported capacity-building and training as normal components of its projects. This is undertaken in the developing country, training in developing countries and Canada, and in the case of collaborative projects as partnerships with Canadian institutions and universities.

New Opportunities
Environment and sustainable development objectives should be made more explicit in new projects and advantage taken of opportunities to support capacity-building of institutions able and willing to follow such research goals.

Unusual or High-Risk Opportunities
Canada is a leader in many fields of development in third world countries ranging from agriculture to hydroelectricity and subways. IDRC has the opportunity for participating with CIDA, Environment Canada and the private sector in elaborating guidelines for voluntary codes of professional and corporate conduct concerning the environment and as a condition of government support.

REGIONAL SPECIFICITY

The role of the scientific and technological community is not region specific.

KEY PARTNERS/OTHER ACTORS

Canada
Virtually all of the professional associations which will be involved in Agenda 21 are represented in Canada.

Other Countries
Scientists and technologists individually and through membership in professional associations are linked to their peers in other countries as well as sharing research results and discussion of policy issues in publications, seminars, congresses and as public action groups.

RECOMMENDATIONS

WHICH NICHES ARE BEST FOR IDRC PROGRAMS?

Program Organization
The objectives of Chapter 31 cut across several IDRC divisions as well as the two programs, Environment & Technology and Sustainable Production Systems in the Environment and Natural Resources Division. The lead could be taken by Environment & Technology.

Process and Project Cycle
IDRC should play a supportive but minor role in the achieving the objectives of reviewing, communicating and preparing codes for the scientific and technological community except where the Centre directly supports projects which can materially influence global outcomes. The fields of interest of the Rio Declaration are too numerous and broad for the Centre to disperse its energies across hundreds of professional associations, scientific and technological disciplines. This depends of course how UNESCO or other UN agency structure the process.

Structure/Staffing
Program Officers and directors may be called upon to participate in committees and panels but no specific staffing is envisioned for the modest level of activity proposed.

ARE ADJUSTMENTS NEEDED AT IDRC IN ORDER TO FILL THESE NICHES?
None.

ARE THERE CROSS-CUTTING ISSUES THAT ARE NOT ADEQUATELY REFLECTED IN ANY OF THE ABOVE?

As mentioned, Chapter 31 on the "Scientific and Technological Community" cuts across other chapters in Agenda 21, such as Chapter 35 on "Science for Sustainable Development" and nearly all other chapters under the heading on means of implementation.

It is becoming recognized that the environment and sustainable development answer to many scientific and technological disciplines. Universities are now awarding degrees in environmental science and engineering. It is also becoming increasingly important for governments and companies to have trained environmentalists on staff to ensure understanding of issues and compliance with regulations. This reality has become part of IDRC's thinking.

COMMENTARY 31

Name of Commentator: Brent Herbert-Copley

1. GENERAL COMMENTS ON THE CHAPTER

- A very uninspiring set of proposed actions, focused on a) improving communications between the scientific and technological community, decision-makers and the public; and b) development of voluntary codes of ethics/practice for members of the scientific and technological community. This chapter could have been subsumed under others (Science for Sustainable Development in particular).
- Very vague about specific roles and responsibilities, except general references to UNESCO taking a lead role.
- The Chapter focuses on "harnessing" *existing* scientific and technological communities to the task of sustainable development. But the key challenge in developing countries strengthening weak or non-existent scientific and technological communities, via training and institutional development.
- Groups like consulting engineers, professional and scientific associations could play a key role in fostering more environmentally sustainable patterns of scientific and technological development. But these are notoriously weak in most developing countries. Such institutional development is essential to linking the scientific community to decision-makers, or promoting codes of environmental ethics.

2. OVERALL COMMENTARY ON THE FIRST REVIEW OF THE CHAPTER

- The review provides a good summary of the Chapter's main points. It is somewhat weaker in identifying gaps or alternative approaches.
- Disagree with some of the suggestions regarding areas for action, and niches for IDRC (see following points).

3. MAJOR POINTS AGREED/DISAGREED WITH, AND REASONS

- Strongly agree with the point made about the abstract and "generic" nature of the term "scientific and technological community". Emphasis needs to be placed, as the review notes, on identifying the institutions and associations which constitute this "community", and working with them to develop specific initiatives.
- Disagree with the review regarding niches for IDRC involvement. The kinds of issues raised in the Chapter are important, but not priorities for future IDRC activity (see below).

4. MINOR POINTS AGREED/DISAGREED WITH, AND REASONS

- The reviewer indicates that voluntary codes of practice are insufficient, but should be enshrined in law. This is premature, and would conflict with the overall emphasis of Agenda 21 of promoting the involvement of key stakeholders, rather than regulating their activities.
- The review suggests a need for "research on professional involvement, human resource development and capacity-building". But these are **all** areas for concrete **action**, not further research.

5. POSSIBLE ON-GOING ISSUES OR CONCERNS FOR IDRC

- The development of codes of environmental ethics and practice (voluntary or not) could have important consequences for any research-supporting agency. IDRC should consider developing its own guidelines (perhaps in conjunction with like-minded agencies like SAREC). At the very least, it should stay informed about the status of international efforts by UNESCO or others to develop such codes.

6. POSSIBLE IMPLICATIONS FOR IDRC

- There are no strong niches for future IDRC involvement. Training and institutional development of the kind normally supported by IDRC will continue to be the best methods for helping to strengthen the scientific and technological communities in developing countries.
- The other area of specific involvement might be work by the Research Utilization Program to investigate ways of involving scientific and professional associations in a greater dissemination of research results.
- IDRC also should:
  a) Renew its commitment to academic rights and freedoms as essential to the promotion of sustainable development;
  b) Task the Centre's Ethics Committee to investigate the possibility of developing guidelines on environmental ethics, and to maintain a watching brief on development in this field internationally.

CHAPTER THIRTY-TWO

STRENGTHENING THE ROLE OF FARMERS

Responsible Officer: John Graham

ABSTRACT

1. OVERALL CRITIQUE OF AGENDA 21 CHAPTER

- The argument presented is that individual farmers, fisher-folk and foresters will automatically use resources under their control in a sustainable manner. Hence, an individual or a "farmer centred" approach to decision-making and policy-setting is recommended as this will promote sustainable farming methods and ultimately prevent the degradation of our natural resource base. Although this is possible, it is more probable if governments set resource use policies and legal and institutional boundaries that limit the freedoms and choices of individuals.
- Governments need to be able to analyze and understand various options open to them and then set policies and programs that allow farmers or other economic agents to work within these bounds. Governments need to review their own economic and development goals, bearing in mind the needs of their people and their resource base, and then develop a time-table that moves current policies and programs towards ones that are more sustainable. The Chapter assumes that this is possible and farmers themselves know which route to take.

2. KEY CONCLUSIONS ARISING FROM CHAPTER

- A farmer centered or participatory approach and involvement in decision making and promoting sustainable resource use is recommended.
- Government policies need to be conducive and allow farmers to manage their resource effectively.
- The strengthening of women's roles and farmer organizations is recommended.
- To assist farmers research is needed on the development of environmentally sound farming technologies.
- Ineffective tenure laws have been an obstacle in some countries resulting in poor land use practices.
- Research, training and capacity-building needs are given.

3. RESEARCH AND/OR IMPLEMENTATION POSSIBILITIES/OPPORTUNITIES

- Research is required on:
    a) Sustainable production systems, management methods for fragile ecosystems, efficient use of water, and integrated methods for the use of natural resource systems;
    b) The design of resource and agricultural policies that result in the efficient and sustainable *use* of resources;
    c) Research on the impact of these policies on household and national food security, on farm incomes, on employment opportunities and on the environment;
    d) How best to involve and strengthen the role of women, farmers and their organizations in participatory, decision-making networks;
    e) Development of location specific and environment friendly farming systems;

f) Indigenous production methods, the low external input nature of these methods, their economic and technical efficiency in the use of all resources including land, water and forest resources;

g) Macro-level/resource use or policy type questions.

4. ON-GOING AND/OR NEW PARTNERSHIPS FOR IDRC

- IDRC has actively promoted and strengthened the role of farmers as decision-makers over the last decade by supporting farming systems research and extension methods. Strong partners have been built. The emphasis has been contacts between farmers and researchers but extension and education agendas have also been positively influenced.
- Spheres of influence need to be broadened to include all decision-makers and agents involved in agriculture or other uses of natural resources.

5. SUGGESTED NICHES FOR IDRC

- IDRC has an established a reputation as one of the leaders in this field. Therefore, build on past activities using established contacts and networks.
- Need to strengthen resource economics and social science dimensions of these research agendas which are very weak.
- Attention should be given to broader policy type research, because traditional partners do not have these skills and long-term training is needed.

6. OTHER COMMENTS

- High pay off activity and a basic principle is central to IDRC's philosophy. Needs to be an important component for the majority of research activities within ENRD.

KEY CONCLUSIONS IN THE CHAPTER

A farmer-centred or participatory approach and involvement in decision making and promoting sustainable resource uses is recommended. Government policies need to be conducive and set a macro environment that will allow farmers to manage their resources efficiently. Specific actions for governments are recommended, including the strengthening of women's roles and farmers' organizations. To assist farmers, research is needed on the development of environmentally sound farming technologies. Ineffective tenure laws have been an obstacle in some countries resulting in poor land use practices. Research, training and capacity building needs are identified.

WHAT IS THERE
Main Conclusions
Rural households, indigenous people and their communities, and farmers (including fisherfolk and foresters) are recognized as being important contributors to our economic system. Many of the world's current farming methods and systems are not sustainable and farmers are faced with the problem of adjusting their methods and being able to produce enough food for over six billion people by the year 2000. A "farmer-centred" approach is recommended as the key to the attainment of sustainable agricultural production methods for both developed and developing countries. This calls for a decentralized

decision-making and participatory approach in the design and implementation of resource and agricultural policies and the promotion of sustainable farming practices and technologies.

In particular, governments need to design and use pricing mechanisms, trade policies, fiscal incentives and other policy instruments to positively influence individual farmers decisions as these relate to efficient and sustainable use of natural resources and also ensure that, in doing so, full account of the impact of these decisions on household food security, farm incomes, on employment and on the environment are considered. This is a difficult task. The participation of farmers and/or their organizations in all decision making processes is promoted. Explicit recognition is given to women farmers and the roles that they can play.

Agreements Reached for International and National Action
Government actions required include:
- The design and implementation of programmes on sustainable livelihoods, agriculture and rural development, for the management of fragile ecosystems, the wise use of water and methods of integrated and sustainable management of natural resources systems;
- Promotion of agricultural and resource use policies that ensure an efficient and sustainable use of natural resources and at the same time account fully for the impact of individual farmer decisions on food security issues, farm incomes, employment and on the environment;
- Involve farmers and their organizations in the formulation of policies;
- Protect, recognise and formalise women's access to tenure and the use land, credit, other inputs and technologies and training; and,
- Support the formation of farmers organizations by providing adequate legal and social conditions and allocate sufficient resources to strengthen such organizations.

Politically Sensitive Issues
Strengthening the role of farmers is apolitical but difficulties are foreseen in attempting to move all of agriculture towards more sustainable production systems. Given the need to feed its own people, to create employment and earn foreign exchange, many governments have implemented agricultural and resource use policies that are not sustainable. High input mono-cropping farming systems account for a major share of the world's agricultural output and these production methods are often directly encouraged by governments by the policy framework that have been set. Individual farmers as decision makers will not shift to more sustainable practices unless this macro economic and policy environment encourages such a shift. Many governments look to rural populations for their political support. Fundamental changes in this policy environment, and in our agriculture, are required if we are to move towards a new agriculture. Studies have shown that food costs will increase and, in the shorter-run, it is virtually impossible to move completely towards more sustainable methods if food needs are to be met at a reasonable cost. Adjustments will need time and will require further research and a new understanding of complex production processes governed by different socio-economic conditions.

WHAT IS NOT THERE
The central argument is that individuals or their organizations will automatically give due attention to the resources with which they work and strive to use these in a sustainable manner. It is true that many individual farmers, both in developed and developing countries, have developed and are practising methods that are ingenious in terms of sustainability. It is also true that many farmers in both sets of countries practice production methods that are not sustainable. They often follow and lobby for non-sustainable production methods for economic reasons and strengthening the role of farmers in the decision-making process will not automatically guarantee sustainability unless the policy environment and other institutional factors are conducive or favour this. This Chapter (and perhaps others) has not

explicitly outlined specific policies that governments can follow in order to promote a sustainable agriculture and it is assumed that governments will automatically know these policies. This link between the macro-policy environment and the micro-agent or farmer is not explicitly detailed. Much more thought and research is required on these broader policy type issues and the role of farmers as agents for the achievement of these goals can then be evaluated.

OVERALL CRITIQUE

Substantive Content

Farmers and their organizations operate within the bounds and limitations of their social, economic, political, legal and resource environments. There are trade-offs that we as individuals are constantly making and these are reflected in the decisions made and indirectly in the outcomes of these decisions.

Farmers who are extremely poor and faced with the problem of attempting to feed a family will tend to place a high priority upon their daily food needs while others who are better off and have solved this problem will tend to give priority to other needs or perhaps investments in their farms. Landless farmers with few rights or resources will make decisions that are substantially different to those made by land owners or farmers with more resources under their control *ceteris paribus*. The authors in their arguments do not recognise these differences and tend to assume that strengthening the advisory and participatory or individual decision making role of farmers will automatically lead to the promotion of Agenda 21 principles. This is obviously not true given some of the serious resource depletion problems that are witnessed.

Farmers, fisherfolk or foresters themselves through their decisions and actions are directly responsible for many of these problems although it is recognised that they operate in an environment that sets bounds and options open to them. Chapter 32 hints at the importance of this general environment but having done so it automatically assumes that individuals will always make decisions favourable to the principles being promoted. It is difficult to pinpoint the exact conditions under which this would be true but given the time preferences of society vis-à-vis that of the individual, governments must regulate and set conditions within which individuals have a freedom to operate. This overall view or framework tends to be ignored and hence the reader can easily assume that if everything is left to the individual decision maker then everything will work out alright.

Design of the Chapter as an Organizing Framework

This Chapter was probably included and is justified because farmers are major users of natural resources. This use can be sustainable or non-sustainable. Resource use decisions that individual farmers make have major impacts both on the input and output side and in many of the poorer countries, agriculture is a dominant economic activity.

Since farmers are involved directly in combating deforestation, in managing fragile ecosystems, in sustainable mountain development, in the conservation of biological diversity, in sustainable agricultural and rural development and in other aspects of the management of natural resources it may have been possible to explicitly detail their role as decision makers in each of these Agenda 21 Chapters. Their role may also be highlighted in Chapter 32 because of the success that has been achieved in development and research activities where farmers have been explicitly brought in as partners. A sustainable agriculture is not possible without their full participation. The overall format followed is consistent with that of other chapters. It highlights the needs and this is probably appropriate.

RESEARCH REQUIREMENTS, CAPACITY BUILDING ETC.

EXPLICIT AND IMPLICIT PROPOSALS FROM THE CHAPTER
Research on:
- Sustainable production systems, on management methods for fragile ecosystems, on water, and on an integrated use of natural resources based on a systems approach;
- The design of policies that result in the efficient and sustainable use of natural resources, on the impact of these policies on household and national food security issues, on farm incomes and employment opportunities and on the environment;
- How best to involve and strengthen the role of farmers and their organizations in participatory action research and the formulation of broader economic social or legal policies to support this involvement. The role that women can and should play in this process;
- Development of location specific and environment friendly farming techniques;
- Evaluating the role that farmers organizations can play in assisting development projects;
- Indigenous production methods, the low external input nature of these and their efficiency with respect to use of land, water and forest resources.

GAPS AND ALTERNATIVE APPROACHES
- Research that explicitly identifies and evaluates production methods in terms of the sustainability or non-sustainability of each option. The benefits and costs of different systems must be measured and presented to individuals or governments in a manner that will allow decision makers to use this information.
- Research of the decision making processes of farmers and other decision makers with special emphasis given to the importance attached and given to environmental factors both in the short-run and the longer run. An assessment of the priority given to "the needs of the present without compromising the ability of future generations to meet their own needs". An explicit examination of the criteria and trade-offs that decision makers use and make is required.
- Research that attempts to define the rights of society vis-à-vis those of the individual farmers on environmental issues.
- Research that examines the role of individual farmers or their organisations as "key actors" in promoting Agenda 21 principles.
- Research that will direct and guide governments in terms of the social, legal, political and economic bounds that need to be set and within which individual farmers or their organizations can operate without compromising Agenda 21 principles.
- Research that will guide governments and help set sustainable resource use policies.
- For desperate and extremely poor farmers find alternatives that will help prevent the depletion of the natural resources base on which their livelihoods are based.

NICHES FOR IDRC
Opportunities that Fit Normal Programming
IDRC has been actively promoting and attempting to strengthen the role of farmers as decision makers for the last decade through its support of farming systems research and extension methods. Initially directed to closer contact between agricultural researchers and farmers the approach has influenced and directed research agendas and it also has, more recently, broadened to influence and help direct and set extension activities, education agendas and agricultural and resource use policies. IDRC and many of our partners are recognised as leaders in farming systems research methods and approaches. This activity should remain important given several of the new global program initiatives identified by the Environment and Natural Resources (ENR) Division. This support has promoted sustainable agricultural production systems and is seen as a strategy with high pay-offs in terms of Agenda 21 principles.

New Opportunities

Many of the research needs as outlined above will require special expertise and more in-depth analysis. Our research partners have, in some instances, began to tackle these questions but difficult conceptual and empirical questions remain. IDRC can and should support this research if we are to understand and influence farmers decisions. There is a need to strengthen the resource economics and social science dimensions of these agendas which are very weak. Attention also needs to be given to broader macro-policy/resource use and agricultural policy questions which will enable micro agents to operate in a policy environment that favours sustainable production methods. Canadian expertise exists and should be drawn upon.

RECOMMENDATIONS

WHICH NICHES ARE BEST FOR IDRC PROGRAM?

High pay-off activity and basic principle is central to our own philosophy. Strengthening the role of farmers or communities as partners in our research processes needs to be a core component for the majority of our research activities within the ENR Division particularly if we are to validate our work and ensure that research findings are acceptable and will be adopted by farmers and their communities. Full participation from the initial conceptual stage is recommended. Traditional niche for IDRC and its partners has been more on farming systems with an emphasis on finding appropriate production technologies. A shift is required giving more attention to the social science component of this work together with a strengthening of the resource economics/policy level type research.

ARE ADJUSTMENTS NEEDED AT IDRC IN ORDER TO FILL THESE NICHES?

Recent restructuring of the ENR Division has left gaps in our traditional areas of strength including agriculture, fisheries and forestry.

COMMENTARY 32

Name of Commentator: Ronnie Vernooy

1. GENERAL COMMENTS ON THE CHAPTER

- The Chapter highlights important issues that relate to farmers who are facing the challenge to produce enough food, maintain their enterprises, and conserve natural resources for the future. In many developing countries they have limited access to means of production (land, technology, credit); operate in an insecure economic, legal and political environment; and lack alternatives.
- Decentralization is seen as a key to these problems. Although decentralization is crucial, it tends to emphasize a top-down approach while neglecting a bottom-up approach, i.e. farmers strengthening their own organizations using tools they consider convenient.
- A major weakness of the Chapter concerns is its failure to differentiate between farmers and communities. Farmers do not all have the same ideas and interests (including gender, race and class), whether at local, regional, national or international levels. In fact, in many countries farmer organizations clash with each other as also happens between countries (viz. GATT negotiations).

2. OVERALL COMMENTARY ON THE FIRST REVIEW OF THE CHAPTER

- In general, agree. This is a very sound, overall critique which points out both the strong and weak points of the Chapter. It also identifies a good set of research requirements.
- Some observations should receive more attention, such as the issue of differentiation.
- Disagree with the statement on page 226 that "strengthening the role of farmers is apolitical but...". It is very much a political issue, both in the top-down or decentralization approach and bottom-up approach (farmers organizing themselves, lobbying, exercising pressure). Becoming more political by involved — participation in decision-making — is at the heart of strengthening the role of farmers. As point 3, a few lines later, says: "Many governments look to rural populations for political support". This is another aspect of the politics of strengthening the farmers' role.

3. MAJOR POINTS AGREED/DISAGREED WITH, AND REASONS

- Agree with the sections "what is there"; "what is not there" (indeed, insufficient analysis of how macro-policy relates to micro-level decision making and changing attitudes); "substantive critique" (the lack of attention given to differentiation); "research requirements"; "research gaps not identified" and "new opportunities for IDRC".
- Disagreed with "political issues" (see above).

4. MINOR POINTS AGREED/DISAGREED WITH, AND REASONS

- Disagree — the whole issue of differentiation requires more attention and analysis.

5. POSSIBLE ON-GOING ISSUES OR CONCERNS FOR IDRC

- See review. IDRC should increase research that links universities, research centres and NGOs with farmers' groups, organizations, associations, including women farmers' associations.

6. POSSIBLE IMPLICATIONS FOR IDRC

- See review.

SECTION 4

MEANS OF IMPLEMENTATION

CHAPTER THIRTY-THREE

FINANCIAL RESOURCES AND MECHANISMS

Responsible Officer: Gary McMahon

ABSTRACT 33

1. OVERALL CRITIQUE OF AGENDA 21 CHAPTER

- This Chapter totals up the bill for Agenda 21 ($US 600 billion per year) and rounds up the "usual suspects" as to who is going to pay for it.
- No discussion of priority areas or evaluation of feasibility of raising significant sums from the various sources. (Note: if all of the Third World debt was forgiven it would only amount to about 2 years of the cost of Agenda 21. Or it could be funded out of the present US $ 1 trillion for the world's arms and "defence", and even from the defence budgets of many Third World countries, which often absorb as much as 30–40% of their rational budgets.
- The presentation of Chapter 33 gives the process an air of unreality, although perhaps nothing more could have been expected at this time.

2. KEY CONCLUSIONS ARISING FROM CHAPTER

- Agenda 21 is going to cost a lot of money and the developed countries are largely expected to have to pay for it.

3. RESEARCH AND/OR IMPLEMENTATION POSSIBILITIES/OPPORTUNITIES

- Most of the proposals have to do with raising money rather than research.
- However, two possible areas are: (a) research on new types of facilities which could channel funds to Agenda 21 as well as the magnitudes that could be generated by the proposed facilities; and (b) research on the distribution of benefits of implementing the provisions of Agenda 21 between developing and developed countries as well as within the developing countries themselves.

4. ON-GOING AND/OR NEW PARTNERSHIPS FOR IDRC

- Global Environmental Facility, Commission for Sustainable Development, the Earth Council, various business and industrial councils/associations, foundations, etc.

5. SUGGESTED NICHES FOR IDRC

- The implementation of Agenda 21 is going to result in both winners and losers in the developing countries thus research on the distribution of the costs and benefits within developing countries seems appropriate for IDRC.

6. OTHER COMMENTS

- None.

KEY CONCLUSIONS IN THE CHAPTER

WHAT IS THERE

Main Conclusions
- Agenda 21 is going to cost a lot of money (US$ 600 billion per year) and the developed countries are largely going to have to pay for it.

Agreements Reached for International and National Action
- Global Environmental Facility to be restructured.
- Re-commitment to achieving 0.7% of GNP for ODA by 2000.

Politically Significant Issues
- Large increase in foreign aid will be required.
- Environment as a global public good.
- Benefits from clean environment appear to be more valuable to developed country citizens than developing country citizens (and therefore the latter seem to be more willing to pay for the clean-up).

WHAT IS NOT THERE

Given the huge (and unobtainable) amount of money that is needed for the "full" job, no discussion of priority areas.

Also, the practicality of raising significant sums from the different measures noted is not addressed.

No discussion of the reallocation of military expenditures ($1 trillion/year) to environment & development.

OVERALL CRITIQUE

Substantive Content
- Rounds-up the usual "suspects" for funding Agenda 21.
- No analysis of feasibility or (when feasible) the amounts they would generate (for example, if the entire debt of the Third World was forgiven and this money used for Agenda 21, it would only amount to the budget for about 2 of the 8 years).
- Design of the Chapter as an Organizing Framework.

Definitely this chapter is needed. However, its presentation gives the whole process an air of unreality. But perhaps nothing more substantive could have been expected at the time.

RESEARCH REQUIREMENTS, CAPACITY BUILDING ETC.

EXPLICIT PROPOSALS IN THE CHAPTER

Most of the proposals deal with how to raise money to finance Agenda 21 and do not lead to much IDRC-style research.

However, there is some room for research on new types of facilities which could channel funds to Agenda 21 as well as the magnitudes that could be generated by the proposed facilities.

IMPLICIT PROPOSALS DERIVED FROM THE CHAPTER

Given the large amounts of resources needed for Agenda 21, it seems likely that resources for more typical development projects will be limited. There seems to be room for research on the distribution of benefits of Agenda 21 between developing and developed countries, as well as within developing countries themselves.

NICHES FOR IDRC

GENERAL

Few good prospects for IDRC research.

Some difficult but potentially valuable research could look at the benefits of Agenda 21 provisions coming into effect. Of particular interest, the distribution within developing countries (Brazil is an obvious example).

KEY PARTNERS/OTHER ACTORS
Canada
Just about everybody.

Other Countries
Just about everybody, especially Western taxpayers.

RECOMMENDATIONS

WHICH NICHES ARE BEST FOR IDRC PROGRAM?

See above.

ARE ADJUSTMENTS NEEDED AT IDRC IN ORDER TO FILL THESE NICHES?

Program Organization
None.

Process and Project Cycle
None.

Structure/Staffing
None.

ARE THERE CROSS-CUTTING ISSUES THAT ARE NOT ADEQUATELY REFLECTED IN ANY OF THE ABOVE?
None.

CHAPTER THIRTY-FOUR

TRANSFER OF ENVIRONMENTALLY SOUND TECHNOLOGY, COOPERATION AND CAPACITY-BUILDING

Responsible Officer: Brent Herbert-Copley

ABSTRACT 34

1. OVERALL CRITIQUE OF AGENDA 21 CHAPTER

- Makes several important points, notably: a) capacity-building is indispensable to efforts to promote North–South transfer of technology; and b) effective transfer demands ongoing effort by recipients, and (ideally) long-term partnerships between recipients and suppliers.
- On the negative side, the document shows little attention to the effects of "environmentally-sound" technologies on employment, poverty, income distribution, gender concerns, etc.
- Excessively broad nature of recommended actions, with little indication of specific steps or responsibilities.

2. KEY CONCLUSIONS ARISING FROM CHAPTER

- The Chapter calls for action on five broad fronts:
    a) Improve access to scientific and technological information;
    b) Promote, facilitate and finance access to and transfer of environmentally-sound technologies;
    c) Facilitate maintenance and promotion of indigenous technologies;
    d) Strengthen endogenous capacity to assess, adopt, manage and apply environmentally-sound technologies;
    e) Promote long-term technological partnerships between owners and users of technologies.
- Two more specific proposals call for: a) establishment of regional information clearing-houses to link existing national, regional and international information systems; b) formation of collaborative network of research centres on environmentally-sound technology (akin to CGIAR, but also drawing on national centres of excellence).
- It adopts cautious note on two most sensitive issues (concessionality and intellectual property rights): document includes (non-binding) call for transfer on "concessional and preferential terms", but only "as mutually agreed"; and stresses need to respect IPRs in order to facilitate transfer (although it talk of possibility of compulsory licensing in some cases).

3. RESEARCH AND/OR IMPLEMENTATION POSSIBILITIES/OPPORTUNITIES

- Ongoing research required in a variety of areas, all of which IDRC could pursue: impact of existing policies (subsidies, tax incentives) on transfer and adoption of technology; alternative approaches to management of technology at enterprise level; evaluation of alternative approaches to intellectual property protection; strategies for promoting research collaboration and technology diffusion among firms, and between firms and public sector bodies; non-commercial sources of technology.

- Two more immediate proposals for action (see 1, above): information clearing house(s); and, collaborative network of research centres. (IDRC should remain active in discussions on both these proposals.)
- Variety of longer-term, more diffuse areas of action, which might involve IDRC: training and institutional development for national research and technology-support institutions; development and pilot testing of criteria and methodologies for technology needs assessment; establishment of "brokers" to act as intermediaries between suppliers and users of technology.

4. ON-GOING AND/OR NEW PARTNERSHIPS FOR IDRC

- Business community — such as the Business Council for Sustainable Development (BCSD), or the National Round Table on the Environment and the Economy (NRTEE), Chambers of Commerce, etc.
- Public sector agencies supporting technology-development in Canada — ISTC, provincial research organizations, NRC-IRAP.
- Technology-oriented NGOs — Intermediate Technology Development Group, Appropriate Technology International, African Centre for Technology Studies.

5. SUGGESTED NICHES FOR IDRC

- As a three-part strategy:
    a) IDRC should monitor the development of the two specific proposals in the Chapter (information clearing-house and collaborative research centres) in order to pinpoint opportunities for IDRC involvement;
    b) Existing program divisions should focus medium-term research support on examination of alternative policy and institutional frameworks to support the development, transfer and adoption of "environmentally-sound" technologies;
    c) Over the next few months, in-house resources should be devoted to exploring some of the longer-term opportunities outlined above, and where applicable developing proposals for specific initiatives.

6. OTHER COMMENTS

- There is considerable overlap between this Chapter and others (Science for Sustainable Development; Role of Business and Industry; Environmentally Sound Management of Biotechnology). These should be grouped pursuit of initiatives outlined above will involve SSD, ENR, CAID (the Research Utilization Program) and, to a lesser degree, ISD; while no formal restructuring is needed, effective mechanisms for collaboration will be needed.

REVIEW 34

KEY CONCLUSIONS IN THE CHAPTER

WHAT IS THERE

Main Conclusions

Five broad objectives:
- Improve access to scientific and technological information;
- Promote, facilitate and finance access to and transfer of technologies;
- Facilitate maintenance and promotion of indigenous technologies;
- Strengthen endogenous capacity to assess, adopt, manage and apply technologies; and,
- Promote long-term technological partnerships between holders and users of technologies.

Agreements Reached for International and National Action

No specific agreements. Like most chapters, this one contains a number of fairly vague calls for action on several fronts.

Two more specific proposals, calling for:
- Regional information clearing-houses to link existing national, regional and international information systems; and,
- Collaborative network of research centres on environmentally-sound technology (akin to the Consultative Group on International Agricultural Research centres, although also drawing on national centres of excellence).

In neither of these two cases, however, does the document outline specific steps or responsibilities.

Politically Significant Issues

The two sensitive issues regarding technology transfer are (i.e., should developing countries pay commercial terms for needed technology) and Intellectual Property Rights (IPRs). Both are complex — in the negotiations over the wording of the paragraph on concessionality, the debate ultimately settled on where to place one comma!

Ultimately the document adopts a relatively cautious note on both. There is a (non-binding) call for transfer of technology on "concessional and preferential terms", but only "as mutually agreed". And while the document talks about the necessity of guarding against abuse of IPRs (and mentions the possibility of compulsory licensing in some circumstances), the overall thrust is to respect IPRs. This is consistent with Agenda 21's overall emphasis on market-based incentives.

The real fireworks regarding IPRs and concessionality, of course, came in the Biodiversity Convention. This is the only binding commitment to transfer on non-commercial terms.

WHAT IS NOT THERE

Nothing really absent, but several issues get insufficient attention:
- Very little concrete discussion of indigenous technology, despite general statement regarding its importance;
- Little attention to the effects of so-called environmentally-sound technology on employment, poverty, income distribution, gender concerns, etc. — an overwhelming focus on the environmental side of the equation (although not just remediation technology); and,

- Overall, too sanguine about how easy it is to identify environmentally-sound technologies. Too little attention to the complexities of technology/needs assessment, which is presented as almost entirely a technical matter (particularly if development concerns are figured in, this clearly isn't the case!).

OVERALL CRITIQUE
Substantive Content
- Not bad. The document makes some real advance over the discussions of 12–18 months ago, in particular by stressing that facilitating North-South technology flow isn't sufficient, but has to be matched by efforts to build domestic capabilities. Early documents concentrated much more exclusively on legal/financial barriers to transfer (particularly patents), rather than on link between tech transfer and domestic tech capabilities.
- The Chapter also moves away from a "technology supermarket" view, by stressing that effective transfer demands on-going effort by recipients and (ideally) long-term partnerships between recipients and suppliers. (In UNCED-lingo, this has come to be known as "technology cooperation", a phrase championed by the Business Council for Sustainable Development). Here and elsewhere, IDRC can claim some credit in moving the debate forward.
- See also points above.

Design of the Chapter as an Organizing Framework
Definite need for a chapter on this, since this is one of the three key cross-cutting issues (along with finances and institutions).

The stress on capacity-building as a complement to technology transfer is important conceptually, but a bit of a morass in terms of programming. It broadens the scope of the Chapter to encompass almost anything to do with technology, and thus increases overlap with other sections of Agenda 21. Not surprisingly, the Chapter has more specific suggestions regarding information systems and technology transfer than regarding capacity-building.

The breadth of coverage also means that the Chapter contains almost no references to specific types of technology which might provide an initial focus for international efforts. Perhaps unavoidable, but it gives the Chapter a very abstract feel.

RESEARCH REQUIREMENTS, CAPACITY BUILDING ETC.

EXPLICIT PROPOSALS IN THE CHAPTER
- Clearing house(s) to provide information on alternate technologies. As a first step, the document suggests a review of existing information systems to identify gaps/opportunities.
- Review of existing policies (especially Research and Development subsidies, tax incentives) to determine impact on transfer/adoption of environmentally-sound technology.
- Training, infrastructure development, etc. to strengthen capabilities of existing national research institutions.
- Creation of network of national, regional and international research centres in the field of environmentally sound technology.
- Training and institutional development to strengthen capacity for undertaking technology needs assessment.

IMPLICIT PROPOSALS DERIVED FROM THE CHAPTER
- Research on alternative approaches to management of technology at enterprise/research institution level ("what works").

- Review of alternative approaches to intellectual property protection.
- Development of criteria/methodologies for technology needs assessment (especially how to mix environmental and developmental criteria).
- Strategies/mechanisms for promoting research collaboration and technology diffusion among firms and between firms and public sector bodies (especially what lessons from Northern experience?).

GAPS AND ALTERNATIVE APPROACHES

- Technology brokering: the document puts a lot of emphasis on improving information on environmental technology. But at least as important as the availability of information on alternative technologies is the ability to effectively assimilate and use this information. This requires new institutional mechanisms — small, specialized bodies which can act as intermediaries between suppliers and users of technology.
- Alternative sources of technology: the document focuses on commercially-owned technology, but in many cases non-commercial technology is crucial — particularly in the areas of environmental management and other "soft technology" fields where universities, public sector agencies have important expertise. Alternative sources in turn demand alternative channels to facilitate transfer, and there is room for considerable research to scout these out and examine "what works".
- Gaps in technology supply: as noted above, the document concentrates on general actions/initiatives (without reference to specific types of technologies). An alternative approach would be to look at specific areas where needed technology is not readily available, and work from there to strategies for its development or transfer (e.g. non-CFC refrigeration technology, which is relatively under-developed despite the Montreal Protocol. There are undoubtedly many more).

NICHES FOR IDRC

GENERAL

Most of the content of the chapter fits in one way or another with IDRC's mandate, given the emphasis placed on capacity-building.

Opportunities that Fit Normal Programming

- Information clearing-house : good in-house expertise and experience in ISD. This deserves a very close look (see below).
- Study of the effects of alternative policies (especially subsidies, tax incentives) on development, transfer and adoption of tech). This is a good fit with the Economic and Technology Policy program in SSD — one project already supported, and a major network on fiscal policy just off the ground.
- Management of technology at the enterprise and/or research institute level: the new Research Utilization Program in CAID is well-placed (in terms of both mandate and staff) to look at this.

New Opportunities

- International network of research centres: There may be an important role for IDRC in getting such a network off the ground, building on our experience in supporting research networks. Pursuit of this would require some immediate and high-level manoeuvring.
- Alternate approaches to intellectual property protection: possible area for collaboration between ETP, RUP and ENR, due to the greatest scope for immediate concrete action is in the field of biodiversity/biotechnology. One proposal for an international meeting to review this subject is already under review.

- Non-commercial technology transfer — good opportunity here for IDRC to review experiences with municipal twinning programs, university-university cooperation, etc., and try to extract some general lessons on elements of success. ENR would probably take lead, with collaboration of ETP and perhaps RUP.
- Technology needs assessment criteria, methodologies — a bit of a long-shot, but IDRC might get involved in conjunction with other actors such as Intermediate Technology Development Group (ITDG).

Unusual or High-Risk Opportunities
- Research collaboration: At one level, this wouldn't be all that unusual. IDRC (ETP and/or RUP) could look at the emerging Northern experience with international collaborative research, and attempt to draw out lessons for LDCs. (Steps have been taken in this direction with Lynn Mytelka's paper on strategic partnering.)
- On a more ambitious level, however, this might be linked to the plans for the Bolivar Initiative, an IDB-financed initiative to fund cross-national research partnerships in the Americas, and thus given a bit more of an action orientation. Discussions are underway regarding possible Canadian involvement in Bolivar, and IDRC (LARO, ETP and RUP) are keeping a watching brief. IDRC would then get involved more directly in fostering such research partnerships, including partnerships involving Canadian firms/research institutes. One weakness in Bolivar is its focus on collaborative research, rather than technology transfer/diffusion.
- Country reviews of capacity-building requirements. This would be a very ambitious undertaking, in which IDRC would support and help to organize assessments of key technology resources/needs in given countries. IDRC could take on responsibility (in conjunction with the UNDP and other actors) for a small number of such reviews as a pilot test of possible approaches to needs assessment at the national level). In LARO, Fernando Chaparro is discussing a possible joint venture with the OECD Development Centre to review experience with "country reviews" of innovation policy.
- Non-CFC refrigeration technology: a major effort is needed to examine alternative refrigeration technologies, and options for the development and/or transfer of such technologies. This would involve a combination of technical and policy research, and would thus require cross-divisional collaboration. As a first step, considerable digging would be required to discover who is at work in the field, and what opportunities exist for IDRC involvement.

REGIONAL SPECIFICITY

Most issues are not region-specific. The Bolivar Initiative (see above) makes LARO a natural point of departure for any work on international research collaboration.

KEY PARTNERS/OTHER ACTORS

Canada
- ISTC, Provincial research organizations, NRC-IRAP — all good partners regarding management of technology.
- Federation of Canadian Municipalities, Association des universités et collèges du Canada (AUCC) regarding non-commercial technology transfer.
- IISD — potential partner if a number of fields.

Other Countries
- UNCTAD — on a number of issues, from research partnerships to intellectual property.
- Business Council on Sustainable Development — on IPR issues, research partnerships, tax incentives.
- African Centre for Technology Studies — on biodiversity and biotechnology issues.

- Intermediate Technology Development Group, Alternative Technology International — on criteria for needs assessments, non-CFC refrigeration technology.

RECOMMENDATIONS

WHICH NICHES ARE BEST FOR IDRC PROGRAM?

As noted above, there is a great degree of fit between this chapter and IDRC's long-standing mandate to support the development of research capacity in developing countries. Much can and will be done without any effort by IDRC to alter its programming. At the same time, there are some real opportunities here, which IDRC can and should pursue more vigorously three-part strategy would include:

- Pursue possible IDRC involvement in the two specific suggestions made in the Chapter (i.e., the information-clearing house and the network of research centres).
- Focus ongoing IDRC research support on examination of alternative policy and institutional frameworks to support the development, transfer and adoption of technologies. This flows naturally from the mandate of ETP, and the emerging mandate of RUP, and would yield a number of topics for individual research projects or networks (alone or in collaboration with ENR).
- Selectively pursue the "new and unusual" initiatives listed above, as resources and opportunities present themselves. Over the next 3–6 months, in-house resources could be devoted to exploring at least the first and third of those outlined above.

ARE ADJUSTMENTS NEEDED AT IDRC IN ORDER TO FILL THESE NICHES?

Program Organization
- No changes required in order to pursue the first two elements of this strategy. Short-term task groups would be required to develop IDRC position on the info clearing house and the network of research centres. Work on the second element of the strategy could be accomplished by existing programs, with ad hoc collaboration among ETP, RUP and ENR staff.
- Pursuit of the "new and unusual initiatives" would require longer-term task groups, or perhaps creation of new activity centres. Active IDRC involvement in the Bolivar Initiative might result in creation of an arms-length office (funded by IDRC and others) to manage Canadian inputs.

Process and Project Cycle
None anticipated.

Structure/Staffing
- No immediate staffing requirements. New RUP staff have improved capacity in this area. Eventually experts might be needed in some fields of technology (e.g., biotech, where IDRC is still somewhat weak?). Pursuit of the "new and unusual" initiatives might necessitate some additional staff resources.
- As noted above, inter-divisional task groups could probably handle most of the areas outlined.

ARE THERE CROSS-CUTTING ISSUES THAT ARE NOT ADEQUATELY REFLECTED IN ANY OF THE ABOVE?
None.

COMMENTARY 34

Name of Commentator: Bill Edwardson

1. GENERAL COMMENTS ON THE FIRST REVIEW OF THE CHAPTER

- The review is comprehensive and well done.
- Many of the issues specifically apply to Chapter 16 (Environmentally Sound Management of Biotechnology).

2. OVERALL COMMENTARY ON THE FIRST REVIEW OF THE CHAPTER

- Agree with all the comments, but would add that there is a specific opportunity for the application of biotechnology to development in the South.
- Also would add the need to link or integrate all the objectives on specific topics (at least initially), e.g. information clearing-houses related to solid waste utilization technologies; promoting, financing, facilitating access to these technologies; promoting indigenous and/or appropriate technology; strengthening capacity to access, adopt, manage and apply appropriate technologies; and promoting long-term partnerships between owners and users of such technologies. If linked, the impacts would be greater and facilitate application to other fields.

3. MAJOR POINTS AGREED/DISAGREED WITH, AND REASONS

- Particularly agree with the Chapter's lack of attention to indigenous technology and South–South opportunities for development and transfer.

4. MINOR POINTS AGREED/DISAGREED WITH, AND REASONS

- None.

5. POSSIBLE ON-GOING ISSUES OR CONCERNS FOR IDRC

- Finding ways for multi-divisional teams to work effectively on such topics in an integrative way.

6. POSSIBLE IMPLICATIONS FOR IDRC

- Experimentation with funding handled by multi-divisional teams, which may change in membership, intensity, and location over time.
- Alternatively, building and funding external teams of individuals and institutions for execution of projects in this field.

CHAPTER THIRTY-FIVE

SCIENCE FOR SUSTAINABLE DEVELOPMENT

Responsible Officer: Anne Whyte

ABSTRACT

1. OVERALL CRITIQUE OF AGENDA 21 CHAPTER

- This chapter is clearly based on a text prepared by scientists and puts forward many of the current "big science" programs in earth sciences as worthy of countries' support.
- It pays passing reference to the need to integrate social sciences with natural sciences but gives no clues as to how this will be achieved.
- There are several interesting references to the earth's carrying capacity and "Limits to Growth" revisited, but at the level of fine purpose and generalities.
- What is most interesting is what is **not** mentioned: which organizations are assigned responsibility for implementation (UNESCO is not even mentioned, nor UNEP, UNDP or ICSU); the key issue of science policy is not developed; nor the free exchange of scientific data (especially satellite derived data).

2. KEY CONCLUSIONS ARISING FROM CHAPTER

- Science is crucial to needed basic understanding of earth's systems, and resource use; and thus is a key component in sustainable development;
- Precautionary principle should be exercised in applying scientific results to policies affecting the environment: the need for more research should not be used as an excuse to delay action;
- Countries should identify national scientific research agenda;
- International cooperation in science is critical and must include developing country scientists;
- Scientific capacity-building is necessary and urgent;
- Long term monitoring and assessment of the earth's natural and resource use systems are a priority.

3. RESEARCH AND/OR IMPLEMENTATION POSSIBILITIES/OPPORTUNITIES

- Much, if not all, of IDRC's program activities already respond to the call in this Chapter for science and scientific capacity-building, with the proviso that this Chapter calls for much more investment in environmental sciences than IDRC currently allocates on a proportional basis.
- Cooperation in environmentally sound technology;
- Integrated and interdisciplinary research for sustainable development;
- Science policy: institutions and process for getting research results effective in improving policies;
- Management of environmental data;
- Support to research networks.

4. ON-GOING AND/OR NEW PARTNERSHIPS FOR IDRC

- Basically all existing partnerships with research institutions;
- Not mentioned but important is International Council for Scientific Unions (ICSU), and the specialized agencies within the UN system, especially UNESCO, FAO, UNEP and WHO.

5. SUGGESTED NICHES FOR IDRC
- Generally, capacity-building in research, and particularly interdisciplinary research that bridges natural and social sciences;
- South-South scientific collaboration and support to research networks;
- Scientific and technical database networking;
- Systems for recording and retrieving indigenous environmental knowledge;

6. OTHER COMMENTS
- This Chapter emphasizes the need for more environmental science and more international cooperation in science at the scale of global projects. It is not unreasonable, given that this type of research produced the data on ozone depletion, climate change, and loss of biodiversity that led to the Earth Summit. The issue for IDRC is that the "big science" research projects are very costly and are dominated by Northern scientists. IDRC could play a role in developing country participation in global change research, or in setting the priorities to respond more to their own research needs, but it would need to take a hard look at how effective this effort would be, given the realities of funding for the natural sciences.

REVIEW 35

Brent Herbert-Copley

KEY CONCLUSIONS IN THE CHAPTER

WHAT IS THERE

Main Conclusions
- The Chapter concludes that improved scientific knowledge of the Earth's systems is crucial for furthering sustainable development. There is a need both to improve the state of scientific knowledge, and to increase its application in decision-making;
- In order to achieve these aims, there is need for the development of improved assessment methodologies and monitoring strategies, the promotion of international scientific collaboration, and the strengthening the scientific capabilities of developing countries; and,
- The Chapter strongly endorses the "precautionary principle". The lack of scientific certainty and the need for more research in some areas should **not** be used as an excuse to delay action on sustainable development.

Agreements Reached for International and National Action
No specific agreements exist, but the Chapter outlines four broad areas of activity:
- Strengthening the scientific basis for sustainable management;
- Enhancing scientific understanding;
- Improving long-term scientific assessment; and,
- Building up scientific capacity and capability.

Politically Significant Issues
Nothing politically controversial here. The endorsement of the precautionary principle is an indication of its widespread support.

WHAT IS NOT THERE

There is no attempt to prioritize the various recommended actions, or to assign responsibility among various international agencies. Many of the relevant agencies (ICSU, UNESCO) are not mentioned.

The emphasis is on the "supply" side. While the document talks at length about increasing scientific knowledge and capability, there is little attention to the barriers which impede the application of scientific knowledge in decision-making, and almost nothing about promoting linkages between the scientific community and the productive sectors. Moreover, there is no discussion of science policy.

OVERALL CRITIQUE

Substantive Content
- A number of worthwhile suggestions exist in the Chapter, but overall the document is general. It does not really serve as a guide to action, but is a "shopping list" of useful endeavours. It calls for capacity-building, etc., need to be backed up with specific actions, targets;
- The Chapter emphasizes "big science" projects, rather than the day-to-day job of building scientific capability. It tends to assume naively that more scientific knowledge will result in more informed decisions; and,
- There are passing references to several key issues (integration of local knowledge, public participation in setting scientific priorities, involvement of women in science). Unfortunately most are not backed up with specific programs of action.

Design of the Chapter as an Organizing Framework
- It would have been helpful to prioritize some of the actions, and perhaps have set up separate sections on "issues for urgent attention"; and,
- The breadth of the Chapter is problematic. It could have shown areas of complementarity/overlap with some of the sector- and issue-specific chapters of Agenda 21.

RESEARCH REQUIREMENTS, CAPACITY-BUILDING ETC.

EXPLICIT PROPOSALS IN THE CHAPTER

The Chapter contains a long list of proposed research and capacity-building actions. Some of the key proposals are as follows:
- National inventories of data holdings, research needs and priorities;
- Development of decision-making tools (quality of life indicators, incentive structures, technology assessment criteria);
- Development of participatory approaches to setting scientific research priorities;
- Expanded monitoring network(s) to collect data on various global cycles;
- Coordination of satellite missions, dissemination of satellite data;
- Development of Earth observation systems from space;
- Coordinations of existing data- and statistics-gathering systems relevant to environment/development issues;
- Development of methodologies to carry out national and regional audits;
- Development and expand national scientific and technological databases; and,
- Compilation, analysis and publishing of information on indigenous environmental and developmental knowledge.

This list is not exhaustive, but it does give a sense of the types of proposals put forward, and the broad scope of the Chapter.

IMPLICIT PROPOSALS DERIVED FROM THE CHAPTER

Almost **any** activity geared to supporting scientific research or research-capacity building activities could be included here. This would include most or all of what IDRC is already doing in the field of environmental science.

GAPS AND ALTERNATIVE APPROACHES

As noted earlier, there is relatively little attention to two important issues:
- Science policy: How should developing country governments address some of the key issues regarding financing of basic vs. applied research, management of scientific research institutions, participation in international scientific fora, design of incentive systems to promote research excellence, etc.
- Linkages between scientific institutions and the productive sectors (handled to some degree in Chapter 30, but from the perspective of the business community).

NICHES FOR IDRC

GENERAL

Opportunities that Fit Normal Programming
- A large variety of initiatives are mentioned which could conceivably fit within IDRC programming. Of the four areas outlined in the Chapter, the fourth ("Building up scientific capacity and capability") is the most obvious entry point for IDRC. Most of the training and institutional support activities promoted by IDRC would fit within this general category;
- One of the activities which fits well with established IDRC expertise is the suggestion for increased work on the development of scientific information systems, databases, and networks; and,
- The Chapter makes reference to the need to integrate natural and social science inputs — this is in area on which IDRC could concentrate efforts.

New Opportunities
- The development and/or testing of tools and methods in a number of areas: methodologies for environment/development audits; development of sustainable development indicators; design of improved incentive systems for better resource management; and,
- The study and cataloguing of indigenous scientific knowledge and practices; information systems for storage and dissemination of such knowledge.

Unusual or High-Risk Opportunities
Many of the proposals in the Chapter call for investment in "big science" programs. While these are beyond the scope of IDRC funding, the Centre might consider supporting participation of developing countries in these programs, and/or of ways of influencing the orientation of such programs to ensure that developing country priorities are adequately reflected. Careful thought would have to be given to the opportunity costs of any such involvement. Overall, IDRC's traditional mandate of building research capability should remain front and centre in its response to Agenda 21.

REGIONAL SPECIFICITY

No specific regional orientation. Capacity-building efforts should be directed toward least developed countries, but the Chapter's conclusions are applicable across the range of developing countries.

KEY PARTNERS/OTHER ACTORS

Canada
- Science-based government agencies — NRC, ISTC, Environment, Agriculture, etc.
- Granting agencies — NSERC.

Other Countries
Almost all of IDRC's existing research partners. ICSU and specialized UN agencies (UNESCO, FAO, UNEP, WHO).

RECOMMENDATIONS

WHICH NICHES ARE BEST FOR IDRC PROGRAM?
There is little need to pursue a specific "niche" — IDRC's long-established mandate makes it well-placed to pursue some of the issues raised in the Chapter.

Increased attention should be given to the development of tools and methods to assist in decision-making (see above, section III.A.2).

ARE ADJUSTMENTS NEEDED AT IDRC IN ORDER TO FILL THESE NICHES?
Program Organization
None anticipated.

Process and Project Cycle
Support systems for building scientific capability need to be considered — especially the balance between institutional support and project-based grants.

Structure/Staffing
None anticipated.

ARE THERE CROSS-CUTTING ISSUES THAT ARE NOT ADEQUATELY REFLECTED IN ANY OF THE ABOVE?
No, but this Chapter should be read in conjunction with some of the sectoral chapters and the other implementation chapters.

COMMENTARY 35

Name of Commentator: Maureen Law

1. GENERAL COMMENTS ON THE FIRST REVIEW OF THE CHAPTER
- The review is clear, concise and entirely appropriate. It does a good job of identifying the particular relevance of the Chapter to IDRC.

2. OVERALL COMMENTARY ON THE FIRST REVIEW OF THE CHAPTER
- Agree completely with the comments, especially the observation that the Chapter is very general.

3. MAJOR POINTS AGREED/DISAGREED WITH, AND REASONS
- Very much support the view that the "big science" research projects would be too costly and too North-dominated for IDRC, and that the Centre should find its niche in areas such as South-South scientific collaboration and in database networking.

4. MINOR POINTS AGREED/DISAGREED WITH, AND REASONS
- None.

5. POSSIBLE ON-GOING ISSUES OR CONCERNS FOR IDRC
- None.

6. POSSIBLE IMPLICATIONS FOR IDRC
- IDRC could play a role in promoting the integration of the natural sciences and social sciences — a subject which receives recognition in this Chapter but which is not dealt with in any substantive way.

CHAPTER THIRTY-SIX

PROMOTING EDUCATION, PUBLIC AWARENESS AND TRAINING

Responsible Officer: C. Smart and D. Morales-Gómez

ABSTRACT

1. OVERALL CRITIQUE OF AGENDA 21 CHAPTER

- With the exception of references to Jomtien and Tbilisi, the Chapter does not recognize that the three themes, education, public awareness and training, are not new and that important work (innovations) has been done (especially in education).
- No clear distinction is made between education, public awareness and training. They each require different technical treatment, with education being more fundamental and complex than the other two.
- There is a danger that public awareness is reduced to propaganda and training to the acquisition of mechanical skills.

2. KEY CONCLUSIONS ARISING FROM CHAPTER

- It is urgent that governments take action:
    a) To ensure that development education is an essential part of learning and that education in all disciplines includes the physical, socio-economic and human elements;
    b) To increase the general level of sensitivity to the challenge of sustainable development by encouraging involvement and devolving decision-making authority; (c) to integrate the notion of sustainable development into the development of human resources for productive work to ensure that training is a two-way learning process.

3. RESEARCH AND/OR IMPLEMENTATION POSSIBILITIES/OPPORTUNITIES

- Education, Public Awareness and Training are all programmatic concerns for IDRC: the Social Policy Program is strongly supporting post-Jomtien activities in education; PIP has many public awareness activities. The question of what resources the Centre will devote to training in support of its Agenda 21 orientation does need to be reexamined with a view to allocating more and better qualified resources.

4. ON-GOING AND/OR NEW PARTNERSHIPS FOR IDRC

- New partnerships are less of an issue than building on relationships with traditional partners (universities) and encouraging incipient partnerships with (Canadian-based) NGOs, the private sector, the First Nations and professional associations (teachers, learned societies).
- Consideration must be given to an expanded relationship with UN agencies (Unesco, Unicef).

5. SUGGESTED NICHES FOR IDRC

- The Centre has well established niches for each of the areas covered by the Chapter.
- The Social Policy Program is able to address comprehensively the issue of education for sustainable development from a policy and planning perspective.

- The call for stronger information exchange by enhancing technologies and the capacity to promote environment and development education and public awareness provides ISS with a particular opportunity.
- Support for PIP activities and training provide the Centre with a particular challenge if it adopts as a major theme the challenge of helping to encourage environment-related changes in behaviour (lifestyle changes) in the North.
- Closer interaction with the First Nations in Canada and indigenous people in the Third World provide a particular niche for most programs of the Centre.
- ENR is especially well placed to provide substantive, professional and scientific inputs in all areas of activity.

6. OTHER COMMENTS

- None of the Centre's efforts made in response to the issues in the Chapter should be offered as particularly new or as the 'quick fix'. All three issues in the Chapter (public awareness being a possible exception) are perennial concerns related to human development and research capacity. They promise much but are totally dependent on prevailing political forces.

REVIEW 36

C. Smart

KEY CONCLUSIONS IN THE CHAPTER

No specific conclusions are drawn in this chapter. All countries are urged to do more under three program heads:
- Reorienting Education Towards Sustainable Development;
- Increasing Public Awareness; and,
- Promoting Training.

The Chapter recognizes that the three are linked to all areas of Agenda 21, particularly to the ones on meeting basic human needs, capacity-building, data and information, science and the role of major groups.

At a broad international level, two conclusions could be drawn: (i) the urgency to act on the proposed programs; and, (ii) the identification of a plan of action including concrete activities and proposals for their implementation.

At the level of each of the "programs," the following could be highlighted:
- In reorienting education: (a) the integration of development education as an essential part of learning; and, (b) the integration of physical, socio-economic and human dynamics (including demography) in all disciplines transmitted through education.
- In increasing awareness: (a) increase sensitiveness and involvement; and, (b) devolving authority in decision-making.

Training: (a) integrate the notion of sustainable development in human resources development for productive work (which is more than training); and, (b) transforming training into a two-way learning process (an innovative notion of training).

WHAT IS THERE

Main Conclusions

The Chapter makes only three references to research. The emphasis in this chapter is to ensure that knowledge (the results of research) are disseminated through education, public awareness and training. The implied conclusion is that these are three virtuous and necessary programs to achieve better environmental management and sustainable development.

The main conclusion of the chapter which is congruent with Jomtien and Tbilisi is: the centrality of education (primarily basic education) and learning (as a process) as a means to develop new values and awareness (about environment and sustainable development) and to change behaviours. To make this effective, the dissemination of knowledge is essential).

Agreements Reached for International and National Action

Throughout the chapter there are references to international programs, conventions, etc. that countries should take into account when devising policy and activities connected to education, public awareness and training, to quote:

- The Declaration and Recommendations of the Tbilisi Intergovernmental Conference on Environmental Education, organized by UNESCO and UNEP and held in 1977, have provided the fundamental principles for the proposals in this document;
- All countries are encouraged to endorse the recommendations arising from the World Conference on Education for All: Meeting Basic Learning Needs (Jomtien, Thailand, 5–9 March 1990) and to strive to ensure its Framework for Action;
- Countries should promote, as appropriate, environmentally sound leisure and tourism activities, building on The Hague Declaration of Tourism (1989) and the current programs of the World Tourism Organization and UNEP;
- UNICEF, UNESCO, UNDP and non-governmental organizations should develop support programs to involve young people and children in environment and development issues, such as children's and youth hearings, building on decisions of the World Summit for Children; and,
- Aid agencies should strengthen the training component in all development projects. The **environmental management guidelines of UNDP** for operational activities of the United Nations system may contribute to this end.

Politically Significant Issues

There are several references that imply a major role for the agencies of the UN system:

- Within 2 years the **United Nations system should undertake a comprehensive review of its educational programs, encompassing training and public awareness**, to reassess priorities and reallocate resources. The UNESCO/UNEP International Environmental Education Program should, in cooperation with the appropriate bodies of the United Nations system, Governments, non-governmental organizations and others, **establish a program within 2 years to integrate the decisions of the Conference into the existing United Nations framework** adapted to the needs of educators at different levels and circumstances;
- The United Nations could maintain **a monitoring and evaluative role regarding decisions of the United Nations Conference on Environment and Development** on education and awareness, through the relevant United Nations agencies; and,
- Countries with the support of the United Nations system should identify workforce training needs and assess measures to be taken to meet those needs. **A review of progress in this area could be undertaken by the United Nations system in 1995.**
- These indicate an implicit need for coordinated actions with UN agencies and governments. The potential implications for IDRC is the pressure of external agendas.
- In terms of this document, how does this affect the actual involvement of NGOs? NGOs are one of IDRC's primary partners. Under the new trends, to whom do we respond?

WHAT IS NOT THERE

A "sleeper" in this chapter, which asserts the fundamental right of access to more and better information about environment and sustainable development, is the issue of "advocacy". If we are people empowered then possibility of the conflict and struggle that characterizes advocacy should be anticipated. (In a recent $ 10 million CIDA grant to the Environmental NGOs in Canada to collect and disseminate information they were expressly forbad to use the funds in support of research and advocacy. The Struggle of the Cree of Northern Quebec with Hydro Quebec is a reminder of the intensity and scope of environmental disputes likely to flow from the successful implementation of Agenda 21.)

The Chapter does not distinguish between the application of three program themes in the North and South. All objectives and activities are treated as generic. The application of the three programs proposed in this chapter require a different emphasis, content and modes of presentation in the North than in the South. Education, public awareness and training for the South, even when they call for a special emphasis on the environment are extensions of the current and ongoing struggle to raise basic levels of literacy and to empower people and communities. In the North effective education, public awareness and training must bring about major changes in attitudes and behaviour towards consumption, economic growth, power sharing etc. which, implies a diminishing of the economic and political power of Northerners in favour of Southerners. Agenda 21 was a document crafted for politicians: the lack of this fundamental distinction is one of the more telling proofs of the level of generality that was required to reach consensus.

Except for the general references to Jomtien and Tbilisi, the chapter does not recognize that this discourse is not new and that important work (innovations) have been done. At least over the last five years, concerns about environment and sustainable development is very much in the framework of those dealing (and understanding) education. By not recognizing that something has been done, the chapter contributes to reinforce trends.

The chapter does not make a clear distinction between education, public awareness and training. These are not the same thing. They are technically different activities, which scientifically are defined on the basis of distinct theoretical frameworks. Education is a foundational and more comprehensive and complex process than public awareness and training. Failing to establish this distinction or to recognize this difference leads to emphasizing the last two and reducing them to sophisticated propaganda and acquisition of mechanical skills.

The Chapter only superficially refers to NGOs. Parallel to what this chapter says, there is a whole Treaty of NGOs on environmental education and sustainable development. The Treaty includes 16 "principles" to base the understanding of environmental education; 22 recommendations for action; 8 proposals for coordination; and, 5 agreements on use of resources.

The Chapter does not make reference to a key point: feasibility. In each of the programs there is a reference to estimated costs, which in most cases are overwhelming. From where these resources are going to come is a question not even raised.

From the point of view of education, the Chapter does not properly address the issues of quality and relevance of education (in the context of access, content, and output) and their importance in sustainable development.

OVERALL CRITIQUE

Substantive Content
See points above.

Fundamental criticisms which apply not only to this chapter but to the whole Agenda 21:
- Despite its discourse, Agenda 21 and the notion of how education fits into this new wisdom is a "Northern product", which satisfies primarily the international political and economic needs and agenda of industrialized countries, and so positions developing countries in a reactive position;
- Agenda 21, and the Chapter on education, does not go far enough in acknowledging the critical problems underlying the environmental issue. Agenda 21 seems to focus primarily on aspects related to political will, awareness, lack of consciousness, etc. It ignores issues of class, capital accumulation, the predominance of the market ideology, unequal distribution of wealth, and relations of political control between the North and the South. This leads to very superficial analyses of the problems.

Design of the Chapter as an Organizing Framework
The first program theme, Reorienting Education Towards Sustainable Development, in general terms resonates with areas of research supported by the Education Program in the past and the Social Policy Program today. The other two themes, Public Awareness and Training, are areas provided for in CAID because they have a Centre-wide support function. The drafters of this chapter stress that it should be read in conjunction with the other chapters. The decision to treat these three themes in a separate chapter is justified given their cross-cutting nature, the degree of dedicated investment and policy commitment they require and the fact that they will require significant reforms to existing practice especially in education.

RESEARCH REQUIREMENTS, CAPACITY BUILDING ETC.

EXPLICIT PROPOSALS IN THE CHAPTER

Each of the three programs lists "activities" for governments to implement. The following are the possible activities for Centre programs:

Education
All countries are encouraged to endorse the recommendations of the Jomtien Conference and strive to ensure its Framework for Action. This would encompass the preparation of national strategies and actions for meeting basic learning needs; universalizing access and promoting equity; broadening the means and scope of education; developing a supporting policy context; and, mobilizing resources and strengthening international cooperation to redress existing economic, social and gender disparities which interfere with these aims. Non-governmental organizations can make an important contribution in designing and implementing educational programs and should be recognized.

With the above as the overarching activity, governments are also asked to take steps to ensure: that environment/sustainable development become a cross-cutting issue in curriculum at all levels of education; that different population groups and communities assess their own needs and develop the skills needed to implement their own initiatives; that effective teaching methods be promoted and innovative teaching methods be sought; that they provide in-service training for teachers, educational planners, and administrators; that they use enhancing technologies for information exchange; that they support university and other tertiary activities and networks placing emphasis on cross-disciplinary courses; that they strengthen national and regional Centres of Excellence; that non-formal education and continuing education be promoted and facilitated; that gender stereo typing be removed from curricula; and, that indigenous people be encouraged to play a role in education and training.

Public Awareness
There is some overlap with the education theme: the main "activities" focus on the collection and sharing of information of environment and development by:

Strengthening existing advisory bodies or establishing new ones for public environment and development information; promoting the co-ordination of national and regional information bodies; providing public information services; encouraging educational establishments in all sectors, especially universities to contribute to awareness building; by promoting a co-operative relationship with media, popular theatre groups, and the entertainment and advertising industries; employing modern communications technologies for effective public outreach.

Of particular note is the appeal to governments:

To increase their interaction with and include, as appropriate, indigenous people in the management, planning and development of their local environment, and to promote dissemination of traditional and socially learned knowledge through means based on local customs, especially in rural areas, integrating these efforts with the electronic media, whenever appropriate; to develop support programmes to involve young people and children in environment and development issues.

Training
From a list of 13 "activities" the following might inform Centre's training policy and programs:

National professional associations are encouraged to develop and review their codes of ethics and conduct to strengthen environmental connections and commitment; environment and development issues should be integrated into existing training curricula including in-service training courses for all vocational and management training; develop a service of locally trained and recruited environmental technicians able to provide local people and communities, particularly in deprived urban and rural areas, with the services they require, starting from primary environmental care; enhance the ability to gain access to, analyze and effectively use information and knowledge available on environment and development; develop training resource-guides; strengthen the training component in all development projects, emphasizing a multidisciplinary approach, promoting awareness and providing the necessary skills for transition to a sustainable society.

IMPLICIT PROPOSALS DERIVED FROM THE CHAPTER
The micro versus to macro levels of intervention are both covered in the range of recommended actions. Appeals to government to endorse the Jomtien Conference to ensure its Framework of Action with national strategies; the strengthening of national bodies for environment and development information, greater co-operations with UN agencies; working with national professional associations on codes of ethics and training that incorporates the concern for sustainable development are examples of macro level intervention. The greater part of the activities invoke micro level actions which focus on the participation of NGOs, teachers, youth, women, communities, and indigenous peoples.

The Centre is debating pros and cons of the macro versus the micro as its most appropriate and effective level of intervention. The program activities suggested in this chapter do not reflect this tension. All three programs, while needing enabling policy at the macro level, can only be put into effect through the associations, communities and particular groups that work at the micro level.

There is a "meso" level of intervention that might assist the Centre to resolve the macro/micro dilemma. It is represented by the universities and perhaps the professional associations. The universities are the Centre's traditional partners in research and training. A reassessment of the scope of this partnership in relation to Agenda 21 is needed. *Creating a Common Future: An Action Plan For Universities*, the report of the Halifax Conference on University Action for Sustainable Development which contains some 85 recommendations would be a good starting point. But the distinction between "micro" and "macro" might be considered artificial.

GAPS AND ALTERNATIVE APPROACHES

A major gap in the document is the lack of attention to issues of quality and relevance (in access, content, and output). Technically, this ignores the claims of international agencies and government currently addressing education issues.

NICHES FOR IDRC

GENERAL

Opportunities that Fit Normal Programming

Education
The Social Policy Program of SSD is already supporting follow-up activities to the Jomtien Conference on Education for All. This covers both enabling policy and regulations and technical support for education and permits a wide range of entry points for research, curriculum, development, teacher effectiveness, computers in the classroom, etc. The question is: will links with environmental issues hinder rather than enhance the more fundamental effort to create the will, the policy, and technical support for good, broad-based general education?

Public Awareness
PIP has a well established base from which to promote public awareness activities related to IDRC's work in Canada. To what extent should the expertise supporting this Canada-focused activity have an international dimension? The Summer Institute is one example of an effective international dimension to the PIP work.

Training
The virtue of increasing the environmental accent on Centre supported training is not at issue. The Chapter implies that a significant "quantity" of training is needed to support Agenda 21 objectives. The question for the Centre is: what portion of its resources (budget and staff does) it want to commit to Agenda 21-related training?

New Opportunities
One persistent thread throughout this Chapter is the need for enhanced use of information technologies. Assuming that countries co-operate in the production of up-to-date teaching and training materials, and make strong commitments to public awareness and training focusing on environment and sustainable development, there is a need to strengthen, within 5 years, **information exchange by enhancing technologies and capacities necessary to promote environment and development education and public awareness.** ISSD is already involved in support of post UNCED regional and international information systems. What is the link between these systems and smaller local, community, school, etc. needs and access to information?

The combination of the ideas in Agenda 21 and the new programming in IDRC opens a new opportunity for addressing comprehensively the issues of education for sustainable development from a policy-planning perspective. Although, this may have less immediate impact on high profile micro-issues, it does emphasize sustainability in a systemic way.

Unusual or High-Risk Opportunities
The most dramatic inference of the UNCED Conference is that the North must change if the South is to develop. "We must change our attitudes. That message hasn't got through to everybody. Current Lifestyles in North America are not sustainable" (Maurice Strong in the New Scientist:June 20, 1992). IDRC could adopt the need for behavioral change in the North as a major theme in its support for public awareness and training. The Centre would build on the relationships it has with teachers, the NGOs, professional associations and especially the Canadian Universities to promote this line.

The risk in the opportunities offered by the Chapter and Agenda 21 is related to the political decision on how to move ahead on the recommendations. The risk of short term political visibility and impact, over the cost of longer term effectiveness, is present in all actions that can be taken on this Chapter.

KEY PARTNERS/OTHER ACTORS
Canada
The Universities are and will continue to be the Centre's traditional partners in research and training. *Creating A Common Future: An Action Plan For Universities* provides a starting point for strengthening the Centre's partnership with Canadian Universities where the recommendations link to the international development research and training themes of the Centre.

The Chapter makes numerous references to the importance of NGOs in education, and public awareness. The focus on sustainable development underscores forcefully the link between problem identification, research and remedial action, especially when the rights and well-being of disadvantaged communities and groups are at stake. The NGOs embody this link. In Canada the role of the Development NGOs (DNGO) is changing as the Southern NGOs grow in strength. The NGO community is beginning to use the same vocabulary as the Centre: they are aware of the importance of research; know that they are being given more space for action by government; and, are alert to their possible role in shaping policy for environmental and development interventions. At the same time they are aware of their institutional weaknesses and the complex political matrix of their sector. They fear co-option by government rather than true and equitable partnerships in the search for alternative economic and social approaches to development. The Environmental NGOs (ENGO) are beginning to extend their horizons from national to international issues. Whether they convert themselves into another set of DNGOs or workout fruitful alliances with the established DNGOs is in the balance. The Centre must be alert to the ways in which it might respond to the NGOs at this critical period of their transformation into more prominent players in civil society.

The Chapter makes several pointed references to the value of indigenous knowledge and communities as a contribution to the search for approaches to sustainable development. The Centre has found ways of forging links with the indigenous community in Canada and can build on this while being conscious of the complexities of a new emerging political order for the First Nations (see HS-Split lake ENV-traditional knowledge).

The PIP program in CAID has laid the ground work for links to several of the other groups mentioned in the Chapter: with teachers and students (the Summer Institute); media (Developing Stories); the broader public (Development Fora); Community groups (the speakers bureau).

Other Countries

The research and training links with universities in the developing world is well established. Increasingly SS and HS have supported participatory research that supports Southern NGOs many of which represent indigenous peoples.

RECOMMENDATIONS

WHICH NICHES ARE BEST FOR IDRC PROGRAM?

Underlying all of the programs in the Chapter is the assumption that there is a reliable and shared source of "science-based" (for which read "research product") information/knowledge. This resonates with the Centre's mission "Empowerment Through Knowledge." The Centre has and will continue to support activities in education, public awareness and training. The Centre must ask itself if it wants to do more in support of the collecting, packaging and dissemination of science-based information, whether based on the research it funds or broadly dealing with science knowledge. This latter is important for sustainable development but often does not reach people who could use that knowledge to negotiate effectively environmental disputes or to improve their lives.

ARE ADJUSTMENTS NEEDED AT IDRC IN ORDER TO FILL THESE NICHES?

Program Organization

Several sections above highlight the need for enhanced relationships with Canadian groups, NGOs, Universities, Professional Associations. The Centre should consider a less restrictive collaborative arrangements with Canadian groups on activities related to Agenda 21. For example, a case might be made for requiring all longterm support for research institutions in the Third World to have a Canadian Partner adequately supported to ensure longer range sustained relationships that would permit the two way exchange of knowledge, and , perhaps as important the exchange of attitudes, cultural perspectives etc.

Process and Project Cycle

None.

Structure/Staffing

If the content and spirit of this Chapter are taken seriously, an adjustment for the Centre is **to educate its staff on what education for sustainable development is all about.**

ARE THERE CROSS-CUTTING ISSUES THAT ARE NOT ADEQUATELY REFLECTED IN ANY OF THE ABOVE?

None.

COMMENTARY 36

Name of Commentator: Necla Tschirgi

1. GENERAL COMMENTS ON THE CHAPTER

- This Chapter deals with a "cross-cutting" issue bearing on virtually all the major substantive topics covered by Agenda 21.
- The three program areas it addresses are loosely-related but quite distinct. The reason they are linked together in this Chapter is because they are considered as the key tools for the promotion, propagation and advancement of new values, attitudes, behavioural patterns and skills necessary for sustainable development.
- The Chapter views each of these intrinsically important activities primarily from an instrumentalist perspective.
- Acceding to political realities, the Chapter limits itself to an identification of the general objectives and activities under each program.
- It explicitly states that "countries, regional and international organizations will develop their own priorities and schedules for implementation in accordance with their needs, policies and programs."

2. OVERALL COMMENTARY ON THE FIRST REVIEW OF THE CHAPTER

- This Chapter is thoroughly reviewed, with the reviewers elaborating on the contents of the Chapter, drawing out its implications for IDRC, and questioning some of the underlying assumptions of the Chapter, as well as its broader practical and political implications.

3. MAJOR POINTS AGREED/DISAGREED WITH, AND REASONS

- Agree that this Chapter reflects the difficulties inherent in trying to accommodate the differing expectations and needs of the South and the North in terms acceptable to all.
- The resultant document is so broad that it incorporates virtually everything. That is one of its main failures: it does not establish priorities, sign posts, concrete targets. Everything is considered important and has to be tackled.
- It is stated, for example, that one of the aims of the education program is "to achieve environmental and development awareness in all sectors of society on a world-wide scale as soon as possible." This is a tall order, especially when it is piggy-backed to existing educational programmes and institutions which, in many cases, are already over-burdened, inadequate, obsolete or weak.
- The challenge, is how to accomplish the goals of Chapter 36 without breaking the back of existing educational systems.
- Agree that, while education involves the transmittal of key social values, these values do not exist in a vacuum. The persistence of values contrary to sustainable development is not simply a function of ignorance, lack of awareness or political will. Values, both in the South and North, are intimately connected to prevailing structures of power, wealth, class, gender, race. Accordingly, it is not sufficient to call for new "globalist" values without changing the basic structural relations that promote those values.

4. MINOR POINTS AGREED/DISAGREED WITH, AND REASONS

- Too many to list; moreover, enumerating them would add little.

5. POSSIBLE ON-GOING ISSUES OR CONCERNS FOR IDRC

- The following issues raised in Chapter 36 fall directly within IDRC's mandate:
    a) Strengthening formal and non-formal educational systems;
    b) Promoting research on sustainable development;
    c) Capacity building;
    d) Information exchange;
    e) Collaborating with international organizations and the UN system in monitoring progress on the program objectives;
    f) Strengthening the role of NGOs and community groups in policy making and resource allocation;
    g) Encouraging governments to create an "enabling" environment for policy innovations.

6. POSSIBLE IMPLICATIONS FOR IDRC

- IDRC's comparative advantage lies in the following:
    a) Educating/sensitizing the educators;
    b) Re-tooling and motivating the policy-makers, educational planners and administrators;
    c) Involving NGOs and Private Voluntary Organizations (PVOs) in public information and awareness activities with direct bearing on their lives;
    d) Enlisting the help of the mass media and other opinion-makers to become engaged in issues of sustainable development.

CHAPTER THIRTY-SEVEN

NATIONAL MECHANISMS AND INTERNATIONAL COOPERATION FOR CAPACITY-BUILDING

Responsible Officer: Anne Whyte

ABSTRACT

1. OVERALL CRITIQUE OF AGENDA 21 CHAPTER

- A fair summary of the capacity and capability-building (CCB) implications of Agenda 21 and the global conventions.
- There is heavy emphasis on the role of the UN and little specificity about CCB implementation.
- Much emphasis on CCB for technology transfer and "know-how" and on the need for CCB for integrating environment into development policies (but no clue given how this might be achieved).
- More attention is given to institutional arrangements and institutional CCB than to human resource development and training.
- The lead role is given to UNDP, although it is specified they must work with UNEP. There is some doubt about UNDP's own capacity in CCB!

2. KEY CONCLUSIONS ARISING FROM CHAPTER

- The purpose of CCB is to improve policy-making both with respect to environmental sustainability and to participatory process.
- CCB requires support of the North, UN organizations and donors.
- Donors should coordinate their efforts, and so should UN system.
- National reports on CCB needs and strategies should be prepared by 1994.
- Countries should establish a central coordinating unit for technical cooperation, priority planning and resource allocation.
- Review mechanisms should be established to monitor progress in CCB for ability of countries to conduct EIA's, fulfill obligations under Agenda 21 and global conventions; conduct participatory process in CCB; etc.

3. RESEARCH AND/OR IMPLEMENTATION POSSIBILITIES/OPPORTUNITIES

- The research possibilities are open-ended:
  a) What are CCB needs for improved policy-making for sustainable development?
  b) How can NGOs and private sector work with government and academic communities to develop and implement an effective and efficient CCB strategy?
  c) Who are the target groups for training in integrating environment and economics?
  d) What are appropriate curricula, institutional linkages for CCB?
  e) Participatory research on developing a national participatory process for CCB.

4. ON-GOING AND/OR NEW PARTNERSHIPS FOR IDRC

- UNDP, UNEP, WB and specialized agencies of the UN system.
- Other donors, especially CIDA and IISD in Canada.

- ICSU and other international scientific organizations and programs.
- International NGOs and ENGOs and their national counterparts.
- Private sector, with respect to technology transfer and training.

5. SUGGESTED NICHES FOR IDRC
- Technology co-operation: CCB for specific sectors; SME's.
- CCB for integrated and interdisciplinary research.
- Project evaluation design and methods to include measures of sustainability.
- Research on participatory research and participatory processes.
- Developing model approaches and information support systems for national CCB plans.

6. OTHER COMMENTS
- Capacity-building is central to IDRC's work and therefore the possible niches for the Centre are many and cross-cutting with almost anything else it will undertakes with respect to Agenda 21. The most urgent challenge is to help developing countries identify their needs for capacity-building in a way that is compatible with their own agendas and capacities to sustain initiatives and institutions. Also to make best use of opportunities for regional cooperation and international institutions, which should be supportive mechanisms rather than driving forces.

REVIEW 37

Claire Thompson

KEY CONCLUSIONS IN THE CHAPTER

WHAT IS THERE
Main Conclusions
- The purpose of capacity-building is to improve policy-making for environmental sustainability on a national and regional level while also promoting and improving the participatory process;
- Building-capacity requires partnership between the South, the North, the UN system and donors. As well, the international community, municipalities, NGOs, universities, research centres and the private sector should be involved;
- Greater coordination should be encouraged both between donors and within the UN system. Each should improve and reorient their own capacity to deal with environment and/or development matters; and,
- Institutional-strengthening and improved mechanisms for technical cooperation will be crucial elements of capacity-building. They must be reoriented to the specific conditions and individual needs of recipients. Human resources development and training are also important.

Agreements Reached for International and National Action
No agreements were reached for international or national action. However, the Chapter mentions two specific objectives and several "activities", some of which are outlined below, which governments and international bodies should undertake. But, no real process or mechanism was put in place to ensure that these occur.

- National reports on capacity-building needs and strategies should be prepared by 1994;
- By 1997, the Secretary-General of the UN should submit a report to the General Assembly on improvements made in the implementation of technical cooperation programs;
- Countries should establish a central coordinating unit for technical cooperation, priority planning and resource allocation; and,
- A review mechanism should be established to monitor progress in capacity-building. Specifically this would monitor the ability of countries to conduct environmental impact assessments; fulfil obligations under Agenda 21 and the global conventions; and conduct the necessary participatory process for successful capacity-building, etc.

Politically Sensitive Issues

Much of the emphasis in this Chapter is on the technical cooperation component of capacity-building. Its recommendations state that it be reoriented to reflect the needs of recipients and that coordination between donors and recipient countries, and among donors, be "improved" and expanded to include NGOs, and scientific and technological institutions. This raises questions about how technical cooperation has been carried out to date and raises the thorny issue of participation, its definition and actual practice.

Technical cooperation, particularly technology transfer, between North and South has never been a simple process, being fraught with diplomatic and economic conflicts. "Reorienting" it to reflect the needs of recipient countries may often conflict with the desires ("needs"?) of donor countries.

Participation, involving all constituents within recipient countries and of recipient countries in regional and international decision-making fora, runs into such potential conflict areas as democracy within a country and North–South imbalances of power. Gender and class issues also arise both settings and can cause serious political differences with major impacts upon capacity-building efforts.

WHAT IS NOT THERE

Missing in this Chapter and throughout much of Agenda 21 are clear definitions of, and practical applications of such loaded terms as participation, technical cooperation, reorienting. The Chapter also heavily emphasizes the role of the UN agencies and international donors, to the detriment of any substantial discussion about the role of the institutions and groups which, might be more effectively targeted for successful national capacity-building efforts (e.g. scientific institutions, research centres, NGOs, women's, indigenous and grassroots groups). The discussion about the improvement and reorienting of international institutions is sketchy, leaving wide open to interpretation (by an undefined body) the areas of those institutions which might need refinement or change or how that is to be accomplished.

There is a lack of continuity between this Chapter and others in the document. Successful capacity-building for environmental sustainability cannot occur in a context divorced from social and economic restructuring. To take this document at face value is to assume that numerous committees and reports will make for successful capacity-building. What about the economic and social implications and complications of "capacity-building" as outlined here? What are the links between capacity-building efforts and the recommendations found in chapters such as "Combating Poverty" or "Changing Consumption Patterns" or "Demographics"?

OVERALL CRITIQUE

Substantive Content

This Chapter is a fair summary of the capacity-building implications of Agenda 21 and the global conventions. However, it does not give the reader a clear understanding of the mechanisms by which capacity-building will be enhanced in developing countries. A document this short cannot possibly give highly detailed specifics about the implementation of capacity-building, but there is a lack of pointers towards specifics. Activities and objectives are suggested only and no agreements were reached for action.

There is a disappointing lack of innovative ideas in the Chapter. Capacity-building is key to all sectors mentioned in Agenda 21. Nonetheless, the activities and objectives outlined in this Chapter are prosaic and traditional (note that a primary role is given to the UNDP, whose own capacity in these matters has been queried).

The "participatory process" is mentioned several times in the Chapter - as a means and a goal. It is a key ingredient to capacity-building and but it also remains undefined, and no guidelines for implementation are provided.

The emphasis throughout the Chapter on increased cooperation and coordination between and among all actors is commendable. The Chapter does not seem to suffer from false premises — just a lack of definition and concrete activities. This may be due to attempting to reach agreement on several sectors or areas of concern simultaneously.

Design of the Chapter as an Organizing Framework

The subject of this Chapter cross-cuts all sectors of Agenda 21 but seems to have been written in a vacuum divorced from the other Chapters. The Chapter would have had more relevancy if it had been designed first as an analysis of the activities included under capacity-building and based on the conclusions drawn from the other chapters, followed by a set of recommendations to support those activities.

RESEARCH REQUIREMENTS, CAPACITY-BUILDING, ETC.

This Chapter concerns itself solely with capacity-building and not with any one sector. Therefore the "research proposals" can be considered primarily as the objectives and activities outlined above. Gaps in these activities are also mentioned above. The implications for the activities of IDRC and like-minded donors have already received much attention at IDRC; please see the following section on "Niches for IDRC".

NICHES FOR IDRC

GENERAL

Capacity-building at IDRC once referred primarily to training for research, for scientists. Its common usage has now come to mean capacity-building for policy-making (as reflected in this chapter) and therefore for all actors or constituents (eg. NGOs, policy-makers at all levels of government). This requires a greater focus on participatory processes, and interdisciplinary and multisectoral research and action. These are the highlights of IDRC's activities in capacity-building. The possible niches for IDRC are therefore many and cross-cut most activities undertaken with respect to Agenda 21.

The most urgent challenge for IDRC is to assist developing countries in putting together their own needs for capacity-building in a way compatible with their own agendas and capacities to sustain initiatives and institutions. In these efforts, best use should be made of regional cooperation and international institutions, which should be supportive mechanisms rather than driving forces for developing countries' institutions.

Research opportunities for IDRC are open-ended, but include the exploration of the following questions (present activities in each area are italicized):

- What mechanisms can IDRC support which will assist countries in identifying their own capacity-building needs for improved policy-making for sustainable development?
- How can NGOs and the private sector work with government and academic communities to develop and implement an effective and efficient capacity-building strategy? How can projects be developed to strengthen the role of NGOs, indigenous and women's groups in civil society?
- Who are the primary target groups for training in integrating environment into economic and social policy, and into national accounting?
- What are the appropriate curricula for the different areas in which training is required? What are the appropriate institutional linkages and how should these be made?
- What participatory research needs to be done, and how, to develop a national participatory process for capacity-building?
- How can project evaluation design and methods accommodate measures of sustainability?
- How can information systems be enhanced to support national capacity-building plans?

IDRC has already restructured its programs and staffing requirements to reflect the demands of Agenda 21, therefore all the above fit a normal programming framework.

REGIONAL SPECIFICITY
Global.

KEY PARTNERS/OTHER ACTORS
Canada
CIDA, IISD, NGOs (e.g. CCIC, CEN, Federation of Canadian Municipalities, Assembly of First Nations), universities and AUCC, professional associations, UN agencies.

Other
UNDP, UNEP, World Bank and specialized agencies of the UN system; ICSU and other international scientific organizations and programs; private sector organizations and companies (particularly with respect to technology transfer and training); international NGOs and ENGOs and their national counterparts.

RECOMMENDATIONS
The best niches for IDRC are outlined above (as they have already been identified and acted upon). No new adjustments need to be made to IDRC's program organization, process and project cycle or structure and staffing; these have been made in the new Corporate Framework 1993–1995.

CHAPTER THIRTY-EIGHT

INTERNATIONAL INSTITUTIONAL ARRANGEMENTS

Responsible Officer: Jingjai Hanchanlash

ABSTRACT

1. OVERALL CRITIQUE OF AGENDA 21 CHAPTER

- It does not provide guidelines for organizations on how to design their programs to fit into Agenda 21, but this could be due to the Agenda 21 drafters wishing to allow a flexible approach to the interpretation and implementation of Agenda 21.
- It does not provide guidelines on the collaboration between regional and sub-regional organizations with the UN system.
- It emphasizes too much the coordination between the UN system and the multilateral financial institutions.
- It does not provide specific functions for the UN Commission on Sustainable Development, but again this is likely due to the drafters not wanting to be too prescriptive.

2. KEY CONCLUSIONS ARISING FROM CHAPTER

- The establishment of the UN Commission on Sustainable Development.
- Recommendations on specific programs for UNEP.
- Need for interaction and cooperation between the UN system and sub-region, regional and global institutions.

3. RESEARCH AND/OR IMPLEMENTATION POSSIBILITIES/OPPORTUNITIES

- Natural resource accounting.
- Environmental economics.
- Policy research on the implementation and impacts of scientific solutions to solve environmental problems.
- Dissemination of environmental information and data to governments.

4. ON-GOING AND/OR NEW PARTNERSHIPS FOR IDRC

- National research institutions.
    a) Non-Governmental Organizations;
    b) Regional and global research institutions;
    c) UN organizations (UNDP, UNEP); and
    d) Multilateral financial institutions (ADB).

5. SUGGESTED NICHES FOR IDRC

- Continue to work with traditional partners.
- Take the lead in the setting up of regional and sub-regional as well as in country research network.
- Play a catalytic role between national research institutions and the UN system.
- Establish closer collaboration with emerging regional groupings such as APEC, PECC.

6. OTHER COMMENTS
- The Centre should take a certain risk in attempting to defuse tension among countries in the region by promoting research cooperation in such areas of environment as are of common interest to them.

REVIEW 38

There is complementarity between this chapter and Chapter 39 on International Legal Instruments.

KEY CONCLUSIONS IN THE CHAPTER
- It recommends the establishment of the UN Commission on Sustainable Development to coordinate the implementation of the Agenda 21 at the policy level.
- It emphasizes the high level inter-agency coordination mechanism between the multilateral financial institutions and other UN bodies.
- It recommends specific programs for UNEP.
- It recommends the interaction and cooperation between the UN System and other sub-region, regional and global institutions, both governmental and non-governmental.
- It does not provide guidelines for an organization like IDRC (research funding) on how to design its program to fit into Agenda 21.
- It does not provide general guidelines for the collaboration between regional, sub-regional institutions and the UN System.

The recommendations for international institutional arrangements could have been better organised by incorporating them in other chapters and not as a separate Chapter.

RESEARCH REQUIREMENTS, CAPACITY BUILDING ETC.
There are several priority areas recommended to UNEP in which IDRC would be able to get involved. These are:
- Support the information system to disseminate environmental information and data to Governments.
- Support research works in the area of natural resource accounting, environmental economics, environmental impact assessment, environmental legislation including related training.
- Support policy research on the implementation of scientific solution to environmental problems.
- Support research network on sustainable development at regional and sub-regional level.

IDRC should interact with UNEP when supporting research works in the above areas. The interaction could be done through the network of UNEP regional offices.

The issue of training needs to be carefully looked into since it is the most important factor, contributing to the capacity-building. Strategy such as trainers training, has to be designed in such a way that it will optimise the benefit of the training program.

NICHE FOR IDRC
- It seems more appropriate for IDRC to continue to work with its traditional partners i.e. research institutions, and especially those at the national level rather than divert the limited resources to the

UN System. It is, however, important for the Centre to take into consideration the UNEP work plan when identifying specific program/project for funding.
- The recently revised program of the Centre can be directed more towards sustainable development research activities without any further major adjustment. What is required is for the Centre to take a more active initiative in helping its research institutions partners to design research program/project to be more in line with the sustainable development.
- One area which may need more resources to be reallocated for is training, especially in the new areas of natural resource accounting and environmental economics.
- The Centre is considered to have a comparative advantage for having the experience in the setting up of research network. Such experience is very useful for the promotion of regional and sub-regional cooperation.

RECOMMENDATIONS

- The Centre always enjoys a very good working relationship with national research institutions. It should take that relationship one step ahead by encouraging them to work together in a more systematic way.
- The creation of research network in the area of sustainable development is a good entry point for the Centre.
- The Centre should whenever possible consider designing the research network to fit with the existing regional cooperation arrangement. A concrete example would be for the Centre to support research network project in the areas related to sustainable development within the framework of APEC (Asia Pacific Economic Cooperation) or PECC (Pacific Economic Cooperation Council). This will make research work more visible at the international level and therefore facilitate the follow-up implementation. The Centre will also benefit from the projection its image as a major player at the international level.
- The Centre should also use its experience to take a certain risk in attempting to defuse tension among countries in the same region by promoting research cooperation in the environmental area which is of common concern. The success of such undertaking will not only be beneficially to countries concerned it will strengthen the Centre's international credibility as well.
- In pursuing the above strategy the Centre should draw on Canadian expertise through various geographical focus centres of different universities. It should also collaborate closely with Canadian organisations with regional mandate such as the Asia-Pacific Foundation and the Canada-Asean Centre.

COMMENTARY 38

Name of Commentator: Robert Valantin

1. GENERAL COMMENTS ON THE CHAPTER

- The Chapter focuses mainly on the UN system and then its interactions with external actors. It does not provide any critical analysis of the existing institutional framework, although it does mention "ongoing restructuring and revitalization of the United Nations".

- The linkage of the Sustainable Development Commission (SDC) to ECOSOC, which is seen by many as a weak body, has led some to be sceptical that the SDC will get the "teeth" needed to do its job properly. How the UN General Assembly handles this will decide the real role of the SDC and its credibility.

2. **OVERALL COMMENTARY ON THE FIRST REVIEW OF THE CHAPTER**
- Succinct, clear, and identifies reasonable entry points for IDRC.
- Agree with its main conclusions.
- Two areas the review could have tackled a bit more are: possible ways IDRC might stimulate the UN system to do its job better, and the potential role of IDRC to stimulate/coordinate initiatives among other actors (perhaps on specific issues).

3. **MAJOR POINTS AGREED/DISAGREED WITH, AND REASONS**
- Agree with an IDRC emphasis on research partners, especially national institutions in developing countries, plus modalities such as networking, information access, regional cooperation.
- Agree with the need for more IDRC research support on monitoring and policy aspects; these will be crucial for follow-up by national governments, the SDC and its "shadow" Earth Council, plus other international institutions and NGOs. This is an area where IDRC can make an important contribution.

4. **MINOR POINTS AGREED/DISAGREED WITH, AND REASONS**
- Agree on the need for more training, but question IDRC's niche in this area (given resource implications, other agency programs, problems with follow-through), which could cause extensive IDRC resources being diverted.

5. **POSSIBLE ON-GOING ISSUES OR CONCERNS FOR IDRC**
- The Chapter assumes that UN agencies will do their jobs well, but the past record shows many weaknesses (e.g. UNDP and ECOSOC). Despite valid program objectives/statements and even good programs, results have often been disappointing, yet these use significant portions of development funding. Can IDRC somehow make strategic interventions without getting mired in UN problems or spending lots of its own money? Some successful examples in information systems area may be instructive.

6. **POSSIBLE IMPLICATIONS FOR IDRC**
- Overall philosophy of the Chapter is positive, recognizing the need for better cooperation/consultation with UN system, among UN and international partners, with other actors (e.g. NGOs), etc. It recognizes that such interactions will require open access to processes and information. IDRC may be able to provide leadership (and leverage) here.

CHAPTER THIRTY-NINE

INTERNATIONAL LEGAL INSTRUMENTS AND MECHANISMS

Responsible Officer: Robert Auger

ABSTRACT

1. OVERALL CRITIQUE OF AGENDA 21 CHAPTER

- This is an important chapter which covers the birth of a new law, i.e. the international law of sustainable development.
- The fact that the document devotes a chapter to legal instruments and mechanisms underscores the significance of the law for the adoption of environmental policies, at the international as well as national levels.
- This Chapter, therefore, constitutes an excellent contribution to the advancement of the sustainable development concept, and also of international law.

2. KEY CONCLUSIONS ARISING FROM CHAPTER

- Two main conclusions can be drawn from the Chapter.
    a) Firstly, it proposes that the international law of sustainable development be established and developed.
    b) Then, it recommends that assistance be given to developing countries, so that they may participate actively in the establishment of international standards and their implementation at a national level.

3. RESEARCH AND/OR IMPLEMENTATION POSSIBILITIES/OPPORTUNITIES

- Several proposals have been made for assistance to LDCs, so that they may participate actively in negotiations regarding international treaties in the area of sustainable development, and implement the obligations which they have endorsed at the national level. In summary, this means assisting the LDCs in establishing their powers to advance the international law on sustainable development as well as its domestic impact.

4. ON-GOING AND/OR NEW PARTNERSHIPS FOR IDRC

- The Centre would wish to establish links with Canadian NGOs, working in the area of environmental law, and even with different bar associations. As regards the LDCs, the Centre could offer its support to governments and NGOs interested in environmental policies and legislation.

5. SUGGESTED NICHES FOR IDRC

- I would propose that IDRC concentrate its efforts on assisting LDCs at the national level, mainly by funding research which could help them bring their internal laws in line with the international development law and to comply with the obligations that they have endorsed by international treaty or agreement.

6. OTHER COMMENTS

- None.

REVIEW 39

KEY CONCLUSIONS IN THE CHAPTER

WHAT IS THERE

Main conclusions
There are two:
- The international law of sustainable development — which reconciles development and environmental concerns — should be developed.
- LDCs should be given financial and technical assistance so as to enable them to participate effectively in the elaboration of this new law and to implement 'sustainable development' obligations they have subscribed to by treaty.

Agreements Reached for International and National Action
There is a section in the chapter entitled 'Activities' which has five sub-headings -two of which stand out in importance:
- "Parties should review and assess both the past performance and effectiveness of international agreements or instruments as well as the priorities for future law-making on sustainable development."
- Financial and technical support should be provided to these LDCs in order to ensure their participation in all activities and others which may be pursued in the future, based on the (above) basis for Action and Objectives. LDCs should be given "head-start" support, not only in their national efforts to implement international agreements or instruments, but also to participate effectively in the negotiations of new or revised agreements or instruments and in actual international operation of such agreements or instruments. Support should include assistance in building up expertise in international law, particularly in relation to sustainable development, and in assuming access to the necessary reference information and scientific (technical) expertise.

Other actions agreed to have to do with narrower issues: large scale destruction of the environment in times of armed conflict; nuclear power, reporting systems on implementation of international legal instruments, and reduction of disputes in the field of sustainable development.

Politically Significant Issues
Given the level of generality at which the proposed activities are expressed, they would not give rise to political issues or difficulties.

WHAT IS NOT THERE?
No comments.

OVERALL CRITIQUE
Substantive Content
The Chapter gives recognition by the international community to a new law: **the international law of sustainable development**, founded on the realization that whatever the subject-matter of an international agreement, it must take into consideration, both environmental and developmental factors. This kind of thinking is already very much evident in the North (e.g. the environmental concerns expressed in connection with the NAFTA treaty). It is likely to gain currency all over the globe in years to come.

Devoting a chapter of Agenda 21 to the law is itself significant. It is a recognition of the fact that law - be it international or national - is the foremost expression of policy. Environmental policy that is not couched in legal terms is likely to be fleeting, ephemeral.

Design of the Chapter as an Organizing Framework
The organization of the text is not ideal: it is not obvious that the proposed activities have been agreed to by the international community, lesser issues are lumped together with the important ones, etc. This should not, however, detract from the central ideas: there is now established an international law of sustainable development; it must be developed, LDC's must participate effectively in this process and need financial and technical assistance to do so.

RESEARCH REQUIREMENTS, CAPACITY BUILDING, ETC.

EXPLICIT PROPOSALS IN THE CHAPTER
The Chapter states that LDCs require financial and technical assistance for the following:
- In order to enhance their **national** legislative capabilities in the field of sustainable development (39.1 d).
- In order to participate effectively in the negotiation, implementation, review and governance of **international** agreements or instruments (39.3 c).
- In order to ensure their effective participation in all activities (and others) listed in the Chapter. LDCs should be given "head-start" support not only in their national efforts to implement international agreements, but also, to participate effectively in the negotiation of new or revised agreements and in the actual operation of such agreements. Assistance should be provided in building up expertise in international law, particularly in relation to sustainable development, and in ensuring access to the necessary reference information and scientific/technical expertise (39.8).

IMPLICIT PROPOSALS DERIVED FROM THE CHAPTER
They seem to be all explicit.

GAPS AND ALTERNATIVE APPROACHES
No comments.

NICHES FOR IDRC

GENERAL
Opportunities that Fit Normal Programming
- Law is policy and, therefore, legal matters should, if they are not already, be integrated in our environmental policy research program.

New Opportunities
No comment.

Unusual or High-Risk Opportunities
No comment.

REGIONAL SPECIFICITY

No comment.

KEY PARTNERS/OTHER ACTORS

Canada
The Centre would want to work with environmental law NGOs. In English Canada, the one that has most visibility is the Toronto-based, Canadian Institute for Environmental Law and Policy.

It might also be worth determining the capabilities of the legal professional association across the country.

Other Countries
There are a number of NGOs which have been active in the past in conducting research on the implementation of national environmental laws. A few years back, the Office of the Secretary General Counsel (OSGC) funded such research with Consumers' Association of Penang (CAP) in Malaysia.

RECOMMENDATIONS

WHICH NICHES ARE BEST FOR IDRC PROGRAM?

I would suggest that we consider supporting environmental law research at the **national** level. Such research could be directed towards: (i) articulating legislation which would conform to internationally agreed upon norms; and (ii) assisting the countries concerned in implementing their treaty obligations.

Research efforts aimed at developing **regional** or **international** environmental norms would require more time to produce tangible results and our supporting them could overly tax Centre resources.

The **national level** niche is, of course, one that could be shared (and therefore lose its status as a "niche") with other donors, as I would imagine that there is considerable work to be done.

ARE ADJUSTMENTS NEEDED AT IDRC IN ORDER TO FILL THESE NICHES?

Program Organization
I am not familiar with the "environmental law" segment of the environmental policy program. I therefore suspect that it is not a big one. If this is the case, then, greater emphasis would have to be given to legal matters, if the niche were adopted.

Process and Project Cycle
Devote more attention to the legal expression of policy in research funded by the programme.

Structure/Staffing
Access to someone with an environmental law background (as staff or consultant) would seem necessary.

COMMENTARY 39

Name of Commentator: Paul McConnell

1. **GENERAL COMMENTS ON THE CHAPTER**
- The review provides a thoughtful analysis of Chapter 39, and highlights the significance of the emerging international law of sustainable development. It reflects Chapter 39's conspicuous focus on the needs and concerns of developing countries in this field.

2. **OVERALL COMMENTARY ON THE FIRST REVIEW OF THE CHAPTER**
- Good review. No problem.

3. **MAJOR POINTS AGREED/DISAGREED WITH, AND REASONS**
- None.

4. **MINOR POINTS AGREED/DISAGREED WITH, AND REASONS**
- Some additional specific proposals in section II A (Research Requirements) and/or III A (Niches for IDRC) could be:
    a) Analysis of effectiveness of existing international agreements/instruments and future needs (39.5);
    b) Analysis of constraints to compliance being experienced by LDCs (39.3.a);
    c) Analysis of the linkages to Trade Policy (as well as to Environmental Policy) (39.3.d).

5. **POSSIBLE ON-GOING ISSUES OR CONCERNS FOR IDRC**
- None.

6. **POSSIBLE IMPLICATIONS FOR IDRC**
- Significant involvement in this field would move IDRC into relatively new territory. Several divisions could be involved. As the resources required would be substantial, IDRC would first need to establish whether it had a comparative advantage in this field.

CHAPTER FORTY

INFORMATION FOR DECISION-MAKING

Responsible Officer: Paul McConnell

ABSTRACT

1. OVERALL CRITIQUE OF AGENDA 21 CHAPTER

- Inclusion of a special chapter dedicated to this cross-cutting topic significantly raises the profile of information needs and problems for sustainable development.
- It provides an effective introduction to the role for information and information technologies to improve planning, decision-making, and monitoring.
- The Chapter 40 addresses only the generic information issues. Specific sectoral information proposals are identified in other chapters throughout Agenda 21 and must also be taken into account.

2. KEY CONCLUSIONS ARISING FROM CHAPTER

- There is a need for better information at all levels of decision-making for sustainable development, whether national/international or grassroots/individual and NGOs.
- Action is required in two Program Areas: (a) "Bridging the data gap" (i.e., improving the collection, quality, standardization, and accessibility of data); and (b) "Improving information availability" (i.e., building-capacity to manage, share, promote and use information for decision-making).

3. RESEARCH AND/OR IMPLEMENTATION POSSIBILITIES/OPPORTUNITIES

- Eleven program activities are identified in Chapter 40, all of which fall within the applied research and capacity-building mandate of IDRC. These encompass development of indicators of sustainable development; promoting expanded use of indicators; improving data collection and use; improving methods of data assessment and analysis; establishing comprehensive information infrastructure and policy; strengthening the use of traditional indigenous knowledge; producing information services better suited to decision-making; harmonizing standards and methods to promote exchange of information; improving mechanisms for documenting sources of information, including projects of donors, NGOs, and other actors; strengthening electronic networks; and improving access to commercial information services.
- The proposed activities closely match the newly-defined program interests of IDRC/ISSD in terms of improving access to information, more collaborative efforts, capacity-building, and applied research on information technologies and systems.

4. ON-GOING AND/OR NEW PARTNERSHIPS FOR IDRC

- Opportunities exist for collaboration on these research and capacity-building activities with all categories of partners for IDRC. These include the traditional ones, e.g., academic, public, private, and donor institutions, but also the new post-UNCED organizations such as the Earth Council, NGONET, the UNDP's Sustainable Development Network, and the Commission for Sustainable Development.

5. SUGGESTED NICHES FOR IDRC

- IDRC can play an active role in all of the 11 generic program activities listed above; these can be related directly to divisional and centrewide objectives.
- Special emphasis will need to be placed on information networking, LDC applications of new information technologies, strengthening the use of traditional indigenous knowledge, and research and development on new information systems, services, and technologies.
- IDRC's substantial experience in the information field will enable it to play a catalytic role as other actors start giving attention to the information issues raised in Chapter 40, and to be a coordinator of initiatives and organizations.

6. OTHER COMMENTS

- This Chapter deals only with generic information problems. It does not assign relative priorities nor make cross-reference to specific information proposals contained elsewhere in Agenda 21. Consequently, implementation of the recommendations of this Chapter must be interpreted within the larger framework. A systematic analysis of the information component of each chapter is now being undertaken by IDRC/ISSD to ensure a convergence of sectoral priorities and information priorities.

REVIEW 40

Robert Valantin

KEY CONCLUSIONS IN THE CHAPTER

WHAT IS THERE

Main Conclusions

There is a need for better information at all levels of decision-making for sustainable development, whether national/international or grassroots/individual (40.1)

Action is required on two related fronts or "Program Areas":
- Bridging the data gap, i.e. the gap (primarily North–South) in the availability, quality, coherence, standardization, accessibility, transformation and coordination of data that would improve decisions (40.2, 40.3).
- Improving information availability, i.e., even where data and information do exist, the management of this information resource is so weak that it is difficult to obtain appropriate information at the right time (40.17), because of shortages of financial resources and trained manpower, lack of awareness of the value and availability of such information, lack of modern information technology, and insufficient funds to gain access to commercial sources of information (40.18).

Agreements Reached for International and National Action

(In this section, "Agreements Reached" is interpreted as the agreed-upon list of actions **required** to meet the program objectives declared for Chapter 40, rather than specific programs proposed or in place by agencies.)

- For "Program Area a." (40.6 et seq.):
  - Development of indicators of sustainable development.
  - Promotion of global use of indicators of sustainable development.
  - Improvement of data collection and use.
  - Improvement of methods of data assessment and analysis (use of modern information technologies, e.g. GIS, remote sensing, etc.)
  - Establishment of comprehensive information framework (information infrastructure and information policy).
  - Strengthening of the capacity for traditional information (indigenous knowledge).
- For "Program Area b." (40.22 et seq.):
  - Production of information usable for decision-making.
  - Establishment of standards and methods for handling of information.
  - Development of documentation about information.
  - Establishment and strengthening of electronic networking capacities.
  - Making use of commercial information sources.

WHAT IS NOT THERE

Critical evaluation of existing systems and institutions dealing with information for sustainable development.

Setting of priorities among objectives and activities, as well as among different groups of users.

Elaboration of the "sustainable development indicators" concept.

Discussion of the problems of sustainability of information systems.

How to monitor progress towards objectives of Chapter 40.

How to identify gaps and problems (e.g., how to seek out shortcomings in information systems, flows, etc.), as well as how to identify opportunities.

Concrete mechanisms to implement ideas and corresponding funding estimates and commitments — an Action Plan.

A discussion of the relationship between sustainable development information more generally and environmental information more specifically.

Cross-references to major information-related program areas described in other chapters of Agenda 21, e.g.,

Chapter 9.	Protection of the atmosphere
	A. Addressing the uncertainties: Improving the scientific basis for decision-making.
Chapter 12.	Managing fragile ecosystems: Combating desertification and drought
	A. Strengthening the knowledge base and developing information and monitoring systems for regions prone to desertification and drought, including the economic and social aspects of these ecosystems.
Chapter 14.	Promoting sustainable agriculture and rural development
	D. Land-resource planning, information and education for agriculture.
Chapter 18.	Protection of the quality and supply of freshwater resources
	B. Water resources assessment

Chapter 19.   Environmentally sound management of toxic chemicals
               C. Information exchange on toxic chemicals and chemical risks.
Chapter 31.   Scientific and technological community
               A. Improving communication and cooperation among the scientific and technological community, and decision-makers and the public.

OVERALL CRITIQUE

Substantive Content

Close match to newly-defined program interests of ISSD in terms of improving access to information, more collaborative efforts, capacity building, and applied research on information technologies and systems.

Recognition of the role of information in sustainable development through planning, decision-making, and monitoring.

Recognition of the importance of information technologies for data collection, analysis, access, and networking.

Useful overview for raising the profile of information issues in sustainable development.

Acknowledges some politically-sensitive issues:
- National sovereignty (who owns the data concerning a country?).
- Sensitivity re indicators of performance on Agenda 21 issues (e.g. environmental management).
- Intellectual property rights (regarding resource information, technologies, etc.).

But

Absence of specific problems, needs, and priorities with different aspects of environmental information. Role of institutions is not clear (e.g., UNEP and GEMS/GRID), nor the rationale for identifying them.

Heavy emphasis on UN target institutions and processes.

Does not address major problem of sustainability of information systems.

Design of the Chapter as an Organizing Framework

It was important for UNCED to devote a separate chapter to this subject. Information issues permeate most chapters and thereby constitute a significant dimension of Agenda 21. But specific sectoral information needs should not be looked at in isolation; otherwise, the important cross-cutting or generic aspects would be missed. And these represent targets for action aimed at bringing about long-term results. Chapter 40, therefore, is ground-breaking in international proceedings in giving full recognition to the importance of concerted action on information problems.

Content is basically OK, but variety and overlap of the objectives and activities of the two Program Areas leaves the impression that dividing the program under these two headings is a bit arbitrary.

No cross-reference from general information problems to specific needs in the various sectors described in preceding chapters of Agenda 21.

RESEARCH REQUIREMENTS, CAPACITY BUILDING ETC.

EXPLICIT PROPOSALS IN THE CHAPTER

This chapter is extremely relevant to the kinds of things that IDRC supports through its dual approach of applied research and capacity-building.

Certain paragraphs call for action to support developing countries in these two fields, i.e., training of decision-makers as information users (40.15), capacity-building at the national level in information management (40.16, 40.29), and research in hardware, software, and other aspects of information technology (40.30).

In addition, more or less specific proposals are contained within each of the topics listed above (IDRC's potential role is also indicated below):
- Strengthening existing UN agencies, etc. — IDRC role would be mainly advisory.
- Development of indicators, statistics, standards, methods — IDRC technical participation.
- Support for national, regional, international information systems and networks — IDRC could provide selective support for "models"/prototypes/novel systems.
- Research on new technologies, methods, tools for data collection and analysis/assessment plus access to data/information/knowledge — program support.
- Use of traditional/indigenous knowledge and also its integration with new technologies — program support.
- Commercialization of information — project follow-up and program support.

IMPLICIT PROPOSALS DERIVED FROM THE CHAPTER

The generic-type information proposals listed above find expression in specific applications within the subject sectors covered by other chapters. Indeed, there are numerous information activities proposed throughout Agenda 21 which can be directly related to the program areas and objectives presented in Chapter 40. ISSD staff undertook a preliminary review of other chapters. Annex I to this document lists over 50 such activities identified within them. Annex II illustrates how one category of information-related research, that dealing with new information technologies, has potential application in most areas of Agenda 21.

GAPS AND ALTERNATIVE APPROACHES

Several apparent gaps can be identified in Chapter 40, e.g., no reference to national information policies, no attention to sustainability problems of information systems, very limited proposals on human resource development and capacity-building, etc. But the question is difficult to answer without having in-depth knowledge of other chapters. It may well be that gaps such as those referred to above may have been addressed in other chapters dealing with cross-cutting topics.

NICHES FOR IDRC

GENERAL

Opportunities that Fit Normal Programming
All of above, but with special emphasis on:
- Information networking.
- Research and development (R&D) on new Information Technologies (ITs); see also Annex II.
- Applications of new ITs; see also Annex II.
- Strengthening the use of indigenous knowledge.

New Opportunities
- Commercialization of information.
- Research on the application of the "indicators" concept.

Unusual or High-Risk Opportunities
None. (Note that some research on new ITs might be considered high-risk, but could be considered within normal programming parameters).

REGIONAL SPECIFICITY
Not applicable to "generic" information problems.

KEY PARTNERS/OTHER ACTORS
Canada
Government, academic and private organizations active in selected fields identified in Chapter 40, such as Remote Sensing and GIS, for collaborative research and training.

Also, for more general capacity-building in partnership with LDC institutions, organizations such as CIDA, IISD, and Environment Canada could figure prominently.

A review should be undertaken of Agenda 21 priorities within Canada (including those being advocated by Canada in the Rio negotiations) and an assessment made of potential partners in these sectors.

Other Countries
UNCED-related institutional mechanisms — SDC, SDN, Earth Council, NGONET

Other donors with a declared interest in Agenda 21, such as Rockefeller, SAREC.

RECOMMENDATIONS

WHICH NICHES ARE BEST FOR IDRC PROGRAM?
IDRC can play an active and productive role in all of the 11 generic program activities listed above. All can be directly related to Divisional and Centre objectives.

Relative priority depends less on the particular program category and more on the merits of the specific proposal (e.g., applied research rather than technical assistance; strengthening an LDC information system rather than a UN one; selecting IT research linked to a utilization plan rather than an exploratory approach).

The criteria on which to base such recommendations do exist. They appear in Strategy 91 and in the ISSD divisional strategy. In summary, these criteria address relevance to identified information needs, extent of collaboration, capacity-building and sustainability, impact of information and information tools, comparative advantage of IDRC, focus on selected priority issues, practical results-oriented approach, innovative research opportunities, stronger linkages to Canadian expertise, and overall clarity of program objectives.

The bigger task lies beyond the scope of this particular questionnaire. This will entail a more formal analysis of generic Chapter 40 program activities in concert with the specific information proposals identified elsewhere in Agenda 21. This will require careful application of the above criteria, together with sectoral priorities to be debated at the centrewide level.

ARE ADJUSTMENTS NEEDED AT IDRC IN ORDER TO FILL THESE NICHES?

Program Organization
No.

Process and Project Cycle
No.

Structure/Staffing
No.

ARE THERE CROSS-CUTTING ISSUES THAT ARE NOT ADEQUATELY REFLECTED IN ANY OF THE ABOVE?

It should be emphasized that Chapter 40 addresses "generic" problems of information access, management, and use. These apply no matter what the specific sector might be — agroforestry, biodiversity, tropical diseases, etc. This point is made in section II.8. above, and in Annex I. Consequently, action to implement recommendation of Chapter 40 should be interpreted within the context of all the preceeding sectoral chapters of Agenda 21. In IDRC's analysis, there should be a convergence of sectoral priorities and information priorities. In parallel with this review of Chapter 40, ISSD will examine the major information problems and proposals raised elsewhere in Agenda 21. This concern over cross-cutting issues was mentioned in section II.C. above.

ANNEX I: INFORMATION ISSUES THROUGHOUT AGENDA 21

Chapter 40 reaffirms that, for sustainable development, decisions at any level must be based on sound information. It draws attention to the fact that there is a serious gap in the availability, quality, and accessibility of data between developed and developing countries. It points out that there is a general lack of capacity in many areas for the collection and assessment of data, for their transformation into useful information, and for their dissemination. It also emphasizes the needs for increased collection of relevant data, for improved coordination among information activities, for improved methods for data assessment and analysis, for application of traditional and indigenous knowledge, and for development of indicators of sustainable development.

The Chapter further points out the problems of inadequate management of information, lack of awareness of value and availability of information, shortage of financial resources and trained personnel, and lack of technology for effective access. It emphasizes the needs for transforming existing information into forms more useful for decision-making, for developing mechanisms for efficient and harmonized exchange of information, for documenting and sharing the sources of available information, and for developing and facilitating electronic networking capabilities.

This call for increased and better coordinated data and information activities echoes throughout the document, with each program area emphasizing specific aspects. The following are some of the typical or notable statements culled from Chapters 1 to 39 of Agenda 21, listed by the breakdown used in Chapter 40.

BRIDGING THE DATA GAP

1. **Development of indicators**
- To develop criteria and methodologies for the assessment of environmental impacts and resource requirements throughout the full life cycle of products and processes and to transform results of those assessments into clear indicators to inform consumers and decision-makers. (4.20)

- To produce better national and municipal statistics based on practical, standardized indicators for improved urban development and management. (6.36)
- To develop systems for monitoring and evaluation of progress towards achieving sustainable development by adopting indicators that measure changes across economic, social, and environmental dimensions. (8.6)

2. **Promotion of global use of indicators**
- To support the utilization of sustainable development indicators in national economic and social planning and decision-making practices to ensure that IEEAs (integrated environmental and economic accounting) are well integrated in economic planning at the national level. (8.44a)

3. **Improvement of data collection and use**
- To collect information on target groups and target areas to facilitate the design of focused programs and activities (3.9)
- To collect, consolidate, and exchange existing information and to establish baseline information on aspects relevant to the program area. (11.33a)
- To collect, analyze, and integrate data on the linkages between the state of ecosystems and the health of human communities to improve knowledge of the cost and benefit of different development policies and strategies in relation to health and the environment. (35.7e)
- To increase the use of appropriate systems and technologies, such as supercomputers, space-based observational technology, Earth- and ocean-based observational technologies, data management, and database technologies, and to expand the Global Climate Observing System. (35.14b)

4. **Improvement of methods of data assessment and analysis**
- To expand or promote databases on production and consumption and develop methodologies for analyzing them. (4.10a)
- To develop methodologies and instruments to identify areas where sustainability is threatened by the environmental effects of demographic trends and factors. (5.26)
- To give developing countries access to modern techniques of land-resource management, such as geographical information systems, satellite photography/imagery, and other remote-sensing technologies. (7.33)
- To continue legal data collection, translation, and assessment and to improve standardization and compatibility of data. (8.24)
- To improve systems for the interpretation and integrated analysis of data on land use and land resources. (10.8a)
- To develop integrated information systems for environmental monitoring, accounting, and impact assessment (12.12b)
- To develop internationally acceptable methodologies for the establishment of databases, description of land uses, and multiple goal optimization. (14.39b)
- To develop databases and geographical information systems to store and display physical, social, and economic information pertaining to agriculture, and the definition of ecological zones, and development areas. (14.41a)

5. **Establishment of a comprehensive information framework**
- To strengthen national databases on demographic trends and factors and environment. (5.25)
- To establish and/or strengthen national environmental information coordination centres and to ensure that national environmental information systems are linked together through a network. (12.6a)
- To establish globally harmonized hazard classification and information systems. (19.29a)

- To develop and link existing national, subregional, regional, and international information systems through regional clearing-houses covering broad-based sectors of the economy such as agriculture, industry and energy. (34.15)
- To encourage coordination of satellite missions, the networks, systems, and procedures for processing and disseminating their data, and to develop the interface with the research users of Earth observation data and with the United Nations EARTHWATCH system. (35.12d)
- To develop Earth observation systems from space which will provide integrated, continuous, and long-term measurements of the interactions of the atmosphere, hydrosphere, and lithosphere. (35.12h)
- To develop and expand regional and global scientific and technological information networks which are based on and linked to national scientific and technological databases. (35.22d)

6. Strengthening of the capacity for traditional information
- To establish grass-roots mechanisms for the sharing of experience and knowledge between communities. (3.7c)
- To ensure that women and men have the same right to have access to the information. (3.8j)
- (International institutions and networks) to enhance their scientific capacity, taking full account of community experience and knowledge and to disseminate the experience gained in multidisciplinary approaches. (5.8)
- To integrate traditional knowledge and experience into national health systems. (6.5aix, 6.27dii)
- To conduct research into traditional knowledge of prevention and curative health practices. (6.5biii)
- To promote the organization of national, intercountry, and interregional symposia, etc., to exchange information among agencies and groups concerned with the health of children, youth, women, and indigenous people. (6.31)
- To promote greater public awareness of the role of people's participation and people's organizations, especially women's groups, youth, indigenous people, and local communities in sustainable agriculture and rural development. (14.17a)
- To promote the wider application of the knowledge, innovations, and practices of indigenous and local communities embodying traditional lifestyles for the conservation of biological diversity and the sustainable use of biological resources. (15.5e)
- To develop gender sensitive databases, information systems, and participatory action-oriented research and policy analyses. (24.8)
- To develop educational and awareness programs specifically targeted to the youth population. (25.9f)
- To document, synthesize, and disseminate local knowledge, practices and project experiences to make use of past lessons for formulating policies affecting farming, forest, and fishing populations. (32.9a)
- To develop methods to link the findings of the established sciences with the indigenous knowledge of different cultures, using pilot studies. (35.7h)
- To compile, analyze, and publish information on indigenous environmental and developmental knowledge and to assist the communities that possess such knowledge to benefit from them. (35.22g)

IMPROVING AVAILABILITY OF INFORMATION

1. Production of information usable for decision-making
- To develop decision-making models and promote their use to assess the costs and the health and environment impact of alternative technologies and strategies. (6.36)

- To improve the decision-making process by ensuring public access to relevant information and facilitating the reception of public views and allowing for effective participation. (8.4f)
- To strengthen the flow of early-warning information to decision-makers and land users to enable nations to implement strategies for drought intervention. (12.47b)
- To improve communication between the scientific and technological community and decision makers to facilitate greater use of scientific and technical information and knowledge in policies and program implementation. (31.1)

2. Establishment of standards and methods for handling information
- To encourage the emergence of an informed consumer public and assist individuals to make environmentally informed choices. (4.22)
- To develop socio-demographic information in a suitable format for interfacing with physical, biological and socio-economic data. (5.10)
- To disseminate results of research concerned with sustainable development issues through technical reports, scientific journals, the media, workshops, forums, etc. (5.13)
- To increase collaboration and exchange of information between research institutions and international, regional and national agencies, and all other sectors. (5.14)
- To facilitate the transfer and sharing of information and expertise, including communication methods and educational materials. (6.7)
- To promote studies to determine how to disseminate optimally the results from research. (6.13gii)
- To implement public awareness campaigns through all available media, translating the knowledge into information easily comprehensible to the general public. (7.60b)
- To develop guidelines and mechanisms to adapt and diffuse information technologies to developing countries. (8.53)
- To document and exchange information and experience for the benefit of countries with similar problems and prospects. (11.16c)
- To strengthen existing regional and global networks for the exchange of relevant information. (11.34c)
- To improve the exchange of knowledge and concerns between the scientific and technological community and the general public to enable policies and programs to be better formulated, understood, and supported. (31.3b)
- To improve the dissemination of research results by supporting scientists, technologists, and teachers engaged in communicating and interpreting scientific and technological information to policy makers, professionals in other fields, and the general public. (31.4e)
- To develop and implement information technologies to enhance the dissemination of information for sustainable development. (31.4h)

3. Development of documentation about information
- To undertake an inventory of existing and international or regional clearing-houses or information exchange systems. (34.17)

4. Establishment and strengthening of electronic networking capabilities
- To employ modern communication technologies for effective public outreach. (36.10f)

CAPACITY BUILDING AND HUMAN RESOURCES DEVELOPMENT
- To develop intensive, short, practical training programs with emphasis on skills in effective communication, community organization, and facilitation of behaviour change. (6.8)
- To utilize the full range of training methods, from formal education to the use of the mass media. (7.23)

- To go beyond the training individuals and functional groups to include institutional arrangements, administrative routines, inter-agency linkages, information flows, and consultative processes. (7.25)
- To improve the scientific capacities by periodic academic update of scientists from developing countries in their respective fields of knowledge. (35.21f)

The above are only samples. The results of AGIS Database searches have revealed the prevalence of the information component throughout the programs. The figures below indicate the number of records with the number of postings in brackets.

Information 426 (852); Communication(s) 34 (39); Knowledge 142 (176); Data 256 (425); Database(s) 52 (64); Awareness 121 (181); Inventors 32 (52); GIS or Satellite or Geographic(al) Information or Remote Sensing 21; Indigenous or Traditional Knowledge 44.

ANNEX II: AREAS OF POTENTIAL APPLICATION OF INFORMATION TECHNOLOGIES

This Annex is intended to illustrate the potential for the application of new information technologies throughout Agenda 21.

The table on the following page shows how many paragraphs in each of the 40 chapters of Agenda 21 were selected as indicating a potential area for the application of a specific information technology. The technologies concerned are among those mentioned in ISSD's Information and Communication Technologies (ICT) program statements. However, because the Agenda 21 examples and recommendations are usually not detailed, it was not possible to pin the technologies down very specifically, and thus they were interpreted as covering broader areas than in the ICT program statements. Some of the technologies were mentioned explicitly in the Agenda 21 text, but in the vast majority of cases it was a judgement call as to their potential suitability or usefulness. If an application was mentioned in two paragraphs (e.g. under both "Objectives" and "Activities"), it was counted only once. The extent to which the application would be "routine" or would require research and development (R&D) could not be assessed.

Thus the numbers shown are rather subjective, but they do highlight potential areas for multidisciplinary work involving information technologies.

Legend for the technologies
RS = Remote Sensing
IA = Image Analysis
DB = Database Management Systems
GI = Geographic Information Systems
OL = Online Access to Databases
EN = Electronic Networking
ES = Expert Systems
KR = Other Knowledge Representation
NL = Natural Language Processing
CT = Computer-based Training
MO = Modelling Tools
R+ = REDATAM Plus

	All Techs.	Technology [see legend]											
		RS	IA	DB	GI	OL	EN	ES	KR	NL	CT	MO	R+
Chapters 1-40	414	12	5	68	33	32	63	51	41	5	53	47	4
Social and Economic Dimensions													
01 Preamble	0												
02 Intl. Cooperation	2			1			1						
03 Combat. Poverty	5			1		1	1		1		1		
04 Change Consumption	3			1								2	
05 Demographic Dyn.	10			1			2	1		2	3		1
06 Health	16			1	1	1	1	5			5	2	
07 Settlement	21	1	1	3	3	1	3	3			5	1	
08 Env./Dev. in Dec.	23			7			3	4	1		1	6	1
Conservation and Management of Resources													
09 Atmospheric Prot.	6			3		1	1				1		
10 Land Resources	4				3			1					
11 Deforestation	13	1		1	3	1		4			1	1	1
12 Combat. Drought	15	1		4	2			1	4			3	
13 Mountain Devel.	7			1			2	2	1		1		
14 Sustain. Agric.	31	1		8	6		2	1	4		5	3	1
15 Biol. Diversity	6			1	1		1	2	1				
16 Biotechnology	9			2		2	1		2		2		
17 Ocean Protect.	45	3		10	6	5	6	2	8		2	3	
18 Fresh Water	31	1		6	4	3	3	3			3	8	
19 Toxic Chemicals	30			1		2	8	10		2	3	4	
20 Hazardous Waste	25			2	3	3	5	5			5	2	
21 Solid Waste	5						2	2				1	
22 Radioactive Waste	0												
Strengthening the Role of Major Groups													
24 Women	6			2					2		2		
25 Children	2						1				1		
26 Indigenous Peoples	2								2				
27 NGOs	2				1	1							
28 Local Authorities	2						2						
29 Workers & Unions	1										1		
30 Busin. & Industry	3			1			1				1		
31 Science & Tech.	5				1	1		2			1		
Means of Implementation													
32 Farmers	0												
33 Financial Means	0												
34 Envir. Sound Tech.	5			1		2	2						
35 Scientific Means	35	3	3	8		5	5	1	3	1		6	
36 Education	17						5		5		7		
37 Capacity Bldg.	1						1						
38 Institutional Arr.	0												
39 Legal Instruments	0												
40 Information	26	1	1	2	1	3	4	5	2		2	5	

Commentary 40

Name of Commentator: Erin O'Manique

1. GENERAL COMMENTS ON THE CHAPTER

- Good overview of the need for better information access and management at all levels for input into decision-making processes.
- Tends to underemphasize accessibility to private information sources and issues related to patents and intellectual property rights, which in some sectors can greatly hinder access to relevant information.

2. OVERALL COMMENTARY ON THE FIRST REVIEW OF THE CHAPTER

- Agree.

3. MAJOR POINTS AGREED/DISAGREED WITH, AND REASONS

- None.

4. MINOR POINTS AGREED/DISAGREED WITH, AND REASONS

- None.

5. POSSIBLE ON-GOING ISSUES OR CONCERNS FOR IDRC

- Information needs on a sectoral basis must be examined within the context of IDRC's priorities.
- As above, some of the barriers to access information are systemic (legal/institutional as opposed to financial) and therefore more difficult to address.
- Ensuring inclusion of indigenous knowledge in data gathering/information processing, and developing systems that are sensitive to the way in which indigenous knowledge is traditionally gathered and stored, without distorting it.

6. POSSIBLE IMPLICATIONS FOR IDRC

- As pointed out by the reviewer, the Information Sciences and Systems Division is heavily involved in this topic; indeed the existence of this division since the beginning of IDRC indicates the importance that the Centre has always placed on capacity-building for developing and managing information technologies and resources. This Chapter serves to support and strengthen what has traditionally been viewed as an IDRC priority.

CONVENTIONS AND OTHER DOCUMENTS

CONVENTION ON BIOLOGICAL DIVERSITY

Responsible Officer: Sam Landon

ABSTRACT

1. OVERALL CRITIQUE OF AGENDA 21 CHAPTER

- Excellent start for action on biodiversity conservation but depends on a lot of follow-up actions for any real impact.
- Recognizes the **intrinsic** ecological, genetic, social, economic, educational, cultural, recreational and aesthetic values of biological diversity and its components.
- Places the main emphasis on national actions, based upon thorough analysis of need and opportunity.
- Calls for the **integration** of biodiversity concerns within relevant sectoral planning. Attention is given to those areas that fall outside national jurisdictions.
- Section on *in situ* conservation deals mainly with protected areas **leaving out** subsistence crops, minor crops, different varieties etc. that cannot be dealt with through *ex situ* conservation which deals typically with the economically important crops. Thus, these crops that are left out are in danger and their loss could lead to medium and long term food insecurity.
- "Environmentally sound and sustainable development in areas adjacent to protected areas" requires increased understanding of socio-economic dynamics, of technical resource management, and of policy measures which will support and encourage effective buffer-zone management.

2. KEY CONCLUSIONS ARISING FROM CHAPTER

- Affirms that states have rights and responsibilities for their biodiversity; recognizes that human actions are a main cause of biodiversity losses (but downplays impact of population growth); notes the general lack of knowledge and the need to develop capacity regarding biodiversity; and, importantly, adds that lack of scientific certainty should not be used as a reason for postponing action — the Precautionary Approach.
- Recognizes that the fundamental requirement for the conservation of biological diversity is in situ conservation of ecosystems and natural habitats and the maintenance of viable populations of species in their natural surroundings.
- Acknowledges that new and additional financial resources and appropriate access to relevant technologies can make a difference and that special provisions are needed to assist developing countries.
- Recognizes that **economic and social development and poverty eradication are the first and overriding priorities** of developing countries.
- Article 6: General Measures for Conservation and Sustainable Use. The signatory nations contract to develop national strategies, plans or programs for the conservation and sustainable use of biological diversity and to integrate these with relevant sectoral or cross-sectoral plans, programs and policies.

3. RESEARCH AND/OR IMPLEMENTATION POSSIBILITIES/OPPORTUNITIES

- Since huge gaps exist in baseline knowledge about biodiversity, a strong program of ecological research is required.
- Article 12 covers, in a general way, research and training obligations and calls for scientific and technical education and training measures, as well as research into, identification, conservation and sustainable use of biodiversity and to provide support in these areas to developing countries.
- Calls for rehabilitation and restoration of degraded ecosystems requiring technical and policy-relevant research.
- Need for more knowledge around how to rehabilitate damaged ecosystems.
- Important task of documenting traditional knowledge that has application in designing strategies for the conservation and use of biodiversity is required.
- Calls for measures to facilitate the exchange of genetic resources and technology.
- Exchange of information and networking is necessary.
- Research on the impacts of population growth on ecosystems.

4. ON-GOING AND/OR NEW PARTNERSHIPS FOR IDRC

- Convention calls for the creation of a subsidiary body on Technical and Technological Advice. IDRC should seek either participatory or observer status on this body.
- On-going partnership of IDRC with International Service for the Acquisition of Agri-Biotech Applications (ISAAA) is tackling the issue of access by developing countries to proprietary biotechnologies through brokered technology transfer agreements.

5. SUGGESTED NICHES FOR IDRC

- Biodiversity fits squarely within the research envelope set out in the Convention. The Biodiversity issue should be treated as a top priority for IDRC. ENRD is intended expressly as an **integrated multidisciplinary** division and is well suited to the kind of research support required by and for the Biodiversity Convention.
- Fits with work proposed for INBAR project and proposed area of work in Resource Valuation, etc.
- Possibility for IDRC to take on the task of working with one or more individual countries to develop a model process for the implementation of the Biodiversity Convention (see full review by Brian Belcher).

6. OTHER COMMENTS

- Biodiversity Convention should be a top priority for IDRC. Training on the meaning, context and importance should be given to IDRC staff throughout the divisions.
- Biodiversity conservation is the best proxy in the absence of a holistic approach to environment and development.

REVIEW

Brian Belcher

KEY CONCLUSIONS IN THE CHAPTER

WHAT IS THERE

Main Conclusions

This Convention, even with all its qualifiers, modifiers and weasel words, makes an excellent start for action on biodiversity conservation.

The Preamble
- The Preamble is intended as a non-binding set of ideas which indicate the intention of the Convention and which provide a context for the interpretation of the Convention. This Preamble seems to be very progressive. It begins by recognizing the intrinsic, ecological, genetic, social, economic, educational, cultural, recreational and aesthetic values of biological diversity and its components.
- A lengthy section, the Preamble continues to affirm that States have rights and responsibilities for their biodiversity; recognizes that human actions are a main cause of biodiversity losses; notes the general lack of knowledge and the need to develop capacity regarding biodiversity; and, importantly, adds that lack of full scientific certainty should not be used as a reason for postponing action (the **precautionary principle**).
- There is recognition that the fundamental requirement for the conservation of biological diversity is in situ conservation of ecosystems and natural habitats and the maintenance of viable populations of species in their natural surroundings.
- There is an acknowledgement that the provision of new and additional financial resources and appropriate access to relevant technologies can be expected to make a substantial difference in the world's ability to address the loss of biological diversity and that special provisions are needed to assist developing countries.
- There is a recognition that economic and social development and poverty eradication are the first and overriding priorities of developing countries.

The Objectives
- The objectives will be referred to in later articles which require specific obligations. The wording is therefore very important. It reads:
"The objectives of this Convention, to be pursued in accordance with its relevant provisions, are the conservation of biological diversity, the sustainable use of its components and the fair and equitable sharing of the benefits arising out of the utilization of genetic resources, including by appropriate access to genetic resources and by appropriate transfer of relevant technologies, taking into account all rights over those resources and to technologies, and by appropriate funding."
- Article 3 represents an important step in international law. It states:
"States have, in accordance with the Charter of the United Nations and the principles of international law, the sovereign right to exploit their own resources pursuant to their own environmental policies, and the responsibility to ensure that activities within their jurisdiction or control do not cause damage to the environment of other States or of areas beyond the limits of national jurisdiction."
This principle has been an unsure part of customary international law. With its inclusion in the body of an international convention it gains considerable strength.

- The Convention calls for cooperation among nations, "as far as possible and appropriate", for the conservation and sustainable use of biodiversity. The two concepts, conservation and sustainable use, are linked deliberately and consistently, throughout the Convention.
- A very important idea is contained in article 6: General Measures for Conservation and Sustainable Use. The signatory nations contract to develop national strategies, plans or programs for the conservation and sustainable use of biological diversity (or adapt existing plans), and to integrate these with relevant sectoral or cross-sectoral plans, programs and policies. This sets the tone for the whole Convention, which serves essentially as a framework for national actions within their own jurisdictions. Cooperation is called for in the sharing of information, provision of access to technology and genetic resources, and provision of financial and other assistance to developing countries.
- Articles 7 to 19 inclusive deal with particular elements of biodiversity conservation and sustainable use programs; Article 20 with financial resources; and, the remainder (Articles 21 to 42 and annexes) with administrative and legal details.

Agreements Reached for International and National Action
The Convention is an agreement for International and National actions.

Politically Significant Issues
- This Convention, and the negotiations leading up to it, were very highly charged politically. Developing countries, and especially those countries possessing high levels of biodiversity, went into the negotiations determined to capitalize on what they feel (rightly or wrongly) is and will increasingly be an extremely valuable resource. In exchange for access to their biodiversity they wanted to extract guarantees of increased aid money and access to evolving technologies. The developed countries wanted to guarantee their own continued access to the genetic resources of the South, while guarding carefully the intellectual property of their nations. The negotiations were made more complex by certain hard-liners on both sides (notably Malaysia and India on one side and the U.S.A on the other). In addition, according to one of the Canadian negotiators, both sides felt they gave away too much on the Climate Change Convention and went to the table at the final session determined to do better.
- The intellectual property issue will be a minefield, both as regards technology and as regards genetic resources and the whole issue of "Farmer's rights".
- Article 15.3 reads:
"For the purpose of this Convention, the genetic resources being provided by a Contracting Party ... are only those that are provided by Contracting Parties that are countries of origin of such resources or by the Parties that have acquired the genetic resources in accordance with this Convention."
This has been interpreted by some as meaning that all genetic resources currently in collections are not covered by the Convention. The implications are unclear, but it will no doubt be an issue of contention. The concern is that countries of origin will not benefit from materials already collected.
- The fact that the U.S.A. declined to sign the Convention is, of course, important. It probably bodes well for the effectiveness of the Convention, as protocols to the Convention can be formulated without U.S. obstruction. The final product will likely come out stronger for it. Perhaps the U.S. will sign on later, and become party to a stronger Convention.
Overall, this Convention is just the first step in a very long process. Considerable detail will be added in the future as separate protocols. Generally speaking, as a first step, it is quite well-rounded.

WHAT IS NOT THERE
Although the definition of the term "in situ conservation" includes the conservation of "domesticated or cultivated species, in the surroundings where they have developed their distinctive properties", there is

very little explicit reference to these valuable genetic resources in the action articles. The section on in situ conservation deals mainly with protected area (i.e. natural biodiversity), while ex situ measures deal typically with economically important crops. Ex situ conservation methods cannot adequately deal with the large numbers of subsistence crops, minor crops, or with the large numbers of different varieties even of the more important commercial crops. Many of these varieties are in imminent danger and their loss may translate into reduced food security for large numbers of people in the medium and long term.

OVERALL CRITIQUE

Substantive Content

This Convention makes a good start. The objectives are sound. The Convention recognizes biological process and ecological functions of biodiversity, and even the inherent value of biodiversity, in addition to its utility value. It places the main emphasis on national actions, based upon thorough analyses of need and opportunity, and it calls for the integration of biodiversity concerns within relevant sectoral planning. There is attention to those areas which fall outside national jurisdiction. And, very importantly, there is a good connection made between development and conservation. It is a good beginning, but it depends on a lot of follow-up actions for any real impact.

Design of the Chapter as an Organizing Framework

The Chapter uses a reductionist approach (see also Chapter 15). But such criticisms notwithstanding, the Convention does provide a good framework for the organization of efforts to improve the conservation and sustainable utilization of biodiversity. Given the virtual impossibility of securing international agreement on the holistic approaches which are really needed, incremental improvements are the most likely, although second-best. The challenge is to incorporate as much as possible of the more holistic approach within this framework.

RESEARCH REQUIREMENTS, CAPACITY BUILDING ETC.

EXPLICIT PROPOSALS IN THE CHAPTER

The main area in which explicit calls are made for research is Article 7, Identification and Monitoring. Huge gaps exist in baseline knowledge about biodiversity, and a strong program of ecological research is required.

In addition, research and training obligations are covered, in a very general way, by Article 12. The Article states (emphasis added):
"The Contracting Parties, taking into account the special needs of developing countries shall:
- Establish and maintain programmes for scientific and technical education and training in measures for the identification, conservation and sustainable use of biological diversity and its components and **provide support for such education and training for the specific needs of developing countries**;
- Promote and encourage research which contributes to the conservation and sustainable use of biological diversity, **particularly in developing countries**, in accordance with decisions of the Conference of the Parties taken in consequence of recommendations of the Subsidiary Body on Scientific, Technical and Technological Advice; and,
- In keeping with the provisions of Articles 16 (Access to and Transfer of Technology), 18 (Technical and Scientific Cooperation) and 20 (Financial Resources), promote and cooperate in the use of scientific advances in biological diversity research in developing methods for conservation and sustainable use of biological resources."

Specific research activities are to be identified by the Subsidiary Body on Scientific, Technical and Technological Advice.

IMPLICIT PROPOSALS DERIVED FROM THE CHAPTER

- Many of the actions called for by the Convention require or will be facilitated by increased understanding of both technical and policy issues.
- The emphasis on the integration of biodiversity concerns with sectoral policy is correct and much needed. However, there are large questions to be answered as to how best to achieve this integration, and what will be the costs. (These questions are a part of ENR's collective research agenda as they are part of any other research organization with interests in sustainability issues.)
- Article 8, In situ Conservation, emphasizes the use and management of protected areas. Article 8(e) calls for the promotion of "environmentally sound and sustainable development in areas adjacent to protected areas". This is particularly important in developing countries where strong competition exists between people and their immediate needs, and longer-term conservation interests. There is a need for increased understanding of the socio-economic dynamics of these areas, of technical resource management-related approaches for these areas, and of policy measures which will support and encourage effective "buffer-zone management".
- Article 8(f) calls for the rehabilitation and restoration of degraded ecosystems. Success in this area will require a combination of technical and policy-relevant research. Like Article 8(i), and others, there is a need for the creation and improvement of conditions which will facilitate the conservation of biodiversity. Yet understanding of what these conditions are and how to foster them is sadly lacking, including among researchers and research institutions. This is a very large area in which research is needed.
- Corresponding challenges await on the technical side. For example, there is a need for considerably more knowledge around how to rehabilitate damaged ecosystems. This is particularly true, in agricultural areas, where increased sustainability may mean slowing the advance of agriculture into pristine and fragile areas which are host to very high levels of biodiversity.
- One of the accomplishments of the Convention is its recognition that there is valuable traditional knowledge that has application in designing strategies for the conservation and wise use of biodiversity. The task of documenting this knowledge has barely begun. The job of synthesizing and applying the useful lessons to solve contemporary problems remains, to all intents and purposes, un-initiated.
 The flip side of this is the agreement within the Convention to seek equitable sharing of the benefits arising from the use of traditional knowledge and from the use of genetic resources (biodiversity). Here again a major research issue lies waiting to be tackled.
- Article 13, Public Education and Awareness, has implications for activities of IDRC and similar donors, as does the Exchange of Information through Networking, etc.
- Articles 15 and 16 call for measures to facilitate the exchange of genetic resources and of technology. An ongoing project of IDRC — with ISAAA — is tackling one aspect of this; the access by developing countries to proprietary biotechnologies through brokered technology transfer agreements. However, it is a very new area, and an important one. Considerably more research is required, with high potential for benefit from collaboration with CAID and SSD, etc.

GAPS AND ALTERNATIVE APPROACHES

See above.

NICHES FOR IDRC

GENERAL

Opportunities that Fit Normal Programming

IDRC's Biodiversity theme fits squarely within the research envelope set out in the Convention, while other themes or programs will contribute strongly to the research needs identified within the Convention. Ongoing and pending projects, including the "value of trees" work, much of the work proposed in the "International Bamboo and Rattan (INBAR)" project, and proposed areas of work in the Resource Valuation, LISA, and other GPIs will address research needs identified here.

New Opportunities

- Biodiversity conservation is a highly important subject area which has, coincidentally or not, found a place of importance on the political agenda as well. It is a natural entry point for efforts designed to link environment and sustainability concerns with development. As a direct result of the UNCED negotiations, and those around the Convention itself, there is a commitment for increased funding from developed countries. There are also corresponding expectations from developing countries that this support will be forthcoming, and commitments on their part to take appropriate action. IDRC is perfectly placed to play an important role as these commitments are honoured. As outlined above, much research is required. Some is explicitly called for by the Convention; much more is implied. IDRC has experience and capacity in supporting research in, by, and for developing countries.
- The Biodiversity theme is a modest proposal for action. If so inclined IDRC could capitalize on the concurrence of commitment and interest in both developed and developing countries and make a much larger contribution to this very important area. This could be done on an incremental basis, increasing resources directed to this subject area.
- The Convention does call for the creation of a Subsidiary Body on Technical and Technological Advice. If IDRC opts to make biodiversity conservation and utilization a high priority, and depending on the scale of intended activity, it should seek either participatory or observer status on this body.

Unusual or High-Risk Opportunities

- As mentioned above, there is an opportunity for IDRC to increase its involvement in biodiversity research. This could be done in several ways. On the one hand, IDRC could simply scale-up activities in biodiversity.
- Alternatively, and probably much more usefully, IDRC could take on the task of working with one or more individual countries to develop a model process for the implementation of the Biodiversity Convention. Here the research issues would be of two orders. First order: research questions would revolve around appropriate methods and mechanisms of implementing the Convention, and the implications of various approaches, with the ultimate objective of designing a model approach for implementation. Second order: questions would address the background research needs on particular issues; i.e. the research questions outlined explicitly or implicitly by the Convention.

An undertaking of this kind would see IDRC collaborating very closely with the participating national government(s) and the Subsidiary Body on Technical and Technological Advice in the coordination and implementation of the necessary research. Ideally, other collaborating agencies (eg. CIDA, SAREC) would be drawn on to provide support for capacity building, etc.

This would truly be a leadership activity for IDRC. The output would be highly valuable (and highly visible) as the numerous signatory nations set about to implement the Convention. It would provide a very valuable service to donor countries as an effective model and would contribute greatly to the efficient use of funds and would maximize the benefits.

- Perhaps the ideal would be to work with two countries with quite different conditions, thus increasing the probable robustness of any resulting model. A country like Laos, in the process of change from a centrally planned to a market economy, might make a good case study. A second, perhaps Costa Rica or Chile, might be chosen because it has a strong economy but recognizes the need to integrate environmental concerns with existing sectoral policy.

Obviously there are concomitant risks to such an undertaking. Success would depend on identifying a partner country(s) committed to full-ahead action. Failure could come at any stage, from an inability to identify an interested participating government, lack of support from other agencies, and lack of ability to attract funds, right through to failure ultimately, to achieve the ambitious objectives.

Success could be measured at many stages, from progress in integrating biodiversity (environmental) concerns at many levels of the economy, through to the drafting of a useable model for the implementation of the biodiversity Convention.

REGIONAL SPECIFICITY

As appropriate.

KEY PARTNERS/OTHER ACTORS

Canada
Some key contacts are:

John Herity, Director, Biodiversity Convention Office, Environment Canada, Asticou Centre, Block 700 B, Rm. 710, 241 Cité des Jeunes, Ph. 953-9669 FAX 953-1765 (re Canadian position on the Convention, political connections, etc.)

Don McAllister, Senior Biodiversity Advisor, Canadian Centre for Biodiversity, Canadian Museum of Nature, P.O. Box 3443, Station D, Ottawa, K1P 6P4, Ph. 990-8819 FAX 990-8818 (re research activities).

RECOMMENDATIONS

WHICH NICHES ARE BEST FOR IDRC PROGRAM?

The Biodiversity issue should be treated as a top priority for IDRC. In the absence of a holistic approach to environment and development, biodiversity conservation is the best proxy. The objectives of biodiversity conservation cannot be achieved without a sane approach to natural resources utilization and development. Ameliorating the problems and moving toward sustainability will require a complete integration of the social sciences and the physical sciences, of policy issues and technical issues. Biodiversity is an excellent point of entry for work in environment and development and perfectly suited to the mandate of the Environment and Natural Resources Division.

The key preference among the above research scenarios is for an integrated, intensive effort focused on one or two countries, with the objective of designing a model approach for the implementation of the Biodiversity Convention.

ARE ADJUSTMENTS NEEDED AT IDRC IN ORDER TO FILL THESE NICHES?

Program Organization

The ENRD is intended expressly as an integrated, multi-disciplinary division. This organization is well suited to the kind of research-support required by and for the Biodiversity Convention.

Structure/Staffing

Present staffing lacks both the depth and the breadth to adequately tackle the biodiversity issue on a scale fitting the lofty title of "Agenda 21 Agency". ENRD staff should be augmented to reach the magic minimum critical mass. This would require the addition, at a minimum, of:
- Biologist/ecologist with biodiversity expertise;
- Plant breeder with genetics expertise especially relating to land-race varieties; and,
- Environmental economist.

ARE THERE CROSS-CUTTING ISSUES THAT ARE NOT ADEQUATELY REFLECTED IN ANY OF THE ABOVE?

Dealt with above.

COMMENTARY

Name of Commentator: Rob Robertson

1. **GENERAL COMMENTS ON THE FIRST REVIEW OF THE CHAPTER**
- The review examines a treaty which deals with scientific, financial and legal issues of immense complexity, which it is very much a first step in ensuring the preservation of the planet's bio-diversity. Thus the review must focus upon the extent to which the three main objectives of the treaty — conservation, sustainable use, and fair and equitable sharing — have been achieved, recognizing that elaboration on many elements in the Convention will be required over many years to come.

2. **OVERALL COMMENTARY ON THE FIRST REVIEW OF THE CHAPTER**
- The review provides an excellent introduction into many of the key elements of the treaty, and in particular those dealing with conservation and sustainability. The importance and place of biodiversity is well illustrated.
- The review also is especially strong in identifying areas for IDRC involvement in treaty implementation, especially in the areas of environmental and natural sciences.
- The review presents a less complete picture of the concepts of equity and fairness, and how numerous articles in the treaty attempt to achieve this. Particularly interesting would have been a more lengthy treatment of the ways that LDCs can potentially make significant economic progress as a result of the Convention, and the potential costs to developed countries in ensuring that. This would highlight the contentious issues such as control of intellectual property and the funding mechanisms.
- Another area deserving of greater attention in the review would have been the on-going mechanisms for Convention implementation and enforcement. Do they permit an adequate assertion of a global perspective, as distinct from a national one, in the area of preservation for example? Will there be room for non-governmental entities or even independent individuals in the process, or will analysis and discussion fall totally under the self-interested control of national governments?

3. MAJOR POINTS AGREED/DISAGREED WITH, AND REASONS

- The review is correct in saying that the Convention is a good start in identifying the proper objectives and in addressing the wide range of questions inherent in dealing with the issue of bio-diversity. Emphasis must be placed on the word "start" rather than "good".
- The success of the treaty will rest upon its elaboration in protocols yet to be developed, in the establishment of many ways to promote inter-state co-operation, and in establishing effective monitoring and enforcement mechanisms.

4. MINOR POINTS AGREED/DISAGREED WITH, AND REASONS

- The review says that on the whole it may be good that the United States has not signed the Convention, as this may avoid obstructionism in the early stages of the elaboration process. While the absence from the room of the "bad boy" of the Western World may seem occasionally convenient, it is hard to accept that it is good that the world's leading state should not be a participant in this question which is so globally important, both from the standpoint of policy development and funding.

5. POSSIBLE ON-GOING ISSUES OR CONCERNS FOR IDRC

- In addition to the many entry points for IDRC which the review identifies, the review could have laid greater emphasis on the important role which Communications (i.e. CAID and ISSD) could play in such areas as technology adaptation and dissemination, and in furthering the Convention article on public information and awareness, including through information exchange.
- The review highlights some areas where IDRC's human resources would require bolstering in order to provide a well-rounded response to the Convention. In addition to those mentioned, a person familiar with legislative and regulatory matters would be essential, given the heavy emphasis placed by the Convention on the legal aspects of such subjects as conservation, impact assessment, compensation, technology ownership and transfer, and the safe handling of organisms.

6. POSSIBLE IMPLICATIONS FOR IDRC

- Involvement with the formulation of national strategies, as suggested in the review, would require significant collaboration by IDRC with bigger donors, given the scope of such an activity.
- Participation in issues like technology transfer, adaptation and ownership would certainly require a more intense and business-like involvement with the private sector.
- Greater concentration in this general area would mean that IDRC would have to be, in a sense, a better-rounded organization, given the multiplicity of disciplines and issues which are encompassed under bio-diversity.

STATEMENT OF PRINCIPLES ON FORESTRY

Responsible Officer: R.D. Ayling

ABSTRACT

1. OVERALL CRITIQUE OF AGENDA 21 CHAPTER

- The Statement contains observations on the importance of forests, viz. related to the entire range of environmental/development issues and opportunities, and essential to economic development and maintenance of all life forms.
- A weak, "non-legally binding" document and, with vague concepts open to interpretation, lacking impact and concrete steps/strategies to implement.
- Encourages governments to promote sustainable management but no incentives for action nor penalties for inaction.
- Suggests but does not require acceptance, commitment or action.
- Fails to recognize principal causes of deforestation (poverty/landlessness; excessive north consumerism).
- Weak linkage to climate warming, hydrological cycles, biodiversity.

2. KEY CONCLUSIONS ARISING FROM CHAPTER

- Recognizes essential role/importance of forest ecosystems.
- Encourages application of principles of sustainable management. These should apply to *all* forest types (temperate and tropical).
- Recognizes sovereign right of States to utilize/manage/develop their own resources in accordance with their development needs/level of socio-economic development and pursuant to their own environmental policies.
- Recognizes need for States to exercise responsibility to ensure activities do not damage environment beyond their borders, but exercising this right is based on the assumption that policies are consistent with sustainable development.
- Suggests the need for international cooperation with costs shared.

3. RESEARCH AND/OR IMPLEMENTATION POSSIBILITIES/OPPORTUNITIES

- Implicit opportunities are provided, especially development of sound national forest/land-use policies; analysis of land tenure arrangements; contributions of forests to national economies; development and testing of guidelines for valuation of forest benefits (productive/service, social/economic/cultural) and for sustainable forest management (evaluation of models); analysis of externalities influencing forest management; identification/testing of ways to ensure all stakeholder involvement; identification/development/access to information and environmentally-sound technologies supporting sustainable forest management.

4. ON-GOING AND/OR NEW PARTNERSHIPS FOR IDRC

- Opportunities exist for maximum Centre impact through existing international organizations in novel/distinct ways. These include: the CGIAR system, specifically influencing IARCs such as ICRAF, IFPRI on policy development. The CG's CIFOR can be positively influenced to develop

policy programs which look at key sustainable resource-use constraints. Other partners include organizations with an international focus such as IIED, ITTO and ODI's Social Forestry Network.
- Canadian partners will include universities, Forestry-Canada, viable NGOs with an international record. There could be opportunities to influence more effective development of the FAO's Tropical Forestry Action Program (TFAP).

5. SUGGESTED NICHES FOR IDRC

- Opportunities exist to support key strategic studies on critical research topics; to identify key institutions and rapidly help them to organize to influence development of specific programs (model forests/biodiversity proposals); to identify and/or influence programs associated with key networks related to policy development/implementation.

6. OTHER COMMENTS

- Several opportunities exist to move this Statement forward, including support for key international organizations such as ITTO/FAO and the CGIAR system.
- National programs can be supported but research should be generic and capable of being transferred to and between countries.

REVIEW

KEY CONCLUSIONS IN THE STATEMENT

WHAT IS THERE

Main Conclusions

There are no "conclusions". Several fundamental but important statements or observations are made, as well as ones which are "qualified". These include (in the Preamble):
- That forests are related to the entire range of environmental and development issues and opportunities, including the right to socio-economic development on a sustainable basis, and therefore a "holistic" and "balanced" approach should be taken;
- That forests embody complex and unique ecological processes, and have the capacity to satisfy both human needs and environmental values — hence "sound management and conservation" are of concern (to national governments);
- That forests are essential to economic development and to the maintenance of all forms of life.

Agreements Reached for International and National Action

No specific follow-up was proposed, hence no agreements were reached.

To the extent the Statement itself represents consensus: signatories accepted that the objective of the Principles is to contribute to the management, conservation and sustainable development of forests, that these Principles **should** apply to all forest types, and that each State **should** pursue these Principles.

It was recognized also that "increased international cooperation" is required, and costs "**should** be equitably shared by the international community".

Politically Significant Issues

The Statement is "non-legally binding". States are encouraged but not required to act. However, there are politically sensitive areas to be aware of. For example, the only clear, unequivocal statement in the body of the Principles appears to be:

> "Access to biological resources, including genetic material, shall be with due regard to the sovereign rights" of countries where forests are located and to the sharing, **on mutually agreed** terms, technology and profits derived from these resources.

This statement does not consider the private sector's interests in germplasm and biotechnology, and therefore control and compensation are only between governments.

Qualified statements from the body of the Principles have political undertones.

> "States have... the sovereign right to exploit their own resources **pursuant to their own environmental policies**" and in so doing, have the responsibility to ensure activities do not damage the environment beyond their borders; further, exercising their right is based on the assumption that national policies are consistent with sustainable development and rational land-use planning;

> "States have the sovereign and inalienable right to utilize, manage and develop their forests **in accordance with their development needs** and level of socio-economic development".

These vague statements are open to individual interpretation and definition of concepts of "rational" and "sustainable development". There is the underlying assumption that everyone understands what "environmental policies" are, that all States have the same, acceptable standards, that "in accordance with their development needs" means rational behaviour.

WHAT IS NOT THERE

The Statement considers **all** types of forests, encourages governments to "promote and provide opportunities for the participation of interested parties" (women, local communities, indigenous people, industries, etc.) "in the development, implementation and planning of national forest policies", and recognizes the importance of international cooperation (including the provision of new & additional financial resources).

- What is missing are firm statements of intent and concrete steps or strategies to implement **any** of the points raised.
- What is also missing is the recognition of the ultimate causes of deforestation — poverty and landlessness (tenure inequities only briefly mentioned) and the excessive consumerism of developed countries (waste and inefficiencies).

OVERALL CRITIQUE

Substantive Content

The Statement lacks impact. It suffers, among other things, from a lack of credibility. If statements such as: "forests are essential to economic development and the maintenance of all forms of life" were **really** understood and accepted, they would not have been followed by a weak set of suggested Principles.

The **central**, pivotal role of forest ecosystems, particularly those of the humid tropics, in influencing climate, maintaining hydrological balances, the principal sources of terrestrial biodiversity, is not emphasized. This is partially due to the inclusion of all forest types in the Statement. All forests are not of equal value. Further, UNCED's decision to consider separately forests, climate change and biodiversity contributes significantly to the weakness of the Statement. Forests are seen as just one among some 40 chapters of Agenda 21.

The Statement is a bland and inoffensive document, consisting of uncontestable "motherhood" statements and others which suggest but do not require acceptance, commitment nor action by governments. While there are points made about the importance of forests, their critical environmental role and their importance in national economic development, these are broad and obvious. What is not obvious is what attention, if any, individual governments will give to the Statement. There are no incentives for action nor penalties for inaction.

Instead of watering everything down to reach a consensus, a forceful document only a few could sign would have been preferable to one anyone could sign.

Design of Chapter as an Organizing Framework
The Preamble is vague. The "principles" lack clear titles or themes, and are merely presented as some fifteen points, some of which are expansive yet often manage to avoid substance. There are no conclusions nor specifics for follow-up action.

The Preamble also lacks substance. Hard data are avoided on the seriousness and magnitude of forest ecosystem disruption and destruction. Linkages, if noted, between forests and other issues (eg; agricultural productivity, river siltation, climate change, etc.) are vague.

RESEARCH REQUIREMENTS, CAPACITY BUILDING ETC.

EXPLICIT PROPOSALS
There are no explicit proposals.

IMPLICIT PROPOSALS
Much is suggested as to what national governments **should** do.

What should be done, however, should be within the framework of sound national forest and land-use policies. The formulation of such policies should be based on the following researchable points (assuming accurate information on forest and land resources):
- Identification/testing of ways to ensure all stakeholders have opportunities for input in policy development.
- Identification of forms of land tenure arrangements which encourage sustainable forest utilization.
- Identification of the contributions of forests to national economies, including employment and energy sectors.
- Development of methodologies for the accurate valuation of all forest benefits (productive and service functions), including cultural and social values of forests.
- Identification/testing of guidelines for sustainable forest management, including evaluation of "models" of conservation (buffer zones, extractive reserves, etc.).
- Identification/analysis of "externalities" influencing forest management, including economic and trade barriers, constraints and incentives, as well as the linkages or relationships between forestry and other economic sectors (mining, industries, agriculture, etc.).
- Identification and/or development, and access to information and environmentally-sound technologies supporting sustainable forest management.

GAPS AND ALTERNATIVE APPROACHES
Some key activities missing include:
- Need to establish a "workable" centralized monitoring system, not only for forest ecosystems but for all land-use activities, especially in the tropics.

- Need to work through existing international organizations and networks.
- Need to recognize and work on the ultimate causes of deforestation — for example, to encourage and promote intensive (but low-input) agriculture and to promote land reform.

NICHES FOR IDRC

The Centre has appeared as an independent (apolitical) organization with the ability to recognize and readily support key strategic studies often overlooked by larger donors. The Centre has supported individuals of considerable promise in developing countries, and needs to sustain this support.

Centre officers should have the freedom and means to identify and to support research which has often not attracted other donors.

The Centre has the opportunity to act as a major catalyst in environment and natural resource issues to help change the development path toward a greater degree of resource sustainability.

GENERAL

Opportunities that Fit Normal Programming
- Support and influence key international organizations such as the CGIAR centres (ICRAF, IBPGR, CIFOR), IUFRO and key networks (ODI's Social Forestry Network);
- Support and enhance methods for evaluating resource values, to recognize relationships between resource base and development, to recognize trade-off factors involved, to recognize and resolve resource conservation and development conflicts;
- Promote a more integrated approach to forestry resource issues;
- Promote a more integrated approach, including multidisciplinary analysis, of natural resource utilization;
- Identify/develop low-input technologies with a sustainability perspective;
- Support resource information studies and policy design;
- Promote more intensive sociological studies to provide understanding of major issues;
- Support and promote the recognition of forest-dwelling people, and provide for direct participation in decision-making processes.

New Opportunities
- Provide material/technical/administrative assistance for development of key institutions (in developing and in developed countries) in areas of policy formulation, resource surveys, conflict resolution, resource valuation;
- Support, within national institutions, environmental specialists;
- Support efforts to identify unique ecosystems, and opportunities for sustainable management, including germplasm collection and evaluation.

Unusual or High-Risk Opportunities
- Support research to identify and resolve land-tenure constraints;
- Provide salaries to scientists/policy makers who make the research possible (in addition to material support).

REGIONAL SPECIFICITY

The Statement encompasses all forested areas in both developed and developing countries. The Centre's focus should continue to be:
- In wet/dry forest systems of developing countries.
- In ecosystems of major importance/significance and where conservation/development conflicts are intensifying.

- Where attempts at resolution are achievable and will have maximum impact (in terms of Centre profile and problem resolution).

KEY PARTNERS/OTHER ACTORS
Canada
Partners with a good international track record and/or prepared to work/share experiences on an equitable basis. These could include NGOs with a "Third World" focus, university departments (e.g. Alberta's Department of Rural Economy; Toronto's Department of Sociology & Geology), institutions (Manitoba's Institute of Sustainable Development). Forestry Canada could also be encouraged to develop tropical forestry expertise.

IDRC–CIDA linkages should be encouraged and made to work.

Other Countries
A number of international organizations should be supported, e.g. the UK's International Institute for Environment and Development (IIED) and the Overseas Development Institute's (ODI) Social Forestry Network.

Several key international organizations/mechanisms are possible partners or foci for support. These include the CGIAR (Consultative Group for International Agricultural Research) which is presently developing an agroecosystem focus for activities and programs on natural resource management. The CGIAR is the largest and most influential system for donor research support. In addition to continuing Centre support for IARCs such as ICRAF, the CG's newest entity, the Centre for International Forestry Research (CIFOR) should receive IDRC support.

Other mechanisms in international forestry, where the Centre could have a positive impact, include support for the International Tropical Timber Organization (ITTO), the International Union for the Conservation of Nature (IUCN) and support for the development/implementation of improved NFAPS (national forestry action plans).

RECOMMENDATIONS

WHICH NICHES ARE BEST FOR IDRC PROGRAM?
The development of "holistic" approaches to national economic planning and development, including the development and implementation of carefully crafted national land-use and forest policies, is critical to the Statement of Principles.

The Centre should move rapidly to:
- Support CIFOR's intended forest policy research program.
- Evaluate and provide input into ITTO.
- Focus on the development/strengthening of regional and/or key national programs on forest/land-use policy development.
- Support national studies on natural resources and development, *and* assist in analysis and follow-up, including support for methodologies for integrating forest valuation into national accounting systems.

ARE ADJUSTMENTS NEEDED AT IDRC IN ORDER TO FILL THESE NICHES?

Program Organization

This might include instituting a third program within Environment and Natural Resources Division which is focused on natural resources — coastal resources, mountain systems, wet/dry tropical forests, rangelands.

Process and Project Cycle

Projects should be network-focused, regionally as well as within a country, to incorporate a more integrated approach to forests and national/regional development. Additional funds should be provided for "holistic" natural resource studies, as well as to major international organizations with national programs to develop, analyze, and implement sustainable forest management.

Structure/Staffing

The proposed activities require additional staff in forest resource management and development, with strong linkages to key regional offices.

ARE THERE CROSS-CUTTING ISSUES NOT ADEQUATELY REFLECTED IN ANY OF THE ABOVE?

Issues implied but not adequately discussed in the Statement of Principles are the biodiversity aspects of tropical forests; the critical role of forest ecosystems in global warming; climate change and hydrological cycles (including regulation of streamflows and maintenance of watertables); the importance of forests and trees in reducing and reversing desertification; and, the potential of sustainable forest management in rural livelihood security, including food security, employment and cash generation and in reducing poverty.

COMMENTARY

Name of Commentator: Cherla B. Sastry

1. **GENERAL COMMENTS ON THE CHAPTER**
   - Given the non-legally binding nature of the document, it is a good starting point for future discussions. The coverage is broad and comprehensive and certainly has a global perspective.
   - Sufficient emphasis has been given the needs of developing countries to enhance their capacity to better manage, conserve and develop their resources on a sustainable basis. Nevertheless, there are many statements that need clarifications and strengthening as ably pointed out by the reviewer.
   - A major limitation for achieving the goals is the enormous funding required for sustainably managing the forests, in particular, the tropical rain-forest which is being depleted at an alarming rate.
   - There is thus need for continuing dialogue amongst the various donor agencies and the countries involved in order to achieve the desired objectives.

2. **OVERALL COMMENTARY ON THE FIRST REVIEW OF THE CHAPTER**
   - The reviewer has done a good job and provided an illuminating insight on the topic. Agree with the recommendations in general, including the suggested approach for the Program Organization.
   - In places, the reviewer is too critical on the intent of the document, confusing a statement of principle with a statement on policy.

3. MAJOR POINTS AGREED/DISAGREED WITH, AND REASONS

- Do not agree with the reviewer's statement that the document "lacks impact" and "suffers ... from a lack of credibility". As noted above, this is a statement of principles for a global consensus and a **starting document** for further dialogue.
- The reviewer's recommendation that "a forceful document only a few could sign would have been preferable" will not achieve the desired results, which is to manage the forests and its resources wisely, as set out in the Preamble.

4. MINOR POINTS AGREED/DISAGREED WITH, AND REASONS

- With the exception of the above. Agree in principle with the reviewer's comments and recommendations.

5. POSSIBLE ON-GOING ISSUES OR CONCERNS FOR IDRC

- As the subject is related to the entire range of environmental and developmental issues, this should be of major concern for the Centre as an Agenda 21 organization. Many of the various divisions' and Regional Offices' priorities are closely tied to this topic.

6. POSSIBLE IMPLICATIONS FOR IDRC

- Adequate provisions (staff and finances) should be made available to address the issues highlighted in the Statement. This should include enhancing "in-house" research capacity by granting internships, hiring research assistants, post-doctoral fellows, and staff sabbaticals.

FRAMEWORK CONVENTION ON CLIMATE CHANGE

Responsible Officer: Hartmut Krugmann

REVIEW

KEY CONCLUSIONS IN THE CHAPTER

WHAT IS THERE

Main Conclusions

The Preamble contains reference to a number of important conclusions, concepts, issues and principles:
- Climate change and its effects are a "common concern of humankind";
- Human activities have increased greenhouse gas concentrations. Such increases have enhanced the natural greenhouse effect. This in turn will result in additional warming of the Earth's surface and atmoshpere, and may affect negatively natural ecosystems and humanity;
- The largest share of historical and current greenhouse gas emissions (GGE) has come from developed countries;
- Per capita GGE from developing countries are still low but their share will grow (quite rapidly) to meet their own social and development needs;
- Different countries have common but differentiated responsibilities and respective capabilities (due to differences in their socio-economic comditions);
- The global nature of climate change calls for the widest possible cooperation by all countries and their participation in an international response;
- States have the sovereign right to exploit their own natural resources but also the responsibility to ensure that this does not cause damage to the environment of other States;
- The principle of the sovereignty of States exists in international cooperation when addressing climate change;
- Environmental standards and legislation enacted by some States may be inappropriate and too costly for others (e.g. developing countries);
- Various actions to address climate change can be justified economically in their own right and may help solve other environmental problems (e.g. by the more efficient use of fossil fuel);
- The need for developed countries to take immediate action (or take the lead) exists;
- Fragile ecosystems, natural disaster-prone areas, and low-lying countries are particularly vulnerable to climate change;
- Responses to climate change should avoid impeding legitimate social and economic development, particularly in developing countries;
- For developing countries to achieve sustainable (social and economic) development, their energy consumption needs to grow, even if energy efficiency and GGE improvements are exploited; and,
- The climate for present **and future** generations (the principle of intergenerational equity) should be protected.

The Objectives section (Article 2) implies two conclusions:
- Greenhouse gas concentrations in the atmosphere must be stabilized at an appropriate level — so as to prevent dangerous human interference with the climate system; and,

- Sufficient time should be allotted to reach that level — so as not to jeopardize such goals as food production and (sustainable) economic development.

The principles presented in the **principles** section (Article 3) have been mostly already introduced or referred to in the Preamble section. The following principles are new or stronger however:

- Precautionary measures are necessary to anticipate, prevent or minimize the causes of climate change and mitigate its adverse effects;
- Lack of full scientific certainty should not be used as a reason for postponing such measures (although the measures should be cost-effective); and,
- Measures used to combat climate change should not constitute a means of discrimination or a disguised restriction on international trade.

Agreements Reached for International and National Action

All Parties to the Convention undertake to do the following (but taking into account differentiated responsibilities and capacities of different countries):
- Preparation of national inventories of anthropogenic GGE by sources and removals by sinks using comparable methodologies; and,
- Preparation and regularly updating of national strategies containing programs (and measures for implementation) to mitigate, facilitate and adapt to climate change.

All Parties should promote and co-operate in:
- Technology development and diffusion;
- Conservation of GG sinks and reservoirs;
- Adaptation to climate change impacts;
- Inclusion of climate change considerations in policy formulation, action and impact assessment;
- Research and development of data archives on climate issues to reduce remaining uncertainties (by fostering international, and intergovernmental programs and networks, capacity-building in developing countries and exchange of data);
- Exchange of relevant climate-related information; and,
- Climate-related education, training and public awareness (by fostering public access to information, public participation, exchange of relevant material, and training of experts in developing countries, among other things).

The Developed Country Parties and Other Countries listed in Annex I of the Convention (countries undergoing transition to market economy) undertake to:
- Adopt policies and measures to limit GGE and enhance GG sinks and reservoirs so as to return to earlier levels of GGE by the turn of the 21st Century; and,
- Communicate (according to a timetable) information on policies and measures aimed at returning (individually or jointly) to 1990 levels of GGE and on their effects on GG emissions and removals.

In this connection, these Parties will coordinate, and periodically review their own policies and practices. The Conference of the Parties will agree on: methodologies for GG emission and sink calculations, criteria for implementation of GGE reduction levels and time frames, and amendments to the list of these Parties (Annexes I and II of the Convention).

These Parties will also:
- Provide adequate (new and additional) resources to:
    - Meet the agreed full costs incurred by developing country parties to communicate the agreed implementation-related information;

- Assist developing countries in meeting costs of adaptation to adverse climate effects; and,
- Promote the transfer of, access to and endogenous capacity in environmentally sound technologies vis-à-vis developing countries.

The degree to which (vulnerable) developing countries will (be able to) implement their commitments, as well as to compile and communicate the necessary information, will depend on the assistance they get from these Parties in terms of finance, access to technology, and technical support.

Politically Significant Issues
- The text of the Convention is vague, tortuous and obfuscating in a number of places. This likely reflects the political horsetrading and hard ball play that went on during the negotiations and behind the scenes. One participant in the INC process described the final text as a "linguistic striptease". But a clearer statement of commitments might not have been acceptable to all parties involved.
- The principal reason for the vague and convoluted text of the Convention, especially those sections spelling out the commitments is that one major industrial power and some oil-exporting developing countries did not see it in their interest (because of perceived cost or development implications) to agree to clear targets for reductions in GG emissions and concentrations. Nor did they see it in their interests to set a time table for those reductions, or to establish clear mechanisms for joint implementation of GGE reductions (e.g. GGE entitlements and tradable GGE permits). (It is interesting to note in this connection that the delegations of several European countries and Japan at the Earth Summit — i.e. just after the completion of the drafting of the Convention — reiterated their intention to reduce emissions of CO_2, the chief GG, down to 1990 levels, and to stabilize them at those levels, by the year 2000.)
- From a Southern perspective, the "commitments" Articles could be seen as paying as much or more attention to establishing and sustainably managing GG sinks (primarily in the South) as or than reducing GG emissions (primarily in the North). In other words, the perception could exist that the North may go on polluting while the South is asked to clean up the mess.
- The question of GGE entitlements — not touched upon in the Convention — is a thorny political issue and has invited conflicting proposals reflecting Northern and Southern perspectives. The extreme positions are: GGE entitlements according to current GNP/capita levels (favourable to industrial countries) on the one hand, and GGE entitlements on a per capita basis (favoured as an equitable approach for developing countries) on the other.
- The Convention does not mention (let alone tackle) the more fundamental issues about international equity (foreign debt, trade patterns, consumption/production patterns in the North, etc) underlying the asymmetry of responsibilities and capacities of North versus South in meeting commitments. Rather, the asymmetry is taken as a given and dealt with in terms of providing (curative rather than preventative) financial and technological assistance.

WHAT IS NOT THERE
- Article 4 (sections 2a and 2b) does not relate GGE target reductions to target dates for GGE reductions. GGE reductions to 1990 levels are not connected to any specific date as to when this might be accomplished, while the 2000 target date is given without specification as to of how much GGE reduction should take place by then. This takes much of the "bite" out of the commitments statement.
- It is intrinsically easier to ensure reductions in GG concentrations in the atmosphere by *curtailing* GG emissions than by relying on the **absorptive** capacity of GG sinks (forests, grasslands, etc.) to absorb them. The possible degree of control over GG emission reductions is much higher than over GG removal into sinks, and the response time of GG atmospheric concentration levels to emission reductions is faster than the establishment of new sinks. This is not or reflected in the Convention.

- The Convention recognizes the need for financial assistance and for the transfer of (environmentally sound) technology to developing countries, as well as the need for strengthening endogenous technological capacities in developing countries to enable them to meet their commitments (sections 3 and 5 of Article 4 as well as Article 11, Financial Mechanism). The Convention even links effective implementation by developing countries of their commitments to the degree by which developed countries keep their commitments of financial assistance and technology transfer ("escape clause" for developing country governments). But, unlike the financial resources issue to which a whole article is devoted, the technology transfer issue is merely mentioned (in section 5 of Article 4) but not detailed. This seems to be a concession to corporate perceptions and interests in industrial countries (e.g. concern about losing industrial property rights).
- See "Politically Significant Issues".

OVERALL CRITIQUE

Substantive Content

The Convention is flexible in its approach and comprehensive in terms of the proposed international cooperation. The flexibility is reflected in the explicit recognition of differences across countries (in particular between developed and developing countries) in responsibilities and capacities to meet commitments. Paragraph 1 of Article 4, for instance, is a comprehensive list of the commitments of all Parties. Because developing countries do not have the capacity and financial resources to fulfill these commitments, they need assistance, which is recognized in the Convention.

However, in a number of respects the Convention falls short of what is needed to address the problem of climate change effectively. For instance, precise and consistently linked targets for GGE reductions, a time table, and precise mechanisms for joint implementation are watered down or missing altogether. And a number of other important issues are either played down or ignored (see above under "What is Not There").

Design of the Convention as an Organizing Framework

Abstracting, from the existing political realities, there are a number of ways in which the Convention could be revamped to make it more transparent and more relevant to tackling the problem:
- Shorten the Preamble and include some of its more important statements in the main body of the Convention. This avoids repetitiveness and increases the relevance of the main text.
- Expand and streamline the list of principles (Article 3). Several important principles were dropped during the negotiations from the initially longer list and would be worth including. Examples are: "right to development", "polluter pays", and reference to sovereignty of states.
- Revise the Article 4 on Commitments including aspects suggested above in "What is Not There".

RESEARCH REQUIREMENTS, CAPACITY BUILDING ETC.

EXPLICIT PROPOSALS IN THE CONVENTION

Paragraph 3, Article 4 calls for financial and technology transfer assistance to be provided by developed country Parties and other developed countries to developing country Parties to meet the agreed full incremental costs of implementing the commitments spelled out under paragraph 1 of Article 4.

These commitments include:
- Preparation of national inventories of anthropogenic GG emissions by sources and GG removals by sinks (except for GG already controlled by the Montreal Protocol), using comparable methodologies to be agreed upon by the Conference of Parties.
- Formulation and implementation of national (and regional) programs containing:

- Measures to mitigate climate change by addressing GGE emissions and removals; and,
- Measures to facilitate adaptation to climate change.
- Development and diffusion of technologies and practices that control, reduce or prevent GG emissions in all sectors (including energy, transport, industry, agriculture, forestry, and waste management).
- Sustainable management, conservation and enhancement of GG sinks and reservoirs (including biomass, forests and oceans as well as other terrestrial, coastal and marine ecosystems).
- Preparation for adaptation to the impacts of climate change, including development of integrated plans for:
    - Coastal zone management, water resources and agriculture; and,
    - Protecting and rehabilitating drought-, desertification-, and flood-prone areas, particularly in Africa.
- Incorporation of climate change considerations in social, economic and environmental policies and actions.
- Assessment and minimization of adverse effects on the economy, public health and environmental quality, of climate change mitigation or adaptation projects or measures.
- Promotion of and cooperation in research, data systems, and the exchange of relevant information aimed at improving the understanding, and reducing remaining uncertainties, of causes, effects, magnitude and timing of climate change, and of the economic and social consequences of various response strategies. (The need for promoting research and monitoring, research cooperation and networking, research capacity-building in developing countries, and the access to or exchange of related information, is highlighted in a separate article — Article 5.)
- Promotion of and cooperation in education, training, public awareness and public participation, including that of NGOs, relating to climate change. (This aspect is further detailed and strengthened in Article 6. Stated commitments include the training of scientific, technical and managerial personnel and the strengthening of national institutions. Obviously, this is of particular relevance to developing countries, although this is not said in the Article.)

A mechanism is set up under Article 11 to expedite the called for financial assistance to developing country Parties and an international entity — assumed, but not mentioned, to be the Global Environmental Facility — is entrusted with its operation, under the guidance of the Conference of Parties. Reporting requirements under the Convention — in terms of national GG emission and removal inventories, national programs and measures to mitigate or adapt to climate change, etc. — are specified in Article 12. These requirements are made less stringent for developing countries, because of their lack of relevant capacity. Developing country Parties are invited to present relevant projects (aimed at strengthening their capacity) for funding from the above-mentioned mechanism.

The promotion and financing of the transfer of environmentally sound technologies to, and development/enhancement of endogenous capacities and technologies in, developing country Parties are covered in paragraph 5, Article 4.

Special attention is given to financial assistance, technology transfer and capacity-building for particularly vulnerable developing country Parties so that the latter can meet costs and other needs or concerns arising from climate change and from the implementation of response measures (paragraphs 4 and 8, Article 4). (A list of the kinds of particularly vulnerable developing countries is added in paragraph 8.)

IMPLICIT PROPOSALS DERIVED FROM THE CONVENTION

Each of the commitments listed above has its research and capacity-building implications. However, research-related commitments (as expanded in Article 5) are worded sufficiently flexibly and broadly as to be interpreted as all-encompassing for both implicit and explicit research and capacity-building requirements.

GAPS AND ALTERNATIVE APPROACHES

The broadly formulated commitment to climate change related research seems to cover the whole range of possible (research) issues. No discernible gaps appear to remain.

NICHES FOR IDRC

GENERAL

Opportunities that Fit Normal Programming

- Identifying and quantifying national GG emissions (by source and sector) in developing countries, and assessement of how the GG emissions are influenced by structural, regulatory and incentive factors.
- Identification and characterization of policy avenues and technological innovations for limiting GG emissions in developing countries. Fostering economic growth and social development, with special attention to those policies, measures and technologies that can be implemented relatively easily and/or that can be justified on other grounds (e.g. economic returns from more efficient use of energy in different applications.)
  A Centre-supported project focussing on these issues for Tanzania and Zimbabwe has just started. This research is closely linked to specific IDRC themes.
- Ways and means of sustainably managing terrestrial, coastal and marine ecosystems. Here the emphasis should **not** be on how the GG sink capacity of such ecosystems could be enhanced (as an overriding objective) but on how the ecosystems could be managed sustainably for the benefit of local communities and developing countries (and with what implications for GG sink capacity, among other things). In other words, GG sink capacity might be considered as just one, and not the most important, variable in the system.
- Possible climate change impacts (economic, environmental, social, human health, etc.) and options for ways of adapting and mitigating them. A variety of impacts could be considered but attention should focus on those which are likely to be the most important ones.

These last two topics may relate variously to different Centre themes: policy-related work; development/transfer of environmentally/climatically sound technology; biodiversity (related impacts of climate change and what to do about it); and communication/information systems and environment, or climate-related systems.

New, Unusual or High-Risk Opportunities

There is a clear need to evaluate the impacts and effectiveness of GEF administered support in developing countries so as to contribute to the improvement of this Facility. This could be done by focussing on selected projects in those areas where support has been provided, including climate-related projects. The Centre has the necessary contacts, expertise and reputation, and hence would be in a good position to sponsor such evaluative work. Local (research) NGOs, among other institutions, could be involved in this work.

REGIONAL SPECIFICITY

There is no clear regional specificity, except that (research) capacity-building aspects gain in importance in the poorer developing countries, particularly Africa.

KEY PARTNERS/OTHER ACTORS

Canada
Environment Canada, External Affairs, and resource persons from universities and other institutions, as appropriate.

Other Countries
Key donor countries (Parties to the Climate Convention and/or contributors to the GEF); UNEP, UNDP and World Bank.

RECOMMENDATIONS

WHAT NICHES ARE BEST FOR IDRC'S PROGRAM?

- Support to "pathbreaking" studies in developing countries on GG emission inventories and policy options to limit the emissions, in a manner that is consistent with the needs for economic growth and social development (e.g. the Tanzania/Zimbabwe GHGE study.) Once more studies have been undertaken and the methodology becomes more established, support to this work should be left to other donors, including the GEF. (Research) capacity-building in this area in developing countries will contribute to a more effective and equitable implementation of the Climate Framework Convention (assuming that the necessary 50 ratifications take place).
- Information systems, regional/global networking and NGO involvement — the Centre has a comparative advantage due to its experience in information systems, (electronic) networking, and working with NGOs.
- Evaluations of GEF supported climate related projects in developing countries. This would have a potentially large impact, given the volume of funds moved by the GEF. Such evaluations could be carried out by developing country institutions, by IDRC program staff, or by a combination of the two. The political sensitivity of the subject may require the work to be carried out (or at least coordinated) by IDRC staff. GEF contributors may be interested in providing funding to IDRC for this purpose.

ARE ADJUSTMENTS NEEDED AT IDRC IN ORDER TO FILL THESE NICHES?

The first two niches can be filled by using regular program delivery mechanisms. The third niche, however, may require some adjustments if IDRC staff are to be directly involved in the work. Secondments and/or (mini) sabbaticals could be used to free participating IDRC program staff from their regular duties for these purposes.

RIO DECLARATION

Below is the full Rio Declaration on Environment and Development, adopted on June 13, 1992, at the Earth Summit.

THE RIO DECLARATION ON ENVIRONMENT AND DEVELOPMENT

PREAMBLE

The United Nations Conference on Environment and Development,

Having met at Rio de Janeiro from 3 to 14 June 1992,

Reaffirming the Declaration of the United Nations Conference on the Human Environment, adopted at Stockholm on 16 June 1972, and seeking to build upon it,

With the goal of establishing a new and equitable global partnership through the creation of new levels of cooperation among States, key sectors of societies and people,

Working towards international agreements which respect the interests of all and protect the integrity of the global environmental and developmental system,

Recognizing the integral and interdependent nature of the Earth, our home,

Proclaims that:

PRINCIPLE 1

Human beings are at the centre of concerns for sustainable development. They are entitled to a healthy and productive life in harmony with nature.

PRINCIPLE 2

States have, in accordance with the Charter of the United Nations and the principles of international law, the sovereign right to exploit their own resources pursuant to their own environmental and developmental policies, and the responsibility to ensure that activities within their jurisdiction or control do not cause damage to the environment of other States or of areas beyond the limits of national jurisdiction.

PRINCIPLE 3

The right to development must be fulfilled so as to equitably meet developmental and environmental needs of present and future generations.

PRINCIPLE 4

In order to achieve sustainable development, environmental protection shall constitute an integral part of the development process and cannot be considered in isolation from it.

PRINCIPLE 5

All States and all people shall cooperate in the essential task of eradicating poverty as an indispensable requirement for sustainable development, in order to decrease the disparities in standards of living and better meet the needs of the majority of the people of the world.

PRINCIPLE 6

The special situation and needs of developing countries, particularly the least developed and those most environmentally vulnerable, shall be given special priority. International actions in the field of environment and development should also address the interests and needs of all countries.

PRINCIPLE 7

States shall cooperate in a spirit of global partnership to conserve, protect and restore the health and integrity of the Earth's ecosystem. In view of the different contributions to global environmental degradation, States have common but differentiated responsibilities. The developed countries acknowledge the responsibility that they bear in the international pursuit of sustainable development in view of the pressures their societies place on the global environment and of the technologies and financial resources they command.

PRINCIPLE 8

To achieve sustainable development and a higher quality of life for all people, States should reduce and eliminate unsustainable patterns of production and consumption and promote appropriate demographic policies.

PRINCIPLE 9

States should cooperate to strengthen endogenous capacity-building for sustainable development by improving scientific understanding through exchanges of scientific and technological knowledge, and by enhancing the development, adaptation, diffusion and transfer of technologies, including new and innovative technologies.

PRINCIPLE 10

Environmental issues are best handled with the participation of all concerned citizens, at the relevant level. At the national level, each individual shall have appropriate access to information concerning the environment that is held by public authorities, including information on hazardous materials and activities in their communities, and the opportunity to participate in decision-making processes. States shall facilitate and encourage public awareness and participation by making information widely available. Effective access to judicial and administrative proceedings, including redress and remedy, shall be provided.

PRINCIPLE 11

States shall enact effective environmental legislation. Environmental standards, management objectives and priorities should reflect the environmental and developmental context to which they apply. Standards applied by some countries may be inappropriate and of unwarranted economic and social cost to other countries, in particular developing countries.

PRINCIPLE 12

States should cooperate to promote a supportive and open international economic system that would lead to economic growth and sustainable development in all countries, to better address the problems of environmental degradation. Trade policy measures for environmental purposes should not constitute a means of arbitrary or unjustifiable discrimination or a disguised restriction on international trade. Unilateral actions to deal with environmental challenges outside the jurisdiction of the importing country should be avoided. Environmental measures addressing transboundary or global environmental problems should, as far as possible, be based on an international consensus.

PRINCIPLE 13

States shall develop national law regarding liability and compensation for the victims of pollution and other environmental damage. States shall also cooperate in an expeditious and more determined manner to develop further international law regarding liability and compensation for adverse effects of environmental damage caused by activities within their jurisdiction or control to areas beyond their jurisdiction.

PRINCIPLE 14

States should effectively cooperate to discourage or prevent the relocation and transfer to other States of any activities and substances that cause severe environmental degradation or are found to be harmful to human health.

PRINCIPLE 15

In order to protect the environment, the precautionary approach shall be widely applied by States according to their capabilities. Where there are threats of serious or irreversible damage, lack of full scientific certainty shall not be used as a reason for postponing cost-effective measures to prevent environmental degradation.

PRINCIPLE 16

National authorities should endeavour to promote the internalization of environmental costs and the use of economic instruments, taking into account the approach that the polluter should, in principle, bear the cost of pollution, with due regard to the public interest and without distorting international trade and investment.

PRINCIPLE 17

Environmental impact assessment, as a national instrument, shall be undertaken for proposed activities that are likely to have a significant adverse impact on the environment and are subject to a decision of a competent national authority.

PRINCIPLE 18

States shall immediately notify other States of any natural disasters or other emergencies that are likely to produce sudden harmful effects on the environment of those States. Every effort shall be made by the international community to help States so afflicted.

PRINCIPLE 19

States shall provide prior and timely notification and relevant information to potentially affected States on activities that may have a significant adverse transboundary environmental effect and shall consult with those States at an early stage and in good faith.

PRINCIPLE 20

Women have a vital role in environmental management and development. Their full participation is therefore essential to achieve sustainable development.

PRINCIPLE 21

The creativity, ideals and courage of the youth of the world should be mobilized to forge a global partnership in order to achieve sustainable development and ensure a better future for all.

PRINCIPLE 22

Indigenous people and their communities, and other local communities, have a vital role in environmental management and development because of their knowledge and traditional practices. States should recognize and duly support their identity, culture and interests and enable their effective participation in the achievement of sustainable development.

PRINCIPLE 23

The environment and natural resources of people under oppression, domination and occupation shall be protected.

PRINCIPLE 24

Warfare is inherently destructive of sustainable development. States shall therefore respect international law providing protection for the environment in times of armed conflict and cooperate in its further development, as necessary.

PRINCIPLE 25

Peace, development and environmental protection are interdependent and indivisible.

PRINCIPLE 26

States shall resolve all their environmental disputes peacefully and by appropriate means in accordance with the Charter of the United Nations.

PRINCIPLE 27

States and people shall cooperate in good faith and in a spirit of partnership in the fulfilment of the principles embodied in this Declaration and in the further development of international law in the field of sustainable development.

ACRONYMS

ACC	(UN) Administrative Committee on Coordination
AECB	Atomic Energy Control Board
ARET	Accelerated Reduction or Elimination of Toxics
ASCEND	International Conference on an Agenda of Science for Environment and Development
ASRO	Regional Office for Southeast and East Asia (IDRC)
BCNI	Business Council on National Initiatives (Canada)
BCSD	Business Council on Sustainable Development (Geneva)
CAID	Corporate Affairs and Initiatives Division (IDRC)
CANZ	Canada, Australia and New Zealand
CCFM	Canadian Council of Forestry Ministers
CCIC	Canadian Council on International Cooperation
CCME	Canadian Council of Ministers for the Environment
CCREM	Canadian Council of Resource and Environment Ministers
CEPA	Canadian Environmental Protection Act
CIDA	Canadian International Development Agency
CMHC	Canada Mortgage and Housing Corporation
CPHA	Canadian Public Health Association
CSD	Commission on Sustainable Development
CZM	Coastal Zone Management
EARO	Regional Office for Eastern and Southern Africa (IDRC)
EC	European Council
EC	European Community
ECOSOC	Economic and Social Council
EEZ	Exclusive Economic Zones
ENRD	Environment and Natural Resources Division (IDRC)
FAO	Food and Agricultural Organization
GATT	General Agreement on Tariffs and Trade
GEF	Global Environmental Facility
GEMI	Global Environmental Management Initiatives
GHGE	Green House Gas Emissions
GIS	Geographic Information Systems
GLWQA	Great Lakes Water Quality Agreement
HABITAT	UN Human Settlements Program
HSD	Health Sciences Division (IDRC)
IAEA	International Atomic Energy Agency
ICC	International Chamber of Commerce
ICLEI	International Council of Local Environmental Initiatives
ICOD	International Centre for Ocean Development
IDA	International Development Agency
IDRC	International Development Research Centre
IFAD	International Fund for Agricultural Development
IIED	International Institute for Environment and Development
IISD	International Institute for Sustainable Development
ILO	International Labour Organization
IMF	International Monetary Fund
IMO	International Maritime Organization
IPA	Intellectual Property Act

IPCC	Inter-governmental Panel on Climate Change
IPCS	International Program on Chemical Safety
IRCWD	International Reference Centre for Wastes Disposal
ISAAA	International Service for the Acquisition of Agri-Biotechnology Applications
ISSD	Information Sciences and Systems Division (IDRC)
IUCN	International Union for the Conservation of Nature and Natural Resources
IULA	International Union of Local Authorities
LARO	Regional Office for Latin America and the Caribbean (IDRC)
MAC	Mining Association of Canada
MERO	Regional Office for the Middle East and North Africa (IDRC)
MSY	Maximum Sustainable Yield
NAFTA	North American Free Trade Agreement
NBS	National Biotechnology Strategy
NEAPs	National Environmental Action Plans
NEIN	National Environmental Information Network
NSCP	National Soil Conservation Program
ODA	Overseas Development Administration
OECD	Organization for Economic Cooperation and Development
PIC	Prior Informed Consent
RAPs	Remedial Action Plans
SARO	Regional Office for South Asia (IDRC)
SSD	Social Sciences Division (IDRC)
UNAC	UN Association of Canada
UNCED	UN Conference on Environment and Development
UNCTAD	UN Conference on Trade and Development
UNDP	UN Development Program
UNECE	UN Economic Commission for Europe
UNEP	UN Environment Program
UNESCO	UN Educational, Scientific and Cultural Organization
UNFPA	UN Fund for Population Activities
UNGA	UN General Assembly
UNIDO	UN Industrial Development Organization
UNNGLS	United Nations Non-Governmental Liaison Service
UTO	United Towns Organization
WARO	Regional Office for West and Central Africa (IDRC)
WCED	World Commission on Environment and Development
WFP	World Food Program
WHO	World Health Organization
WICEM	World Industry Conferences on Environmental Management
WMO	World Meterological Organization
WRI	World Resources Institute

Note: This is a partial list of the acronyms used in this publication.

LIST OF REVIEWERS AND COMMENTATORS

Chap #	Title (abbreviated)	Abstract	Review	Commentary
1.	Preamble to Agenda 21	—	—	—
2.	International Cooperation	P. English	P. English	H. Krugmann
3.	Combating Poverty	D. Morales-Gómez	D. Morales-Gómez	—
4.	Changing Consumption Patterns	T. Carroll-Foster	D. Brooks	G. McMahon
5.	Demographic Dynamics	F. Farah	F. Farah	—
6.	Protection of Human Health	M. Law	M. Law	—
7.	Sustainable Human Settlement	L. Mougeot	L. Mougeot	D. Massé
8.	Environment and Development Decision-Making	R. Spence	R. Spence	R. Medhora
9.	Protection of the Atmosphere	S. Tyler	S. Tyler	D. Brooks
10.	Land Resources	H. Krugmann	H. Krugmann	—
11.	Combating Deforestation	R. Ayling	R. Ayling	E. Rached
12.	Desertification and Drought	E. Rached	E. Rached	R. Ayling
13.	Sustainable Mountain Development	H. Li Pun	H. Li Pun	C. Thompson
14.	Sustainable Agriculture	R. Vernooy	R. Vernooy	H. Li Pun
15.	Biological Diversity	S. Landon	B. Belcher	—
16.	Biotechnology	B. Edwardson	B. Edwardson	—
17.	Oceans & Their Living Resources	T. Carroll-Foster	B. Davy	A. McNaughton
18.	Freshwater Resources	T. Carroll-Foster	B. Davy	J. Hea
19.	Management of Toxic Chemicals	P. Zaya	P. Zaya	A. Gyi
20.	Management of Hazardous Wastes	J. Verastegui	J. Verastegui	S. Dufour
21.	Solid Wastes and Sewage	G. Forget	A. Sanchez	D. Anton
22.	Radioactive Wastes	S. Dufour	S. Dufour	J. Verastegui
23.	Strengthening Role of Major Groups: Preamble	—	—	—
24.	Global Action for Women	T. Carroll-Foster	T. Carroll-Foster	R. Wiltshire
25.	Children and Youth	J.-M. Labatût	J.-M. Labatût	C. Lim
26.	Indigenous People and their Communities	T. Carroll-Foster	Y. Lambrou	G. Morin-Labatût
27.	Non-Governmental Organizations	T. Carroll-Foster	T. Carroll-Foster	C. Smart
28.	Local Authorities' Initiatives	D. Deby	D. Deby	—
29.	Workers and Trade Unions	G. McMahon	G. McMahon	D. Morales-Gómez
30.	Business and Industry	S. Mukerji	S. Mukerji	—
31.	Scientific and Technological Community	J. Hea	J. Hea	B. Herbert-Copley
32.	Strengthening the Role of Farmers	J. Graham	J. Graham	R. Vernooy
33.	Financial Resources and Mechanisms	G. McMahon	G. McMahon	—
34.	Transfer of Technology	B. Herbert-Copley	B. Herbert-Copley	B. Edwardson
35.	Science for Sustainable Development	A. Whyte	B. Herbert-Copley	M. Law

Chap #	Title (abbreviated)	Abstract	Review	Commentary
36.	Education/Public Awareness/Training	C. Smart and D. Morales-Gómez	C. Smart	N. Tschirgi
37.	Capacity Building	A. Whyte	C. Thompson	—
38.	International Institutions	J. Hanchanlash	J. Hanchanlash	R. Valantin
39.	International Legal Instruments	R. Auger	R. Auger	P. McConnell
40.	Information for Decision-Making	P. McConnell	R. Valantin	E. O'Manique

CONVENTIONS

Title	Abstract	Review	Commentary
Biological Diversity	S. Landon	B. Belcher	R. Robertson
Forestry	R. Ayling	R. Ayling	C. Sastry
Climate Change	—	H. Krugmann	—
Rio Declaration	—	—	—

The International Development Research Centre is a public corporation created by the Parliament of Canada in 1970 to support technical and policy research designed to adapt science and technology to the needs of developing countries. The Centre's five program sectors are Environment and Natural Resources, Social Sciences, Health Sciences, Information Sciences and Systems, and Corporate Affairs and Initiatives. The Centre's funds are provided by the Parliament of Canada; IDRC's policies, however, are set by an international Board of Governors. The Centre's headquarters are in Ottawa, Canada. Regional offices are located in Africa, Asia, Latin America, and the Middle East.

Head Office
IDRC, PO Box 8500, Ottawa, Ontario, Canada K1G 3H9

Regional Office for South Asia
IDRC, 11 Jor Bagh, New Delhi 110003, India

Regional Office for Southeast and East Asia
IDRC, Tanglin PO Box 101, Singapore 9124, Republic of Singapore

Regional Office for Eastern and Southern Africa
IDRC, PO Box 62084, Nairobi, Kenya

Regional Office for Southern Africa
IDRC, Ninth Floor Braamfontein Centre, Corner Bertha and Jorissen Streets, Braamfontein, 2001 Johannesburg, South Africa

Regional Office for the Middle East and North Africa
IDRC, PO Box 14 Orman, Giza, Cairo, Egypt

Regional Office for West and Central Africa
IDRC, BP 11007, CD Annexe, Dakar, Senegal

Regional Office for Latin America and the Caribbean
IDRC, Casilla de Correos 6379, Montevideo, Uruguay

Please direct requests for information about IDRC and its activities to the IDRC office in your region.

IDRC AND AGENDA 21 — FURTHER READING

I would like to be informed of new IDRC publications on development and the environment.

❑   Please add my name to the IDRC Agenda 21 Mailing List. (Please print)

NAME:

TITLE:

DEPARTMENT:

ORGANIZATION:

ADDRESS:

This is my ❑ HOME / ❑ BUSINESS address.   DATE:

Principal business of my organization:

❑   Education (401)
❑   Research (801)
❑   Government (101)
❑   Library (no affiliation) (301)

❑   NGO (201)
❑   United Nations and Affiliates (501)
❑   Media (601)
❑   Private Sector (701)

I would like to order the following titles on IDRC and Agenda 21:

❑   *Agenda 21: Green Paths to the Future*
    An introduction to Agenda 21 as a response to the global environmental crisis
    $14.95   ISBN 0-88936-689-6

❑   *A Guide to Agenda 21: Issues, Debates, and Canadian Initiatives*
    A reference guide to Agenda 21, and issues surrounding its implementation
    $24.95   ISBN 0-88936-687-X

❑   *Agenda 21: Abstracts, Reviews, and Commentaries*
    A chapter by chapter critical analysis of the Agenda 21 document
    $24.95   ISBN 0-88936-688-8

❑   *UNCED Archives CD-ROM*
    The complete UNCED archives on CD-ROM.
    Regular price US$495; US$395 before September 1, 1993
    (Payment for CD-ROM in US funds only)

Please send payment by cheque with your order to:
IDRC Books, P.O. Box 8500, Ottawa, Ontario, Canada, K1G 3H9
Telephone (613) 236-6163 extension 2110; Facsimile (613) 563-0815

Agenda 21 new releases by IDRC Books

To mark the one year anniversary of the United Nations Conference on the Environment and Development, IDRC has produced a number of other excellent publications that provide extensive coverage of the Earth Summit and beyond. **IDRC's Guide to Agenda 21** is an indispensable reference book that summarizes each of the 40 chapters, its parameters, and Canadian initiatives. For a chapter by chapter critical analysis of Agenda 21 and an insight into IDRC's opportunities for moving the global agenda forward, interested parties should read **Abstracts, Reviews, and Commentaries. Agenda 21 — Green Paths to the Future** is intended for the general public. It is a comprehensive guide to Agenda 21 and describes IDRC's work as an Agenda 21 organization. Researchers will be particularly interested in the **UNCED Archives CD-ROM**, which is the only official record of all the documentation pertaining to the Earth Summit.

No matter what type of information you require on Agenda 21, IDRC has it. Take the high road to Rio and find out how knowledge knows no boundaries. Contact IDRC Books at IDRC, PO Box 8500, Ottawa, Ontario, Canada K1G 3H9.

Telephone (613) 236-6163 ext. 2110
Fax (613) 563-0815

DEC 12 1991